WITHOUT RESERVE

A MEMOIR
PART TWO

To Nancy,

Life is full of wonderful possibilities. The older we get the more I know the best is yet to come.

Love,
Dorinda

DORINDA VOLLMER

 FriesenPress

Suite 300 - 990 Fort St
Victoria, BC, V8V 3K2
Canada

www.friesenpress.com

Copyright © 2019 by Dorinda Vollmer
First Edition — 2019

All rights reserved.

No part of this publication may be reproduced in any form, or by any means, electronic or mechanical, including photocopying, recording, or any information browsing, storage, or retrieval system, without permission in writing from FriesenPress.

ISBN
978-1-5255-4354-8 (Hardcover)
978-1-5255-4355-5 (Paperback)
978-1-5255-4356-2 (eBook)

1. BIOGRAPHY & AUTOBIOGRAPHY, PERSONAL MEMOIRS

Distributed to the trade by The Ingram Book Company

Table of Contents

Dedication v

Acknowlegements vii

About the Book Cover Art Work ix

Prologue x

Get out of town Reverend Squaw 3

Three Wonderful Friends 29

Leaving Grand Valley 44

Transitioning to New Liskeard 60

Conflict and Resolution 67

Eighteen wonderful Months 88

A Terrible Loss 98

Leaving New Liskeard 104

Warsaw United Church 130

Millbrook, a Period of Transition and More Changes 189

A Wedding and a Death in the Family 203

Another Milestone and Moving on 218

Orono, Coming Full Circle 232

A Wedding and More Funerals 251

A New Baby and Conflict in the Church 274

Retirement 293

Epilogue 339

Dedication

I dedicate this book to all those people in the churches I have served over the many years.
Trinity United Church, Grand Valley, Ontario, and Monticello United Church, 1981-85
St. Paul's United Church, New Liskeard, Ontario, 1985-89
Warsaw United Church and Bethel, Zion, and Carmel United Churches near Warsaw, Ontario, 1989-92
Millbrook United Church, Millbrook, Ontario and Cavan United Church, 1992-93
Port Perry United Church, Port Perry, Ontario and Prince Albert United Church, 1994-99
Kirby United Church 2000-2004 at Kirby, Ontario and Orono United Church, 2000-2009
Alderville United Church, Alderville First Nation 2013-2019

Many have passed away and I remember these dear friends in my congregations :

Trinity United Church - Jean Boggs; Monticello United Church - Ross Brown, Betty and Brian Johnston

St. Paul's United Church - Len and Lila Fielder, Nora Ladacoeur

Warsaw United Church - Edna Clysdale, Lu Cooper, June Clysdale, Reg Payne; Bethel United Church - Ron Frankish, Ron Darling ; Zion United Church - Marta Hamilton; Carmel United Church - Maida Ormsby

Millbrook United Church - Marg Clifford, Leo Fallis

Port Perry United Church - Grace and Les Beacock, Lillian Peake, Ena Harris, Clarence Fair; Prince Albert United Church - Reverend Charles Clarke and Lila Clarke

Orono United Church – Ed and Olive Millson, Minnie Taylor, Joyce Willis, Wayne Bailey, Ed Coatham, Faye and Carman Cornish, Betty and Jim Major, Francis Cowan, Muriel Patton, Muriel Patterson, Shirley Moffat, Elaine and Jack Mercer, Vera Staples, Lloyd and Flo Sharpe, Don and Jeanne Staples, Edna and Earl Taylor, Thelma Vagg, Carol Yeo, Derek Barnett, Margie and Clarence Gunter, Ruth Grady, Gary Hancock, Bill Hooey, Dave Kilpatrick, Hilda Caswell, Dr. Fraser McKenzie, Anna Marie and John Allin, Roy and Marion Scott, Bev Cowan, Matthew Robinson, Charlie Campbell, Jean Bemrose, Hazel and Alf Pigott, Jack and Bernice Moffat, Ross Mercer, Don Lycett, Doreen Wood, Dini and Klaas Schoenmaker, Ken Gray, Laurence Sherwin; Kirby United Church - Isabel and Don Hamm, Annie Fischer, Leland Ball, Jim Rutherford

Alderville United Church – Brad Crowe, Ray Stanlick, Don Isaac, Gary Crowe, Hailey Holmes, Wally Crowe, Daxton Crowe-Marsden, Bobby Gray, Audrey Hagar, Evelyn Wannamaker, Alton and Fran Bigwin

This book is also dedicated to my two friends and colleagues in ministry and they have not been forgotten:

Reverend Joan Henderson died very suddenly in her 30's. At the time she was serving at Westminster United Church in Peterborough. She is still remembered for the love and friendship she gave to so many.

Reverend Marion Davis had retired and was helping at Queen Street United Church in Lindsay when she was killed in a tragic car accident. She is also remembered for the love and friendship she gave to so many.

Acknowlegements

I can't thank my sister Jana Purcell enough for being there for me throughout my life and especially during the time I was writing my memoirs. She has always been there to encourage and support me as I have been there for her.

My son Warren Vollmer has been the joy of my life and I have seen him grow into a wonderful man who deeply cares for his family and friends and for the people in his congregations that he has been privileged to serve. I am so proud of him. He has helped me out in troubled times always giving me wise counsel and love and he has supported me in the writing of my memoirs.

My daughter-in- law Susan is very special. Warren and Susan were married in June 1995 and I could not imagine a better match. They have great love and respect for each other. Susan has been a wonderful support to me in the last four years as I was writing and working on these two books and there were times when I really needed her help and she was always there.

Since they were very small my grandchildren, Rachel and Sarah, have asked me to tell them stories of my life and the people who impacted my life. They were always keen to listen and take it all in. What a gift they have been to me. They have brought me such love and joy and when I started writing these two books, they continued to still ask me to tell them more stories.

Then there are my three special friends, Karen Kastner, Ruth Gray and Laura Head who were kind enough to volunteer to read my memoir from cover to cover and they read all 800 original pages and offered me positive feedback. They were very much part of my book in the early stages and they have given me great encouragement which helped me to feel very confident about my writing. For that I can never thank them enough.

I wrote my memoirs while I was at Alderville First Nation. I am still serving at Alderville United Church as their minister. Mary Crowe, Tim Smoke and Evelyn Jewell read the section in my book about the Roseau River Indian Reserve and only had positive things to say. I can't thank them enough for doing that for me. I also want to thank Chief Jimbob Marsden, and councilors Jody Holmes, Julie Bothwell, Pam Crowe and David Simpson for the support and encouragement they have given to me and to our congregation.

Anita Locke has been a wonderful friend. She is also an editor and offered to proofread my second book in August, 2018. When I went to Lakefield to give her the last six chapters, she had already done the proofreading on most of my book. I asked her how it went and she said she couldn't put my book down. I told her it did my heart good to hear that. She helped me feel very confident about what I had written which I very much appreciated.

My editor, Myrna Riback has been a special gift to me. She was there every step of the way for me - the content and every word, paragraph and chapter helping me to make these books the best they could be. From the bottom of my heart I thank Myrna because I could never have done this without her guiding me, encouraging me especially in those times I wondered what I was doing. She kept me on track and always helped me move forward.

About the Book Cover Art Work

I did this pencil crayon drawing in 1978. When I finished, I called it *White Teepee* and I decided to put it on the cover of the second book of this memoir as I did for my first book because it has deep spiritual meaning for me that transcends culture. The white teepee in the drawing is the symbol for me of pure spirituality. The background colour of this book cover is green. This is for me the colour of creation and is a symbol of mother earth that nurtures and reminds us of how much we are given by the Creator that is truly beautiful. We are given special gifts that we are to use to enrich this world which is our home.

Prologue

In the first book of my two-volume memoir, *Without Reserve, A Memoir* I wrote about my early life. My mother gave me up when I was three years old. I grew up in Oakville, Ontario with my grandma and grandpa and my two aunts Louise and her husband Phil and, Susie and, later, her husband Hugh. My Aunt Louise was a fine pianist and when I was four years old, she realized that I had a real gift for music and especially the piano. When I was nine years old she sent me to study with concert pianist Mona Bates in Toronto. I had a wonderful childhood filled with music, art and poetry. My aunts and uncles gave me a love for history. My grandmother had a very strong faith in God and I attended Sunday School at St. John's United Church in Oakville and I later sang in the Junior and Senior church choirs. My mother and father and my sister Jana, who was three years younger than me lived in Port Colborne. My sister came to live with us for a year when she was nine and she has been my confidant and friend throughout my life. We have a bond that has never been broken but only become stronger through the many years.

My family told me that, when I was five years old, they remember me telling them that I wanted to be a minister when I grew up. That call was there from an early age but it took me years before I could accept it. The year I graduated from the Oakville Trafalgar High School my parents and my sister moved to Sacramento, California. That was a huge loss for me and I missed them terribly, again. I studied for a year at the University of Toronto, Music Faculty but my family didn't have money and I couldn't continue.

It was a very confusing time for me and I left Canada and drove to California with two friends to see my parents and sister. It was not a good experience and the three of us ended up back in Canada in British Columbia where I lived for six and a half years. There, I attended the Music Faculty at the University of British Columbia in 1968. I returned home for the summer in 1969, fell in love and found I was pregnant. Back in British Columbia I had a beautiful baby boy, Warren, who was born April 1, 1970 while I was continuing my studies. I graduated with the Bachelor of Music degree in 1971 and returned to Oakville the following year. Not long after I came home, my mother died. Once again I felt abandoned.

The call I felt from God as a child became stronger over the many years and finally I accepted that call. It was a huge struggle to be accepted as a candidate for ministry since I was not married and had a son. My family supported me as did St. John's United Church and the minister there, Reverend Jim Campbell. I was ordained in 1976 and felt a call to serve on an Indian reserve, and after ordination, I went to the Roseau River Indian Reserve in southern Manitoba and was there for four years. I tell many stories about the people on the reserve and their struggle just to survive. I also made many wonderful friends there. During that time, Warren and I lived in Dominion City, Manitoba which is four miles from the reserve. The last year I was in Manitoba we lived in Winnipeg. In July 1981, we left Manitoba as I had taken a call to the Grand Valley,

Monticello Pastoral Charge which is where this book begins.

My second book is about how we deal with people in ministry, in our families, in our communities and how we are influenced by others and their opinions. It is about how we handle ourselves when we are frustrated and angry. This is again a very personal story about my life experiences and about my ministry and how I have dealt with very conflicted situations with people who seem to need to be in control and make life miserable for everyone else. It is also about those who live their faith and lift us all up which is much needed in our churches, our mosques, our synagogues and in every place we worship. We need positive people who care and who love and most importantly live their faith. People who are not afraid to gently remind others that they need to be more careful, more kind and more respectful towards others and especially to those who have no voice.

Life is difficult enough as it is without people beating us up emotionally to get their own way. My book talks about some of these people in churches I have served who were determined to get their own way at any cost and how I dealt with these disruptive people as their minister. It is a story that can translate into any situation at work, at school and in our social encounters. It is a story about reconciliation and transformation when we bring out the best in our ourselves and in others.

CHAPTER ONE

Get out of town Reverend Squaw

From a very young age, I had a love and a gift for music. Music was always there for me. I would play the piano for hours on end, putting my heart and soul into every piece, losing myself as it carried me to another place. The composer that moved me the most was Chopin. He was born March 1, 1810 and when he died on October 17, 1849 at the age of 39, he was the most famous Polish composer and virtuoso pianist of the Romantic Era. He became passionately involved with George Sand, the 19th Century French novelist. She was a widely acclaimed writer who lived a bohemian lifestyle and was a great personality, not afraid to be loud and shocking and scandalous. Her relationship with Chopin was one of the great relationships in history and his music reflected the passion and love he felt for her.

My music had taken a back seat over the last 10 years. In the early 1970's, I had discovered new gifts and my creativity exploded in the work I did as the Administrative Assistant and, later, the General Manager of the Kelso Music Centre where I worked with the Orford String Quartet and helped to create new programs for the Oakville community. That was a very exciting and rewarding time for me. Then began my studies at Emmanuel College at the University of Toronto in 1973. I had two summer fields as a student minister, which gave me all kinds of opportunities to be creative in worship and preaching, and in my ministry with young people. When I was in Oakville I sang in the senior choir at St. John's United Church which was my home church and where I was a candidate for ministry.

Sadly, though, I didn't have any opportunity to pursue my music at the Roseau River Indian Reserve where I had served as their minister in southern Manitoba from 1976-1980. But I desperately needed a creative outlet. It was there that I discovered art. Although the hard work of making the Roseau River Children's Centre a reality certainly challenged me and gave me a use for those creative gifts I had discovered in the early 1970s, I needed something more. I started drawing in 1978 using pencil crayons and continued doing this off and on over the next five years as my creative urges would not be stilled. But I always knew that music was too much a part of me to be left behind. Now, as Warren and I prepared to begin our new adventure at Grand Valley in July, 1981, I was unaware that the music that still lived deep inside of me and recreated my soul was about to resurface.

On our way to Grand Valley, we stopped at Oakville and had a wonderful visit with my two aunts, Louise and Susie, who had raised me. Warren was also able to see his dad while we were there and it was always good for Warren to be able to spend time with him. Then we continued on to Grand Valley, only an hours drive from Oakville, and, as we drove through Grand Valley to the large, two-storey, four bedroom manse that would be our new home, I had a wonderful sense of hope and joy. I knew this was the place that God had called me to. It would be a new ministry for me at Trinity and Monticello United Churches and a new beginning for my son too, a new town and a new school, and he was excited to be there.

I had the keys to the manse and, as I opened the door and stepped into our new home for the first time, it felt great. All our boxes and furniture were already there, all laid out in the different rooms as I had requested. We headed upstairs first. At the top of the stairs on the right, there was a small bedroom which I turned into my office. Across from this room was a full bathroom and going down the hall on the right were two bedrooms with a large bedroom at the end of the hall on the left. Warren and I chose the two bedrooms facing each other at the end of the hall as our own and that left the bedroom next to the bathroom for guests. Coming downstairs there was a large living room on our left with a long and large adjoining dining room that could easily seat 25-35 people for a dinner. That's how big it was. From there you walked into a good-sized kitchen with a medium size room opposite it where we put some of our living room furniture and our television and it became our family room. There was a door just past this room which led down to an old musty basement where the furnace was. And next to that there was a small room where there was the washer and dryer and a toilet.

After Warren and I looked through the house, we went outside to the very large backyard. There was a building at the very back of the yard that looked like a barn where horses might have been kept years ago and Warren was excited to see it. When Warren finished looking through the barn, we went to see the church which was directly across the road from the manse. Trinity United Church was a beautiful old Methodist Church built in the 1800's. We saw how well looked after and cared for it was. We loved the numerous stain glass windows that surrounded the inside of the church and made it look so beautiful and welcoming. Warren was surprised at how big it was. I told him the church could seat at least 250 people but that our congregation was smaller. I also told Warren that, in comparison, Monticello United Church was almost 100 years old and it only seated 70 people. I showed him the pipe organ at the front of the church where the organist sat with her back to the congregation facing the Senior Choir and we also had a Junior Choir and an active Sunday School which Warren would be attending. We both loved the feel of this church.

We went back to the manse and started unpacking. It took us the better part of that first week to get moved in, but Warren and I were good at this and we were soon comfortable in this old, solid brick home. During that first week, I met with the people who had interviewed me and everyone had a chance to meet Warren. I was also very pleased to see Jean Boggs again. Not long after we arrived, Blake Witmer, the Chair of the committee that had interviewed me, wrote an article about me in the *Star and Vidette* newspaper introducing me to the community. It was accompanied by a picture of me with my hair braided. I had long hair at that time and often wore it in braids as the women at Roseau had shown me. The article came out July 15, under the title, "First Female Minister for Grand Valley" and in the article he wrote:

"Grand Valley and Monticello congregations of the United Church will welcome their new minister, Rev. Dorinda Vollmer, at a joint service in Trinity United Church this Sunday, July 19th at 11:00 a.m. After the service a potluck luncheon will be served to provide an opportunity to welcome the new minister and get to know her. Knox Presbyterian congregation will also worship at this service as part of the summer exchange. Rev. Vollmer comes…...from Carmen Presbytery in Manitoba Conference where she served for four years after her ordination in 1976. Her work there was … with Canadian Indians on the Roseau Reserve and… led in worship in Valley Pastoral Charge. During the past year she has been working with the Federal Government trying to identify and propose solutions to the problems encountered by Indians when they migrate from the reserves to large cities. It is a first for any congregation in Grand Valley to invite a woman to be their minister. Rev. Vollmer was born in Niagara Falls, Ontario and grew up in the Oakville area….She has her Bachelor of Music degree from U.B.C. and is an accomplished pianist. She also has her Master of Divinity from Emmanuel College in Toronto. Warren Vollmer will come with his mother to Grand Valley. Warren is 11 years old and interested in sports---especially soccer. The sermon title for Rev. Vollmer's first service in Grand Valley will be, "A Time of Change and Renewal." We welcome the Vollmers to our community and hope their stay here will be productive and rewarding for all."

I remember spending 20 hours preparing my first sermon for Grand Valley, doing the research for the scripture and trying to keep it personal as well. In those days, I wrote my sermons out by hand which took a long time. At the Roseau Reserve where I had served there had been no opportunity to preach. I volunteered my time to lead in worship and preach every Sunday in Valley Pastoral Charge that was made up of three congregations. I shared the pulpit with Reverend Bill Whetter, the minister of that Pastoral Charge. Preparing a sermon every week forced me to take time to think and process what was happening in the church and the community, and even in my own life. It gave me time to reflect on my faith and my spiritual journey. This time in Grand Valley it was no different.

That first Thursday night, I met the organist, Irene Newson, and the choir. They were rehearsing the hymns and the anthem for my first Sunday and welcomed me with open arms. At my first church service July 19th, I met most of the members of our two congregations. They had a combined service for our two churches and there were also ministers and some members of their congregations who came from other churches in town to welcome us. It was hard to remember who everyone was that first Sunday. I was very well received and there was a wonderful reception afterwards. I felt right at home in Grand Valley and Monticello. It was a great beginning. At this first church service, Warren met Paul Hunter who was his age. They immediately liked each other and became friends. They would also be in the same class at school. Paul's mother Ruth had multiple sclerosis but she brought her children, Paul and his younger sister Sheila, who was nine, to church every Sunday. Because of his mother's illness, Paul had a lot of responsibility at home helping his mother. Warren was often at their home and I dropped in regularly to visit

Ruth. I also met June Maycock that Sunday. June and I would become good friends. June and her husband Wayne lived across the road from me next to the church with their three children, Warren, the oldest, Adrienne, who was about 14 and did a lot of babysitting for me, and Julie who was my son's age. June was a member and Elder at Knox Presbyterian Church. She was also one of the most respected public school teachers in the school district. Wayne didn't go to church but I got to know him and really liked him. I would often go over to visit them.

I was still processing what had happened in my life in the previous five years and how that experience had affected me. But I wasn't thinking about that as I settled into life in Grand Valley. Everything was new and very different and I was just focusing on that. I wrote to Lloyd Axworthy when I arrived at Grand Valley to tell him where I was and what I was doing and, on July 20th he wrote to me and said: *"It was nice to hear from you and good to know where you are located. Good luck on your new pastoral charge. Kindest regards. Lloyd"*

I spent a lot of my time that first summer easing my way into the ministry by visiting families in Monticello and Grand Valley, going over the lists of families in our church and preaching on Sundays. I knew that from September on, more of my time would be taken up attending all the meetings of the two Sessions, the Official Board of the Charge and any Congregational, Presbytery and Conference meetings that came up from time to time. Warren and I saw a lot more of Louise and Susie. In August, I brought them up to Grand Valley for a visit and they loved the house and the church. We often went to Oakville and they were so happy we lived so close. Warren and I also loved swimming in the pool at the apartment building with Susie. Louise never learned to swim, so she never went down to the pool with us. Warren and I loved to race each other from one end of the pool to the other and I always beat him. We would laugh but then he would ask me to do it again and try even harder to beat me. It would be another two years before he would get the best of me and, from then on, he won all the races we had. Susie wasn't a strong swimmer and always did the breast stroke in the pool. She loved to sing when she was in the pool and Susie had had a beautiful voice at one time but she could still sing. Her voice would echo all the way up, throughout the apartment building, and people always knew when Susie was in the pool. Life was good.

Sometime in early August, Campbell Cork, a freelance writer from Mount Forest, wrote me and asked if he could come and talk with me. He said that he had seen the article about me in the *Star and Vidette* in July and thought I would be a very interesting person to interview. I said he could come but that I wasn't so sure about having an article written. When I met him I was very impressed by his sincerity and I told him he could interview me. The article came out August 26, 1981 and it was a very good article. He called it *"Minister Brings Benefits of a Varied Background"* and it was accompanied by a picture of Warren and me. Here are some excerpts from it:

> *"A woman as minister of the United Churches in Grand Valley and Monticello is new, but it doesn't appear as though Reverend Dorinda Vollmer will have trouble overcoming any opposition there may be to the idea. Her capabilities and enthusiasm are matched*

only by the firmness of her conviction that the role of a spiritual leader, regardless of sex, is needed by all members of the congregation.

Her grounding in reality is evident in her ability to relate with people from all walks of life. Reverend Vollmer says she knew when she was 12 years old that she would eventually join the ministry. That was in 1956, and at that time, a woman in the ministry was still a relative novelty. It was another 17 years before she actually enrolled in Emmanuel College at the University of Toronto to study Divinity with the idea of becoming a minister. During those 17 years Dorinda travelled the continent, and lived in the midst of some turbulent times that have compelled many people to question the values of our society and that have thrust the spiritual aspects of our life into sharp relief. It was those experiences as much as her social conscience that guided Dorinda to be ordained in the United Church.

Dorinda describes her family as being very close and open. Discussions at the family dinner table were always freewheeling, covering any and every subject. She was always encouraged to speak her mind… … Now, sitting in the United Church manse and talking to Reverend Vollmer, the Indian reserve seems far away. By the stereo record player sit records of everything from Rimsky-Korsakov's 'Scheheraezade' to Tanya Tucker and Elvis Presley. Prints of Indian life on the prairies during the mid 1800's and the Reverend's tightly braided long hair are the only hints of five years spent working with one of this country's most neglected and oppressed people, the Canadian Indians. Won't life in Grand Valley be hard to adjust to after working on the Indian Reserve? "There's a tremendous amount of work to be done here," Reverend Vollmer declares…… She says that her duties here will include the concept of a ministry of presence; being available for people in their time of need, at times of sickness and of death. People also have a need, Reverend Vollmer feels, to talk about their faith, God, the Church and life and death issues… …The change from the Roseau Indian Reserve to Grand Valley may seem great, but the challenge of maintaining spiritual integrity is something that has to be renewed in everyone no matter where they live. Reverend Vollmer… … feels that ultimately the measure of a society is determined by how we care for each other; leadership in that aspect of life is the church's role. It is a role that Reverend Vollmer is both able and eager to assume."

After this article came out, Campbell called me and asked if he could approach *The Toronto Star* or *The Globe and Mail* to see if he could do an article for their Religious section. I told him it was alright with me but I didn't really expect anything to happen. Perhaps I should have thought this through more carefully at the time because there were repercussions to come.

I had worked with many of the young people in The Tempus Youth Choir back in the early 1970s when I was part of the program we created called *Discovering Old Oakville*. The choir sent me an invitation to attend its 10th Anniversary celebration on August 29th in Oakville. Brian Turnbull was the founder and director of Tempus and an amazing musician. He had taken this group of teenagers all over the world where they even sang for the Pope in Rome. What an accomplishment! Their home base was St. John's United Church where I had had the privilege of singing in the Senior Choir from 1971-1976 when Brian was also our Choir Director. It was a great evening and a wonderful celebration to see some of the young people I knew and had worked with, like Fran Lunshof, Cindy Craig, Ellen de Boer, Mike Dinsmore.

Near the end of August, I got a phone call from a young woman who lived near Monticello. She asked me if I would come out and talk with her. She said she had seen the article written about me in the local paper and needed someone to talk to. When we met, she told me she having a great deal of trouble with the death of her father. He had died the year before. Her father was Catholic, as she was, but he had not attended the church for years. She said that was a type of sin according to her church so she didn't believe that her father had gone to heaven. She had these terrible nightmares about her father buried in the ground unable to go anywhere and reaching out to her. I could feel this young woman's pain and I told her what I believed - that God loves us, is merciful and never lets us go even when we turn away. From what she told me about her father I said I thought he was a good man and I believed God loved her father and had taken him home. I prayed with her and I told her that God loved her and didn't want her to suffer. I told her I believed that her father was with God and when God calls her home, she would see her father again. About a week after we met, this young woman called me and thanked me again for coming and told me she didn't have those terrible nightmares anymore. I was angry at a Church that could cause such pain. All I could do was share my faith and what I believed as a Christian. I truly believe that we have to believe in something good and beautiful about this life, how we come to be created and what happens when we die. No one can prove anything but we need to be reassured from time to time that we are loved no matter what.

The members of Monticello United Church were a group of people who really took their faith very seriously and lived their faith. Being a very small church with about 20 families, they all worked together and supported each other. As with the Session at Trinity United Church we met once a month except for July and August. There was Arnold Townsend who was the Chair of the Board of the Pastoral Charge, as well as an Elder on Session at Monticello. He was good to work with and his wife Nina was very active in the church. Fledda Hillis was the church Treasurer and was on the Committee of Stewards. She was in her 70s when I knew her and she had been a widow for many years. She lived in a wonderful old, big house that reminded me of my home in Oakville. Fledda would give her heart to anyone. I loved visiting her and we always had tea in the most beautiful teacups along with her homemade cookies. She reminded me of my Aunt Louise who loved to have nice things and made you feel right at home whenever you came to visit.

Then there was Ioan and Elmer Shortt who for me were the most wonderful couple. Elmer and I spent time together because he was the Clerk of Session and he was wonderful to work with. He was looked up to in the church as their lay leader but he never made a decision without consulting with the Session or the congregation for their input. Elmer and Ioan had six children and owned a dairy farm so they were always very busy but I was often invited to their home for lunch when I was out visiting in Monticello. On a farm, lunch is dinner. For our meal there would always be roast beef or chicken, mashed potatoes, vegetables and dessert. The food was always amazing because Ioan was a wonderful cook and a very kind woman.

There were also Ross and Grace Brown. Ross was on the Session and the Official Board of the Charge and he was good to work with too. Grace owned the insurance business in Grand Valley and was one of the first people I met when I came. I needed to change my car insurance and I heard that Grace was the person to talk to. I phoned her and she came over to the house. She was in her 40s and had beautiful red hair. She had met Ross not long after his first wife died in a terrible car accident which left him with four young children to raise. Neither Ross nor Grace were prepared to change churches but agreed, that, if they had any children together, Grace would raise them in the Catholic church. They had one 12 year old daughter, who attended the Catholic Church with her mother in Orangeville but their daughter was also active in the youth group in Monticello United Church. It was an interesting arrangement considering Catholics and Protestants usually kept themselves pretty much separate one from the other. But it worked for them, as unusual as that was for its time everyone in Monticello respected their decision.

Bill Gooderham was on the Session at Monticello. His wife had died some years earlier and he only had one daughter. He came to church for the fellowship and the congregation was good to him. He was the only person I know of in all my years of ministry that fell asleep during my sermons and, every time I saw that, I had to smile. I went to his house many times to visit and it was packed with stuff everywhere. He always bought things when they were on sale but, not just one item, five or six of each. All the things he bought were lying unopened on his dining room table, the floor and all around his living room. His house was so full of stuff you could hardly move. I felt so badly for Bill because I understood that this obsession expressed his deep loneliness. I also worked very closely with Shirley Bruce, John Hunter and Brian Johnston who were also Elders on the Session. Marg Hunter didn't come to church as often as her husband did, but I enjoyed my visits with her because of Marg's great sense of humour and her Scottish brogue which reminded me of my neighbour Margurite in Dominion City, Manitoba when I lived there. Marg always helped out when the church needed her, as did Betty Johnston, Brian's wife. Betty and Brian and I became friends. I worked very closely with all these Elders at Monticello and it was a joy to work with them. They were the finest group of Elders that it was my privilege to do ministry with. They truly lived their faith and took their calling to look after the spiritual needs of the members of their congregation seriously.

An Official Board of the Charge is made up of all the members of a Session as well as all the members of the Committee of Stewards that deal with financial matters. The Board also includes the Chair of the Ministry and Personnel Committee for the Charge, the Chair of the Christian Education Committee for each church and the Stewardship Committee for the Charge. According to the Manual which contains the United Church of Canada's official rules as how we are structured as a church and what responsibilities each committee has, the Official Board of the Charge is required to meet three times a year and the minister, or a lay member of the Board, chairs the Board meetings and a Secretary is chosen from the Board's membership. At some of the Official Board meetings, more members from Monticello attended than members of Trinity United Church which, in attendance and membership, was at least five times larger with about 120 families. Monticello United Church, being a small rural church, gave much less financially to the Pastoral Charge and, even though their families had more difficulty financially, they always lived up to their financial commitment to the Charge and never complained. The three people who were instrumental in keeping this Pastoral Charge focused on what was most important in terms of faith and Christian love were Arnold Townsend who chaired the Official Board, Elmer Shortt, Clerk of Session and they were both from Monticello and Jean Boggs who was Clerk of Session at Trinity United Church . Arnold and Jean were good friends and respected each other and neither one suffered fools gladly. Both had a wicked sense of humour which I enjoyed immensely, particularly at our Board meetings.

Being the Clerk of Session at Trinity United Church meant that Jean Boggs was looked up to as the lay leader in her church. She worked closely with me on matters of faith and spiritual concerns. As the nurse for the local doctor in town, Jean knew everyone and was known and respected by everyone in the community. Her husband Bil had passed away suddenly in 1969. He had been the pharmacist in the drug store in town where everyone went to him to get their prescriptions filled. They were a couple who deeply cared for the people in their community and Bill's death had been a huge loss for Jean. She still grieved and missed her husband terribly. Jean had grown children and grandchildren and was in her 60's. She had the most beautiful white hair and always looked elegant in whatever she wore. Jean took me under her wing and we spent a lot of time together. We had hit it off from the moment we met at the airport back in March and she supported me through the good and the bad. She never let me down during the four years I was the minister at Grand Valley. When I first met Jean, I felt I had known her all my life and she became my dearest friend. Few people have that kind of impact on me but Jean was one of those people that I just knew would always be in my life. She sensed it too. Jean knew how difficult it was to be a minister in the church because her father had been a minister and she saw firsthand as a young person how that worked. As she said, there were always some people who were very negative and whom you could never please no matter what you did.

I learned early on that there was a very small group of people who ran Trinity United Church and everyone went along with them. The minister was expected to as well. I knew there were two ways I could go. I could sidle up to the power brokers in the church and go along with whatever they wanted to do or I could keep my own counsel and be concerned for the members of the congregation as a whole and do what I felt was the right thing to do, especially in matters of faith. The first way would have been so much easier but I could never take that path. So, from the beginning I knew that, at Trinity United Church I would ruffle some feathers whenever I didn't agree with people whose only concern was to have it their own way. I knew that Blake and Norma Witmer were the king and queen bee in the congregation. Since they were married, it made it even more complicated and more difficult. Blake was Treasurer of Trinity United Church and Norma was President of the United Church Women's group. She was also the Presbytery representative from our Charge. They were into everything and it was important to the congregation that the minister at least be perceived to get along with them. Blake and Norma had gotten along really well with the former minister and Norma always sat with him at Presbytery meetings. I had been at Unity Saskatchewan and Valley Pastoral Charge in Manitoba where I had preached and led in worship in their churches but I wasn't their minister and I didn't have to deal with the politics and inner workings of a church. This was my first Pastoral Charge but I wasn't naïve. I had grown up in St. John's United Church and got a taste of how mean people can be in the church. When they didn't want my Aunt Louise to work with young people in their church in 1947 they pushed her out. She was so hurt that she never went back to the church.

Now I was the minister and I worried about how I would handle this situation and I was so thankful Jean was there. I knew in my heart that I could talk with her about anything and it would go no further. Every month before our Session meeting, Jean and I would go out for dinner at the Garafraxa Inn in Belmont. We always had a great time talking about our families and laughing, but, of course, we always also discussed the church. Those discussions were a great outlet for me, because I could say anything to Jean and she never betrayed my trust. Even though she was a very kind and loving person, Jean had a very sharp mind and a way of putting things that let you know you really didn't want to mess with her. I had told Jean I could play the piano, and early on, she said she wanted to loan me her piano because she knew how important my music was to me. Besides, she said, she would love to see it used again. I didn't want to accept her kind offer, but she insisted. Jean arranged for her piano to be delivered to me early in September and I can't begin to describe how I felt when that piano arrived at my home. Until the moment that I sat down and started playing I hadn't really realized how much I missed it. My fingers just flew across the keys as if I had never stopped playing. Warren was so happy for me and my soul came alive as our house was once again filled with music. It was a great source of comfort for me as I played Bach and Beethoven, Chopin and Mozart, Clementi and Padereski and I couldn't thank Jean enough. I called Louise and Susie that first night and to tell them. They were so pleased and looked forward to hearing me play for them again.

Irene Newson, the organist at Trinity, was a very interesting woman. She was German and had lived in East Germany during the Cold War at the time when East Germany was under the communist domination of the Soviet Union. During that period of history, there was a massive buildup of atomic bombs by America and the Soviet Union. Things were so tense between the superpowers that people were in a panic and began building bomb shelters in North America in preparation for a Third World War. On August 13, 1961, the Communist government of the German Democratic Republic (East Germany) began to build a barbed wire and a concrete 'antifascist bulwark' between East and West Berlin. The official line was that this Berlin Wall was to keep western 'fascists' from entering East Germany and undermining the socialist state but it was built primarily to stem mass defections from the East to the West. Nevertheless, thousands of people from East Germany regularly tried to climb over the wall to get to West Germany and were routinely being shot down by guards. Before the wall was built, Irene had made the difficult and dangerous journey from East Germany to West Germany and, 10 years later, she immigrated to Canada on her own. Irene was probably in her late 30's when she came to Canada and met Stan Newson who lived just outside Grand Valley on a farm. They married and had one daughter, Vicky, who, when I met her, was in her early teens. I liked Stan very much. He was a member of the Committee of Stewards that looked after the finances of Trinity United Church and he was good to work with. He was a very intelligent man and had a great sense of humour.

Irene was short and feisty with grey hair and was a wonderful organist and musician. She was very intelligent like her husband but stubborn and independent and determined she was always right. We certainly had a love for music in common but, even though we both respected each other, Irene and I would always disagree about something. Stan loved his cigars but Irene hated him smoking them so he always went outside to smoke. I loved the smell of cigar smoke because my father had smoked cigars, so it annoyed Irene when I encouraged him. Stan understood Irene and was patient and kind and he dearly loved his wife. He also immensely enjoyed our disagreements. Irene and I chalked our sparring up to two strong-willed Germans butting heads. To try and make our relationship a little smoother, I invited Irene over to my home after choir practice one Thursday night in September. I knew she liked brandy and I bought a bottle so we could have a drink when she came over. We sat and visited and talked about all kinds of interesting things and then I brought out the bottle of brandy and two glasses. She was shocked and I didn't expect that. She said no, she couldn't possibly have a drink because she was afraid of what people would think about her drinking with the minister. I finally convinced her it was alright that it was just a glass of brandy. Besides, I told her, I had bought the brandy for her because I knew she liked it and this was a special occasion. She finally gave in and was enjoying the brandy when suddenly there was a knock at my door. Poor Irene was in a panic. I told her it was fine but she wasn't convinced and started to hide the glasses and the bottle as I went to the door. It happened to be her brother-in-law Bill Newson. I had forgotten that I had called him earlier in the day about a problem I was having with the furnace and he had come to fix it. I told him to come in and when he did, he saw Irene, said hello and went downstairs to the old musty basement to fix the furnace. Irene was beyond upset. I rarely drink and then never brandy but I thought I was doing something nice for Irene. I felt badly but, truth be told, I actually found the incident really quite funny. It made me realize the difficulties that members of congregations, and ministers as well, can have if they take themselves too seriously.

About a week after our ill-fated get together, I went to the IGA in town to do some shopping and saw a pipe on a shelf there. I had never smoked a pipe before and thought I would like to try it so I picked it up with some tobacco. I had smoked Cigarillos and Mores and, once, even a cigar, but rarely cigarettes. Why not try a pipe? It was a nice autumn day and, that afternoon, I sat outside with this pipe trying to figure out how to work it. I put the tobacco in and lit it up but it was hard to keep it lit. Finally, I got it going just as Irene came around the corner and saw me smoking this pipe. She was not impressed and told me so. I never really consider these things to be a problem because I felt strongly that I had to be who I was and not lose my identity and become 'the minister'. Unfortunately, these two incidents cemented Irene's opinion of me. They were probably the reason she was always nervous when I was around her daughter who, as all teenagers are, was wanting to break out of her shell. I liked Vicky and we became good friends and kept in touch over the years as I also did with Irene.

In early September 1981, I felt quite settled in the communities, and was getting a good feel for who people were. Warren was at school and making new friends and I was beginning to feel really good about my two churches and the people who came to services. I enjoyed leading in worship and preaching and was visiting families, going to the hospital in Orangeville once a week and visiting the nursing home in Shelburne. I was getting a good feel for who people were. I also wanted to do something for the young people in the community and initiated an open house at my home on Thursday afternoons after school from 3:30 p.m. to 5:30 p.m. for young people ages 6-12 who wanted to come. I put feelers out and the word spread. Ten children came the first Thursday and played together, made a meal together and had fun together. It didn't take long before I had a list of 70 children with at least 25 children coming to my home every week and 35-39 coming for the four parties I had at Halloween, Christmas, Easter and the end of June. I once even had a two year old show up with her sister but I had to discourage that. I had five long tables and 30 chairs set up in the dining room which extended into the large front room which also had my piano in it and a chesterfield. It was that big. Everyone was eager to cook the meal and all the children took turns deciding on the menu. It could be pancakes, eggs and bacon, hamburgers, hot dogs or macaroni and cheese and they would always make a cake for dessert. They also all took turns in the kitchen, cooking and cleaning up afterwards. We all sat around the table for a full dinner together and, just before the meal, I would tell them a bible story and say a prayer and we would sing some songs. There was always a topic for the day around world issues and concerns and the young people would talk to me about this while we made dinner. The children also loved the horse barn in the back yard and had lots of fun in it. Those were great times and Warren had a lot of fun with everyone who came. We both looked forward to Thursday.

They were good kids and I was so happy to be doing youth work again. I was also very happy with the response because the children loved coming to my place. I just wanted them to have a safe place to come and to know that there was a minister who wanted to spend time with them and just be a friend. It was important to me that they know the church cares and that there are no strings attached. I have always enjoyed young people. The children were very respectful. Rarely did I ever have to take a young person aside and, if I did, I told them they couldn't come anymore if they couldn't play nice with everyone. My congregation was surprised at the response and were very supportive and encouraged me in this endeavor. Many parents sent cake mixes, packages of hot dogs and Kraft macaroni and cheese, which I appreciated. I had only been doing this for about five months when the *Star and Vidette* wrote an article April 7, 1982 titled "Informal and Fun" and these are some excerpts from the article:

> "Thursday afternoon has become something to look forward to for a good many Grand Valley children between the ages of six and twelve….they go over to the residence of Dorinda Vollmer, Trinity United Church Minister, where they play games, draw, sing

songs ... .and Rev. Vollmer talks with the group about different concerns. "If God came and talked to you what would you say about the state of the world?" was the topic last Thursday. The children mentioned concern about nuclear weapons and pollution. Last Thursday there were 24 there which is a fairly average number. Rev. Vollmer says she enjoys children and likes seeing them enjoying themselves... Many of the children who come are from the United Church, but there are many from families that go to other churches or none at all......Larger crowds show up at the parties which are held about four times a year, ... Christmas, Easter, Hallowe'en and just before the group breaks up for the summer in June."

There were a lot of churches in Grand Valley, a town of about 1,200 people. All the churches in Grand Valley were represented by the Ministerial Association, which included the Presbyterian Church, the Baptist Church, the Latter Day Saints Church, Church of Christ, Trinity and Monticello United Churches and the Anglican Church. All leaders in these churches except for myself, were all men. Apart from those churches in the Ministerial, there was also a Kingdom Hall in town but they weren't part of the ministerial. About a month after I arrived in Grand Valley, there was a knock on my door and I opened it to find two people standing there. I invited them into my home and we talked in my hallway. They were both Jehovah Witnesses and they had their bibles with them that had many small pieces of paper sticking out of their Bible so they had easy access to certain passages. They knew I was the minister at Trinity United Church but started reading some of these passages to me, believing that I really needed to hear the Word. I wasn't impressed and told them so. "Don't you believe in the Bible?" they asked me. "No," was all I answered. They looked at me in shock and horror and didn't know what to say. So I continued and told them I didn't believe in their interpretation of the Bible. I told them I knew a family in town that was divided because of them. The family was distraught that their mother had left Trinity United Church and gone over to the Jehovah Witnesses. She never celebrated birthdays or Christmas again with her family. Every time she met with her family, she felt compelled to tell them they needed to come to the Kingdom Hall too. It was so hard on that family. When I had only been in Grand Valley two weeks, the family talked to me about this. They loved their mom and grandma so much and they were torn. I railed at these two people for creating such a rift in a family. I told them I knew that this was part of their tactics. I told them that if they had come to my home to welcome me and have a conversation that would have been fine, but they knew I was a minister and I knew they had ulterior motives in coming to see me. I told them to get out of my home and not to come back. They never did.

One day the members of the Ministerial Association came to talk with me about the teenagers in town. There was nothing for these kids to do and there were problems with drugs and drinking. In the summertime, they would walk through some of the older people's gardens and pull things up. Teenagers also came to Grand Valley from other towns to do drugs and drink. The members of the Ministerial told me that the police detachment in Shelburne was about 30 minutes away and the young people knew that, if the police were called, they had lots of time to take off because the police had a very large area to cover. The members of the Ministerial told me they wanted to meet with the Reeve and Councilors in Grand Valley and ask them for help. They said the Reeve and most of the Councilors were members of Trinity United Church and said they would appreciate it if I made the presentation. They suggested that maybe we could ask the Council about building a roller skating rink. I was surprised they asked me to make the presentation, since I had only been in Grand Valley for two months but the members of the Ministerial seemed really sincere about making a presentation to the Council so I agreed to do what they asked. We set a date near the end of September to meet with the Council and I suggested to them that, since this would be an official visit, we wear our collars when we go to the Council. After the members of the Ministerial left, I called Jean to confirm that the Reeve and Councilors were indeed members of Trinity United Church. She confirmed they were but said she couldn't remember when they were last in church. I was excited about the possibilities of working for the community with the Ministerial but I had no idea what I was getting into. Jean tried to tell me what I could expect going to the Council but I was hopeful. Perhaps I should have asked more questions at the time.

When the time came, we went to the Council meeting and were asked to make our presentation. I talked with the Council about the young people and teenagers in the community and the need for more facilities for them, like a roller skating rink. They were not at all supportive, which is not what I expected. Not only did they not come up with a single suggestion, they showed no concern about the problems young people were having. It was clear to me they were not interested in doing anything for young people in the community. As a newcomer with an 11 year old son, I was not impressed. Then something disrespectful was said to me. I can't remember exactly what it was but I got angry. I told the Council that I had come from an Indian Reserve where the government does little to help the people and now I felt like I was on a white reserve where there was no concern for the needs of young people in their community. That ended the presentation and we left. The members of the Ministerial apologized to me and told me they realized that the Council had no interest in helping anyone but themselves.

The next day around 4:00 p.m., Adrienne Maycock, the daughter of my neighbours across the street, came over to my home. She was very agitated and told me that someone had spray painted something about me on the bridge coming into town. She said they had written, "Get out of Town Reverend Squaw". How ignorant could people be? It certainly showed me the temper of the community. I realized that the article that had been written about me when I first moved to town included a picture of me wearing braids. Obviously, someone thought that I was an Indian. All I could do was smile and be proud. Adrienne's mother June came over to apologize for her daughter telling me what had been written about me. I told her not to blame Adrienne because I didn't take it as an insult. I was sure it was no coincidence that this had happened the day after our meeting with the town council.

Then, Jean Boggs came over to talk with me. She was very upset and told me that earlier that day she had talked to Les Canivet, the Town Clerk and an active member in our church, and told him to have someone paint over those words which he had done. I told Jean that I would have preferred they leave the words on the bridge because it showed the character of the community. Jean said she thought it was probably a young person who had done it but I told her that I believed it was adults that did it. Jean tried to help me understand the community and told me that, several years earlier, a family had moved into town and bought the only gas station there. She said they were good people but the people in town refused to buy gas from them because they were black. The situation got so bad that, eventually, this family had to leave Grand Valley because they couldn't make a living. Jean said she had been very upset about how that family was treated. I was as shocked at what Jean told me about that family as I was at the attitude of the Reeve and Councilors toward the members of the Ministerial and the young people in their community. Living here in this community, I had already begun to experience negative things within the church, the community, the Jehovah Witnesses and now the Town Council.

It is hard to stay positive when there are negative forces around us trying to pull us down, but I was determined to remain positive and faithful to what I believed although I knew that was not going to be easy. I realized that people saw everything I did and took notice so I began to feel like a goldfish in a bowl and I wasn't totally comfortable with that. Now it became even more important to me to continue the work I was already doing with young people and raise that up as a positive force in the community. Yes I was angry and upset at the stupidity of people in this community and in the church, but I knew I couldn't afford to take it personally. This wasn't so much about me as about the community acting out and showing its true colors. I had learned at Roseau, and in the communities that surrounded it, that life is not always what it seems on the surface and I was discovering that is true everywhere. It was certainly true here in Grand Valley. Small and racially discriminating minds live everywhere. But life had to go on and I was determined to keep my life and Warren's as normal as possible.

When my dryer broke down I called Blake, to come and look at it. He did and told me it couldn't be fixed because it was too old. He also told me he wasn't sure when he would be able to get a new dryer because they were expensive and it would take time. I had reached my breaking point and I was tired of feeling pushed around. I was really upset with Blake. He was taking it upon himself, without any consultation with his committee, to tell me that he wasn't prepared to look after this which was disrespectful to me and not acceptable. I was angry and I pushed back. I told him that, in that case, it would now take me longer to do our laundry without a dryer and I wouldn't be able to visit as much or do some of the other things I normally had time to do. I went on about that and how I would have to cut back the hours I spent doing ministry and he heard me. He went to Toronto, bought a new dryer and installed it all in two days. Why did Blake try to make things more difficult for me? Was he showing me he was the boss and in control? I just needed the dryer replaced. It was part of my contract and I wasn't asking for anything that the Charge was not required to do. Why did I have to go through this with him? I was becoming very frustrated and wondering whether I had made a mistake coming to Grand Valley. Manitoba started looking pretty good to me but there was a ministry to do here and I had just begun.

Back in September, I had talked with the Ministry and Personnel Committee about taking a course on Stewardship from October 19-23 in Toronto. I thought taking this course, with its focus on finances and mission, would be helpful to the ministry I was doing. The committee had agreed and, while I was away, Warren stayed with the Rowes next door. This course was great and I learned a lot. As we all gathered at 9:00 a.m. for our last session I heard someone say that we had a celebrity in our midst. I looked around like everyone else did to see who it was when someone came over and told me it was me, that I was the celebrity. I was on the front page of *The Globe and Mail* and the title of the article was "Unwed Mother Wins Respect in Ministry". I was shocked and embarrassed. No one had contacted me from *The Globe and Mail* and I didn't know what to think. The Bishop of the Latter Day Saints Church from Guelph came over to me and asked me if I had read the article. I told him I hadn't and that I didn't even know what was in it, why it had been written or even who had written it. He told me that he had read the article, and thought it was a good article. He said he was proud to be in the ministry with me. I thanked him for his comments and really appreciated it but I was very embarrassed. Then someone else came over to me and asked me if I would like to read the article. I said no, not right now. My head was still swimming and I felt so disconcerted that I don't even remember saying goodbye to the members of the group.

On the Go Train going back to Oakville to get my car, I kept seeing pictures of myself and Warren on the front page of *The Globe and Mail* as people sat reading the paper. I was so embarrassed that I just wanted to crawl under my seat. I don't remember driving home, but I know I couldn't wait to get there and close the door. When I did get home, Warren was there and came running over to me with a copy of the paper a neighbor had given him and said the neighbor had told him that *The Globe and Mail* had sold out for the first time ever in Grand Valley. He was so excited. After all, he was on the front page of *The Globe and Mail* and he thought that was just too cool. Warren gave me the paper and I thought I looked very stern in the photo. But then aren't ministers supposed to look that way? That thought made me laugh and just looking at Warren, who was so happy, was infectious. I took a deep breath and sat down to read the article. It actually turned out to be quite good. Here are some excerpts from this article published October 23, 1981:

> *"Dorinda Vollmer has her work cut out for her. She's 38, unmarried and the mother of an 11 year-old boy – and she is also a United Church Minister….Miss Vollmer pads around the large two-story manse in purple and white checkered slippers….The hard-edged symbolic paintings she does as a hobby hang in the living room. She watches football on TV, smokes small cigars after dinner and does not mind using a curse or two to make a point in conversation….Of Warren's birth she says, "I was 25. I should have known better. But he was a child of love, regardless of the circumstances. It wasn't right, but let's get on with it." …..*

> *Rev. Jim Campbell of the Oakville church Miss Vollmer first attended supported her in her fight to become a minister. He agrees that she had a difficult time of it and had to be pretty tough to survive. "There was a precedent set and the church didn't want anybody*

at the time to say the church had done this without any thought. "Dr. William Fennell, Principal of Emmanuel College... .where Miss Vollmer studied divinity, remembers her as strong and "very interesting." He said, "The church must stand for its principles but must recognize that there are tragic situations and exceptional circumstances when to adhere to these norms would be in humane."...

Miss Sanderson, who is in charge of placing new United Church (student) ministers across the country said the West accepts women more easily. The second single-mother minister came from the East Coast, and the Maritime Presbytery of the United Church, which recommended her for the ministry, "had a lot of trouble with that one."

"Acceptance is all up to the congregation, which can make a minister's life heaven or hell. Some congregations can be open and accepting, but some can be very narrow," said Rev. Norm Greene of Caledon, chairman of Miss Vollmer's Presbytery of Dufferin-Peel....

"Dorinda has been very well received by the congregation," said Blake Witmer, a member of the Grand Valley congregation and head of the church committee that chose Miss Vollmer. "It's fair to say that there were reservations among the congregation, but we felt her strong points are sufficient to overcome what some might consider a handicap. If we are as Christian as we claim to be, we must use Christian principles at the very least in our work within the church."

Miss Vollmer has stood in her pulpit where she looks tiny in her crimson robes, preaching on such touchy topics as rowdyism on the main street and uncommitted parents. "After last Sunday, I thought they might tar and feather me," Miss Vollmer said with a laugh. "You can't miss the point she's making," Mr. Witmer said.

"The power of her personality is probably the greatest factor in her success." Miss Sanderson said, "Someone else in Dorinda's circumstances would probably not have made it. But her determination and commitment to the ministry are both very strong and they come across. With someone else, being an unmarried mother would have been the overriding factor."

Then I remembered that Campbell Cork had called to ask me if he could write an article about me that might be placed in the religious section of *The Toronto Star* or *The Globe and Mail*. I had said yes and he had come to my house and taken pictures of Warren and me and asked a lot of questions for this article. I didn't think any more about it at the time, but now that decision was coming back to haunt me. That evening, I got a phone call from Campbell apologizing for what *The Globe and Mail* had done, especially for the title they had chosen, "Unwed Mother Wins Respect in Ministry". He told me he had sent the article to *The Globe and Mail* with the understanding that, if they put it in their paper, it would be in the religious section. I had grown up in a newspaper family and I told him that I knew it wasn't his fault. You can't tell the editor of a newspaper where to put an article in their paper. He told me that, when he found out from *The Globe* earlier that week that the article would be in the paper on October 23, he had called me but I was away, so he had sent me a letter. I told him that I had just gotten back and hadn't had a chance to look at my mail yet. I told him what had happened to me that morning and how embarrassed I had felt. I told him I only read the article when I got home and that my son had been very excited about being on the front page of *The Globe and Mail*. I told him it was a very good article and I thanked him for it. I really appreciated his phone call. There was a letter in my mail from Campbell and he wrote:

> *"I called Wed and Thurs before this came out, Warren said you were away for the week. I must say I was surprised they used it on front. Too bad they felt it necessary to choose such a sensational headline. I guess that's newspapers for you. All in all, I was pleased with the way it turned out and I hope you are too. I expect you've probably seen it already, but here's the tear sheet for the old scrapbook. Call me anytime if you have any comments good or bad. Thanks for your help. I have never interviewed anyone quite so courageous and honest."*

It was now late in the evening and I finally got Warren settled down for bed. I made myself a coffee and was just relaxing when someone knocked at my door. It was Blake Witmer. He told me that, as the Chair of the Pastoral Relations Committee that had asked me to be their minister, he was not pleased about the article. When I asked him whether he had read it, he told me he hadn't and that he had not even read the first article Campbell had written about me in *The Star and Vidette*. He told me that both congregations knew of my situation but it was not for the public to know. I was not happy at all with what Blake was saying to me. I was annoyed with him again! I told him how the article had come about but he was not impressed. He said what he came to say and then I walked him out. At the door, he said he hoped this incident wouldn't change anything between us and I answered, "Blake, I always have the pulpit". He turned and left.

The fallout from this article kept me busy for months after it came out. Not long after it was written, The Niagara Falls Review wrote an article with much the same information only much shorter and then my friend Audrey Pearse, sent me a copy of the write up she did in her weekly article in *The Red River Valley Echo* on November 4, 1981. I also received the following letter from Janet Turpin dated October 27, 1981:

> *"I read the article about you in The Globe last week and decided after much thought to write to you. I am a social worker and I run a Women's Issues group at a high school here in Burlington. There are a dozen teenage girls in my group and we talk about anything and everything that affects them as women growing up in this society....The girls are enthusiastic and extremely eager to express their opinions and feelings concerning many different issues.... Lately a number of girls have expressed a concern with God and religion.*

They seem to believe very much in God and want to live their lives in ways which would please God. However they have some problems with the teachings of organized religion regarding the position and role of women. I think they are experiencing a clash between a literal, and quite rigorous, interpretation of the Bible and their desire to live good and moral lives without confining themselves to traditional woman's roles. For myself, I believe in God. Long ago though, I rejected organized religion……I'm not certain that I can answer all their questions, though I think a person like you could. You're a woman, a single parent and a minister. I imagine there were times when you fought a mighty battle in your own heart over such an apparently unorthodox lifestyle. Would you consider coming to a group meeting we have them every Wednesday from 3:15-4:30 to talk to the girls? You could start by talking about anything you wanted –Why you became a minister, the problems you have encountered as a single parent etc. I'm sure the girls will have endless questions for you. I feel that you could have a very strong impact on them and hopefully help them work through some of the confusing thoughts they have right now. I'm certain you will inspire them."

In her letter she gave me her phone number and not long after I called her. I went to Central High School in Burlington to meet her and talk with these 15 girls aged 14-15 and they were as enthusiastic as Janet had said they would be. I told them my story and said I felt called to ministry when I was only five years old. Then I explained my journey to ordination. I talked with them about my love for God and my faith journey and I told them about my two summers as a student minister and how I felt about doing ministry. They were all very responsive and asked lots of questions. How did I know I was called? What did it feel like to grow up in a church? How do you know God loves us? The questions went on and on. We had a great discussion and then I told them that I had three questions to ask them. I assured them they needed only to respond if they felt comfortable by raising their hands. I asked them if they had already had sex and more than half of the girls raised their hands. I asked them if they drank alcohol every week and most of them raised their hands. Finally I asked them if they did drugs and some of them raised their hands. Frankly, I was surprised they raised their hands at all but I guess I had earned their trust. " If you are doing all these things now," I said to them, "what's left?"

Then I talked quietly with them about love and God and Jesus and how my faith had helped me and how much I have needed my faith, especially when I made mistakes and when I lost someone I loved. One young person told me that one of her parents was Protestant and the other was Catholic and they decided not to raise her in any church because they couldn't agree on which Church. They told her she could decide for herself when she grew up. She told me she was confused and asked me how she could ever decide when she didn't know what it was like to be raised in the Church. We talked about that. I understood from what they told me that all of them had parents who were powerful people in their professions and all of them were well off. Some parents left their daughters alone when they went away on weekends and that was when some of these girls had their parties. These were intelligent, beautiful girls who didn't have a strong faith base on which to build their lives. I felt this was a very emotionally distressed and confused group of young girls who just wanted to feel loved. I told them that they were all going to have great influence on other people when they finished high school and asked how they were going to use their education and privilege to help people or just help themselves. I challenged them and I was honest and open with them. I felt sad that they felt so conflicted and unsure of who they were. I told them about Roseau and the Indian people and the poverty and racism there and how that can destroy not only individuals but a whole culture. Because the church is a wealthy institution in itself I asked them how they thought the Church should use its power and influence. I was presented with an opportunity to talk to these young people and I rose to the challenge. I could only hope that down the road something I said might help them in a time they were trying to make a difficult decision. I really enjoyed my time with these young people. I often wondered what became of them.

The fallout from the *Globe and Mail* article didn't end and even Menno Wiebe, Director of Native Concerns, Mennonite Central Committee in Winnipeg, saw it and wrote to me on October 26:

> *"I was on my way out of the door the other morning, en route to Roseau River, when Vern Ratzlaff threw me a copy of the October 23rd issue of The Globe and Mail. On the way south, I read the very interesting article on the front page "Unwed Mother Wins Respect as Minister."*
>
> *Having been close to the scene of your significant ministry here at Roseau and especially the many chances we had to share about your strong visions for that community I felt particularly gripped with the good news of your pastoral assignment at Grand Valley. May the Good Lord give strength to your words and love to your actions as you give pastoral leadership to your church… … .*
>
> *While there are clearly many ways to assess any ministry, I feel convinced that your work at Roseau was a demonstration of what could be done when the vision is sufficiently strong. The firmness with which the band and council have tackled some tough issues, including the construction of an arena and band hall and the birth of a new school with goals and purposes designed by the Ojibway people of Roseau, are but some examples of such determination following strong visions. Your non-preaching ministry at Roseau was a demonstration of making great achievements against considerable odds."*

It was wonderful and heartwarming to receive this letter from Menno whom I greatly respected and it was good to be reminded that the ministry I had done at Roseau was not only important but significant. That same day I received a letter, also dated October 26, from Reverend Bob Smith who would go on to be elected Moderator of our Church in 1984. He wrote:

> *"I read with great interest the article in The Globe and Mail and felt good about being in the same Church as you are. I hope you felt good about the article as well and, since any kind of publicity tends to encourage the crazies to come out of the woodwork I just wanted you to have a letter of a different sort. Kind regards to you and Warren."*

It was good of Bob to write to me and I also appreciated his concern about 'the crazies' which proved to be true. Around the end of October one of the people at *The Globe and Mail* called me. She said they had received a lot of mail in regards to the article that was written about me. She said they had opened the mail, but it was mostly hate mail and she wouldn't send it to me but would send on what she felt she could. I was shocked. I really was. First of all, I hadn't expected I would get any mail and then to think it was hate mail. She did send two pieces of mail from people whom I would consider evangelists from the extreme right or just simply crazy. They were tame in comparison to what she told me people had sent. I threw them out. I wasn't naïve but it was hard to believe people could write things that were so hateful.

I was having trouble with these articles because the focus of them was on me and my being an unwed mother. I had sorted all that out years ago and here it was coming up again. It had all started with Blake writing an article in the local paper when I came to Grand Valley. I had never asked for any of these articles to be written. At Roseau, I had been interviewed many times in regards to the Children's Centre but the focus had been on the Centre not on me and I was fine with that. Now I was feeling uncomfortable being in the spotlight like this. The one good thing that had come out of this notoriety was talking with the teenage girls at the high school in Burlington but I didn't have any other requests. I wasn't sure where all this was going but it didn't sit well with me, especially with articles pointing out my not being married and having a child. It was embarrassing and I didn't know how to handle it. My music became a source of solace for me in that time.

Early in November, I got a phone call from one of the producers of *"That's Life"*, a TV series on Global Television. The producer had seen the article in *The Globe* and he asked me if I would be interested in having them come and bring a TV crew out to tape a Sunday service in Grand Valley and interview me. I wasn't sure about this, especially since not even a month had passed since *The Globe* article had come out. I told him I would have to talk with the Session of our church about this at our meeting that evening and I would call him the next day. There was lots of business to discuss at the Session meeting, and under new business, I talked with them about the television show and told them that they wanted to come and tape a segment at the church. At first, the Elders weren't sure what to say and then Anne Young, one of the Elders asked me what I thought. Until that moment I hadn't known what to think really, but I said, "If doing this helps one woman out there, I want to do it." They thought about that for a few minutes and then the Session agreed to let the crew come. I called the producer the next day and said they could come. We discussed the details and he told me that the crew would come in January with their host, Peter Feniak. They would tape part of the church service and then come to my home and talk with me and my son. He asked if I had other family and I told him that my aunts lived in Oakville. He asked if it was possible to have my aunts there and I said yes. Although I had mixed feelings about the television show, it still seemed far enough away that I could put it out of my mind for the moment. In the meantime, a brutal winter came to Grand Valley. We had storm after storm which Warren loved but I didn't. I was glad I parked my car near the road and because now the snow was over two feet high and I was having to clear the driveway often and the winter had just started.

Then we prepared for Christmas. Of course, Louise and Susie came and we had the most wonderful Christmas together, continuing all the traditions my family had when I was a child growing up. We all loved Christmas but for Warren it was magical. My first Christmas Eve service at Trinity United Church was wonderful. Irene literally pulled out all the stops on the organ to make the music just perfect, and the Junior and Senior Choirs were at their best. When Warren went to bed that night, I read the *Charlie Brown Christmas* to him as well as *The Christmas story* and *'Twas the Night Before Christmas*. He was up very early Christmas morning, opened his Christmas stocking and was happy to see Santa had eaten the cookies and drank all the milk we left out the night before. We had our usual breakfast and then opened presents, laughing and having fun all the while as we listened to the beautiful Christmas carols on my tapes. Warren loved Star Wars and he got lots of those toys and figurines from his aunts and from me. He also got an astronomy set that year and some string art because he liked rug hooking. Of course he loved reading, so he always got books to read. The older he got the more he went from the classics to science fiction and fantasy. All afternoon we played bridge while we waited for the turkey to cook. This time I had a large kitchen and didn't have to worry about how big the turkey was for our Christmas Day dinner. After dinner, I played Jean's piano and we sang all the Christmas carols. Louise was especially happy that I had a piano again. It was a wonderful Christmas and I was feeling right at home with my family.

Before I turned around, though, it was January and time for the TV show taping. The congregation knew what was happening and seemed to be fairly upbeat about it. I had gone down to Oakville on the Friday before the taping and brought Susie and Louise to Grand Valley for the weekend. They were thrilled to be part of this and, of course, they were always happy to spend time with Warren and me. The TV crew showed up before the service on that Sunday and did the set up as people came into church and saw all the cameras and were very excited. After all, it wasn't every day a camera crew came out and filmed a church service. Many of our members watched *That's Life,* never thinking we would be on the show. Before the service began, I talked with the congregation about what the crew would be doing and I introduced the three members of the crew and Peter Feniak, the host. I also mentioned that he would like to interview members of the congregation after the service. I have no idea what I preached on that Sunday but I do remember that, after church, people told me they appreciated my sermon and that it had been a great experience. I was relieved that we had got through the service just fine. After the service, Peter interviewed quite a few people in the church and then the crew took all the equipment down and came to my house. We all had lunch together and then Peter started the interviews with me. I felt nervous about being filmed but Peter was a wonderful interviewer and he made me feel that just the two of us were talking. He asked me how I came to be in Grand Valley and I talked with him about my call and my time in Manitoba at the Roseau River Indian Reserve and how I felt about the Church and the Church's responsibility to serve and be present to those in need. The more questions Peter asked me, the easier it was for me to talk.

Warren was so excited to be interviewed and Peter interviewed him in his bedroom. I stayed downstairs with my aunts. I didn't realize until afterwards that Warren sat on his bed which only had a sheet on it and with his comics spread around him. As they filmed him Peter asked him what it was like to have a mother for a minister and what he liked to do in church and in the community. Then my aunts were interviewed together and they talked about my music and my love for the ministry.

When they were done, they started to get ready to leave. But It was a very cold blustery winter day in Grand Valley that Sunday and we already had lots of snow on the ground. By the time they were packed up and ready to go, the roads were closed because of a blizzard and they ended up having to stay overnight. I hadn't counted on that. Warren and my aunts were thrilled, but all I could think about was what I had in the house for dinner and where I was going to put them all. I called my next door neighbour, who was the owner of the IGA store in town, and explained the situation. He sent over steaks and potatoes and salad for which I was very grateful. Then I phoned June and Wayne Maycock, across the street, and they sent over some bottles of wine. We had a great dinner and they were all impressed with the small town hospitality. After dinner, one of the crew members and Warren played the new video game he had just gotten for Christmas and my aunts even taught two of the guys how to play bridge while I talked with Peter. It turned out to be a great evening. A couple of the crew slept downstairs on the two chesterfields while one of the crew slept in the small office upstairs. Louise and Susie had the spare bedroom. Unfortunately, Warren had to give up his bedroom and go to the neighbours to sleep so Peter could have his room. He was not impressed.

In the morning, I made pancakes for everyone and just when they were getting ready to go, someone knocked at the door. It was Jack Morrison, a member of the church. He said he just wanted everyone to know that the roads were clear and it was time for them all to go. Jack, who was in his late 50s, had been sneaking around to see his girlfriend every week for years, a secret that everyone knew so I was very amused by his concern. He was all worried about me and my reputation with four men in my house. My aunts asked Peter if he could possibly give them a ride home and Peter said they would. They had a big van and lots of room for everyone. It was a little out of their way but they didn't mind. The crew told us how much they appreciated our hospitality and what a great time they had had. Then they were off. Nothing in town seemed to get past the local newspaper and when *The Star and Vidette* came out January 13, 1982 with a short note titled *'That's Lifecrew Stranded'* it read:

> *"A filming and interviewing crew from the popular Global TV program "That's Life", got more than it bargained for during its visit to Grand Valley this past week-end. The crew was in the village on Sunday morning to film parts of the United Church service as part of*

a feature being done on Rev. Dorinda Vollmer of Trinity United Church. The crew filmed parts of the service and conducted short interviews with some of the people present... ... Rev. Vollmer was interviewed at her home on King Street and interviews were conducted with her son Warren and (her) aunt(s). About 5:00 p.m., the crew, including show co-host Peter Feniak, decided it was time to leave for Toronto, however weather conditions soon changed their minds and they settled down to enjoy a stormy evening in the village. By noon Monday, conditions had improved enough to allow the crew to return to Toronto."

When the show came out in February, we really enjoyed watching it. Audrey Pearse from Dominion City sent me an annoucement that she wrote in *The Red River Valley Echo*, February 3rd about the show and it said: *"Dorinda Vollmer phoned the Sawatzky home the other day and asked about everyone. She also mentioned she would be on TV on Channel 9 CKND sometime in February, so if you watch That's Life on Saturday at 12 noon and Tuesday, Wednesday and Thursday at 2:30 in the afternoon you will see Dorinda, Warren and Dorinda's two aunts."*

I later heard from friends in Dominion City that many of them got together when they found out when the show was on and had tea and cookies and watched it more than once. So much had happened over those previous six months. I had had to deal with a great deal of negativity from many different sources which was wearing me down. Even if it hadn't been all bad, it took so much energy for me to keep the negativity at bay and stay focused on the positive. I wasn't the only one affected by the negativity. I didn't realize how Warren was affected by all of this until one day when I was going upstairs and I heard him crying. He was sitting on his bed and I went and sat with him and asked him what was wrong. He found it hard to talk about why he was upset but finally he said, "Everyone is the same." When he said that, I realized he missed the diversity, the different cultures he had gotten used to at Roseau and at Crane Public School in Winnipeg. Warren missed his friends. It was obvious to me that those five years in Manitoba had been good for my son. Like Warren, I missed the diversity and relating to different cultures and I understood exactly what he meant. I told him I missed that too but there wasn't anything I could do about it right now. He said he understood but he just felt sad. This was the only time, in all the moves we made, that Warren felt this way and I was glad we could have a good talk about it. It was becoming clear to me that Grand Valley was not an easy place for us to live and I understood that perhaps I had been blindsided by all the positive and comfortable aspects of living and working there. If I was to be honest, I wanted to have some semblance of a normal life for myself and my son after the previous five years that had almost broken me. But the first six months in Grand Valley had been anything but normal and most of what happened was totally unexpected. I had been doing very well and I had been very busy, but the concerns my son had, made me realize that it wasn't easy for him either.

I was becoming quite a celebrity and soon had another phone call, this time from the *Sunday Sun*. They told me they had also seen *That's Life* and wanted to do a write-up on women in ministry to be featured in their Sunday Showcase section. The ordination of women had only been approved by the Anglican Church of Canada on November 20th, 1976 where six women were ordained. I agreed to do this since there would be three of us interviewed. The reporter who came out brought a photographer with him who took pictures of me. The photographer wanted to take these pictures outside with me wearing my robes, and asked me if I would stand on top of the snow bank in front of the church because he said it would make a better picture,. Warren was home from school when he took these photos and he thought it was really funny. That 11x15 picture turned up in colour on the front page of the Sunday Showcase section on March 7, 1982 with the caption: *"Women of the Cloth. Religion comes of age in Ontario."* On page 3 there was a full page write-up titled "Women priests flock to the call" written by Lee Lester and the three small photos were by Ken Kerr. The first write-up was titled, "A few thorns in the path", and was about The Rev. Ruth Pogson who had been recently ordained and was the minister at Grace Anglican Church in Arthur and St. Albans on the Hill in Grand Valley. Ruth was 58 years old and a very good minister and had come to Grand Valley a few months after I did. Ruth had invited me to come to her covenanting service and I remember it well. There was a lot of pomp and ceremony with many priests attending and I was asked to wear my robes and be in the procession. I went into the hall of the church where everyone was getting ready and, as I put my robes on, one of the priests came to me and said that I needed to wear white. I was wearing a white vestment under my red robe, which is what I always did, but the priest was asking me to wear only white. I told him as nicely as I could that this is what I always wore in my church and I would do the same in this church. We all walked in together and sat in the pews set aside for us. There were two full rows in front of me on either side with priests and important officials all in white vestments. It was slightly overwhelming but I wanted to be there to support Ruth. When it came time for communion, I knew members of my congregation would follow my lead and so I went up with everyone else to be served communion.

The second woman interviewed was Reverend Doris Way, a minister in the Crawford Street Congregational Church in Toronto. Her husband was the pastor and when he became ill, she took over many of his duties. After his death in 1957, she became their lay minister and was ordained in 1965. She was also 58 years old. The write up on Doris was titled, *"Pastor's wife to Minister."* The third write up was on me and was titled, *"Unwed mom earns respect"* and it said:

> *"Women ministered to Christ on the cross. They anointed him. Women have always been at the centre of Christianity," says the Rev. Dorinda Vollmer, 37, of the United Church, Grand Valley... ... she is an unmarried mother and her son, Warren, is now 11. She says the United Church had to be very careful in accepting her for ordination in 1976. Nevertheless, her congregation has supported her and she says: "I can relate to kids who are pregnant because of my experience. I have washed floors in hospitals, waitressed, worked four years on an Indian Reserve... ...People feel very comfortable talking to me. I do not put myself above them. I am one of them."... "It is becoming in our church more accepted to have a woman minister but there is still a lot of work to do," she says.*

Along with all the articles that came out, I was very busy in the ministry. I was doing 20 hours a week preparation on my sermons, and spending another 40-50 hours a week preparing and conducting services, visiting, doing funerals as they came up, holding Baptism classes when needed, going to meeting after meeting and doing the administrative work that was required. Since December, I had officiated at seven funerals and at the end of March I had one of the saddest funerals. Bill Sime was the Funeral Director in Grand Valley and, like many Funeral Directors of his day, he also had a furniture store alongside the funeral home. Bill and his wife Dorothy were wonderful people. One day in the spring, he called me before church to tell me a young man, 20 years old, had committed suicide and had used a rifle to kill himself. The police had called Bill and they needed him to go out and get the body. Bill told me he had gone into the bush to retrieve the body as it was muddy and impossible to take a car in so they had had to walk in by foot and bring the young man out on a stretcher. I could tell by Bill's voice on the phone that he was very upset, which was unusual for him. I asked him who this young man's family was and where they lived. He said it was a long ways out in the country and he wasn't sure I should go out. I insisted and told him I would go out and see the family after church was over and he gave me directions.

The family lived off the beaten track, far from town and when I drove into the driveway, I could see from the house and surroundings that the family didn't have very much. I went up to the door and knocked. I waited a long time and began to think that no one was home when a young woman, probably 18 years old, opened the door. She had a blank look on her face and when I introduced myself, she simply walked ahead of me back into the house. There was hardly any furniture in the room and she told me to sit on the chesterfield and we both sat down. It was hard to get any information out of her. Then she suddenly got up and went to the kitchen saying she would make tea. As I looked around the room, I saw a woman up on a ladder behind me and she appeared to be washing the walls. She was older and I thought she might be the mother. As I started to get up to go to her, I realized there was no pail of water and that she was using a dry cloth to go over and over the same spot on the wall. As I began to take this in, I heard the kettle boil and the daughter came back from the kitchen and said that she would take me to her father. As she ushered me out of the house the kettle was still boiling.

We got into my car and I drove out of the driveway. The daughter said little except to point to where to turn as we drove deeper and deeper into the woods. I knew this girl's mother had some problems and I began to wonder what problems this young girl had. I was getting concerned as to where she was taking me. Finally, she had me turn onto a dirt road, if you could call it that as we went even deeper into the woods now. I couldn't imagine where on earth we are going as branches hit against my car. Then I saw a truck up ahead and she told me to stop. There was a man standing by the truck and I assumed he was this girl's father. Without thinking, I got out of my car and went up to the man and told him how sorry I was about his son. He looked at me and I will never forget the look of pain in his eyes and the feeling of overwhelming helplessness that I felt from him. He apologized to me for having to come out to see him and then talked to me for a long time about his family and how hard he had tried to help his wife and children. He knew how sick his wife was and knew she had a mental illness, but he couldn't put her away, he told me. He apologized to me for having to come out to see him. His son had taken his own life and he felt it was his fault. He was so sad and lost. Life had beaten him down and he had nothing left to give. We talked about the funeral service and he said he didn't know if his wife even knew what had happened even though he had told her. He also said he didn't know how she would be at the funeral but that he needed to bring her. I listened and offered whatever support I could. It seemed surreal, standing there in the woods alone with this man as he shared his life with me.

It was a very small group of people who gathered for the funeral but his wife did come. The dead boy's mother sat quietly throughout the service and only whimpered from time to time, rocking gently back and forth. Even today, I can still see them and I can still feel their pain. I will never forget that husband and father who did everything he could to keep his family together. Their pain has stayed with me and is still so much a part of who I am today. Perhaps that is why it has taken so long for me to write this story.

CHAPTER TWO

Three Wonderful Friends

Things finally settled down in the next few months and there were no more reporters wanting to interview me. Warren had done very well at school and made new friends - Mark Spencer, Paul and Sheila Hunter, Brandon and Meredith Borman and Julie Maycock. They all came to the Thursday afternoon drop- in at my home and had formed a bond with Warren. By March I was very busy with the day to day ministry. I went to the monthly meeting of Dufferin Peel Presbytery and I enjoyed the fellowship with other ministers representing about 25 Pastoral Charges. Because I was in Toronto Conference, I also attended their yearly three day meetings in May to do the business of the Court, along with about 400 other delegates. All the ministers in their Pastoral Charges were expected to attend these conferences, which also included the lay people who were elected by their Pastoral Charge to represent them in their Presbytery and at Conference. I enjoyed those Conferences because they always had wonderful speakers and great music.

Irene Newson, the organist at Trinity United Church, announced she would be retiring at the end of June, 1982. She was having trouble with her eyes and it was becoming more difficult for her. We were sorry to see Irene go because she was such a wonderful organist and musician but we had no choice but to set up a committee to find a new organist. Someone suggested we approach Liz Borman, who was a piano teacher in town and she said she was interested. The committee interviewed her and discovered that she was a very good organist and hired her to start in September.

I didn't know Liz. She was not a member in our church nor did she attend church, so, after she was hired, I called her and we set up a visit. I went to her home and was greeted by a woman in her middle 30s, who seemed very nice but very nervous when she led me into her kitchen and made us a cup of coffee. No sooner had she handed me the cup of coffee she reached into her dining room cabinet, brought out a bottle of Irish Cream and asked if I would like to have some in my coffee. That took me by surprise since it was only 11:00 a.m. in the morning so I said no thank you. She put the bottle back in the cabinet, turned to me and said, "I don't know what I was thinking." That started us both laughing and broke the ice between us. She told me that part of the reason she was nervous was because she had heard what a good musician I was. I assured her that I appreciated the music of every organist I worked with. That seemed to put her at ease and then she told me about herself. Liz said she was raised in a Baptist Church but hadn't been to church in quite a few years. She said that her husband was an electrician and they had three children in school, Brandon and Marilyn who I knew because Warren was friends with them at school, and a younger daughter Meredith. We liked each other right away and I looked forward to working with her. When Warren came home from school that day, I told him I had met the new organist who was starting at our church in July and talked with him about taking piano lessons. He said he didn't want to but it was the only time I insisted he do something he really didn't want to do. Warren was grumpy about it but, once he knew he had to this, he took it seriously. Liz agreed to teach him starting in September and within two years he got his Grade Three piano exam and his Grade One Theory and I was proud of him.

My sister Jana lived in Sacramento, California and we had had many conversations over that first year at Grand Valley. We talked once or twice a month and she would tell me all the news about Ken's children - Derek, Steve and the twins Nicky and Monty. Their mother was in jail serving a long sentence for drug possession and none of her children wanted to see her. They really liked my sister and called her Mom. Jana also told me all the things that her children Stacy and Scott were doing and how well everything was going with her and Ken. I filled her in about Warren and Louise and Susie, how things were going at my churches and how I was feeling about everything. I told her all about the reporters who came and went that first year, the newspaper articles and the television show, *That's Life*.

In June, Jana told me Steve wanted to come for a visit in July. He was 15 and old enough to travel on his own. If I would like to have him for two weeks, Ken would pay for the trip. I told her I would love to have him. Warren thought that was a great idea too. It would give him a chance to get to know his cousin better. We picked Steve up at the airport early in the evening and got home around 9:00 p.m. He was very excited and happy to be with us and loved our big, roomy house and the spare bedroom which would be his room while he was with us. We were just sitting around trying to keep cool on that hot and humid evening when someone knocked at my door. It was 10 year old Johnny and I knew his mom Trisha. She didn't go to our church and I didn't know her very well but I knew who she was and where she lived. Johnny told me his mom was having her baby and needed to go to the hospital but her boyfriend was at work and there was nobody to take her.

Warren and Steve, Johnny and I got in my Volkswagen Beetle and headed over to pick up Trisha. Steve was excited by this turn of events and up for the adventure. When we got to Trisha's apartment, I could see she was ready to give birth and I drove as fast as I could to the hospital in Orangeville. This was the one time I hoped the police would chase me down for speeding but no luck that night. I got her to the hospital around 10:30 p.m. and they took her in right away. I decided to wait and make sure everything was alright since I expected the baby would be delivered very soon. We waited for over two hours and I became very concerned because we could hear Trisha crying out in pain. The nurses knew I was a minister because I visited at the hospital every week. One of the nurses came and talked with me a few times. The last time she talked to me, she seemed nervous and I asked her if everything was alright. She said the doctor was having a problem but assured me Trisha would be fine and there wasn't anything more I could do and we should go home. She said they would look after Johnny because his stepdad had called and was coming off his shift and would be at the hospital soon.

We got home about 1:30 a.m. and Warren and Steve went right to bed. I had trouble falling asleep because I had a bad feeling about what was happening at the hospital. I couldn't say why. I just hoped Trisha was alright. About 3:00 a.m. in the morning the phone rang and woke me. It was a doctor calling me from the hospital. He told me that the doctor who saw Trisha was drunk and he had expected Trisha to give birth naturally and had kept telling her to keep pushing. But he was too drunk to realize it was a breach baby and he wouldn't listen to the nurses who became so concerned they had called him and asked him to come to the hospital. He said he took over and Trisha delivered a healthy baby boy. Both were fine he said but, if they had waited much longer, it would have been very serious. He also told me that it wasn't the first time the other doctor had been drunk on duty. I was surprised to hear what had happened and was very disturbed by it. The doctor assured me that this matter would be dealt with at the next hospital board meeting and I believed him. He didn't have to be honest and tell me the truth but I appreciated that he had. I was so relieved everything was alright. The next day, the boys and I went to Orangeville to visit Trisha and her new beautiful baby boy.

We had a great time with Steve on that visit. We went on picnics, I took him to Niagara Falls and to Stratford. At church, I introduced him to members of my congregation and everyone enjoyed meeting him. We also went to Oakville to see the aunts. They loved him and Susie even tried to teach him how to play bridge. In Oakville we picked up Danny, Warren's friend whom he had met at Theresa's, his babysitter when we lived in Oakville in 1972. Danny was coming to visit with us for a few days in Grand Valley. We also picked up Cathy in Burlington, who was Steve's age and her mother Ursala and I had been friends for many years. Whenever I had to go out visiting families in the church, I dropped Warren, Steve, Danny and Cathy over at the Dobson's a few times. They were a family in my congregation who had a farm just outside of town. They had three girls. The kids all swam in their pool and I picked them up when I finished my visiting. The Maycocks also enjoyed meeting Steve and he and Warren also spent time swimming in their pool and visiting with their daughters, Adrienne and Julie, while I was busy. Warren and I had a great time with Steve and he loved being with us. Our lifestyle was totally different than what he was used to at home because Jana and his dad both worked and they had a very small, three bedroom house raising six children ages 11-15. I don't know how my sister coped with it all.

After Steve went home, we got ready to go on our annual holiday. This year, Warren and I were going to Winnipeg and would be tenting on our way there and back. We went to St. Joseph's Island, to Sault Saint Marie and Thunder Bay and had great fun at the campsites where we stayed. It was so relaxing to sit at the campfire at night. We went on boat trips and went swimming. It was wonderful. We saw the amazing monument in Thunder Bay dedicated to Terry Fox (1958- 1981) who inspired all Canadians in his attempt to run across Canada on his artificial leg to raise money for cancer. When we got to Winnipeg, we stayed a few days with Bill and Gertrude Whetter and Warren got to spend time with his friend Philip and his family. It was wonderful to see Bill and Gertrude again and they were always so kind to us. They took us to see the production of *Oliver* and it was spectacular. Then we went to Dominion City and saw Margurite and Ann Pearce, Jill and Bruce Boredenko, Mary and Alf Sawatsky and their children, Audrey and Stan Pearce and other friends from town when we lived there. Warren was so happy to be able to spend time with his friends David and Stuart.

At Roseau we had a great visit with Mary Ann Patrick and her sons Rodney and Jay and many other friends. But the highlight for me was seeing my dear friend Betty Martin and her husband James and their family. When we first arrived at their home, their children Lorraine, Lydia and Gerry and their grandchildren were there and they were very happy to see us again. Betty took me to her bedroom and closed the door. She went over to her bed and lifted the mattress and took out something wrapped in wax paper. We sat on her bed while she opened it. It was piece of fried bannock and told me she had made bannock that morning but, because the kids were crazy for it she had to hide this piece for me or I would never have gotten any of the bannock that she knew I loved. We had a good laugh over that. Before we left, Betty said she had something for me and gave me a beautiful painting she had won at Bingo. It was pretty special and I didn't want to take it because she didn't have very much but she insisted. Finally, I agreed to take it and I am so glad I have it because, every time I look at it I am reminded of Betty and her family and what a truly beautiful person she was and how much I loved her as my friend. As I looked at that painting, I realized that there was still so much pain inside of me concerning Roseau and that, at some point, I would need to deal with it.

Warren and I also went to the Band Office and we saw Joyce there which was a wonderful surprise. It seemed like forever since we had seen each other. We talked and laughed a lot and that did my heart good. Warren was really happy to see Aunty again too and they had a great conversation. We told Joyce we had just come from seeing her parents, Alice Littlejohn and Sam Hayden and she told me she was working for the Band and living in Letellier. I remembered back to all the times we had spent together, talking and sharing, and how we had really opened up to each other. I missed her. She had wonderful gifts that she had used to make a difference in the work we did at Roseau through the Children's Centre. I felt a great sense of loss leaving Roseau after this visit. I also felt some guilt at having moved on even though I knew in my heart it had been the right thing to do. But knowing that didn't make it any easier. The poverty at Roseau was still there and people still suffered and I felt that all over again. Then I called Mary Rance because we wanted to see Stephanie and Nina, Joyce's children, who had lived in my home with us in Dominion City. Warren and I went out to Sperling to visit them and we had a great visit with Stephanie and Nina. By the last week of August, it was time to head home. It was a great trip and a much needed holiday after all the craziness of our first year at Grand Valley.

In September, Liz and I talked about us doing some duets together. So the next time I was in Oakville, I went to Leslie Music, a business owned by Joan Leslie who ran it out of the basement in her house. I asked her if she had any organ piano duet music and Joan took me to the back part of her basement where there was a lot of it in a big box. I was thrilled as I looked through all this music and bought two copies of at least eight music books for organ and piano. I phoned Liz when I got back and told her what I had done. We got together the next day and it was wonderful to play through some of this music and pick out pieces we liked and would learn to play. That Thanksgiving Sunday was the first time the congregation heard us play together.

They loved it and so did we. It felt wonderful to be back at the piano, especially with Liz who really encouraged me as I encouraged her. I had played a few solos in church the previous year but now I was slowly beginning to really perform again and I loved it. We ended up with a huge repertoire of music, and over the next year, we learned many new pieces and every time we worked up a piece we felt comfortable doing, we played it for the congregation. Eventually, we would have enough piano organ duets so we could give concerts. I was so thankful for my new friend who loved music as much as I did and it really helped me in ways I could not have imagined. I had so missed my music.

One of the first things I had done when I came to my new charge in Grand Valley was to find someone who would represent me on the Ministry and Personnel Committee. This is a very important committee that deals with issues that come up between members of the congregation, or the minister and a member of the congregation. The committee also works with the minister in regards to establishing when the minister's holidays are and the three continuing education weeks. There was one person in town I really thought would be a good person to represent any concerns I might have in the charge and that was Les Canivet, the Town Clerk. I liked Les and his wife Mary who was a lovely person. They were regular attenders at our church and he knew Church procedures which was also important when dealing with church issues. I asked Les if he would sit on the Ministry and Personnel Committee as my representative and, at first, he wasn't really sure about it. I told him that if I got into trouble for any reason and if I wouldn't talk to anyone, he would have the right to come to my home and tell me exactly what he thought and I would listen to him. I told him that I did not expect him to agree with me but I needed his counsel. He took up the challenge and I really appreciated that.

Well, the first year we had no issues that I couldn't deal with but the Sunday after Thanksgiving into my second year proved to be a bit more difficult. I had been having some issues with Norma Witmer who was an Elder on Session, who was also in the choir, was the President of the United Church Women and was our Charge's representative on Presbytery which meant she also went to the yearly Toronto Conference meetings. She seemed to be involved in everything in the church and could be very blunt and annoying. But everyone put up with it. In every congregation there is a queen bee and a king bee. At Trinity United Church they were married to each other and Norma and Blake weren't always easy to deal with.

In September, a couple of people had come and talked with me about Norma and how she upset them in Sunday School and on Session because she was so opinionated and usually got her way. But these people didn't want to take it any further so there was really nothing I could do. Norma was very close with Elizabeth Taylor, a member in our congregation who helped with the Sunday School and Elizabeth had a lot of clout in the congregation. Along with Blake and Norma, this threesome could make any minister's life miserable, as well as any members of the congregation. Where I was concerned, Elizabeth kept a low profile but I could feel her presence. Her father, Reverend Wanless, had been the minister many years ago in this charge. By all accounts he had been very much loved and a wonderful minister. At one point in his ministry he had a heart attack and ended up in the hospital. Finally he was well enough to come home and took his first Sunday service after his illness. Everyone was so happy to see him back. When the service was over, he walked across the street to the manse, walked in the door and had a massive heart attack and died instantly. It was a huge shock and loss to his wife and young children and devastating to the congregation. According to the rules of the United Church of Canada's Manual, in a matter such as this when a minister dies in a Charge he serves, his family is welcome to stay in the manse for six months and then the family has to move out. In the case of Elizabeth's family, they were encouraged to move as soon as they could find a place to live. The Charge wanted to move on and they found a new minister. Elizabeth and her family were not treated kindly by the congregation at that time and Elizabeth never forgave Trinity United Church for how they had treated her family. Her mother had to take on jobs cleaning people's homes because with her husband gone they had very little money.

Elizabeth liked the fact that I worked with young people because that was something she herself was keen about so she stayed out of my way. But she was making things difficult in the Sunday School because she thought she knew what was best for the young people and, usually she had her way there with Norma's help . Two of the teachers in the Sunday School had talked to me more than once about Elizabeth and also about Norma who supported whatever Elizabeth did. The teachers were very upset and felt their opinions didn't matter.

One Sunday morning, Norma was being particularly obnoxious and vocal. She was already mad at me about the previous Presbytery meeting where I hadn't agreed with her on some issue and she let me know it and now she was going on telling the choir members what they should or shouldn't be doing. I had had enough and I lost my temper with Norma. The Junior and Senior Choirs were about to go upstairs to sing and I was about to say the prayer when I dressed Norma down in front of everyone. Then I said the prayer and we went upstairs. The choir went into the choir loft behind me and I was standing at the pulpit. Liz was at the organ in front of me. She had this strange look on her face because she could see the choir was very upset. When the service was over Liz and I had planned to go out for lunch and a movie in Orangeville since we both wanted to see the new movie *Ghandi*. On the way, I saw she was upset and she asked me what I had done to her choir. I told her I was frustrated with Norma and lost my temper with her. I also said I realized I shouldn't have. She said she understood because she had her own issues with Norma but my actions hadn't helped the situation. Liz and I let it go at that and we had a nice lunch together. We also really enjoyed the movie. It was a good afternoon.

But the situation I created that Sunday morning didn't end there. On Monday night Les came to see me. He said he had heard about what I had done on Sunday morning before church and he did not agree with what I did. He felt the way I handled the situation was wrong, especially since the Junior Choir was present. We had a long and serious talk about Blake and Norma and some of the issues I had had with Blake in the last year and he understood my frustration. Nonetheless, I told him, I knew he was right about what happened on Sunday and that I was very sorry. But what could I do? He said he would set up a meeting in the church with me and the choir and the organist to iron things out and he said that he would take charge of the meeting. It was hard for me to agree to do this because I had created the problem by handling the situation very badly. I had let my emotions get the best of me but I agreed to go to the meeting. Everyone came and we all sat together in the choir loft and Les talked with us. He said I was wrong to have done what I did, and that it had not been the way to handle the situation, especially when the Junior Choir was there. I told them how sorry I was and how badly I felt about what I had done and that it would not happen again. I apologized to Norma personally. Les was very helpful to all of us in clearing the air. He was respected by everyone in the church and in the community and there would have been a very different outcome had Les not been there, not only for me but for the choir and the congregation. After the meeting was over, every member of the choir except Norma came over and said how sorry they were which surprised me but I appreciated it.

Around the same time, a situation came up in Monticello United Church that made it clear to me the difference in the attitudes of the two congregations. Elmer, the Clerk of Session was a man of great faith and dedication. At one of our Sessions meetings we were discussing four people who wanted to join our church. Three of these people were already members of a Protestant Church who had their certificates of membership and wanted to transfer to our church. The fourth man raised some problems because he was originally from Switzerland and had been a member in the Catholic Church there. The Session said that a Catholic would have to join by Profession of Faith. I found that strange and asked why. They said because he is Catholic and this is how we do it when someone who is Catholic joins the church. I told them that I didn't think that was right because everyone joining was Christian. Why would we need to make that distinction? It didn't seem fair. They said they had never thought of that and we ended up having a great discussion around why we think what we think and, why we do what we do in terms of how people become a member in our Church. I was amazed and impressed at the faith expressed by these members of Session and their willingness to have an open discussion with me and take the time we needed to make an informed decision based on what we believed as Christians. In the four years I served with them as their minister, every decision they made was based on their faith. They listened to each other and to their minister and challenged me as I challenged them and only then did they make a decision. In the end, for the first time in the 99 years of their history, the Monticello United Church Session decided that this man who was Catholic could join in the same way the other three people were joining even though the Session understood that the Catholic church did not acknowledge us so we would not be able to get a letter from the Catholic Church in Switzerland that this man was in fact a member of the Catholic Church. What impressed me the most in this discussion was the respect the Elders had for each other and for their minister. Without any reservation, I would have to say that this was the finest group of Elders I ever had the pleasure to share in ministry with.

After coming back from holidays in September, 1982, I was definitely having some issues. Being back at Roseau in August had triggered a lot of feelings in me but I didn't take the time I needed to address the concerns I had. I was still doing a lot of visiting every week, preparing services for Sunday and attending the many meetings which came up from time to time. I knew I was where I should be and I was feeling very confident about being a minister in a Pastoral Charge. I loved the ministry. I was especially enjoying playing music with Liz and it really helped me because I could just let myself go in the music and it took me to a different place. Liz was as good on the organ as I was on the piano. Playing together took me back to the time when my Aunt Louise and I did our two piano duets together. Liz and I liked each other and we became good friends. Jean Boggs had also become a really good friend and I often went to her home just to talk about my feelings in regards to the church and she always listened to me and offered good advice. I trusted her implicitly and she never let me down. It is hard being a minister and as a minister you have to be so careful as to who you can trust. I was very fortunate to find a real friend in Jean.

Sometime near the end of November, I got a phone call from a woman who said her name was Lee and she had seen one of the articles written about me and she thought I would be someone she could talk to. She said she wasn't interested in coming to church so she didn't know if I would talk with her. I told her I didn't have a problem having a conversation with her and that sometimes people who weren't in the Church would ask me to visit them and I was always open to that. So I went out to see her. She lived on what she called a hobby farm about five miles out of town. It was a long driveway into the farm and, as I drove in, I could see a small barn and a farmhouse. Lee invited me to sit down and offered me coffee. She told me her husband was an architect and they didn't have any children. She was my age, petite and about 5'4", and she had a good energy about her. They had moved to Grand Valley from Toronto in March because they were tired of city life and her husband didn't mind the drive to Toronto. She said she was a freelance writer so it didn't matter where she lived. At first, her husband had come home every evening but his work load had become too hard for him to do this and in October, he rented a small apartment and was now in Toronto Monday to Friday. She was finding the adjustment hard even though he came home every weekend.

She talked with me about her life and I shared with her as well, something I don't normally do, but she asked me about myself and was interested. Because she was a writer, I talked with her about my Aunt Louise who wrote poetry and tried writing a book and I talked with her about my Uncle Phil who had been a newspaperman. It was obvious we had things in common and she invited me to come back and visit again which I did a few times over the next year. I enjoyed our visits and she was easy to talk to and so we became friends. She would tell me how her latest article was going and she would discuss it with me and ask my opinion and I really appreciated that. She was a very good writer. I told her about the church and that it wasn't easy to be a minister and she understood how that might feel. As a child she had gone to Sunday School but as an adult she had no interest in the church. I loved having a friend who wasn't in the Church and someone who was interesting and interested in many things. I looked forward to those visits where I could just hang out with Lee and be myself. It felt good and gave me a great sense of freedom. It took the edge off the nosy parkers who always wanted to know what I was doing, like Jack Morrison and Harold who lived about four doors down from me and was about 80 at the time. He had the most beautiful wife, Mary, but he was often ringing my doorbell and finding a reason to poke his nose in. I knew others watched me too. It was the goldfish bowl syndrome.

I got to really know Lee over the next 19 months. She was interested in me and my friends at Roseau. It was hard at first to talk about what I had experienced there because I had never talked to anyone about my life in Manitoba, never. But she cared about me and empathized and was a good listener. As I talked to her I found I was very emotional and sometimes I found it hard to talk but she was patient and kind and nurturing and encouraged me to take my time. It was hard because I felt I had let the people down at Roseau and my heart was still breaking for my friends there and what they suffered through and nothing had changed. Lee asked me if I had done any writing about those experiences and I told her I hadn't and she encouraged me to think about writing. She was very sincere and said she wanted me to talk to her because it could only help me. She reminded me how good I had been to her and how much I had helped her and that I was the first friend she made in Grand Valley. I really needed to talk because there was so many feelings unresolved inside me from my time at Roseau. The more we got together and visited the more I trusted her. I also shared with her my deep loneliness and pain as a child because my mother had given me up. I didn't write stories but I started to write poetry, hundreds and hundreds of poems over the next 19 months. Poems about my mother, my father, my uncles and aunts, and poems about people at Roseau, poems about suicide and rape and a poem about Jamie. They just poured out of me in an endless stream of conscious and unconscious thought. It was cathartic and Lee was a gift sent to me by God. I really believed that. I hadn't realized how badly I needed someone to listen to me. A minister is expected to listen to people and their concerns but who listens to the minister? And there was Lee who encouraged me to talk about my life and open up because she cared about me. Every time we got together, I brought the poems I had written and read them to her and she read her most recent article to me. She encouraged me to write more. We had a huge connection through her writing and the poetry I wrote. One day she invited me to come over for dinner and meet her husband. John was a really nice man and very handsome and I could see how much she was in love with him. He loved the farm as much as she did but he had so little time to enjoy it with his work in Toronto but he never missed coming home for the weekends. Lee missed the night life in Toronto and often when she wasn't as busy with her writing she would go down for a couple of nights during the week to be with her husband.

Lee helped me open up a door inside myself and let out all my own personal pain and suffering. I was fearless, thinking all things were possible, and in that time they were. I had incredible energy writing poetry and I even started composing music. I had unlimited energy for the ministry as well and I became a better preacher, digging deeper into the spiritual aspects of faith that can transform us and allowing myself to let go of some things I needed to let go of. Lee was instrumental in helping me and I looked forward to our visits and reading her next article. She was even thinking of writing a book and I encouraged her to do that. I was feeling really good. I had three wonderful friends who were all very different. Liz and the music we loved to do together, Jean who I confided in about the church and she was always there for me, and Lee who I had recently met who was a writer and helped me to listen to myself and encouraged me to write. I couldn't be more thankful for these three amazing friends.

Our Christmas Eve service at Trinity United Church was very special that year with the Junior and Senior Choirs singing and there was lots of Christmas music and, of course, Liz and I played some Christmas organ piano duets which the congregation loved. Louise and Susie came and stayed until the New Year. They were there for the service and were so happy to see me playing in church. Even though they had stayed over the Thanksgiving weekend and the Easter weekend, Christmas was always the most special. Those were our special family times together.

After Christmas June Maycock mentioned that Knox Presbyterian Church was trying to raise money to buy a new organ and I talked to her about how I might be able to help. I really wanted to challenge myself and try doing a concert again. It had been a very long time. I asked her what she thought of my giving a piano concert at her church to help raise money for their organ. She was very pleased to think I would do that and took my offer to the next meeting of their Session. They were also very happy to take me up on my invitation and we set the date for May 15th. Now, along with all the work of ministry, writing poetry and composing, I spent hours practicing on the piano. I was really looking forward to the concert. Liz and I continued to get together when we had time and we took on some fairly difficult piano organ duets. Her organ lessons were paying off and she was becoming a great organist so we pushed each other to be our best. This was one of the most creative periods in my life.

I had two weeks holiday left and I went to California to visit my sister and her family in February 1983. Warren was used to me being away from time to time and he stayed next door with the Rowes as he was friends with their two boys, Jimmy and Robby. I had a great visit with my sister and we did everything together that we could. We talked and talked and were never bored. Jana was very happy for me that I was back doing my music and also writing poetry. She thought the poems I brought for her to read were really good. It was great to see all six children again and be called aunty often. We had lots of laughs and good times. Ken had a great sense of humour and was a really good guy. Dad had been gone almost two years and my sister seemed happy and settled. Jana didn't have the problem with Dad's passing as she had had when Mom passed away. I told her I wanted to go to the cemetery to see where Mom and Dad were buried and we went. It was very emotional as Jana and I sat at the graveside and told stories of our family. It was hard but it was good for us to be there. Jana was doing really well at work and loved her job as a waitress at Kalley's Restaurant. Stacy was 15 then and Scott was 11 and he was still having a hard time because he really missed his dad and didn't see him as often as he would have liked to since his dad had remarried and his wife had two daughters. Steve was 16 at the time, Derek was 13 and the twins Monty and Nicki were almost teenagers. I just loved being with my sister and she felt the same way so it was always hard to leave and go back home.

It was wonderful to see Warren when I got back and he was very happy I was home. When May 15th came and it was time for me to give the concert at Knox Presbyterian Church, I was very excited to be performing again. I was playing Bach, Chopin, Mendelssohn, Clementi, Beethoven, Mozart, MacDowell, Rameau, Shubert and one of my own compositions. The church was packed. Many people came from my congregations and Warren, of course, was there with Louise and Susie. It was wonderful to be giving a concert again and also to help the church raise money for their new organ. There was a lovely reception after the concert and I was very proud of myself. It had gone so well and everyone seemed to appreciate what I had done. Louise and Susie were thrilled and Warren, as usual, was proud of me. June Maycock a member of the Organ Committee wrote me this note:

> "The congregation of Knox Church wishes to express sincere thanks to Rev. Vollmer, not only for the artistic skill with which she has graced our Sanctuary this evening, but also for her most generous and encouraging gesture of support for our Organ Fund. We shall remain deeply indebted to Dorinda, and we shall continue to value her as a great friend of Knox Church."

One day In early June, after I had been out visiting families in our church and had just come home for lunch, the phone rang. It was one of the nurses at Orangeville Hospital calling me. As the minister in Grand Valley and Monticello United Churches, I visited families in the hospital once a week so this nurse knew me. She was calling to tell me that a baby had just been born at full term but was not expected to live and the parents were asking for a minister to baptize their baby. She told me the family lived in Monticello and asked if I would come. I could tell by her voice that she was very upset so I told her I would be there as soon as possible. After I got off the phone, I phoned Elmer Shortt. I knew he would be home at noon for dinner as that's when farmers had their big meal. I told him what had happened and that I would appreciate it if he could come with me to the hospital. Elmer and Ioan had six children and he knew how terrible this was for the parents. He asked if we could baptize the baby if it died because he didn't know if we could. I said that, if this is what the parents wanted and would bring some comfort to them, it was the least we could do. He understood and agreed.

Elmer was at my home in 10 minutes and 20 minutes later we were at the hospital. The nurse who had called me was there and I introduced Elmer to her. She took us to a room where the mother was in bed holding her baby and quietly weeping while the father was sitting on the bed with his arm around her trying to comfort his wife. They were both in their early 20's. There were three nurses in the room with them and they were visibly upset. They had helped to bring this baby into this world and now the baby was gone. My heart broke for them as I introduced myself and Elmer to them. We talked quietly for a few moments and I said a prayer with them. Then the mother gave me her baby to baptize. Chills went up and down my body as I took this lifeless baby in my arms. It was a natural physical reaction to all the pain I was feeling in that room from the parents and the nurses and Elmer. Elmer stood beside me and I was so grateful to have him there. I looked down at this baby and it was so sad. I performed the rite of Baptism, giving the parents hope that their child was now with God in Heaven. It was heartbreaking.

When I finished, the parents told me they wanted their baby buried in the Monticello cemetery and wanted to know if I could do the funeral. I said I would. Elmer looked after the cemetery for the church and he told the parents he would make the arrangements. As I drove Elmer back to my place to pick up his car, we did a lot of talking on the way. Elmer was visibly shaken and didn't know how, as ministers, we are able to do the things we had to do in such difficult circumstances. I told him it is hard, sometimes very hard, and I told him how grateful I was that he was there with me representing the church because it is so important for people in their darkest hour to know that we really do care. Two days later, we met the parents at the cemetery. The funeral director brought the casket and it was so small. I did the best that I could do in this service but, truly, there are no words. I believe in God's love and that God had taken this baby home. But I wonder what people think who have no faith, nothing that they believe in, because I know there are people who do not believe. But these young parents believed and wanted to do give their baby a service to honour the life that their baby had for those brief moments he was with them and that meant so much to them. After the service, the parents just wanted to go home and Elmer and I said goodbye to them and gave them a hug. That was all we could do. It had been such an emotional experience that it stayed with me a long after I left the cemetery.

Life goes on and I was glad the next morning that I would be practicing with Liz for the concert we were giving at Trinity United Church October 2nd. The music gave me something to pour my heart and pain into. I also had the young people who came to my home every Thursday afternoon to look forward to. We had had another great year together, including some great parties, and before the summer break I told them I would be doing this again in September and looked forward to seeing them all again.

I was also looking forward to a very big party that was coming up at Monticello United Church. On Sunday, August 14th, 1983 the church would be celebrating their 100th Anniversary and everyone in the church had been working very hard all year to do everything they could to make this anniversary service one no one would ever forget because their church meant so much to them. They had kept wonderful records, so they wrote to everyone who had ever come to Monticello United Church and invited them to the celebration. They were also creating a booklet which included a Dedication on their front page which was written by Ioan and Elmer Shortt:

> *"This history of Monticello United Church is dedicated to the pioneers of this community who, out of their small substance provided the funds and material and built this church to the glory of God in 1883. It is also in honor of subsequent generations who have supported it and kept it alive by their faithfulness down through the years."*

I was asked to write a message which would include a photo of me as well. In part, I wrote:

> *"It is my privilege to be your minister in this, your year of special celebrations. I know how very hard you work at what you do in the church. I know how very much you love your church, and that is a real tribute to those of your ancestors who gave so much of themselves to their church, that it is still here today for us to gather to worship God. This is truly God's house and you are truly God's people. Your love for God and for each other cannot help but inspire all who enter. For me, Monticello United Church is a gospel church, a living reminder to all who enter, that Jesus Christ indeed has risen. Jesus lives in the hearts of*

each one of you. God is indeed with us… … … May God continue to richly bless us and I hope and pray that Monticello United Church may still be a thriving, vital, gospel church another 100 years from now."

Warren and I were going on holidays at the end of July and part of August and I had to make sure I got back before August 14, which we did. I remember them telling me before I left that they were renting a tent for 500 people. I didn't know everything they were planning but I thought that a tent for 500 was a little excessive. The church might hold 70, but a tent for 500? But I said nothing and Warren and I left for California to have another wonderful holiday with my sister. To see Jana twice in one year was amazing and I was making the most of it. Warren and I had a lot of fun with all the family at Jana and Ken's home in Sacramento, California. Jana and I took Nicky and Monty, Warren and Scott paragliding on the water and they loved it. Jana and I went to Disneyland with Warren and Stacy and Derek and also saw the Spruce Goose and the Queen Mary Ocean Liner. Jana and I had lots of time to talk, even though we had talked many times on the phone since February. Jana said she was doing fine with the family, as hard as it was sometimes to be raising six teenagers. It was glorious to be together and to have our children be able to spend time with each other. I came home relaxed and refreshed, ready for the 100th Anniversary service at Monticello.

Two days before the Anniversary, I decided I needed to buy my own piano so I went to the Remenyi Piano Store in Toronto. I saw a really nice black upright piano, a Rosler, which was handmade in Czechoslovakia. It was a very good one and I bought it on August 12, 1983. Mrs. Remenyi herself sold it to me and she said they would deliver it the next week. I was very excited about this and when I got home I called Jean and told her what I had done. It had been so kind of her to let me use her piano in my home but now I would have my own. She was so happy for me and said she would arrange to have her piano picked up.

I was making the finishing touches on the 100th Anniversary service at Monticello and still wondering about that tent for 500 people they were renting. But I needn't have worried, because almost 700 people showed up for their anniversary celebration. It was an amazing thing to see. The tent was all set up with chairs and the church looked beautiful, decked out with flowers and decorations, a mike system was set up in the church and outside and five former ministers were taking part in the service. It was quite something to see how much this small church on the side of a road meant to so many people. What a tribute to those who built it and those who continued to worship here. It was indeed a blessing. It was a great service, a great day and we had a wonderful reception afterwards. A picture was taken of all the ministers for *The Star and Vidette* on August 14, 1983: there was Reverend Jeff Davison, Reverend Bruce Besley, Reverend Cerwyn Davies, Reverend William Parrott, Reverend John Huether and me. The Elders on the session were Arnold Townsend, Bill Gooderham, John Hunter, Elmer Shortt, Gordon Brayford, Ross Brown, Reta Hills, William Townsend and Audrey Bruce. The Stewards were Brian Johnston, Bill Hunter, Ken Kratky, Fledda Hillis and Nina Townsend. The Centennial Committee members were Nina Townsend, Susan Simpson, Reta Hills, Fledda Hillis, Kathy

Shortt and Elmer Shortt. They did an outstanding job.

What an amazing summer it had been and everything was going so well. My piano came the next week and Warren was very excited to see it. He was still taking lessons at that time and doing exams and now he had a new piano to play on and so did I. Liz came over and tried out my new piano and thought it was wonderful and she was so happy for me. I put the word out that I would be holding confirmation classes for any young people who would like to attend and 11 young people signed up from the two churches, including Warren. When I met with the young people for the first time at the end of September, I told them we would be having the confirmation service in June, 1984 at which time they would be confirmed. I also told them I expected that each one of them would write a 5-8 minute sermon and present it to the congregation on one of the Sundays over the next eight months. They were nervous about that but I gave them lots of resources and suggestions and they did very well. They were a really good group and we had a lot fun at the classes learning about God and Jesus, the Bible, discussing current affairs and how our faith informs our decisions. There was always lots of questions and discussion.

Meanwhile Liz and I were working hard on the Piano and Organ Recital we were giving on October 2, 1983 at Trinity United Church to raise money for our church. The concert itself was a great success. I played a few of my own compositions as well as some Bach, Mozart, Shubert and Chopin. Liz played solo organ pieces too, then we played six organ piano duets which everyone loved, especially *The Holy City* by S. Adams arranged by Ellen Lorenz. It was a showstopper. It was such a great evening that, after the concert, we decided to call what we did "Duo Keyboards - Elizabeth and Dorinda in Concert" and began planning a concert to perform at St. John's United Church in Oakville in April 1984. Liz was looking forward to going to my home church in Oakville to give a concert there but I think she was even more excited to think she would be playing the amazing pipe organ they had at St. John's.

Jean and I continued to go out for dinner once a month before the Session meetings and I loved those times with her. She was such an interesting person. I also know how much she had loved her husband and how she suffered and still grieved. In November, my sister told me she wanted to come for a visit and see the family. I suggested she plan her trip around the concert Liz and I were giving at St. John's in April and she thought that was a great idea. I also told her I would be so happy for her to meet Liz and Jean because we were such good friends. Of course, I told Jana she would also meet my friend Lee. It meant the world to me for my sister to meet my three friends and they all looked forward to meeting Jana. I was so excited that my sister was coming for a visit and so were Warren and Louise and Susie. We would make it very special.

All in all, life was going along really well and my ministry was busy and fulfilling. There were services to prepare and a sermon to write every week, funerals to do, meetings to chair, hospital visits to make as well as the Thursday afternoons with the young people and the confirmation classes. I was very creative in this period, composing my own music and still writing poetry every day. Liz and I continued our organ piano practices and we looked forward to the concerts we were planning. Winter came in like a lion that year and the world was once again white and beautiful. But the winters in Grand Valley were hard with lots of snow and drifts sometimes over four feet high. We put up our Christmas tree and Warren excelled at decorating it. He loved setting up the tree with me, probably because he couldn't wait to see what presents would be put under it. I wasn't good at it but we always had fun doing it and I was amazed at how beautiful it looked, with an angel or a star on top, when we finished. We had our yearly Christmas shopping to do to get presents for Louise and Susie and we looked forward to that. It was a lovely Christmas outing because all the stores always looked so beautiful at that time of year. We usually did most of this shopping in Oakville, staying over on a Friday night with Louise and Susie. We played bridge and laughed and told stories and had fun swimming in the pool. Warren would tell them about school and his friends and Louise always wanted to know how his music lessons were going. He was working on his Grade Three piano exam and his Grade One theory exam for June 1984 and I had agreed that he could stop after that. I realized that piano wasn't Warren's thing and didn't push it further but I was glad he got a very good grounding in music with Liz, taking piano lessons for as long as he did. This helped him in his music classes at school and with reading music in the Junior Choir and, later, the Senior Choir. Those were good times with the aunts.

The churches at Monticello and Grand Valley were all beautifully decorated for Christmas, with lights and decorations and a beautiful Christmas tree. Christmas music wafted through the air and you heard it everywhere. It was Christmas card perfect. Once again, the Christmas Eve service was inspiring and Liz and I played some organ piano Christmas duets. After the service, when we were home, Warren got to open a present before he went to bed and then I read him the stories I always read to him. But he was getting older now and growing up so fast. He was 13 that Christmas and would be in high school come next September. That was so hard to imagine. Where had the time gone? We had another wonderful Christmas Day, doing the things we did as a family that made everything so special and I wondered what a New Year would bring.

CHAPTER THREE

Leaving Grand Valley

As I looked back over the past two and a half years, I felt very good about the ministry I had already done and confidant in my abilities as a minister. At the same time, I didn't know how long I would stay. When a minister feels called to a particular Charge and the congregation agrees, there is no term on that call. As long as everyone is comfortable with their minister and the minister feels the same way, this relationship can go on for many years. Ministers in a Pastoral Charge such as this one usually stayed four to six years and I was sure that those who preferred another minister had already decided they could 'wait me out'.

Warren was happy and doing well and he loved seeing his great aunts and being with them. He had many friends and was growing up before my eyes. He enjoyed participating in the Lions Clubs speaking contest on February 13, 1984, talking about the Roseau River Indian Reserve and his experience there. I was very proud of him. This was his last year at public school and I knew that he would have to take a bus to the high school in Shelburne in September. Changes were coming for Warren, but I had a feeling that this would be a critical year for me but for now, I felt everything was good.

Coming into January 1984 I thought I could become a better composer if I took lessons. I made an appointment to see Robert Dodson, who was the acting Principle at the Royal Conservatory of Music in Toronto. I knew Robert, who was the cellist with the Vaghy String Quartet who I had worked with at the Kelso Music Centre. It was good to see him again as he took me on a tour around the Conservatory. In one room there was a painting of Miss Bates, the same painting I had seen every time I went to her studio for my piano lessons. It was wonderful to see that painting again and it brought back a lot of memories. Robert told me he would talk to Alexina Louie, an up and coming composer, to ask her if she would give me lessons and I really appreciated that. When I phoned her, she agreed to teach me and I began going to Toronto every two weeks to study with her and I got more serious about composing. Alexina and I realized that we had both studied at UBC at the same. time She was doing electronic composition and my locker was right next to the room where she composed. I saw her coming and going but had no idea who she was. Here we were 13 years later, and she was my teacher. I enjoyed my lessons with Alexina. I learned a lot from her and wrote many pieces for the piano during that time. After three months I realized that this was too much for me. I had so many creative interests and only so much energy. My poetry, solo piano work and the piano/organ duets with Liz were all I could handle besides the ministry. My real creative focus was the poetry I was writing, the concerts that Liz and I were giving and the sermons I was writing. Those were the most satisfying.

I went to a Toronto Symphony concert to hear one of Alexina's compositions being performed and that was wonderful. In an article written by *The Toronto Star* on July 23, 1988 on women composers, it was said of Alexina that, "Toronto's Alexina Louis has become arguably the best known Canadian composer of her generation, a prolific note smith". She later won two Juno Awards, was made an Officer of the Order of Canada and a recipient of the Order of Ontario and the Queen's Golden Jubilee Medal. She also received the Queen's Diamond Jubilee Medal. Alexina's compositions were the most played of any Canadian composer and she was the most influential Canadian composer of her generation.

Jean Boggs continued to be a very good friend to me. She was always there for me to talk to about anything that was on my mind and I often dropped in at her home which was a five minute walk from where I lived. She understood the tribulations of being a minister because her father was a minister so she knew how difficult some people could be in the Church. Also, being a nurse, Jean was pretty realistic about people, their personal agendas and how disappointing they could be at times. I felt that way too. I wasn't having concerns with anyone in particular at Trinity United Church but it was the pettiness and snide comments people made from time to time against other members at the church that wore me down. I hated that kind of gossip and negativity because it took that much more out of me to be positive and upbeat. Jean and I had very interesting talks over dinner before the Session meetings. I trusted her completely and she was my rock and a wonderful support. She never let me down. She also had a great sense of humour and we laughed a lot. She had taken me under her wing from the start as Betty had at Roseau. Every minister needs a Jean or a Betty. We need at least one angel to love us, accept us for who we are and believe in us.

Now I was focusing on the ministry and upcoming concert on April 8th that Liz and I were gearing up for at St. John's United Church in Oakville. The *Oakville Beaver* wrote an article about our concert which came out March 28, 1984:

> *"Musician Dorinda Vollmer made her Oakville debut in 1963, and then quietly slipped away. It was not until 20 years later that she regained her interest as a concert pianist,…..*
> *In 1983, she gave two concerts in Grand Valley and now Vollmer returns to Oakville. Accompanied by Elizabeth Borman, organist at Trinity in Grand Valley, Vollmer presents an evening of classical music and call themselves, 'Duo Keyboards'… ….The concert will be dedicated to Louise Thompson of Oakville, who taught piano here for 30 years and encouraged her niece to study music beginning at age three……… in July 1981, Vollmer returned to Ontario, accepting a two-point Charge at Grand Valley, 10 miles west of Orangeville… …. Vollmer lives with her 13 year-old son, Warren, in Grand Valley and all her parishioners just call her Dorinda."*

Before the concert date, Liz and I went down to St. John's United Church in Oakville twice because we needed to find a good balance between the organ and the piano when we played our duets together. Liz also needed to become familiar with this powerful pipe organ. We were doing this Benefit Concert to raise funds for a facility for the handicapped in Trinity United

Church in Grand Valley. Warren was growing up so fast and would soon have his 14th birthday party on April 1st. I always made his birthdays as special as possible and that year would be no exception. Again, he invited Paul, Brandon, the Rowe boys and Mark to his party. I brought Louise and Susie up for the weekend to celebrate his birthday. Warren was getting older and so were my aunts. Whenever there were things to celebrate, my aunts were always part of that. We had a great time and made the most of our time together.

My sister arrived for a visit in early April and it was wonderful to see her. Louise and Susie were thrilled to see her again. We had great times together in Oakville and in Grand Valley. Jana and I went to see the Phantom of the Opera at the Princess of Wales Theatre in Toronto. It is still the best musical I have ever seen. Jean and Liz joined Jana and me at my home for tea one afternoon. We talked and laughed and told stories and it was just wonderful. Jana and my dear friend Jean Boggs hit it off right away. Jana could see that Jean was a very special person and understood why I trusted her and loved her as my friend and colleague in ministry. Jean thought my sister was pretty special too. It was also important that Jana meet Liz and they got along really well. Jana understood how wonderful it was for me to work with someone who loved music as much as I did. Jana also met Lee when we went to her home and we had a great conversation around writing and poetry. Lee showed Jana some of her writing and my sister was very impressed and she could see what a kind person Lee was. Finally, the evening of the concert came. Liz was driving to the church with her family and we had agreed to meet at the church about an hour before the concert so we could get set up. Jana, Warren and I drove down to St. John's and met Louise and Susie there. I was stressed and nervous and excited about the performance, all at the same time. I couldn't believe I was going to my home church to give a concert and I knew how much Louise and Susie and Jana were looking forward to it. They had always loved to hear me play the piano. I also knew that there would be many families coming from my two churches and, of course, friends from Oakville and others as well. Bill would also be there and I knew how much he loved my music and he was taping this concert for me from the balcony. It was wonderful to see Bill. Warren was very excited to see his dad and sat with him in the balcony.

It was a great concert and Liz and I thoroughly enjoyed ourselves. We played about eight organ piano duets and ended the first half with The Holy City, for which we received a standing ovation. Liz played a few solo organ pieces and I played some classical pieces along with four of my compositions. The repertoire choices we made pleased everyone. There was a wonderful reception after the concert which Louise and Susie, Jana, Warren and Bill attended. They were over the moon about the concert. Bill told me that he would give me the tape of the concert once he got it sorted out. My family was so proud of me and it warmed my heart to know that. It was a great evening. After the concert and reception Jana and Warren and I cleaned up and then we drove back to Grand Valley. Warren went up to bed to read and Jana and I talked into the wee hours of the morning. A childhood friend of mine in Oakville, Barbara Ryrie Davidson who had been at the concert sent me a note on April 9, 1984 where she wrote:

"What a wonderful concert last night! Your playing was beautiful and it was so nice to see you at a piano again. It took me back a few years to the good old days. I loved your compositions and do hope you have success on their publication… … …Thank you again for your nice letter and tickets. By the way, you're so slim and trim now I hardly knew you – looks terrific.. Take care and all the best in your future piano endeavours. I feel honoured to know a composer."

I really appreciated getting Barbara's letter. It did my heart good as I remembered back to the good times we had together growing up just down the street from each other. Maureen Forrester kindly wrote me a letter on July 13, 1984 and said:

"I am very sorry I did not answer your letter written way back in February. It was mislaid in a pile of brochures, magazines, etc. and has just come to light. I am way behind in my correspondence as I am performing at Stratford as well as carrying out my duties as Chairman of the Canada Council. The tickets to your organ piano duets were very much appreciated and I would have been pleased to attend. However, I was on tour at that time. I am sure your concert was a great success and please keep me in mind the next time you perform."

While Jana was in Grand Valley with us, she was able to attend two church services at Trinity United Church. On one of those Sundays, she even went to the service at Monticello United Church and met everyone there. She loved the services and the people. The Stewards at Trinity invited Jana and me to come to the church after their meeting was over because they had a surprise for Stan Newson. The day of their meeting was also his birthday and Jana and I went to help him celebrate. Stan really appreciated my sister coming for this and we had a lot of good laughs.

I talked with Jana about a trip I was thinking of taking to Germany with Warren in July and asked if she wanted to come with us. She said she didn't think she wanted to. Our mother had gone with Dad to Germany but it had taken him a long time to convince her to go with him. I had told Dad that I would go with him anytime he wanted, but he never seemed interested. I had always wanted to meet my father's family but my sister didn't feel the same way. She told me that it would be too expensive for her with all the children she and Ken were raising and, besides, she wasn't interested in the way I was but she looked forward to hearing about our trip. When it was time for Jana to leave I couldn't believe how quickly the two weeks had gone by. Warren also loved having his aunt around and, as usual, it was hard for us to say goodbye. After Jana left, I talked to Warren about taking a tour in Europe. He was very excited about this but he was really interested in England. I went to a travel agent and started planning this trip which would end up being 27 days. We would spend two days on our own in England, then take the tour of England and Europe for 15 days and spend the last 10 days of our trip in Freiburg, Germany where my father's sister Maria lived. I had been corresponding with my cousin Marion, Maria's granddaughter. Marion was about my age and spoke English because she had been a nanny in Texas and was now back with her family in Germany. After spending time in Freiburg with the family, we would take a train to Frankfurt and fly home from there.

It seemed that I could not stay out of the public eye for long because a reporter from *The Star and Vidette* heard about the confirmation classes I held and wanted to write an article. He came to the church and took photos for the paper. Needless to say, all the 11 young people in my confirmation classes were very excited to have their photo in the newspaper. The article said:

> *"Last week's church service at Monticello, conducted entirely by members of the combined youth confirmation class of Monticello and Trinity Churches was the first time that Rev. Dorinda Vollmer chose to use this method for preparing young people for official acceptance into their congregation. Eleven young people will be formally made members of their congregation on June 10……. Guy Bruce, Keli Brown, Kelly Robinson, Barb O'Connor and Paul Hunter each gave a short sermon last week at Monticello while six others accepted other roles in the hour-long service, and Rev. Vollmer said afterwards that she was very pleased with the caliber of their work and that each of them had a supporting elder. Preparation for their place in the church has included Bible study, weekly meetings at the Grand Valley manse. At the April 8 service at Trinity Church, it will be the turn of Warren Vollmer, Gwen Farnell, Brandon Borman, Brian Ross and Donna Mae Ross to give their sermons (and Rodney Montgomery will take part). Those who delivered their sermons last week were honoured afterwards with a St. Patrick Day's cake and luncheon."*

I was very proud of the sermon Warren wrote. He called it "Civilization" and I quote from part of it. He chose the Gospel of John 13:1-17 as his Scripture:

> *"Are we really civilized? Do we even know what it is or how to be civilized:… My interpretation of civilized is when people live in a technically advanced era in peace, loving one another and sharing everything or, in other words, very ethically advanced… …..if we really were very ethically and technically advanced we would not have poverty, greed, pollution, money, nuclear waste, nuclear bombs, wars, weapons for either defense or offense… …Well, as for poverty, that is tied in with greed and money… …You see whenever war strikes there are always refugees or people that have had everything torn apart before their very eyes so they have to take refuge somewhere else… …..Pollution we could have a lot less pollution except for the fact that the guys in charge of the places that give off the most pollution will not put in the devices that will cut down on pollution because they cost too much. Then there is nuclear waste. You cannot get rid of it so why did we start using it in the first place. Well it is cheap and economical. But which is more important, destroying nature and saving a few bucks or saving nature and using nature to make our energy? ….the ever popular sun or solar energy, building dams in strong current rivers to make the fast moving water turn generators and many other such things. So now we*

have problems and lots of them. Maybe we have forgotten what is most important. That we love each other and are considerate. Why do we do this? Because God loved us and created every one of us in his image.

How do we do this? Jesus showed us how. Remember that passage in the Gospel of John read earlier where Jesus shared his last supper with the disciples and washed their feet. Does that not prove that Jesus was the most civilized person that ever lived? Because who here would humble themselves like that?........is there anyone here who would risk his or her life for someone else?. … … …. If it was a total stranger you probably would not but if it was a friend you might. Think about that, is that what God wants? No! He wants us to save that person on risk of death without hesitation and that is what God sent Jesus to do to show us the way to real civilization. To follow Jesus' commandment and to be his friend first we have to change what it is in our heart that is not right. Only when we make room for Jesus can we change our lives, and begin to make this world the kind of place God intended it to be."

Sunday, June 10 was a wonderful day when the young people who had taken the confirmation classes with me were confirmed at Trinity and Monticello United Churches. The congregations were so pleased to see these young people in their congregation take a real interest in their church. Each of the Elders had mentored one of the young people and they had taken their role seriously and met and talked with the young person they sponsored many times over that year. It was a great day for everyone involved and I felt very proud of these young people and the ministry I had done with them. June 10th was also the 59th Anniversary of the United Church of Canada. We were still a young Church, struggling with the issues common to all churches such as attendance, finding more members, finances and balancing the understanding of our faith with social justice concerns. I was beginning to feel a change was coming. I had been at Grand Valley three years and felt I had done a good ministry but I was starting to wonder if there was something more I needed to do. For the time being, though, Warren was finishing Grade Eight and had another good year at school. Warren also did his Grade One Theory exam and his Grade Three Piano exam. He got 90% in his theory and over 70% in his piano. I was proud of him and he was happy with his mark and even happier that he didn't have to have piano lessons any more. I couldn't thank Liz enough for teaching my son.

Now we were packing and getting ready for our trip to England and Europe. The flight to England was at night and we got in around 9:00 a.m. We were so tired that we took a cab to the hotel, went to our room and slept until 4:00 p.m. When we got up, we decided to take a taxi tour around London and we had one more day in England before joining the 15 day tour beginning with a two-day bus tour of England. Then we crossed the channel and spent nine days in Paris, France and in Italy in Pisa, Rome, Florence and Venice. Then we had four days in Innsbruck, Austria, Germany and Holland. The tour was amazing. On the bus, our tour guide talked about the histories of the countries we were in. On the walking tours, we had local tour guides take us around in England, France, Germany, Italy and Austria who told us the history of the cathedrals and other places we visited. Warren always made his way to the front of the group and stood next to the local tour guide so he could hear and see everything. We loved it and finally we were in Freiburg, Germany.

Our cousin Marion was at Maria's place to meet us when we arrived and told us she was so sorry to have to tell me that her grandmother was ill and she couldn't have us stay with her. Now I had to book a room for the 10 days we would be in Freiburg, something I didn't expect to have to do, but we had no choice. We visited with Maria about four times at her home. But she couldn't speak English so it was frustrating. Marion helped us twice and Maria had a friend who spoke English and she helped us once. It was obvious to me in our conversations that Maria thought the world of her brother but it was really difficult to communicate and that was disappointing. Maria had a few pictures of my father and I remember one in particular that he had sent to her when he was in Saskatchewan. In the photo, Dad had on a white cowboy hat and looked very young. Maria loved her brother and told me how sorry she was when he passed away.

Marion's parents took us to Durbach where Dad grew up and showed us the cemetery where my grandparents were buried. I was struck by how pristine it was and how, everywhere we went, everything was so clean. I asked Marion about that and she said it was because of the guilt the German people felt about the Second World War. She asked me what I thought of Europe and I told her I found the countries very small. No sooner had our bus driven into one country we were in another country. I told her it made me feel closed in and she said she understood that having lived in Texas. I told her that seeing all the countries, like France and England and Germany and Italy, made me wonder why they had constantly been at war with one another through the centuries. Marion felt the same way I did. Marion's parents were very kind, as was her great aunt who also lived in Durbach and had been Dad's sister-in-law. Her husband, Dad's brother, had died years earlier. They took us to the Catholic Church in Durbach where Dad had gone as a child. It was a huge church but, for the German people, it was too small to be considered a cathedral. It was wonderful to go through the church and see where Dad had been. Because I was a minister they asked me many questions. Could I do baptisms? Could I do Holy Communion? Did I preach? They were surprised I answered yes to all their questions because no women in the Catholic Church in Europe could do that. They were in awe and shocked that a woman could have the authority from her Church to do those things. After seeing the church, we had a wonderful dinner with the family. One other day, Marion's parents took us out and showed us around Freiburg.

In all the visiting I did with Dad's family, I felt closest to Dad's sister in Freiburg but there was such a disconnect that I didn't feel strongly one way or the other and I know Warren felt the same way. I don't know what I had expected but I only knew that I needed to make this journey. I also realized I didn't need to go back. I had identified more with Marion, who was my age and had the same thoughts and feelings that I had, but we didn't spend that much time alone together where we could really talk. The last four days in Frieburg were difficult because we didn't see the family again and we didn't know what to do. Adding to the difficulties was the fact that we couldn't speak the language and the people there didn't speak English. I have to admit that we were glad to finally take the train to Frankfurt and fly home. Warren said the best part of the trip for him was England and, when he asked me what I thought, I was surprised to say that was true for me as well. I didn't expect to like England as much as I did and, in the end, I wasn't as impressed with Germany as I thought I would be. Warren and I had had a lot of fun together on this trip and we had learned a lot.

I must say we were glad to get home and spend a couple of days with Louise and Susie before heading back to Grand Valley to get ready for September. I had the month of August to prepare for my fourth year of ministry in Grand Valley. Warren wasn't happy at all about taking the bus to Shelburne High School every day and I encouraged him to be positive about it and see how it went. It turned out to be a long 30 minute ride. Every day for a few weeks he came home with a headache because the kids on the bus yelled and threw things. Warren was very unhappy and that really upset me. I was wondering whether it was time for me to leave, to move on. I did a lot of praying about this while I continued to do what I needed to do in ministry, but I was struggling with my call. In the end, I really felt I was being called somewhere else, but I had no idea what that meant. Still, I trusted in God and my faith helped me believe that it would work out in the end. One day toward the end of September, I went to see Arnold Townsend, the Chair of the Board for the Charge. When he saw me at the door, he said, 'I hope you are not here for what I think you are here for'. He knew instinctively why I was there. I handed him a letter telling him I was resigning as of June 30, 1985. He read it and asked if there was any way he could change my mind and I told him I was really sorry but I wouldn't change my mind.

I knew in my heart that this was the right thing to do. Warren was unhappy at his high school and, even though he was only four weeks into it, I knew my son, and I knew that he would continue to be unhappy as long as he had to take the bus to school. When I told him I had resigned as of the end of June and that we would be moving, I can't begin to say how happy Warren was. And it was not just about the high school. I remembered back to that day when we had been there only seven months and I had found him in his room crying because everyone was the same in Grand Valley. He missed the cultural differences. I knew he would have a better year at high school knowing we were moving and it turned out he had good teachers. What I didn't know was that there were going to be significant tragedies at Warren's high school that year. The one teacher in particular that he liked so much turned out to need serious heart surgery in January, 1985 and was unable to return to teach the rest of the year. That upset Warren very much. In February, two of the most popular teachers at his high school who were married to each other were killed in a serious car accident during a snow storm and that was so tragic. On several occasions, some kids tried to get Warren to drink alcohol that they had brought to school in a flask. Drugs were also prominent at the school. He told me all about the alcohol and drugs and assured me he had always said no. I was proud of my son because he had good values, a good sense of himself and was confident in who he was.

I phoned Jana again and told her I would be leaving Grand Valley in June, 1985 but she wasn't surprised. She thought I had made a good decision and that I would find the right place to go because she knew I had faith and how important it was for me to go where I was called. I told her it would take time for me to sort out my feelings and be open to that inevitable call but, at the moment, I didn't know what would happen. I also talked with Louise and Susie about my resignation. I told them how unhappy Warren was taking the bus to Shelburne High School and I felt there was something more for me to do in ministry. Of course they were sorry we would be leaving because we lived so close to Oakville and there was the uncertainty for them that we didn't know where we would be in July. But, like my sister they understood, and felt that perhaps, being in a larger community would be better. Although my aunts were very supportive, I knew this was hard on them, especially Louise. I put my name on the United Church of Canada's national list indicating that I was looking for a Pastoral Charge and I received the list of Pastoral Charges looking for ministers across Canada. When my congregations found out I had resigned, they were very sorry that I was leaving and I appreciated that. Then I sent a letter to my Presbytery informing them that I had resigned as of June 30, 1985 so they could help my Pastoral Charge in their search for a new minister.

Jean felt really badly when I told her I was leaving but she understood. She knew it hadn't been easy for me in Grand Valley with some of the people who were so negative. She was also sorry to hear that Warren was having difficulties going on the bus. I told her that I knew we would always be friends and that I would come back to visit her. When I told Liz, she was surprised and really sorry I was leaving. We so enjoyed doing music together and I had appreciated her support and encouragement. We were a good team and the music we did had inspired many people. We were both going to miss this collaboration and friendship we had. I had not spent a lot of time visiting with Lee over the last six months with all the things I had to do in the ministry and with my music and I was still writing poetry almost every day because of Lee's encouragement. I went out to visit her. I had helped her with the concerns she had and had listened to her and supported her in what had a difficult time for her when I first met her. Now Lee and John had made some significant changes over the summer. They were selling the hobby farm and moving back to Toronto. It had been so hard on them to be separated during most of the week. They had tried this for three years and finally realized it wasn't working and they were both so unhappy. I told Lee about my decision to leave Grand Valley. I told her how much I appreciated her friendship and support from the time we had met. I knew what a wonderful writer she was and she was now more determined than ever to put a lot of her time and energy into writing a book. They put their house up for sale and it sold very quickly which surprised them both. They found a lovely home in Toronto and moved in just in time for Christmas. I don't know what I would have done without Lee at the time we met because I didn't realize how overwhelmed I was by the things that had happened at Roseau and that haunted me. Because she had encouraged me to talk and then put in writing what I was feeling I now had hundreds of poems I had written over the last three years which helped me put some of the broken pieces of my life back together. She was a good friend and I told her I would miss her.

The Newsons, Ann Young, Ruth Hunter, Ruth Hambleton, Dorothy White, Irving Potter, Les and Mary Canivet and other families at Trinity United Church with whom I was close were so sorry I was leaving as were all of the people at Monticello United Church. I just carried on as I always had with the ministry until it was time to leave. Liz and I gave another great concert at Trinity United Church on November 11th and it was well received by everyone who attended.

Christmas came and once again we had a wonderful Christmas Eve service and a wonderful Christmas with Louise and Susie. It was our last Christmas in Grand Valley and I had mixed feelings. I realized how much I loved being in the church doing all the things a minister does. It would be hard to leave because there were so many wonderful people in these congregations. Louise and Susie just wanted me to be alright whatever happened. But I had yet to get an interview. Even in January, I wasn't working very hard at it. I sent out some resumes but I didn't seem to feel a great need to even do that. By March, Grand Valley and Monticello had called someone to be their minister as of July 1st and the people at Monticello were very concerned because I didn't know where I was going. It was as if I was waiting for a sign, strange as that may sound. Then I got a phone call. Marg, the Chair of the Pastoral Relations Committee at St. Paul's United Church in New Liskeard was calling to ask me if I would come for an interview. They had already asked for and received my resume. I was very surprised and didn't even know where New Liskeard was until Marg told me it was five hours north of Toronto. I told her I could come up on Sunday after church and stay over but I had to be back Monday night and she said that was fine. I told Warren and he got very excited. As for myself, I wasn't sure how I felt. After church, the last Sunday in March, Warren and I headed up to New Liskeard. It was not a nice drive, with wet, blowing snow most of the way. It seemed to take forever to get to North Bay and then it was another hour and a half drive north, with 3-foot snow banks and lots of blowing snow. At one point, Warren turned to me and said, "We aren't coming here Mom are we?" And I said, "Probably not."

We arrived at Marg's home about 6:00 p.m. and she had dinner ready for us. She advised me that there were 10 people interviewing me including a minister and lay representative from Temiskaming Presbytery, and the meeting was set for 7:30 p.m. She seemed very nice and we chatted and made small talk. Warren was already downstairs in the basement watching TV when people started to arrive. The people on the committee began by telling me all about their church, that it seated about 300 people but only about 125 came on Sundays. They said they had a nice manse that they were planning to repaint inside and I could pick any colours I wanted for the rooms. We talked about the ministry and they said they would really like their minister to visit and work with young people. I told them about myself and the ministry I was already doing. I remember Isabel who was probably in her late 70's and the oldest on the committee. She seemed very kind and sensitive and I liked her. In fact, I liked everything I had heard that evening. They said they were very interested in me being their minister and that they had not had a woman before but thought I would get along really well with the congregation. I felt very good about the interview but told them it was already dark when I arrived and I had to see the town, the church and the manse before I could make a decision. They said they knew I had to return home the next day. They said that Marg would take me out in the morning to see everything I needed to see and we would meet again at 11:00 a.m. at her home. Before they left, Warren came upstairs to meet them and they were very nice to him.

In the morning, after we had breakfast, Marg gave us the tour. The church was a newer church, built in the 1950s, and was quite large inside with very high ceilings and a large choir loft and organ. It had a lectern and a pulpit, which was different from Trinity United Church which only had a pulpit. Next to the sanctuary were two offices for the secretary and the minister. Downstairs, in the church's basement, there was the washroom and a very large kitchen. Marg drove us to the manse which was about three minutes away and it was a large, three bedroom house. There were two bedrooms upstairs with a full bathroom between them and downstairs there was a good size bedroom and a smaller room that could also be used as a bedroom and a full bathroom beside it. There was a large living room and dining room side by side, with a beautiful dining room table with chairs and a buffet which Marg said I could use while I was there. There was a really good sized kitchen and also a finished basement. It had a lovely back yard that backed onto a ravine where you could walk down to the Wabi River. We were impressed. Then Marg drove us to the high school and told Warren he could walk home for lunch because it was only 5 minutes away, a far cry from the 30-minute bus ride. I could feel Warren getting really excited about this. New Liskeard was part of the tri- town: New Liskeard, Haileybury and Cobalt. New Liskeard had grocery stores, a drug store, a hardware store, many restaurants as well as McDonalds and Tim Hortons and two Chinese food restaurants, a Giant Tiger store, a Prebyterian and Baptist church, and beautiful park areas, an arena, a Canadian Tire store, a movie theatre and much more. Finally, Marg took us on the scenic drive around Lake Temiskaming. It was a beautiful drive.

When we came back to her house, Warren and I had time to go out for a short walk in the snow before the meeting and we talked. I asked him what he thought and he was beyond happy and excited and very impressed. So was I. He asked about Louise and Susie and I told him I had asked how they would get there and was told there was a train that came right into New Liskeard from Toronto. I told him I really felt this was the place I was to come and there was no doubt in my mind. He looked so happy and that was all that mattered to me. Once we got back to Marg's house, Warren went downstairs and I met again with the committee. They asked me to be their minister because they really thought I was the right person for them. I accepted their call and they were very pleased. Then we talked about salary and travel and I asked to be paid twice a month and that was agreed upon as were other relevant matters. It was done and I would start July 1st. They asked me to get three quotes from moving companies and when they said that to me, it suddenly became very real. We were moving! Warren and I talked all the way back to Grand Valley and we both felt very good about the decision I had made. As soon as I got home, I talked to my sister about where we were going and she said that sounded more like it. My aunts were happy for us too because we would only be five hours away and it would be no problem, they told me. They would get a taxi to Toronto for the train ride to New Liskeard when they came to visit.

Now, Warren and I had to start packing and Liz and I had to get ready for the Maple Syrup Festival on April 6th. that 'Duo Keyboards' was taking part in. We would be playing at Trinity

United Church and we now had a good selection of more than 12 duets we could play together that were fairly difficult and we felt very comfortable with. I told Liz where we were going and she was sorry to see me go because she had enjoyed doing the music we did together as much as I did, and I told her how much I also appreciated her friendship. When I told my congregations where I was going, there was a sigh of relief from them that I had found a place to go and had accepted a call. I was never worried. I really wasn't. I knew that, if it was right for me to move and I was really called away, then there was something more out there for me to do. I had faith and, if it didn't work out, I would find other work to do. Now there was still a lot to do in my present congregations before I left and I knew that, in the end, it would be hard to say goodbye.

At noon on Friday, May 31, Susie called and said Louise had had a minor stroke and was in the Oakville Hospital. I told her I would be on my way as soon as Warren was back from Shelborne. I was upset and called my sister to tell her what had happened, that we were going down to see Louise and I would call her as soon as I knew anything. When Warren got home, I told him what had happened and, as we drove out of town, the sky was so black it almost felt like the middle of the night, even though it was only four in the afternoon. Warren was worried about Weisa and so was I and I told him we were going right to the hospital. As soon as we got to the Oakville Hospital, we went right to the room where Susie had told me Louise would be and Susie was there. Louise seemed fine but I could see she had been frightened by what had happened. Dr. Soanes, our family doctor, had been in to see her and everything was looked after. We stayed a couple of hours and then we went out to dinner with Susie before going back to the hospital. We said goodnight to Louise and I told her we would see her in the morning before we went back home.

We had a good night's sleep and, in the morning when we got up, Warren went in to watch cartoons and Susie was in the kitchen. I was in the bedroom getting dressed when I heard Warren yell, "Mom, Mom come here quick." Susie and I both ran into the living room. The television was reporting a tornado had touched down in Grand Valley around 4:30 p.m. the day before. It had gone right through Amaranth Street and the main street in town destroying everything. I was stunned and then I remembered that huge, dark cloud that had covered the whole sky as we drove out of town. I told Susie we had to go back right away and she got worried so I had to reassure her that the tornado was gone and we would be alright and I would call her later. I called Louise at the hospital and told her what had happened and that I was very sorry but we had to go home. She understood and told me she was feeling much better. Then I called my sister and told her that the worst was over with Louise and I told her about the tornado. We had no idea what we were going back to or, if we even had a house or a church there. Warren was upset and wondered what we would find when we got home and I tried to keep him calm as we drove. We had to stop for lunch on the way back because we hadn't eaten and we didn't know what to expect when we got home. We stopped half way there at a restaurant we often ate at on our way to or from Oakville and, while we were having lunch there, a family from our church in Grand Valley who were heading to Toronto to stay with their family also stopped in for lunch. They saw us and came right over. They said it was terrible in Grand Valley. They said it was hard to know where to start because so many homes had been destroyed. People whose homes were gone were told to go to the arena for water, for meals and a place to sleep. I couldn't believe what I was hearing. I asked about the church and the manse and they said people had been asking about me because the tornado had hit the barn and the back of the manse and the office was damaged. The tornado had bounced off the manse and gone straight down the driveway where I usually parked my car and then the tornado hit the church. No one was allowed to go into the church because they weren't sure how badly it was damaged.

We finished our lunch as quickly as we could and headed home. As we drove into town, we could feel the tension in the air. Our street looked alright but, looking ahead to Amaranth Street, we saw pieces of houses everywhere. It was scary as if the town had been bombed. I looked at the church and it had a sign on it that said: 'No entry, unsafe'. We went into the manse and looked around and only my office upstairs was damaged by the tornado but we were lucky and it was safe to be in our home. We went back outside and saw that the barn in our back yard was destroyed. We saw some of our neighbours who were still in shock and we talked with them. Then we drove over to the arena where lots of people were packed in. Many people had come from other communities to help and the Mennonites had come to help rebuild homes. I saw many families I knew and they were also in shock. Their homes were gone. Jean saw me and came running over. She was so relieved to see me and told me how worried she had been about me. I asked Jean about Ruth Hunter and her family and she said it was a miracle. Apparently Ruth had been sitting in her kitchen when the tornado hit her house. After the tornado moved on Ruth was still sitting in her kitchen but her house was badly damaged. Her next door neighbours ran over to help Ruth and found that there was not a mark on her. Jean also said it was a miracle that only one man had been killed in this horrendous tornado. He was visiting from the British Isles and was in the library which had been completely destroyed as was the building that had the doctor's office in town where Jean worked. Luckily no one there was hurt.

We went back home and were hardly in the door when some of the members of the ministerial who had heard I was back home, came to see me. They said two of the smaller churches in town were destroyed and they wanted to see if we could have a community service for everyone tomorrow, Sunday, at the public school. I told them I thought it was a great idea so they said they would get everyone together later that day and we would all meet at the school to plan the service. I went over to see Liz and was relieved to see her home wasn't hit. She was so glad to see me because Jean had told her they didn't know where I was. I explained to Liz, as I had to Jean, that my aunt had gone into the hospital the day before and I forgot to call Jean to let her know where I would be. I felt badly about that because normally I always let Jean know when I left town but I had been more upset about Louise than I had realized and had neglected to tell anyone where I was going. That afternoon, the ministerial gathered and planned the service for the next morning. When they asked me to give the sermon, I said I would. The gym in the school was packed that morning and everyone appreciated what we were doing. Needless to say, it was a very difficult and emotional service for us to conduct but we did the best we could. As the spiritual leaders of the community, most of us came together in solidarity. After the service, one of the Latter Day Saints Elders came over and talked with me. He said he knew that our church could not be used for worship and he offered us their church. I thought that was so kind. I hadn't even thought about where we would worship, yet here was a very generous offer. I thanked him, and said that we really appreciated this. I led in worship at their church until I left.

A Planning Committee for Trinity United Church was quickly formed that consisted of Ruth Hambleton, who was Secretary of the Congregation and wonderful to work with, Alan Irwin who was Chair of the Property Committee, Irving Potter who was our Clerk of Session, Stan Newson, who was Chair of Stewards and Ian Reed, a Member at Large. Certain things had to be done immediately. There was a huge amount of work to do. Fencing was immediately put around the church: Denton's from Hamilton were called to remove the organ before more damage was sustained; the stained glass windows were taken out by Classical Stain Glass from Hamilton and each pane was taken out and numbered; insurance adjustors and structural engineers met with us and Summit Restoration was on site to gather information; Rev. Cline, the Executive Secretary of General Council from our head office, came to give us support; our insurance company gave the church a cheque for $15,000.00 to cover immediate expenses.

By the middle of June, we had received a preliminary estimate to restore our church or build a new church. The Maycocks were very concerned because bricks were falling from the church very close to their home so scaffolding was erected by Summit Restoration to protect their house from any damage. We were busy with all of this construction, day and night, trying to figure out what to do. Could we save the church? Was that practical or should we build a new church? These were hard decisions to make and very emotional ones. Some members from our church were designated to go and visit smaller new churches that had been built in the last 10 years to see if it was more practical to rebuild with the insurance money we would receive. The church had bellowed in all directions and only after the plaster and lath were removed could a more thorough examination be made regarding the structural damage. The subsequent report from Rand Valley Structural Engineer Brian E. Boyle and Robert Halsall and Associates Ltd., Consulting Engineers in Toronto, told us we would need to rebuild the north and south walls, the top corner of the north gables and the south and west walls. We would also need to replace the wood deck on the high roof. The list went on and on.

It was an extremely busy and crazy time for both me and Warren. Most of the day, my phone rang off the hook. I had already had three different movers in to give me an estimate to move us to New Liskeard and I was constantly trying to pack up our things but there was so much to pack up. It was a struggle to get everything done in time for the movers. At the same time, I had to prepare weekly services and visit people who were really grieving, especially those who had lost their homes. I was so worried about the church but I knew the congregation would make an informed decision in the next couple of months as to whether to undertake the renovations needed for the church to be safe or to tear it down and build a new but much smaller church. I also knew that, by the time I was gone they would have a new minister.

I didn't expect any kind of going away party before I left because of the tragedy all around us but Monticello United Church stepped in and did it. On June 21, 1985, Warren and I went with

Jean and Liz to the party they planned and it was a very special celebration. The basement was packed with about 100 people who were there from my two churches including lots of young people, which I really appreciated. There were also many, many families there whom I had ministered to and with whom I had become friends with and I was happy to see them there. They gave me a rocking chair to relax in, as well as beautiful watches for Warren and me. They sang songs, told stories and jokes and three men from Monticello - Ross, Elmer and Arnold - did a skit dressed as women. It was hilarious and so wonderful and after all the heartbreak of the previous month, everyone had a great time. It was also bittersweet as I looked out over the crowd that had gathered and saw Jean and Liz sitting together and I knew how much I would miss them. Ioan Shortt from the Monticello congregation wrote a poem that said it all:

> *We've come here for a night of fun Of music, songs, and skits well done. We've tried to do our very best Not just so you would be impressed. But furthermore, to let you know We really hate to see you go. Four years is not so very long to try to teach us right from wrong. But still with patience, you have tried You've laughed with us and oftimes cried. At times, we've even made you cross Then you've tried to show us who was boss. When you showed up a blonde so neat You nearly swept Arnold "off his feet". But he's recovering every day No wonder that his hair turned grey. But with all joking put aside Our love for you, we cannot hide. You've nurtured us with love and care In times of need, you were always there. Then when disaster struck our town You surely didn't let us down. You prayed with us and in our grief Strengthened us in our belief. That God must have some distant plan though now it's hard to understand. The walls that crumbled will again stand tall And in their pews, on His name we'll call. Sometime we'll give thanks I know For these are the things that help us grow. But tonight we're here to honour you and hope that all your dreams come true. As we present these gifts tonight We hope they'll make your future bright. But alas we know you'll never find a group like the ones you're leaving behind… … (Signed on behalf of members and friends of the Grand Valley Monticello Pastoral Charge)*

Ruth Hambleton one of the members of Trinity United Church said this:

> *"I thought it would be nice to say a few words of thanks to you Dorinda on behalf of the congregation of Trinity. We may not have always agreed with your ideas but often yours was the better way. Our Session has a better understanding of its responsibilities. Our Sunday School has grown and more families are part of our Church Family. Your pre-marriage counselling has been of great benefit to those that have attended. Even the classes for baptism have given better understanding.The work you have done to keep us on track during our TORNADO DISASTER has been tremendous and I think it's mainly because of your organizational skills that every thing came so quickly together.Our thanks to you Dorinda. May we continue to grow in God's love and we wish you well as you head north to New Liskeard and new challenges."*

It really was the most wonderful sendoff for us. I couldn't thank all the people in my two congregation enough for this special celebration and party for Warren and me. It was hard to leave. At the end of June, my last service for Trinity United Church congregation was held in the Latter Day Saints Church. We had the Sunday School graduation of our young people and the teachers did a beautiful job to make it very special for them. This was Warren's last year at Sunday School and he received the last of all the pins that he would receive for perfect attendance. He was very proud as Irving Potter pinned it on him and I was very proud of my son. It was a great service and a wonderful way to end my last Sunday at Grand Valley. After the service, Jean wanted to know how to get to New Liskeard because she was coming to my covenanting service which had been set for the next Sunday by Temiskaming Presbytery. I looked forward to having her at our new home on Friday. After the service in Grand Valley, I went on to Monticello United Church and it was just as hard to do the service there and say goodbye. When I hugged Elmer and Ross and Arnold after the service I told them they probably wouldn't be hugging their next minister and they agreed. We all laughed because they were back to having a man again. We had had a lot of great times together.

The movers had come and taken everything and we were packed and ready to go. After the services we came back home, finished loading up the car, took our last walk through our home and then went across the street for the last time to say goodbye to our neighbours June and Wayne Maycock and their children Julie, Adrienne and Warren. As we drove off, we took with us wonderful memories of all the good people in Grand Valley and Monticello. I never looked back. We were moving on to another ministry, another school, another church and another congregation.

CHAPTER FOUR

Transitioning to New Liskeard

Before I moved to New Liskeard, I took some time in June 1985 to reflect on the past four years at Grand Valley. In the spring of 1983 I was having a very difficult time with issues from my childhood that had surfaced. I remembered back when I was 12 years old and my mother and I were sitting on the steps of the porch of their house in Port Colborne. It was a hot, humid night and my sister and father were already asleep. We were talking when my mother stopped for a moment and went into her bedroom. She came back with some photos and love letters from her hope chest. They were from her former husband Win Nixon. When she showed me the pictures, I thought he looked a lot like Errol Flynn, a famous Hollywood actor, and that he was handsome and debonair. She read me a couple of the love letters he had written to her so long ago and told me how much she had loved him. From the way she was talking, I knew she still did. That made me wonder if she really ever loved my father.

This was the only time my mother and I ever had a meaningful conversation. Now, 27 years later in April 1983, I decided to try to contact Win. I hoped he was still living and I found a phone number under his name in Toronto where my mother and Win had lived after they married. I wasn't sure if that was him but I finally gathered up my courage and dialed the number. A man answered and, when I asked if I was speaking to Win Nixon, he said yes. I told him my name but I was sure he didn't know who I was. When I said that I would like to meet with him and that it was important, he was very abrupt and cold on the phone and asked me why I wanted to meet with him. All I could think of was that he had a niece, Adrienne, whom my mother had talked to me about and felt close to. So I told him it had something to do with Adrienne, but that I couldn't discuss it on the phone. He tried to get me to tell him what it was about but I wouldn't. Finally, he said he would meet me in the lobby of his office in downtown Toronto at 10:00 the next morning. He gave me the address, and the conversation was over.

I had mixed feelings about seeing him after I got off the phone but I knew I needed to meet him. My mother had been married to Win for 10 years and even though my mother desperately wanted to have a baby, he didn't. She left him and met my dad. They got involved and nine months later she had me. I was very nervous about going to meet Win and it didn't help that the lobby where I was meeting him was in one of the huge, cold skyscrapers in Toronto's financial district. As I entered the lobby, I saw a man sitting there who stood up when I walked in. I went over to him and introduced myself. Win was about 74 years old at that time and very handsome. When we sat down, I tried to start up a conversation with him but he wasn't having it and very abruptly insisted I tell him about Adrienne. "You were married to my mother," I said to him. He stopped talking then and I took out the pictures I had brought of Mom to show him. He told me I had my mother's eyes and he asked me how she was. When I told him she had died in 1972, he became emotional. I told him that when I was young, I thought he might have been my father but he assured me he wasn't and I believed him. I told him about the conversation I had with my mother when I was 12 years old and that she had showed me pictures of him and the love letters he had sent her. I also said she had told me how much she had loved him. Then he told me that, one night when they were together in their bedroom, they had been drinking and she was being very silly, as only she could be. She wanted to tell him something and he kept asking her what it was and she kept teasing him. Finally she said, "I will come back and tell you". In those days, he said they didn't say they loved each other and he said we probably should have. Then Win looked right at me and said, "Here you are telling me how much she loved me". I knew in that moment that he still loved my mother. He told me that he had remarried and they also lived with his mother but they never had children either and his second wife had died a few years after my mother. His mother outlived both his wives.

We weren't together for very long and, walking away, I felt I had done the right thing in meeting with Win. Through me, my mother had come back to him to tell him how much she loved him. That felt good but this meeting had also opened up some things in me and I needed to look at them. At the end of April in 1983, I had asked Dr. Soanes to recommend a counsellor for me to go to. I felt I needed someone to talk to about my childhood and begin to sort things out that had always bothered me about being given up. He had suggested I see Dr. Zaborowska who had been my grandmother's doctor and the person who had named our home in Oakville, 'The House of Seven Confusions.' She now practiced Family Psychiatry out of her home in Oakville. She agreed to see me in May and I saw her every month for nine months. I don't remember much about our time together but it helped me to just go and talk to her because she was very helpful and reassuring. When I was leaving Grand Valley to go New Liskeard, Dr. Soanes gave me my medical file to take to my new doctor and as I browsed through my records, I found a letter Dr. Zaborowska had sent to Dr. Soanes on March 21, 1984. I quote from parts of this letter:

> *"Dorinda came to see me … … . I knew her and her family which we found very helpful… … When she came to see me, Dorinda was in a turmoil. She was suffering feelings of rejection because, when she was just a little girl, her mother placed her with two aunts and a grandmother in Oakville… …she has begun to write poetry – beautiful, disciplined – real art. Some time later she started composing… .She is now taking a course in composition… Her compositions (she lent me tapes) are excellent… We have done a lot of hard work. I hope it will be helpful. Thank you for this very interesting referral."*

In November, 1983 I was wondering how long I would stay in Grand Valley and where I would go next so I went to Toronto and talked to Reverend Don Gillies, the Personnel Officer at Toronto Conference. Don had 500 ministers under pastoral care and I was one of them and he was wonderful to me over the years I was at Grand Valley and I trusted him. I asked him if there was a place I could go to get an assessment of my vocation and calling and he suggested I go to the Career and Life Planning Consultation/Interfaith Pastoral Counseling Centre. Don told me the Conference often sends ministers there for consulting and assessment. After our meeting he called them, and referred me and they sent me an application to fill out with all the information they needed before they saw me. I returned all of the documentation and references they required and, when they were ready to see me they set up two days of intensive interviewing, assessment and consultation for February 7th and 8th 1984. In early March I received their report and read it and promptly filed it away. I learned a lot about myself but I wasn't ready to process what I was reading because I didn't want to hear it at the time. Now 15 months later, I felt I was ready to really look at this report with an open mind and take it more seriously. In the Introduction of the report, it said the following;

> *"Since her ordination in 1976, Dorinda has served in a variety of unusual and demanding settings…..She has been effective in all her endeavours and her references speak appreciatively of her energy, talent, sincerity and sensitivity. She does however experience periods of 'burn out'. Indeed, her adult working life has been characterized by relatively short periods of intense, energetic involvement followed by periods of burn out…..Dorinda is a single parent with a 13 year old son. She has been clear that his needs will be important in planning her future for at least the next four or five years."*

They were right about the burn out I experienced from time to time but I didn't realize the impact it had on me or how often it had happened until it was pointed out to me. As a minister, I observe people's behavior and try to see the good in people and help them see that in themselves. People tell me their secrets and talk with me about their own personal pain and suffering and some of that stays with me.

I remember a phone call I got one evening from the wife of a member of our choir at Trinity United Church. Peter was a faithful attender but his wife never came to church. She was calling to say that Peter was dying and he wanted to see me. I went right over and his wife showed me into his bedroom and left. He was very weak but also very agitated. He wanted to confess his sins to me and the terrible things he had done when he had been in the Second World War. Peter was from Holland and had been in the army fighting for his country at that time. He had also been a member of the Roman Catholic Church and was asking me for absolution. I listened to him and talked quietly with him. I knew Peter as a good man and I knew terrible things were done in that war so I gave him the absolution he needed to bring him some peace. I prayed with him and I blessed him. When his wife came back to the bedroom, she could see he wasn't agitated anymore and she couldn't thank me enough for coming. Peter died the next day and his funeral was in our church that week. I felt it was a privilege to be with Peter in that sacred time as he was dying. But those times also take their toll on me because I care and I don't want to see people suffering, whether it be physical, mental or spiritual pain. It is my call as a minister to relieve suffering wherever possible and bring a sense of calm and peace to those who suffer. I need to let people know they are loved in spite of the fact they do things that cause other people pain and suffering. We all do hurtful things if we are truly honest with ourselves. Situations like this dredge up deep seated insecurities within all of us so that we feel we are not good enough to be loved by another person or by God. It was easy for me to understand how burn out caught up to me from time to time when I gave so much of myself to others who needed someone to care. The next part of the report was very hard for me to read the first time I read it. Reading it now, I could be more objective as I was trying to understand what drives me to do what I do. In the Pertinent Life History Date of the report, it said:

> "On the whole, Dorinda must have felt alone as a child. The early shift from her parents' home to her grandparents' home was traumatic. She lived in a world of adults and was separated from her only sibling. This perhaps accounts in part for her long talks with God and her deep sense of God in her life. The early traumatic event was replicated when at 12 her mother refused to allow her to return home. Her hurt and angry response to these events may be the fuel for her later anger in situations where there is injustice. As well, the difficult financial situation of the Oakville family must have given Dorinda a sympathy for the struggles of the poor. Dorinda describes the death of her grandmother in 1960 when she was 16, as "very, very difficult". Her parents' (and Jana's) emigration two years later must have increased her sense of aloneness. In 1969, Dorinda fell in love and had her son out of wedlock. While she has continued to receive support from her former lover and father of her child, it did involve another loss and this has not been replaced. This loss was followed in 1972 by her mother's death – another difficult experience. In many ways Dorinda's adult life patterns replicate the emotional dynamics of her childhood. There have been the same short, intensive episodes followed by break offs into new areas. The discontinuity in the flow of her living has meant intense involvement with pressure to master the situation, a breakoff and loss of those relationships, another new situation and new family is created with its cast of good and bad participants. A recurring sense of sadness and loss as relationships are left behind seems inevitable."

I could now understand what the report was saying and it was really helpful to read this again and think about who I was. I do enter into situations with people and give my all. I am a very good listener and use those painful experiences from my past to relate to those who talk with me. The heart is very fragile and people trust me as their minister and that is a sacred trust. I also recognized that I have found ways to cope with the demands of ministry. I pour my heart and soul into my music and use it to let go. While I was at Grand Valley, that was a great release. I used my poetry to put on paper my thoughts and feelings, my love and joy and the painful experiences of my life and the pain I saw and felt in the lives of others. I also love the movies that take me away from it all and, once in a while, a really good movie helps me write a sermon. I think a lot and do a lot of reflection so I need my quiet time. And, of course, the joy of my life is my son Warren who makes me laugh and we have great times together. Over the years, I have often talked to him and sought his counsel, asking him for advice and consulted with him on major decisions that affected us both. I can't change my past but I can learn to accept it for what it is and to realize the gift it is, every time I give back, again and again, to people who come to me with their concerns and pain and need to talk to someone they hope and pray will understand them. The section on Pertinent Personality and Vocational Factors said:

> 'Vocational test results indicate that Dorinda's interests are most congruent with individuals in the artistic world (musicians, artists, photographers, reporters…)….While interest in religious activities specifically is moderately high this does not translate into liking and disliking the same things as the criterion group of ministers used in the reference samples do. In terms of shared interests, Dorinda may have little in common with her colleagues, most of whom are male.'

It surprised me that the report suggested that I would fit in best with people who are in the artistic world. A part of me knew that but seeing it in writing was a different matter. I felt I got along well with my male colleagues in ministry but I recognized that there were definitely differences and, although I didn't have a lot to do with them, I was respected by them. Reading this part of the report challenged me and confirmed for me that my artistic temperament was an integral part of why I was called to ministry. At that time I was looking at doing the Doctor of Ministry program that in part was congregationally based. This is what the report had to say about that. *"Dorinda's academic comfort scale suggest she might not enjoy…...pursuing doctoral studies."*

After reading what the report said, I recognized I was really not suited for more academic studies and I was relieved. I am very much a hands-on person and I couldn't see myself studying in a library, writing papers and then writing a thesis. I had already done a four year degree and the three year Master of Divinity. Seven years was enough and I knew I really didn't want to do more academic studies. I have to be honest and say that the concluding remarks below were true and insightful and very helpful to me. They were hard to look at and read again but I have looked at them many times since, tried to address them so I could bring out what is the best in me. They have certainly helped me to understand why I do what I do and who I am. I still need to be reminded and do a check in from time to time.

> "Dorinda is not highly devoted to societal norms and is willing to risk ostracism for her own beliefs. She is likely to deny some of the implications of her individualism and externalize the blame when people may criticize her for her style or method. She frequently seems astonished when people react negatively to her unorthodox position or her criticism of their hypocrisy. Dorinda is very sensitive to rejection and thus suffers somewhat from her individualism due to her emotional sensitivity. Self- regard is positive and high but it likely requires some effort on her part to maintain that positive outlook given the sensitivity. This could account for the periods of depression she experiences. All evidence supports Dorinda's value that it is important to be nurturant and supportive to other people. People who know her speak of her sensitivity to others and Dorinda describes herself this way… .

she also has a high personal need for the support and succorance of others. This seems to conflict with her desire to be independent. A primary motivation for Dorinda is the need to understand motives behind behaviours and why people act as they do. Our sense is that she focuses outward on other people and on doing so may avoid facing her own internal process, i.e., feelings, awareness of needs, perceptions etc. Perhaps the resurgence of the need to be creative is reflective of this.

*Dorinda needs a good deal of challenge and variety in life. She has a low need for order suggesting she can be quite flexible and finds routine boring. This accounts for the boredom she experiences in meetings and perhaps the frustration she experiences in her present charge. Dorinda, according to the tests, perceives herself as one who strives to be friendly and diplomatic even when this is personally exacting. She likely is this way in most situations. In the broader context, i.e., the organized church or the treatment of native peoples, she does not suffer fools gladly. She has a ready reservoir of anger and intolerance for the 'good' people who don't measure up. This anger against hypocrisy and lack of social justice is a positive resource and there are theological precedents for it. it is good for the Church and society in general to have 'gadflies' who sting us into awareness and action. We have however several concerns about how this affects Dorinda. It creates frustration inside of her when people (as we all are at times) are petty, unmoveable, hypocrites etc."
"It appears that she may not always be aware of the frustrations building until her anger suddenly erupts. This results in criticism from others which astonishes Dorinda and then hurts her. She ends up feeling misunderstood and projects this on others, thereby starting another cycle, whatever, she ends up alone".*

I really looked at what was said here. I remembered back to that incident in the choir in the fall of 1982 where I got angry at Norma and let out my anger without thinking. I know it can happen but it wasn't right. I learned a good lesson then and it is a lesson that needs to be remembered.

"In our opinion, some of this anger stems from her childhood experiences where she was let down by others. Attention to this would make the positive aspects of her legitimate anger at social injustice have more credibility and more power."

This was also hard to read but, if I am to be honest, it is true. I have learned to be more aware when I get frustrated and I take more time to try to understand why I am feeling that way and address whatever concern I am presented with in a more positive way. It is not easy to do.

SUMMARY:

"Dorinda is a competent, sincere person with tremendous energy. She had a storehouse of ideas and gets excited by projects that appeal to her sense of social justice or simply change for the better. She is an individualist who is willing to stand by her beliefs even at personal cost. She excels in preaching, fund raising, getting people involved and creative endeavours like music. She is a gifted, likeable person who can ruffle feathers and pour oil on troubled waters. She can function with great sensitivity or a lack of awareness of how others will be affected by her words or actions".

I didn't know, at the time, how much I needed to take a hard look at this report before I left Grand Valley. I knew some of the issues I had and I found the report honest and truthful even though it was hard to read parts of it again. This report reminded me of who I was and affirmed for me how capable I was. I also realized that I needed to find a way not to take things so personally when I get angry. It was good that I read it when I did because I didn't know what was about to happen at St. Paul's United Church in New Liskeard. I would need all my strength, faith and resources to face the challenge that lay ahead.

CHAPTER FIVE

Conflict and Resolution

When Warren and I drove away from Grand Valley, I had a lot of mixed emotions. The tornado had wreaked terrible damage on our community and I felt really badly that so many families had lost their homes. The issue of whether to renovate the church or tear it down and build a new church was not decided and I felt a lot of guilt leaving without this matter being resolved. It was also hard leaving my congregations and the people I deeply cared about. They had been so good to Warren and me. I thought about Jean and knew how much I would miss her. She had been a wonderful support to me through all the ups and downs of those last four years. But I knew it was time for us to move on and I was excited by the prospects that lay ahead. The moving van had already come and taken all our things which would be waiting for us in New Liskeard when we arrived. When we got to our new home, the key was in our mailbox and we opened the door and walked in. It was a wonderful feeling to be here and I had high hopes and expectations. All our boxes and furniture were in the rooms where I had asked them to be put by the movers and Warren ran upstairs excitedly to see that all his things were there. We unpacked the boxes downstairs first and started by organizing the kitchen. Then Warren set his room up the way he wanted it. The bathroom upstairs was to be his and the bathroom downstairs was across from the large room which would be my bedroom. At my request, the congregation had left the dining room table and chairs with a buffet in the dining room. It belonged to the church in the day when churches had to provide a manse with furniture. They had also left the ping pong table in the basement for us to use.

Over the next couple of days, we continued to unpack. When we were done, I called Charlie Reid, the Treasurer at St. Paul's, and told him I needed to talk with him about when I was to be paid. He said he would come to the church and meet me at my office. When I went to the office, I met Dorothy McLaren who was the church Secretary and she seemed very friendly and happy to meet me. Dorothy was in her early 60's, short and heavy set and had lovely, wavy grey hair. While I was waiting for Charlie, we talked and got to know each other. We discovered that her birthday was April 1, the same day as Warren's and she told me that she worked 25 hours a week for the church. Dorothy's husband Jim had a serious heart condition and she was the only one who brought in an income. When Charlie arrived, I showed him my contract where it specified that I was to be paid twice a month and told him that I hoped that was alright with him. "No," he told me, "it wasn't alright because a Pastoral Charge only has to pay the minister once a month". I told him that I knew that and that was why I had specifically asked to be paid twice a month in my contract. The congregation and Temiskaming Presbytery had agreed to that. I was very surprised at his tone and his indifference but I didn't argue with him. After he left, I phoned Marg Taylor who was the past Chair of the Official Board and now the Chair of the Administration and Personnel Committee and she was also on the Executive. I told her I needed to talk to her and she invited me to her home. When I got there, I told her what Charlie had said and I could see that she was angry. She told me there would be no problem and that she would talk to him and look after it. I took her at her word. The next day, Marg called me and told me that Charlie had resigned as the Treasurer of the church and that he was also leaving St. Paul's and going to Haileybury United Church. She said that I would be paid twice a month and she would look after things until a new Treasurer was in place. Marg was not the least bit worried.

I had only been in New Liskeard for less than a week and, to say the least, I was shocked by this turn of events. I understood Charlie had been the Treasurer for many years and was a very active member at St. Paul's. I also knew I hadn't done anything wrong and I wondered whether he didn't like the fact that I was a woman or if he just liked doing things his way and wouldn't change. It didn't make any sense to me for him to resign as treasurer and leave the church. There had to be a lot more to it but I let it go for now as I had my Covenanting Service coming up that first Sunday evening and I had to prepare for that. Besides, Jean would be arriving Friday and Warren and I were looking forward to having her at our new home. The incident did start me thinking about what I had gotten myself into. It is the norm for a Covenanting Service to be held within two months of a minister arriving at a new Charge which gives the minister a chance to get to know the congregation. I hardly knew anyone and they didn't know me so I didn't understand why Temiskaming Presbytery had scheduled my Covenanting Service within a week of my arrival and now I wondered if they thought I was going to change my mind.

Jean arrived and it was so wonderful to see her. She told me she couldn't remember when she had driven anywhere for five hours and we should feel honoured that she had. We laughed about that and looked forward to a great visit. It was so kind of her to come because I know it was hard on her knowing I wasn't the minister in Grand Valley anymore. She attended my first service that Sunday morning and everything went very well. The people who came to the service were very friendly and happy to meet me and that was a great feeling. That evening, a lot of people came to the Covenanting Service at St. Paul's including ministers from the Tri Town Ministerial (New Liskeard, Haileybury, and Cobalt) and many came from Temiskaming Presbytery which conducted the service. In this service I made promises to the congregation to support them and care for them and lead in worship and conduct the Sacraments. I also made promises to the Presbytery to be an active member of Temiskaming Presbytery and agreed to be under the discipline and authority of Presbytery. Then promises were made by the congregation and the Presbytery to support and work with me in the ministry we would do together. Reverend Murray Binstead, the minister at Haileybury United Church, was the Chair of Temiskaming Presbytery and he warmly welcomed me as did Reverend Bill Jones, who was the minister at Cobalt United Church and the Secretary of Temiskaming Presbytery. At the reception afterwards, the lay leader from the Latter Day Saints Church in town welcomed me and said he had heard wonderful things about me from the Latter Day Saints Church in Grand Valley. I really appreciated that. The ministers from the Baptist Church, the Presbyterian Church and the lay representative from the Anglican Church also warmly welcomed me. It was great to meet most of the United Church ministers in the Presbytery which then consisted of about 15 Pastoral Charges. Reverend Cliff Plant, the Personnel Officer from Manitou Conference in North Bay, was also there to say a few words and welcome me. Members from the congregation, Judi Campbell, President of the Board, Marg Taylor, the former Chair of the Pastoral relations Committee, and Doriel Poupore, the organist, also spoke and welcomed me warmly. It was a great beginning that helped me feel right at home in New Liskeard.

Jean enjoyed her visit with us very much. Warren and I loved having her with us and we all had so much fun together so it was hard to say goodbye to her when Monday morning came and she headed back to Grand Valley. When she left, I set to work in earnest in my new ministry. One of the first families I visited in my second week was Keith and Louise Reid. They were a wonderful older couple who were in their early 70's and very involved in the church. They were very easy to talk to and were so pleased to meet me. I had a good visit with them and they asked me lots of questions about myself and Warren and how I was feeling in my first two weeks as their minister. I was still concerned about what the treasurer had done and I talked to them about my worry that I may have done something wrong. Then Louise told me that Keith was Charlie's brother, at which point I stopped breathing for a moment. But Louise assured me that I had not done anything wrong and that Charlie just liked doing things his own way. Keith said he didn't always agree with his brother and, besides, Charlie's daughter Nancy attended Haileybury United Church and that was the reason he went there. They didn't say it outright but I got the impression that there were problems with the Church Council structure and with certain people on the Executive.

By the end of July I had made quite a few visits and was getting to know people, especially Doriel Poupore, our organist and her husband Don. They were in their 50s and lived in the country. Doriel worked as the Secretary in the Public School near her home and was well liked and respected. Don was a truck driver and was also in the choir along with their youngest daughter Tammy who was the same age as Warren. Don and Doriel had two older children who already had their own families. We hit it off very well and I told Doriel about the organ piano recitals that Liz and I had done. She said she would like us to try playing together in the fall and that Warren and I were welcome at their home anytime. They were a wonderful family. I also visited Sharon Reynolds, Ellen and Bruce Lang and their two sons Randy and Martin, Wendy Whalen and her children, Connie Moore and Lila and Len Fielder. All of us became good friends.

When I met my neighbours down the street, Nora and Fern Ladacoeur, I liked them right away and we became very good friends. Although Fern didn't go to church, Nora was always there on Sunday. Their younger daughter Donna lived in Toronto and had a good job as a librarian. Their older daughter Lee had been killed in a terrible car accident a number of years earlier when she was driving home from university and the man driving the car behind her pulled out to pass and didn't make it. The car coming toward him hit both their cars and Lee was killed instantly. The driver in the passing car was seriously hurt and he was in the hospital in New Liskeard for a few months. It turned out that he was the son of the minister at St. Paul's

United Church in New Liskeard at that time, and, like Lee, had also been heading home from university. It was a terrible tragedy all around and it was so hard on Nora and Fern. It also made their relationship with the minister very difficult and complicated. Although he officiated at their daughter's funeral, he never visited Nora and Fern after the funeral. They showed me a picture of Lee and I could see that she was a beautiful young woman who had had a wonderful future ahead of her and my heart went out to them.

Bill and Elaine Glassford lived in the country. She was a nurse and Bill worked for the township and was the Chair of the Membership Committee which looked after almost everything the Session did in The United Church of Canada's original church structure. Bill and Elaine both had a great sense of humour and we got along really well. I also liked their two boys, Ronald, who was the same age as Warren, and their younger son, Bruce. Both Glassford boys had disabilities. Ronald had been born with one leg a little shorter than the other and, although, he had had many surgeries over the years, he still walked with a limp. Bruce had a serious hearing problem from the time he was born. They were a wonderful family and were always good to me and Warren. Ronald and Warren met at high school in September and immediately liked each other since they both had a love of technology and they became best friends. I knew I would be working closely with Bill so it was important for me to get to know his wife Elaine and see if she would be alright with that. It turned out she was happy for Bill that he wanted to be involved in the church and, over the next few months, Bill and I spent hours on the phone talking about the congregation and what more we could do to build it. Bill was also very eager to learn about the structure of the United Church and how it worked.

At some point in my second week, I went over to Marg's to talk with her about some things and more specifically about Official Council business as they didn't have the Official Board structure, so I was also having difficulty sorting out St. Paul's church structure. I was used to the Session and Stewards structure where the Session looked after the spiritual needs and concerns of the congregation and the Stewards looked after financial concerns and the maintenance of the building. But St. Paul's had changed over to the new unified board structure where there was a Council in place of the Official Board and about six committees that met ten times a year and an Executive that met every month which was made up of the Chairs of those committees. The full Council only met once a year, instead of three to four times a year, which didn't make sense to me. The congregation had thought that, by moving to this new system of governance more people would be involved but it turned out not to be the case. The congregation came to understood that a few people on the Executive were running the church. It was during this meeting with Marg that I saw a different side of her. She told me very bluntly that I was there to visit and that she and the members of the Executive were there to run the church and see that things got done. She made it clear that it wasn't my business to be concerned about how they did things. I tried to talk with her about this but she wouldn't listen. I found this very hurtful and disrespectful and realized it was going to be very hard on me and very stressful doing ministry in an atmosphere of such distrust and uncertainty. I was now sure that she and Charlie had had disagreements in the past and that she felt threatened by anyone who had opinions as strong as hers and who didn't agree with her. Now I felt used because she must have known that Charlie wouldn't pay me twice a month and that that would be the tipping point for him which it was. He was fed up and left the church and Marg got her way. All of this made me very angry but I knew I had to control my anger and frustration.

Still, I didn't know how to react to what Marg had said to me so, later that week, I called Reverend Murray Binstead at Haileybury United Church and went over to see him. I told him about the situation with Charlie and Marg and he said he wasn't surprised at what had happened. He told me that Marg had wanted Charlie out of the church for a long time. Murray knew all the key players at St. Paul's and he knew the difficulty that their former minister Lorne had had. I asked him how Lorne dealt with it and he said he just visited and stayed out of the business of the church. He also said Lorne was well liked by his congregation but he didn't get along with Marg and stayed out of her way. I told Murray I couldn't do that and he understood and said he would help in any way he could and, if I asked Presbytery for help, they were there for me. I felt reassured that I had the support of Presbytery but that didn't help me at this point since I needed to understand the dynamics of how things worked at St. Paul's and who was running the church besides Marg.

As I continued to visit people they talked to me about many things. I found out that Marg didn't like the former minister because she felt that he always wore clothes that made him look like he was the custodian at the church. But, people told me, Lorne had a very good ministry at St. Paul's and the congregation felt very badly when he and his wife left. I slowly began to understand that there was a definite problem at St. Paul's but I wasn't sure exactly how to deal with Marg's tone and attitude as to what ministers' roles were. It was obvious to me that she expected the minister to do what she said a minister should do. My high hopes and expectations were dashed in less than a month. While I was thinking about all of this, I got a letter on July 24, 1985 from Ruth Hamilton, the Secretary of the church committee in Grand Valley, regarding the question of whether to renovate Trinity United Church or tear it down and build a new church. She wrote:

> *"Sure enough as you figured everything has come to a dead stop. Ian has been working very hard at his work and can't be reached. Allan.....is soooo negative; Irving is good but busy with haying; Stan seems to think everything is coming from his pocket and then there is me, what can I say? Dorothy is very good with our money...... Our new minister I have not seen since you saw him last..... Dorinda I don't know what to do, I'm flustered by this whole setup. Bricks are falling, and more cracks have appeared.....Blake and Norma are at it. Having little meetings here and there. Blake was here putting his two cents in about the ballot, wanting to change everything around as to who can vote.......I do not see anything happening in the near future with our church. I'm trying to get a letter together so a vote can be taken soon, like after our presentation on July 31.......Now you have gone, our congregation realizes how good you are when it comes to organizing... I've heard so many times, "Dorinda kept everything moving". I sure hope this new fellow is a mover and a shaker or we're in deep trouble. I wish you were here to help us in our time of decision.*

It really is a difficult time. This isn't much of a letter but at least you know I'm thinking of you and hope somehow I conveyed how everything is. I'll keep in touch."

When I read the letter, I felt so badly for Ruth. She had a lot of responsibility as the Secretary to keep things going but obviously it was becoming more difficult for her. Since I was having my own issues here at St. Paul's, strange as it may sound, Ruth's letter to me was very helpful because she helped me put things in perspective. I realized that there are always a few people in every congregation who are negative, who seek out power and want to be in control and rule over the congregation and the minister. I decided to let all the church politics go for the time being because Warren and I were leaving on holidays for the month of August to visit my sister in California It was really hot in California that summer so Warren and his cousins spent a lot of time in the small above ground pool. I was just happy to be on holidays and it was wonderful to be with my sister again. When we got back, we went to Oakville to see Louise and Susie. We all went up to Barrie to spend a couple of days with our cousins Al and Jessie Stebbings. Their children, Diane and Heather, were there too and we all had a great time together. But a strange thing happened while we were visiting. We stayed over one night and, when we got up in the morning, we couldn't find Louise anywhere. The bed she slept in was empty and we had no idea what happened to her. We were getting really worried when the phone rang and it was Louise asking us to pick her up at the Holiday Inn and bring $25.00. When we walked into the lobby, there was Louise looking very sheepish and dressed only in her housecoat. She told us she got cold about three in the morning and didn't want to wake anyone so she called a taxi to take her to the Holiday Inn. Then she said she only had enough money for the taxi and had a hard time convincing the desk clerk to let her stay the night until she told him her family would pay for her room when they picked her up in the morning. Somehow she convinced him to give her a room. We were all shocked, and Jessie was very upset that Louise hadn't woken them instead of calling a taxi and leaving. Actually it was quite funny and we all had a good laugh.

All in all, it was a good summer and when it was time to go back to New Liskeard, I was feeling more relaxed and hopeful. The first thing I did was take Warren over to the high school and get him registered for Grade 10. He was excited about going to school and couldn't wait to start. He told me he would be coming home at noon and would make his own lunch. I got started again in my ministry but, this time in the office, things with Dorothy felt different. She was not quite as friendly as she had been and I didn't understand why. Whenever I asked her for some specific information, she said she didn't have it or couldn't find it and I had no choice but to search through my office for records and files. I even went to the safe to look things up but only found the old records there. It seemed that this attitude applied to everything until, finally, the next time I asked Dorothy for something, she told me I would have to talk to Marg about it. So, even though Judi was the Chair of the Council and the Executive, it was Marg Taylor I needed to talk to about everything. When two members of the church, Pat and Hope Birnie, arrived to see Dorothy, I asked Hope, who was the Chair of the Finance Committee, for some financial statements. She tried to stonewall me and finally said I would have to talk to Marg.

It was becoming increasingly difficult in the office. I soon realized that Dorothy answered to Marg, the ringleader, along with Hope Birnie and Judi Campbell, the Chair of the Council. This meant that I had limited access to important records like financial reports, minutes of the various meetings, annual reports and correspondence which would give me a better understanding of how the church worked and where it was financially. It became clear to me that Dorothy also reported everything I was doing to Marg. I didn't like that but I also recognized that Dorothy was in a difficult position because she and her husband Jim did not have much money. Dorothy's job afforded the only money that came into the household. So she did as Marg told her. I was beginning to feel very uncomfortable about my situation so I called Marg and went over to see her. Again she told me it was none of my concern. She told me that, at the next Executive meeting I would be informed about everything going on in the church. She also expected a report from me at that meeting.

One of the couples I visited was Madge and Maarten Hogerland. Madge was the Presbytery representative from St. Paul's so she knew the ministers and lay people in the Presbytery and introduced me to many of them. We started to meet for lunch a couple of times a month and enjoyed that time together. But because I didn't know her all that well, I couldn't talk about my concerns about the church with her. However, after a month of this intrigue at the office, I had had enough. I called Murray Binstead at Haileybury United Church and asked him to call some members of Presbytery together to meet with me. Murray set up a meeting a week later and I went to his church and met with him, and Reverend David Bould, the minister at Kirkland Lake, and Reverend Bill Jones from Colbalt United Church. I told them what a hard time I was having and was asking them for help. They suggested I continue to visit the families in the church in order for me to get a really good overview of the congregation and attend the Executive meetings to see how things were done. They told me they would look at it again in the new year and advised me to just give myself time. The Presbytery knew these people and they had experience with them so I took their advice. But it wasn't easy to keep my own counsel and I kept telling myself not to take things personally. I began to spend a lot less time in the office, except to check in, and I had Dorothy make appointments for me to visit families, something she had not been asked to do before, but she said she didn't mind doing that. Whenever I came into the office, if Hope, Judi or Marg was there talking to Dorothy, I was friendly, said hello and left.

I attended the three Executive meetings that were held in September, October and November and said very little at these meetings. But I did a lot of listening. I became aware of the dynamics between members of the Executive and observed the body language of the people there. I made very detailed reports to the Executive about my ministry in regards to the visiting I did and the Presbytery meetings I attended as well as the monthly Tri-Town Ministerial meetings. I worked very closely with Bill Glassford, the Chair of the Membership Committee, and attended their meetings. I knew that, as the minister, I had the right to attend any or all committee meetings except for the Administration and Personnel Committee because that was the committee that dealt with any issues a member had with another member of the congregation or with the minister. I also knew I couldn't bring any concerns I had with any member of the congregation to this committee since Marg was the Chair of the committee. I was also fully aware that nothing I said would be kept in confidence. So I only went to the committee to talk with them about my continuing education courses and salary and benefits for the new year. It was all business.

I found out that there was a jail in Haileybury. I made a few phone calls and went in to see the person in charge of the Haileybury Jail to ask if there would be a possibility for me to visit the men there once a week. I was told that I was more than welcome to come and visit and they explained the rules and regulations to me. They said that their facilities were limited but, if someone wanted to talk to me alone, there was a small room that would be available to me for the four hours I was there where the guards could bring a prisoner to me so we could talk in private. They also explained that I had to have a full police check and be finger printed and have my picture taken. I remember that the guard who was to take my picture jokingly asked me if I wanted an 'official' mug shot taken and I said, "Sure. Why not"? So he took a photo of me with the Polaroid camera, collar and all, holding a criminal number and gave it to me, something he really wasn't supposed to do. I visited inmates in the jail for the first two years I was at St. Paul's and felt I was doing a real service to the men there. There were hard cases in that jail. There were men who beat their wives or girlfriends and, sometimes, even their children. Some told me they found Jesus and I had interesting discussions with them. I am not saying they didn't find Jesus but I was skeptical and challenged them. There were also some very serious, angry-looking guys who didn't want to talk to me. I often talked with those guards who wanted to talk to me and most of them told me they had trouble maintaining relationships with their wives or girlfriends. Some were divorced and many admitted they had an alcohol problem. Being a guard wasn't a job for the faint of heart as they were called all kinds of names by the prisoners. But all the guards were very respectful to me and said the prisoners were quieter when I was there.

Sometimes when I went, there were new prisoners and I would ask them if they were from Kirkland Lake or Timmins because that is where most of them came from. At one point, I met two Indian guys who were in jail for petty theft charges. I got to know them and looked forward to seeing them when I was there. I had told them about some of my experiences at Roseau and they knew I understood about their culture and history. One time, they asked me if I would do them a favour. On my way home, they asked if I would stop at the lake and find a piece of wood by the shore. They would give me some tobacco to put on the wood and asked me to push it out on the water as I said a prayer for them. That seemed alright to me and I took the tobacco from them and, on my way home, I did what they asked me to do and said a prayer for them. The next week when I went into the jail and saw the two Indian men, they told me I hadn't done what they had asked. When I assured them that I had, they asked me to tell them exactly what I had done and I did. Then they said it didn't work and I asked them, 'What didn't work?' They told me that, later that same night, they were able to disconnect the dryer and get out of jail by squeezing through the air vent. They started running up the hill but were seen and caught. I must say we all had a good laugh. "So, you made me part of your escape plan?" I told them and we laughed even harder. Even in jail some people didn't lose their sense of humour. It wasn't easy going to the jail every week and talking to the prisoners but my congregation was very appreciative of the ministry I did at the Haileybury Jail.

Meanwhile, Warren was doing very well in New Liskeard. He was loving school and had made a good friend in Ronald Glassford. Warren had a good tenor voice and loved to sing so Doriel invited him to be in the Senior Choir and he accepted. He enjoyed singing in the choir where he sat next to Don in the choir loft. He also met other young people in our church, like Sally Holdsworth and Bruce Haslam and Randy Lang. Sally was very keen about starting up a youth group so I was helping her with that by providing a space in the church for them.

Warren heard about the Army Cadets at school and told me he wanted to join the troop in town. I wasn't so sure about that but I knew his grandfather, Hugh Carson, had served in the army in the First World War in Europe, Warren's father had served in the Air Force in the Second World War in British Columbia and his cousin, Al Stebbings had served in the Army in the Second World War. Al had told Warren many stories about being on Juno Beach where he had been shot on D Day. He had also taken him to Camp Borden whenever we visited Al and Jessie in Barrie. So, in a way, I shouldn't have been surprised Warren was interested in joining the Army Cadets and I told him I was fine with him doing that. He had to have his uniform cleaned and pressed for the weekly inspection and his boots polished to perfection as well and I told Warren I would buy an iron for him. The meetings were two hours, one evening a week, where they did a lot of marching. Warren loved it. He thrived there and did very, very well. He was respected not only by his peers but also by the officers who ran this program.

I was about four months into the ministry and had been through a lot because I was frustrated time and time again. But I just couldn't let my anger and frustration determine my ministry. I couldn't control what these mean-spirited people were doing to me but I could control how I reacted. I was not going to let small-minded people control me. That took a lot out of me emotionally. I was not going to lower myself to their level because the congregation deserved better from me and I was doing the ministry I felt called to.

Almost by accident, I found that Jane Sullivan, whose family were members of our church, was in her 20s and was going through for ministry. She was studying at a theological college and was a candidate through St. Paul's United Church. When I heard she was coming home for the Thanksgiving weekend, I made arrangements for her to come to the church and talk with me. I was very happy to meet her and told her about the three summer students I had working with me at Roseau and that I was very pleased she was a candidate for ministry at St. Paul's. She told me how frustrated she was because no one from her church had kept up any contact with her. I was surprised and, yet, knowing what I had experienced from certain people in the church, I could see the problem. I liked her and could see she was very intelligent and keen about the ministry so I asked her if she would be willing to preach on Sunday. She didn't know what to say at first and finally said, "But you have Baptisms on Sunday and this is your first Thanksgiving service and there will be a lot of people at the service to hear you preach." This was a wonderful opportunity for Jane and for the congregation to get to know each other better. I told her I knew that but I would love it if she would preach because I thought it was so important for the congregation to realize they had a student minister at their church who had grown up in New Liskeard. I knew I was asking a lot from her to preach on Sunday only two days away but I saw great potential in her and felt she would rise to the task. That Sunday, Jane preached and talked about inclusive language and how important it is to be aware of the words we use. This was very new to the United Church, inclusive language, and controversial but she put it out there. She also talked about corporate greed, something that I knew would also make some people uncomfortable. After the service, a few people on the Executive, were upset with some of the things Jane said but I held my ground and supported her. I was sure she would make a wonderful minister and St. Paul's was very fortunate to have her as their candidate for ministry.

When we had been in California in August, I told my sister that I wanted to do something different with my hair but I didn't want to cut it. My sister suggested that I get a couple of wigs so I bought a brown one and a blonde one just to change things up once in a while. One Sunday, I decided to try out my new blond wig and, after the service a seven year old girl from our Sunday School came over to me and asked me where our minister was. I said I was the minister and she said "No, where is *our* minister. Our minister has brown hair." Her father was standing next to her trying not to laugh. I had to explain to her that I had brown hair, but had decided to wear a blonde wig that day. I don't think I convinced her and she was glad to see *her* minister with the brown hair back the next Sunday.

In many ways, I was very happy in New Liskeard. I met so many wonderful people in this congregation and I was not going to let them down. I had to believe there was a reason for what was happening and that, in the end, whatever would come, would work out to the benefit of the congregation. I focused on Warren and the ministry and I put all my time and energy into visiting and getting to know the people I felt called to serve. Warren was growing up before my eyes and making his own choices and decisions and I was so proud of him. I loved living in New Liskeard and the lake that was only two minutes from my home. If we walked down the hill at the back of our house there was the Wabi River. It felt right to be here and of that I had no doubt. I had also started to make good friends like Sharon, Madge and Martin, Elaine and Bill, and, Ellen and Bruce. People were starting to know me and trust me and were opening up about their concerns in the church with the lay leadership they were also subjected to so I was beginning to understand the issues and concerns they had. I was able to open up to Doriel, whom I trusted implicitly and I shared my frustrations and concerns with her. She did not betray my trust and became the one person I could talk to about anything. I had a lot of support and control in the ministry I did, apart from the business aspects of the church and the congregation could not have been more supportive, which I appreciated. But I knew that, at some point, there would have to be some resolution in regards to the three people who were running the church.

By December, I had made about 1,100 visits and it was all in my report to the Executive in January. Most visits took place in people's homes, but some were visits on the street, people talking with me on the phone, visiting in the seniors' residence and my visits in the Haileybury Jail. Many visits were also in the hospital in town where I went once or twice a week. I always wore my collar when I went and, once, just as I was finishing my last visit and leaving after visiting with a member of my congregation, a woman in the bed opposite indicated she wanted to talk to me. I went over to her and she told me she wasn't a member of my congregation, that she was Catholic, but asked me if I would visit with her and I did. Before I left, I asked her if she would like me to say a prayer and she said she would so I prayed with her and blessed her. She was so happy I was there. I was always sensitive to the fact that people from many denominations were in the hospital at any given time and that my role was simply to visit people from my congregation but, if anyone asked me to talk with them as this woman did, I would never turn anyone down.

Then, before we knew it, Christmas was almost here. I took Warren out of school near the end of November for two days and we went to Sudbury to do our Christmas shopping in the bigger stores. It was a lot of fun and very relaxing and we had a great time together. Then I sent over 100 Christmas cards to my friends and family including one to Reverend Don Gillies, the Personnel Officer for Toronto Conference. He was the first to send me a Christmas card that year and on December 4, 1985 he said:

> *"Thanks for the greeting. It is good to hear that things are looking good for you. Certainly, some of the 'colour' went out of Toronto Conference when you left. All the best to you and Warren at this Christmas time."*

It was wonderful to hear from Don and I had so appreciated his counsel and support when I had been in Toronto Conference. Soon after, Warren and I decorated our Christmas tree. Everything looked lovely in our home when Louise and Susie came on the train for Christmas. They were so happy to see our new home and loved the Christmas Eve service I conducted. Louise and Susie felt warmly welcomed by the many wonderful people in the church and Doriel and I played two organ piano duets together, which everyone really appreciated. At home we played bridge and sang Christmas carols and had the most wonderful Christmas together. Like Warren, Louise and Susie were getting older. Louise was now 78 and Susie was 77 and, happily, they were both doing very well. Louise had high blood pressure, but Dr. Soanes monitered her and saw her once a month. I had no cause to worry about Louise because Susie would tell me if anything was wrong. We welcomed in the

New Year together and then Louise and Susie went back home and Warren settled back into Grade 10. He was doing fairly well but I sat him down before he went back to school and told him that he could do better than the 70 percent average he was getting. He told me he knew he could, but he wanted to spend time with his friends and at Cadets where he had made a new friend in Greg Moore. His friends were important to him, he said, and he didn't want to spend hours every night studying to get higher marks. I understood where he was coming from and I told him that as long as he kept a 70-75 per cent average, I was fine with that. It had been so nice to hear from so many people I cared about at Christmas. I had also received a Christmas card and note from the Rt. Reverend Wilbur Howard dated January 21, 1986. He had been a wonderful support to me at Westminster College back in July 1976 at London, Ontario before I went to Roseau and we wrote every Christmas:

> "How well I remember your visit to Ottawa. Margaret Kerr still speaks of it and it remains a highlight for her. I think that you will leave an indelible imprint wherever you go. You will find those things which need to be done and rouse up the people to be actively concerned. You say that you arrived in New Liskeard in July 1985. I would expect to hear explosions from the northland any time now. Over the years I have been in your part of the country many times for a great variety of things…. I have been up to Camp Lorrain a few times starting back in the days when Dr. Beacroft was the great cabin builder. Cobalt, Haileybury and New Liskeard used to gang up on visitors to see that everybody got equal time. I think that the last time I was in New Liskeard was for a Sunday School Convention when the Ontario Religious Education Council used to send a team of leaders through the north on a Christian Education tour. This was long before your time because you likely do not remember the great fire or the time Champlain came through. Hope you are continuing to find the church challenging and exciting and creatively demanding."

It was great to hear from Wilbur and I appreciated his comments and his humour as well as some of the interesting history. Those first seven months, from July to February, were very busy with visiting some of the 250 families in our congregation, going to the jail, visiting in the hospital, the nursing home, the seniors' residence, going to Presbytery meetings, preparing a service and sermon every Sunday and attending Executive meetings. But the tension was always there. I called Murray again in February for help but the Presbytery was not responding to my concerns. The atmosphere in the church office left a great deal to be desired. It was just so hard because Dorothy was the church secretary and my secretary and I couldn't talk to her or discuss anything with her and she wouldn't give me any information. If Marg was there, she would just glare at me or walk away whenever she saw me coming. It was just painfully unpleasant and I hated that feeling. Doriel was the one person I talked to about this and I told her I just had to do something because I felt almost no support from the leadership in the church even though they were there to work with the minister. It was hard.

One bitter cold winter day in February, I talked with Warren about how unhappy I was due to the lack of respect I felt from some of the leaders which had not changed since I had come to New Liskeard. I told him that I had talked with Presbytery about how I felt and they had done nothing to help me and I told him I couldn't work like this anymore. I had to take a stand, which might mean we would have to leave New Liskeard. I knew how happy he was there and that made my decision to do something much more difficult. Warren really surprised me and said it was alright because he knew how hard this was on me. He didn't want to leave but, if we had to, it was alright. I told him that I hoped we didn't have to leave but I could no longer continue to do the ministry I was doing in an atmosphere of such distrust and disrespect. I told Warren I had gone through the Manual of the United Church of Canada and found some sections where, as the minister, I could charge these three people – Marg, Judi and Hope - with disturbing the peace of the Charge and I thought this was the right thing to do. He gave me his support and encouraged me to do it. My son always gave me good advice when I needed it. He was also a good listener and mature well beyond his years. I trusted his judgement. I didn't want to leave New Liskeard. Warren was so happy there and so was I, but I had to trust that there would be a way through this. In truth, I was angrier than I was afraid because these three people in my congregation were holding our church hostage and I had to do what I felt would break this open without reservations. For me, it was a matter of justice and I was willing to suffer the consequences of my actions. Not to act at that time would have meant that I was as much a part of the problem as they were. So I called a meeting of the Executive Council of St. Paul's United Church and asked the Presbytery to have the members of their Pastoral Oversight Committee there.

This meeting was held on Tuesday, March 6, 1986 at 1:00 p.m. in the Board Room at St. Paul's. Present were: the Chair of the Council, Judi Campbell; the Recording Steward, Dorothy McLaren; the Chair of the Administration and Personnel Committee Marg Taylor; the Chair of the Finance Committee Hope Birnie along with Bill Glassford and all the other heads of the committees of the Council. Reverend Murray Binstead, Reverend Bill Jones, Reverend Tim Hayward and Reverend David Bould were there from Presbytery as was Madge Hogerland who was St. Paul's Presbytery representative. I absolutely knew that what I was about to do was the right thing and I wasn't worried or afraid. I believed that with all my heart and soul. As soon as we were gathered, I read to them my Statement of Grievances and I quote from that document:

> *"At the outset I wish to state that the only person I have discussed this statement with is my son Warren. I have found myself in a very difficult and painful situation these last four months. I have tried to make the best of the situation and remain effective in ministry…..*
> *St. Paul's has some of the most caring and loving people in its congregation that I have ever met… … I do not wish to hurt anyone… But at the risk of being misunderstood I feel I must state my grievances. Regarding the President of the Board, Judi Campbell; the Past President of the Board and Chairperson of the Administration and Personnel Committee Marg Taylor; the Past Chairperson of Administration and Personnel Committee and now Chairperson of the Finance committee Hope Birnie; and the Recording Steward of the Charge Dorothy McLaren – there has been minimal to no consultation and cooperation with the minister on church matters. The minister has been told to leave them to run the church…. . People should be treated fairly in the Christian Church and there must be trust and respect among members and the minister with confidentiality maintained at all times. At present, this church at its level of government is a tight closed shop run autocratically by the few. I am tired of being treated like a second class citizen in this church and treated like the hired help. I am tired of decisions being made behind my back. I am tired of a conspiracy of silence. I am tired of being told to leave meetings. I am tired of being told what I can or can't do by the few who decide what rules to play by… I have had enough. I do not see this situation getting better. Over these past seven months it has gotten worse. There is little if any cooperation from the first three people mentioned above toward the minister and there is certainly no trust and very little respect for the position of minister at*

St. Paul's Church. This whole situation causes me great stress and anxiety. From my point of view ministry is stressful enough without stress being caused by those people named above who should know better and who should be giving the minister of St. Paul's United Church 100% support and cooperation.

I understand that when the Unified Board was originally discussed part of the reason for the change was that more people could be involved. Yet at the Executive level I see more than one person holding two Executive positions. And people whose two year term is up have themselves nominated to chair another committee without either the committee concerned being consulted, and without the nominating committee's advice being sought. I ask the four people named to let go and to not accept an Executive position in St. Paul's United Church for a period of two years, so that the peace of this Charge can be restored and maintained. I recommend that Judi Campbell resign, or be asked to resign by the Council of St. Paul's U.C. from her position as President of the Board. I recommend that Marg Taylor resign or be asked to resign by the Council of St. Paul's U.C. from her position on the Executive Council and as a member of the Administration and Personnel Committee. I recommend that Hope Birnie resign or be asked to resign by the Council of St. Paul's U.C. from her position on the Executive Council and as a member of the Finance Committee. I recommend that Dorothy McLaren resign or be asked to resign her position as Recording Steward of this Charge… … … … In the position of Secretary of the church which is a paid position, the Secretary must be loyal to the minister. It is essential to the wel being of any Christian church that confidentiality be maintained in the church office.

Today I make a formal request to Temiskaming Presbytery, through its Pastoral Oversight Committee, to attend and chair our next Official Council meeting to be held at St. Paul's U.C. on March 17, 18 or 21 at 7:30 p.m… … I call this meeting so that these grievances I present here today may be openly discussed. If these matters are not able to be resolved either by the resignations of the people named above or by the Council's recommendations or by both, I am prepared to lay formal charges against Judi Campbell, Marg Taylor and Hope Birnie under section 74 of the Manual of the United Church of Canada and request that an Informal Hearing be set up under section 76 of the Manual of the United Church of Canada. Since we do not have a Session and work instead under a Unified Board System, the court in this case would be the Council of St. Paul's United Church.

In conclusion, let me say, that if the minister of this church was treating the congregation in the way in which ministers here have been treated by "the few", the minister would be asked or told to resign. At the very least the Presbytery would be called in to discipline that minister. It is out of concern for our congregation as a whole that I respectively submit my grievances. Reverend Marion Dorinda Anne Vollmer

When I finished reading these Grievances and passed out copies to everyone, I was met with total silence. Then everyone began to express how upset they were with me. But I held my ground. I had gone through enough without any help and now it was Presbytery's turn to help this Pastoral Charge and this minister. Presbytery asked me to leave the meeting and told me they would have to discuss my grievances with those gathered. As I left the meeting, I felt such a sense of relief, as if a weight had been lifted from my shoulders. It was now up to Temiskaming Presbytery to deal with this matter and I would respect whatever decision the Presbytery made in consultation with my congregation and, of course, Manitou Conference. When Warren got home from school I told him what had happened and that now it was out of my hands. I had to trust that the Presbytery would do what needed to be done to bring some resolution to this conflicted situation. I also told my son how relieved I felt. He just gave me a big hug and, that night, we went to Koe's Chinese Restaurant for dinner.

The next day, Reverend Cliff Plant, the Personnel Officer, called me from the Conference office. He had heard from Presbytery about my grievances and wanted to come and talk with me. I invited him to come to my home and we had a good talk. He said that he had read my grievances and he knew it took a lot of courage to do what I had done. He told me there had been 'clergy abuse' in this Pastoral Charge for 35 years. I had never heard that term used before but it was a good way to describe what I had been going through. Cliff had good advice for me. He told me to keep my head down and not talk to anyone about these concerns. He also said that, if I heard anything that people were saying that I knew wasn't true, I needed to look into it and then take the correct information to someone in the church I trusted implicitly who could get the word out to counteract any lies that were being spread to scare the congregation. Otherwise, I should keep a low profile. That turned out to be very good advice. The Presbytery acted and chaired St. Paul's Council meeting in March and, in consultation with Manitou Conference, asked two Conflict Consultants – Reverend Louise Cummings and Reverend Don Lockett - to come to St. Paul's and meet with me and any members of the congregation who would like to talk to them, as well as members of the Council, and in particular, those members of the Executive I had named. They were coming to hear everyone's concerns and then would follow up with a written report of their recommendations for the congregation. There would then be a congregational meeting for the congregation to decide whether to accept this report, change parts of it or not accept it. There was certainly anxiety on the part of many people in the congregation, and myself as well, and we asked that this matter not take a long time. The consultants understood that and did the best they could. They would have their report ready to present to the congregation on May 3, 1986 and Presbytery would be there to chair that meeting. I was very relieved and happy that there were conflict consultants coming to listen to everyone.

While the conflict consultants were at St. Paul's, I heard only one rumor and that was about finances. The word was being spread around the church that, if these three people left St. Paul's, the church would lose $15,000.00 a year of donation income which it could not afford to lose. I had no idea what people gave to the church so, one night, I went to the church, opened the safe and took out all the donations receipts and records that were kept there. It was a daunting task but I found all the information I needed from charitable receipts filed over the last five years. The next evening, I went to see Don and Doriel Poupore. They had already heard we would lose a lot of money if Marg, Hope and Judi left the church. I asked Don and Doriel if they trusted me and they said absolutely, so, in confidence, I told them that I had gone through all the charitable receipts over the previous five years the night before. I told Don and Doriel that one of the people I had grievances against gave about $1,800.00 a year, a second person gave about $1,200.00 and a third person gave nothing at all. Don and Doriel were very surprised at what I was telling them. I also told them what Reverend Cliff Plant had advised me to do and that I was there talking with them because I knew people in the congregation trusted them and I trusted them to get the word out. They said they had no problem doing that. Normally, I would not have done what I did next, but this was not a normal situation. I told Don and Doriel that they were the largest donors in the church and they were genuinely shocked to hear that. They mentioned the name of a wealthy business man in town who, they were sure, he gave at least $5,000.00 a year and I said he didn't give half that amount. Here was confirmation for me that people who have money do not always give generously to the church, yet they want a major say in how things will be done and want to make sure that people are elected to the Council and committees to help them do just that. Don and Doriel got the word out and the talk stopped. They had real heart and faith and lived it.

In the midst of all the concerns in the church, this was a happy time for Warren as we celebrated his 16th birthday on April 1st. He had a great party at the house with Ronald, Greg, Tammy, Bruce, Sally, Randy and a couple of other friends from school. I couldn't believe my son was 16. He was growing up and mature beyond his years, but, physically, he looked much younger and his voice was just starting to change.

The Conflict Consultant's Report came out May 3rd and everyone got copies of it to read and think about before the congregational meeting. I quote from parts of that report:

> Observations on the situation at St. Paul's: *Over the last nine months, an atmosphere of increasing tension has arisen between the minister of St. Paul's United Church and some members of its Executive Council. ......On Monday, April 21st, we (the consultants) interviewed 32 people from St. Paul's, representing a variety of perspectives and positions within the congregation, including most of those directly involved. The following are our observations.*
>
> *We noted from all accounts that the Congregation is experiencing a time of vitality and growth. Attendance at Sunday worship is up, and people seemed willing to be involved in the life and work of the church. We celebrate with you this time of renewal. We recognize however, that any kind of change, even desired change, can be stressful. It is evident that the conflict has already brought a great deal of pain to a number of the individuals who make up the community of faith at St. Paul's......preventing them from working together. It was our sense that a key element in the conflict was what we can only call an "attitude" regarding the role of the minister in relation to the running of the Church. The most*

poignant phrase we heard used in this regard was that the minister was a "hired hand". In other words, to quote another remark voiced in our presence, "the minister should do the work of ministry, and let us run the Church."

Other indications of this same attitude i) the minister was excluded from the ad hoc committee established to set the budget; ii) the Constitution of St. Paul's precludes the possibility of the minister being President of the Official Board or Chairperson of the Executive Council (contrary to the Manual, Section 251a); iii) a seeming inability to ensure that the minister's paycheque arrive on time… …; iv) the Constitution's description of the responsibilities of the Administration and Personnel Committee seem to emphasize salaries and evaluation more than support and liason (compare with Manual, section 251).

We sensed that this "attitude" was a factor, not just in the present conflict, but also in several of the previous pastoral relationships. This was the opinion of a number of the people interviewed. We believe that such an attitude not only fails to reflect the intention of the Manual of the United Church of Canada, but also works against the establishment of a cooperative and fruitful pastoral relationship. It was the consensus of most of the people interviewed that the present minister is a strong-willed individual. Clearly, this is regarded by many people as one of her assets, and we would concur with this judgment. And yet, within the context of pastoral ministry, this is a gift that needs special care in its expression. We sensed that at times, perhaps due to an increasing level of frustration, such care was not exercised… from reactions to the minister's Statement of Grievances.

Some people said that over the last few years the Congregation had left responsibility for its governance in the hands of a "faithful few"… .We suspect however that one of the results of this history has been to effectively undermine several aspects of the original intention of the Constitution. That is, from our reading of the Constitution, it was the hope and plan of the Church that turnover of membership on its governing bodies would ensure both "continuity" and "the gradual infusion of fresh talent" (Articles 10a) & b). Furthermore, the desire was to have as many laypeople as possible involved in the life and work of St. Paul's. In addition, the Official Board was to be the main governing body of the Church, with the Executive Council accountable to the Board.

It seems now that in practice the members of the Official Board have felt cut off from any real participation in the decision making process.This seems inevitable with the Board meeting only once a year. Decision making has been the responsibility of the Executive Council which meets monthly. There seems to be some confusion now as to the roles and inter-relationships of the Official Board and the Executive Council, due to the Constitution itself… . The Constitution as it stands has not guaranteed the regular renewal of membership on the Executive Council that was originally hoped for.

Recommendations *a) That the Official Board strike an ad hoc committee to review the Constitution and prepare it for submission to the Congregation, and subsequently to Temiskaming Presbytery b) Given that the minister's Statement of Grievances no longer serves any fruitful purpose in the situation at St Paul's, we recommend that she withdraw it. c) It appears that the working relationship has broken down between the minister, and the President of the Official Board and the Chairperson of the Administration and Personnel Committee. And yet the minister appears to have the support of a substantial percentage of the congregation. We therefore recommend, for the "peace and welfare" of the larger St. Paul's community, that Judi Campbell and Marg Taylor withdraw from holding church office for a period of one year d) That the Administration and Personnel Committee work with the minister and the paid Secretary to establish office procedures satisfactory to all concerned, with special attention to the question of confidentiality e) That the Finance Committee ensure that the minister's salary is paid according to the procedures agreed to by itself and the minister. f) That the minister and the Worship Committee make clear to the Trustees and to the Property Committee their intention to abide by the Insurance regulations regarding the use of candles within the Church.*

I was very happy with this report and all the conflict consultant's recommendations as I read through it. A meeting of the congregation was called and Presbtyery chaired it. Reverend Cliff Plant, the Personnel Officer, came to sit with me and support me at this meeting. I remember us going downstairs to the basement of the church where the meeting was being held and I had been sure that only a few tables would be set up. But there were only chairs and the room was filled with people. Cliff and I had to find seats about halfway toward the back of the room. Cliff said he counted over 250 people there. I was stunned to say the least. I didn't talk to anyone nor did anyone talk with me before the meeting and I had no idea what would happen so I was a little anxious and nervous. I had no idea what the outcome would be, but I didn't feel any resistance or negativity from anyone as I walked in. I also felt a deep sense of sadness that we needed to be here at all. The meeting wasn't long, maybe an hour, but it seemed longer. There was lots of discussion as the meeting was called to order. At the beginning of the meeting, the Chair asked Dorothy McLaren, the Recording Steward, if there was any correspondence and she said there was none. As I looked around the room at the people gathered, I saw many people I had never seen, but I had to assume this was their church and they came to have their say, which they did. I did not see Marg Taylor, Hope Birnie or Judi Campbell at this meeting and that surprised me. In the end, by a show of hands, the vote was almost unanimous to accept all the recommendations with only two people voting against the motion. After the vote was taken, I felt relieved and vindicated because the members of the congregation had come out in full force to have their say and it was obvious they wanted the ministry to continue and change the way things were run in the church.

As the meeting was about to end Dorothy said she had some correspondence and I could see that the Chair was very annoyed. He told Dorothy that he had asked her if there was any correspondence at the beginning of the meeting and she had said no. Dorothy told him that the people who wrote these three letters asked her not to present them until the end of the meeting. The Chair didn't have any choice at that point and the three letters from Judy Campbell, Hope and Pat Birnie and Marg Taylor were read. All of them said they were resigning from their positions on the Council and the Executive and leaving the church. They would be attending the Presbyterian Church across the road. Obviously, they thought the congregation would not support them and they were right. They didn't even have the decency to attend this meeting and that spoke louder than words to me and showed little to no respect for the congregation they had been elected to serve. Now it was over and I was thankful for that. So many people came over to me after the meeting and thanked me for what I had done because they felt they had their church back and we could all move on. When I got home, Warren was waiting anxiously and I told him everything was alright. He was so happy that we were staying, and so was I. We had a good talk about everything that had happened and I felt that I had finally arrived. We didn't have to move and that was great.

An ad hoc committee was set up by the Council to revisit our constitution, based on the concerns and recommendations of the Conflict Consultants Report, and positive changes were made to honour the original intent of St. Paul's Constitution. I think it was Don Haslam that stepped up and was elected Chair of the Council. He was highly respected by the congregation. Ivan, a businessman in town and a member of our church, was encouraged by the Council to chair the Administration and Personnel Committee and I was so pleased he agreed to do that. He was a good man and understood how the United Church worked. One of the first things he did was call his committee together to meet with both Dorothy and myself. Ivan had already talked with me privately as to whether Dorothy should continue to work as the paid Secretary for the church. I told Ivan that I felt she had been used by the three people I had had an issue with. I also told him I knew Dorothy needed the job and was worried about being let go. I told him I could work with her and he said we would talk more about this when the committee met. At the meeting, Ivan was very direct with Dorothy and very clear that her loyalty must be to the minister and the congregation and that confidentiality was crucial. I really felt badly for Dorothy at this meeting because Ivan wasted no words on her. I told her in the meeting that I was more than willing to work with her and that I didn't feel she had initiated anything but had just followed orders. So, when all was said and done, Dorothy stayed on as the church secretary and we started working together.

Looking back over that last year and all that had happened, I thought back to June 1985 when I had done some real soul searching after I read Dr. Zaboraska's letter for the first time, and then I had read again the assessment report. At that time, I had faced some things about myself that I had not wanted to look at and realized I could do better in handling my emotions when things didn't go my way and when people pushed me to get their own way. I felt I had handled this very difficult situation at St. Paul's very well. I contained my anger and frustration and did not take personally what was happening to me in the church. I kept my own counsel most of the time. Most importantly, throughout all of this conflict, I was able to do a meaningful ministry. In the end, I stood up for what I believed was the right thing to do. I felt I had matured and grown that past year and was more capable of dealing with conflict with a lot less anger and because of that, the outcome had been very positive for everyone in the congregation.

June was a good month. I attended the regular meeting of Temiskaming Presbytery and we had our nominations. I had been nominated for the position of Secretary of the Presbytery and, as there was no one else wanting that position I was elected. I would be working with Reverend Richard Lougheed who had been elected as Chair of the Presbytery. He served in the only Pastoral Charge just inside Quebec. I looked forward to working with him. My neighbor and good friend Nora went with me to the Cadet's year end event in June where the Cadets marched and demonstrated to all their families and friends the different activities they had been involved in. It was very impressive. There were army officers who came from Toronto or Ottawa every year to do an inspection and this particular Army Cadet Branch had a very good reputation. Warren had done so well in Cadets the first year that the officers had encouraged him to consider a career in the army. Warren wanted to check out that possibility so his Cadet leader arranged an interview for Warren to meet with someone at the Royal Military College in Kingston in early July. I wasn't thrilled about this but I also know that Warren was only 16 and he had three more years of High School to complete. A lot could happen in that time. So, I supported him in this because this was something he wanted to consider. Before my first year at St. Paul's ended, I was asked to address the 1986 Graduation Class at the New Liskeard Secondary School that Warren attended. It was really an honour and I was very pleased to be invited to do this. This is an excerpt from my remarks of June 27th, 1986:

> *"You have come to a point in your life where you belong to the world. You have been raised in a family. I hope you feel loved. It makes all the difference. But never forget you belong in this world. You were created for a reason, a purpose. You will search all your life to understand the meaning of your own existence. It is your personal quest for truth and for understanding. Tonight you have reached a threshold, a new beginning. Your parents are proud and happy and sad all at the same time. It means changes for you and for them. New beginnings for you, new adjustments for your family. As you leave home in the near future you will be dearly missed. But wherever you go, your family, your teachers, your school, your friends are all part of your life, part of what makes you who you are. You come from a community you can take great pride in. What you become is now up to you. Reach for the stars. Celebrate your life wherever you go in this world. Be proud of your family, your school and your community which has nurtured you and helped you grow and develop these past 18 years. Your whole life is before you. Take your first steps into the world on your own with eagerness and great expectation. It is like learning to walk all over again. Life is full of wonderful surprises. Keep an open mind and an open heart that you might keep wondering and learning all your life about this beautiful world in which you have been blessed to live."*

It was a wonderful and positive way to end my first year at New Liskeard as I spoke to these graduates. Having gone through everything we had at St. Paul's, I really believed now that the best was yet to come.

CHAPTER SIX

Eighteen wonderful Months

At the end of June 1986 Warren and I picked up Jana and her son Scott at the Toronto Airport. We were very excited to see them. Scott was now 14 years old. We brought them back to our new home for their two week visit. We had a great time taking them to see the families in the church I felt really close to, like Don and Doriel Pourore, Bill and Elaine Glassford, Sharon Reynolds and her children and many others. I had told Jana about the conflict in the church many times over the past year but now that it was resolved, she could see how relaxed and happy I was. I had taken the month off so we could travel around, but we spent the first week in New Liskeard. Jana and Scott loved Lake Temiskaming and the way that it wound around the Tri-Town and the trips we took to the parks and the surrounding countryside. We went down to see Susie and Louise and used their apartment to come and go from. Jana was so happy to see them again and to introduce them to her son. They had met Stacy at my ordination in 1976 but not Scott. We showed Scott the house in Oakville where I had grown up and my sister had lived with us for two separate years. We also went to Kingston so that Warren could have his interview at Royal Military College. When Warren got back from his interview he had lots of brochures and information and said they encouraged him to consider applying to the College once he finished high school. After a nice picnic lunch and a lovely cruise, we headed back. We also went to Port Colborne so Jana could show Scott the house where she grew up. Everyone was happy to see Jana and me again and meet Scott and also Warren. We had a great time visiting the Busse's, the Sveda's, the Gilmour's, the Bandura's. Then we headed off to Niagara Falls to see Aunty Marion, my godmother. She was so happy to see us and meet Scott and Warren. Jana and I had spent wonderful times visiting with Aunty Marion and Uncle Frank when we were young and going to The Falls. From there we went to Welland to see Mary-Jane Ferrell (Bandura) who had been Jana's best friend when they lived across from each other in Port Colborne. Finally, we ended up at Olive and Peter Habjan's home in Wainfleet. Olive's mom was Tina Matthews, who had treated us to a day at Crystal Beach every summer. Jana was so happy to have Scott meet all these people who were so much a part of her life growing up. I also took Jana, Scott and Warren to the Sandbanks where Jana and I relived all the wonderful times we had at the cottage with Aunty May, (Susie) and Uncle Hugh. It was wonderful to revisit all the memories and it was particularly special with my sister. Back in Oakville, we had lots of time to talk and visit. Jana showed Scott Brantwood Public School where she had gone to Grade 4 and the Oakville Trafalgar High School for Grade 10 before she, Mom and Dad moved to California in 1964. All in all, it was really quite a trip down Memory Lane for both me and my sister. Warren and Scott got along really well and, of course, every chance they got when we were at the apartment, they were downstairs swimming in the pool and having fun together.

Our time together went by quickly and Jana and Scott were soon on their way back home. Warren and I stayed with Louise and Susie another week and then headed back home so that Warren could get ready to leave for cadet camp. Every year, the officers tried to get some of their cadets into a camp for a month of cadet training. Since there were limited openings, they really pushed hard for those cadets they felt would benefit most. Warren was fortunate to have been chosen to go to Camp Ipperwash near Windsor for three weeks in August and he was looking forward to it. I drove him to the camp and it took eight hours. When we got there, he was told which cabin was his. I went in with him. There were about 10 bunk beds and 20 Cadets and it would be crowded. Then the Warrant Officer came in and started giving orders to the cadets in a very loud voice. When he was finished he saw me and came over and said he was sorry for yelling. I told him Warren would fit right in because he was used to it at home. We laughed and I said goodbye to Warren. I could see he was in his element and was very happy.

I had a great month on my own and a really good time visiting families, going to the hospital, the jail and the nursing home, and preparing services. Now that the tension was gone at St. Paul's, I enjoyed going into the office in the mornings, seeing Dorothy and getting started for the day. I visited her husband Jim at their home and he was such a nice man and we got along great. I also had a very active social life. Nora Ladacoeur and I went out for walks a few times a week and Sharon Reynolds and I went out for dinner a couple of times a month. Madge Hogerland and I continued to go out for our usual lunches. Tuesday night was movie night and five or six of us went out for dinner and the show but if it was a horror movie only Benica and I went. I think we were the only two people in the whole congregation who appreciated horror movies. Ellen Lang and I became friends as well and I enjoyed her company. Benica and Eldon Barton had me over for dinner and Eldon and I got into some great conversations about faith, spirituality, the church and how it all fits together. I really loved visiting Don and Doriel Poupore and Tammy and having dinner with them. After dinner, Doriel and I always went for a long walk and I could talk with her about anything.

Soon it was time to pick Warren up from Camp Ipperwash and attend the closing ceremonies the cadets would be putting on before they went home. It was a Saturday and I had to preach the next day, so I knew it would be a very long day. I left about 5:30 a.m. to get there in time for 2:30 p.m. and it was very hot and humid. All in all, though, it was a spectacular event. Lincoln Alexander, the Lieutenant-Governor of Ontario, was there for the ceremonies. He had been the first black Member of Parliament in the House of Commons, the first black Federal Cabinet Minister serving as Federal Minister of Labour, the first black Chair of the Worker's Compensation Board, the first black (and the 24th), Lieutenant-Governor serving Ontario from 1985-1991 and the first person to serve five terms as Chancellor of the University of Guelph 1991-2007. He had been invited to review the cadets and as he did, he stopped on occasion and talked with some of them. Warren told me the Lieutenant-Governor stopped to talk to him and it was one of the highlights of his summer. Warren looked just great and I could see how much he had matured over that last year. I could also see how much the Cadets had helped him.

Warren had found something he just loved being part of and I was so proud of him. When he was packed and ready to go, we headed home, stopped for dinner on the way and got in about five in the morning. It was very hard for me to get up three hours later and do the service at St. Paul's but it had been worth the effort to see my son so happy.

When some of the women in the church said they wanted to get together and have fun once a month, I told them they were welcome to come to my place, but I had to choose carefully who I trusted enough to come to this monthly gathering. There were seven of us including Sharon Reynolds, Benica Barton and Ellen Lang. The idea was to have a pot luck dinner, lots of wine and play Pictionary. The first night we did this, everyone brought a bottle of wine and some even brought a double bottle. We had so much fun! We laughed until the tears came and it turned out that Benica and I could read each other's thoughts so we usually won at Pictionary. That first night, we put all the empty wine bottles in the garbage to be picked up the next day and the girls told me they hoped the neighbours next door didn't look in my garbage because they might think I was an alcoholic. We all laughed. The youth group was going well and Warren was an active member of it along with about 15 other young people. When they wanted to hold dances in the church once a month, they had to have the approval of the Council which they got. The dances were actually a great success and there was lots of visible adult supervision. The young people charged a small admission and sold pop and chips to raise money for their group.

I have to say that I had never felt so happy and so at home in a community. I loved going to church on Sunday mornings with Warren and when we got to St. Paul's, Doriel was there a half hour before the choir. Don was there too with Tammy, who always came running over to see Warren and the two of them would chat together a mile a minute. Doriel and I had learned a few Christmas pieces and we had performed them at the Christmas Eve service the December before and we continued to enjoy playing organ piano duets together.

Back in September, I had received an invitation from St. John's United Church in Oakville inviting me to participate in their service on November 16th when they would be celebrating the Anniversary of the Ordination of Women to the Ministry of the United Church of Canada. I was to be one of two women to preach that Sunday and I was very excited about that. Warren and I went down for that weekend and stayed with Louise and Susie who both came to the service. Warren decided to ask Brian if he could sing in the choir. Brian was so pleased to see him as were all the members of the choir. It was wonderful to be back at St. John's and I got to see many people I knew at the reception after the service. Christmas was creeping up on us again and, not long after we got back home, I took Warren out of school again for a couple of days during the week to do our Christmas shopping in Sudbury. When we got home, we put up our Christmas tree. Later that week, when I was out walking along the main street in New Liskeard, I looked in one of the store windows and saw a small dog looking back at me. It was a brown beagle mix and very cute. Without another thought, I went in and bought her. When I got home, I picked up the dog and went into the house with her in my arms. Then I called Warren. When he saw the dog he was so excited. He looked at me and said, "Is this our dog?", I said yes. We called her Frisky and went out and got a dog house for her which we put in the back yard and a dog bed for her to sleep in the kitchen. I took her to the vet and got her shots and later I got her spayed. She was a really good dog with a great personality.

Back in the summer, Maarten Hogerland had come over to talk to me. He knew about the art work I had done and asked me if I would do a piece of art for the Christmas Eve bulletin. He told me he did silk screening and would reproduce my art work for the bulletin cover. I took on the challenge but had no idea what I would do. In the end, I figured it out and called it *In Search Of*. I finished it on December 12 and was really pleased with the result. On the top right of the bulletin cover was a star and, inside the star, a cross and a picture below of a Viking ship. In front of the ship was a rocket and on top of the rocket was a space shuttle. I was proud of this.

Louise and Susie came for Christmas with all their parcels and suitcases. We picked them up at the train station in New Liskeard. They had heard about Frisky and were very happy to meet this new addition to our family. They were used to dogs because when I was growing up, we had always had a dog in our house. The Christmas Eve service was as special as it always was and Christmas Day was wonderful again with my family. After breakfast, we listened to the Queen's speech as we had done every year and then, finally, we sat down and opened our presents. We played bridge while we waited for the turkey to cook. After dinner, we had the Christmas cake that Susie had made but it tasted even better than usual and I asked her what she put in it. She told me the usual ingredients but said she had gotten mixed up about the brandy and had put the whole bottle in by mistake. Well, it was some Christmas cake. It was wonderful. I did notice that Louise didn't look as well as she had. She was still trying to get her degree, which she had been working on for the past few years, but I could see she was really struggling physically. Attending classes at Woodsworth College for seniors at the University of Toronto was taking a toll on her. She had only two courses to finish and she wanted so badly to do that. Susie kept busy swimming every day, reading and going to the senior's centre to play cards with the people who were there. She kept the apartment clean and did all the shopping. I had a lot to be grateful for that Christmas. Everything was going so well.

In January, I was invited to put on an Art Exhibition for the month of March 1987 at the Temiskaming Art Gallery in Haileybury. It was quite an honour to be asked and I said I would be pleased to do this. They needed 20 framed pieces of art, which I had, so I was ready. I was very nervous about this but it was a good experience and my art was warmly received by the people who came. Elizabeth Bishop, Curator of the Temiskaming Art Gallery was very pleased with the response. Then the Temiskaming Community Choir invited me to be their guest pianist for their spring concert in April. I had been helping them out when they needed a spare pianist to accompany them at their rehearsals and they had so much enthusiasm for everything they did and were so much fun to work with. I played four of my own compositions, which I thoroughly enjoyed doing. It wasn't long after this event that someone knocked on my door and asked me if I would consider teaching piano. I had actually been thinking about doing that and asked this person why she had approached me. She said it was because there weren't enough qualified music teachers in town for all the young people who wanted to learn to play the piano. The Tri-Town, and in particular New Liskeard, was very keen on the arts and, particularly music and many students competed in the Kiwanis Festival when it came to town once a year. The organizers rented St. Paul's United Church for the event and always enjoyed great success. I told the woman I would be willing to teach piano in the fall but that, with the ministry, I could only take a limited number of students. She was thrilled I said I would. All in all, I just loved being the minister at St. Paul's and I had such a wonderful congregation to serve. I felt right in my prime, which I suppose is the way you are supposed to feel in your 40s. I never felt better. The women's get togethers at my home was still going strong and we still laughed and enjoyed each other's other company and, of course, the wine as well.

The congregation in Grand Valley had to tear down the beautiful old Methodist church and build a new church. Warren and I got an invitation to return to Trinity United Church for the Cornerstone-Laying Ceremony of this new church on Sunday, May 31st at 2:30 p.m. They asked me to take part in the service along with their minister Reverend Martin Garniss and say a few words at this event. This is what I said:

> *"Thank you for inviting Warren and me to come back today. It is our privilege to be here to share with you in worship on this special occasion… Two years ago today when that tornado hit Grand Valley it was like a bad dream, a nightmare. Well that bad dream is over. The church is rebuilt and God's work does go on. I felt badly leaving but I knew when I left that I had done everything I could to help you begin again in the rebuilding of our church. That last month was the busiest I have ever been in my life, as was true for most people in this community. We didn't have time to sit back and let it all sink in. We had so much work to do to begin again that it was hard to know where to start.*
>
> *But start we did, as people we never heard of came to our community to help clean up and help rebuild the many homes that in a split second had been levelled to the ground. It was a time of testing for all of us and we were not found wanting. We continued to worship God with praise and thanksgiving. We wondered again about our place in this vast universe and why this had happened to us. When I left, I left knowing you were moving ahead. You had a new minister to welcome into your community as Martin and his family arrived. Some homes had already been rebuilt. Many more were just beginning. You have a lovely church and I am very impressed. The stained glass windows look so beautiful. As hard as it was to make some of the difficult decisions you had to make, you made them and you moved on. This church here today stands as a tribute to your faith in God and in Jesus Christ as your Lord and Saviour. Remember the church does not belong to one person or to the powerful few, this church is God's house and every one of God's people are welcome. May this new Trinity United Church, dedicated to the glory of Almighty God become a blessing to you and your children for generations to come. God bless you all. Amen.*

I was so glad to be there for the Congregation at Trinity United Church in that moment. It gave me closure and a sense of a ministry well done. There was a lovely reception afterwards where I got to meet everyone. It was, of course wonderful to see Jean again and my neighbours June and Wayne Maycock and their children. There were also people there from Monticello United Church and it was wonderful to see them.

In June, the cadets had their presentation and Norah came with me and enjoyed it as much as I did. That summer, Warren went to Camp Borden for three weeks and loved it. He was doing so well in the cadets. He learned how to shoot at the Camp that year, something I wasn't thrilled about, but he did so well on the shooting range that they invited him to go to England as their representative in their rifle competition coming up the next summer. It wasn't something Warren was interested in, but he felt it was an honour to be asked. During the time Warren was away at camp, I went to visit Jana for three weeks and had a wonderful time with my sister and with my niece Stacy who was 19 years old at that time. I took her out shopping for new clothes. I was so pleased to see her so happy as she tried them on. She wrote me a lovely thank you note on August 10th which I appreciated:

"Dear Auntie Dorinda, I wanted to thank you again for everything. You don't know how much I needed and appreciate the clothes…... It's been great having you here this summer. I love to see mom when she's this happy. It makes me feel good. Besides, she's not yelling. Love ya, Stacy."

When I got back from California, I spent a few days with Louise and Susie before heading home to start packing for our trip to Winnipeg. Then I drove to Camp Borden to attend the ceremonies the Cadets put on. From there Warren and I drove to Winnipeg, where we stayed four days and visited all our friends in Dominion City and Warren got to see David Ballast and Stuart Smoley and we saw Stan and Audrey Pearce and Jean Baskerville. We had a wonderful visit with Betty and Joyce and other friends at Roseau and it was good to be back. We also visited with Bill and Gertrude Whetter in Winnipeg and Warren got to visit with his friend Phillip. On our trip back I dropped Warren off to spend time with his Dad at his cottage near Parry Sound. Bill told me where to meet him and he took Warren across the lake to his cottage for a week. Warren was very excited about being with his dad and they had a great time together boating, canoeing, fishing and swimming. That did my heart good. While Warren was with his dad, I flew back to California. I was taking an eight-day course on Supervising Ministry Students at the Baptist Seminary. Jana picked me up at the San Francisco airport and drove me to Mill Valley near San Francisco. She would pick me up after the course and that would give us three days to visit with the family again before I had to return home.

I had to fight to get the funding to go to this course in California because there were lots of courses in Canada run by the United Church that they would have preferred I attend, but I had taken three of their courses on supervision and I wanted something different. Besides, the United Church listed this Baptist Seminary as a place to go to take a refresher course on supervision. The book the United Church of Canada used for those who wanted to supervise candidates for ministry was produced by this seminary so I was going to the source to get my training. I persisted and finally got the funding I needed. There were 15 ordained men in the group and five women "Ministers of Music" as they were called. I was the only woman there who had been ordained. The men who were taking this course with me talked with me about ministry and one of them told me I wasn't saved. This embarrassed many people there but I didn't take it personally because I know how some evangelical ministers think and like the Jehovah Witnesses there is no point whatever arguing with them. It only fires them up more. I was secure in who I was as a minister and being saved is not part of the way I think about who I am as a Christian. We had some good discussions in this course about how to be a good supervisor and bring out the best in the students we supervised. I didn't hold back because I was there to learn and to understand. One of the men talked to me over lunch about having been in the Southern Baptist Convention but, because he and his wife had divorced, he could no longer serve as a minister there and could only get a call from the Northern Baptist Convention. He told me that was very hard for him but that was the rule, you had to stay married if you wanted to be a minister in the Southern Baptist Convention. I felt badly for him. It just pointed out to me how progressive and far ahead of its time the United Church of Canada was in its openness.

All our leaders were good. One of them was a wonderful Baptist minister from Texas who taught us a course on counselling. He asked for someone in our group to talk about a real situation they had been struggling with back home and he would interview that person about their situation and listen to their concerns. No one in the room raised their hand but I had been dealing with a very difficult situation that summer. I really didn't want to offer myself up for this interview but I felt it might help me to talk this out with someone who had a lot of experience in ministry. I wasn't sure about everyone in our group and what they might think so I hesitated. Finally, I raised my hand and I could feel great relief in the room that someone had volunteered, but it was getting late and our leader said we would have to wait to do this exercise first thing in the morning.

Now I had to wait a whole night to tell my story and I fretted and worried a lot about it. I shared a room with a young woman whose title was "Minister of Music", and that night, she asked me all kinds of questions about what I was allowed do as a minister. She was shocked to hear that my duties were no different than what a male minister could do and that I could perform the Sacraments, preach every Sunday, chair meetings if I needed to, pray with people, attend all church meetings including Council and Congregational meetings, help with the yearly budget, as well as conduct funerals and weddings. The more I talked, the more she became confused. It was so strange for her to hear the things I was telling her because women could not be ordained at that time in the Baptist Church and, in her mind, that was the right way. She simply couldn't understand how I could be ordained.

In the morning, my stomach was in a knot at what I had gotten myself into and I wondered if I was doing the right thing. However, I did have a real concern and I knew it would be helpful to have some advice and I was open to that. Our leader had us sit face to face so I could concentrate on him and forget that anyone else was in the room. That was very helpful and I focused only on him as I told my story. I absolutely trusted him and that helped me to share. I told him that a

28-year-old woman had come to Temiskaming Presbytery for the summer to work as a student minister in a small Pastoral Charge in the country. I had been asked by my Prebytery to do some supervision with her but I informed them I wasn't going to be around most of the summer and the Presbytery said that was fine. I met with the student and told her I wasn't able to do the kind of supervision for her that I had done with student ministers in the past because I was going to be away much of the summer. I told her I could only meet with her a few times to touch base and talk with her about what was happening. She was agreeable to that.

One day, I got a call from a member of her congregation who was very active and highly regarded in her church, her community and in Presbytery. I knew this woman and had met her many times at church functions. She came to my home and talked to me about this student minister with whom she was working at a summer camp. I could see she was very upset. She told me that this woman student minister was harassing her and she didn't know what to do. The student had been following her around and, at first, she said that didn't seem anything to be concerned about, but then she started getting notes from this young woman and then more notes and valentine cards. The more this continued, the more this woman didn't know how to react or what to do. She said it was really hard in a small community to say anything because everybody knew everyone. I could see that she was frightened,and she asked me to keep her name out of whatever conversations I had with the student and the Presbytery. It became clear to me that this woman student was infatuated with this older woman. The woman told me that the student had never talked to her openly about her feelings but, every once in a while, she would give her a 'love note'. She told me she was happily married and had talked to her husband about this and shown him the notes and cards. I asked her if she had any real proof of what had been going on and she took out a large envelope with over 20 notes and cards in it and told me I could keep them. I could tell she was really relieved to be rid of them. As I read through them, it was obvious to me that this young woman had a kind of fatal attraction to this older woman which was disturbing. I then told our leader that I wasn't sure how to deal with this situation but I knew I had to do something.

He asked me what I was thinking of doing. I said I would talk with the student about this situation when I got back from holidays and I would also have a meeting with our Presbytery to bring this up and have her quietly removed. Our leader was very helpful because he was a very good listener and able to clarify with me from time to time what he heard me say. No one in the group knew what questions to ask because they realized what a difficult situation this was. He suggested they translate this situation into the scenario of a young male student doing ministry and being infatuated with an older man in his congregation and doing the same kind of things this young woman was doing. Of course that really made every male minister in our group feel uncomfortable. But I didn't mind because I was uncomfortable too and I was the person who had to go back home and deal with this situation. I really appreciated the confidence our leader had in me and found it helpful to be able to talk about this. I thanked him for listening to me and offering his support. All in all, it was a very good week and I learned a lot. I enjoyed meeting everyone and getting to know the people and the leaders there who led us through that week. I received my certificate and was again an accredited Supervisor for student ministers.

When I got home I did two things. I made an appointment for the student minister to come and talk with me and bring me up to date on what she had been doing. Then I called the Chair of the Students and Education Committee to make an appointment for me to meet with the committee and bring my report. I knew that the student would soon be leaving and I wanted this matter brought before them before she left. It was tricky meeting with the student because I couldn't come right out and tell her what I knew but I wanted to try to get a read on her. As we talked, she mentioned a Valentine's Day they had had at camp and then went on to tell me some other things. As I really looked at her and talked more with her, I began to see some things that just didn't fit together and I could clearly see why this older woman had been so disturbed. The student went off in tangents, she wasn't focused and, the more questions I asked, the more agitated she became even though my questions really didn't require difficult answers.

When I met with Reverend David Bould, Reverend Murray Binstead, Reverend Bill Jones and other members of the Students and Education Committee from the Presbytery at St. Paul's United Church, I told them at the outset that this matter had to be handled with absolute confidence and that I had given my word to the woman who had brought the complaint to me that her name would be kept out of it. I told them everything except the older woman's name and I asked them to trust me. I told them what was happening. Reverend David Bould said he couldn't just take me at my word and kept asking me how I could know this was true and suggested that this woman who had come to me could have misunderstood the intent. "Not a chance," I said. I was annoyed with him but I had to find a way to assure him that this young woman was a disaster waiting to happen again. Someone then asked me if I had the notes and cards this woman had given me and I said I did. They asked that we take a short break so I could go home and get them and I did. I came back with them and I passed them out to everyone. There was no name on them but the intent was very real and everyone was very quiet after they read all these notes and cards from the student. They asked me to destroy them, which I did. I went home and called the older woman. I told her the outcome and she was very relieved. I had my report prepared for this student minister and recommended as her supervisor that she not continue in ministry and gave several reasons why. The Presbytery backed me up and added a few more reasons of their own. The student did not agree. When our meeting was over I was relieved to have closure on this incident.

I came into September 1987 feeling very confident about the course I had just taken at the Baptist Seminary and about my ministry at St. Paul's. I also felt fairly good about the supervision work I had done in the summer. Aside from my work, my personal life was also flourishing. I put the word out that I was willing to teach piano and theory lessons and I had eight students. There was Aaron Fisher and his sister, Stacey McClaherty, Angie and Lynn Hutnick, Jo-Anne Jelly and Erin Bolger. There was also David Johnson who became friends with Warren and started staying after his lesson so they could visit. Every couple of months, I held a Master Class for an hour and a half in the evenings which included a discussion on the lives of four composers and learning about an important period in music history. The students also had an opportunity to play their pieces for each other. We had great fun together at these classes that reminded me of the Master Classes Miss Bates had held in the 1950s. That year, I prepared my students for the Toronto Conservatory exams and the Kiwanis Festival. I have to admit I loved teaching again but I did stop going to the Haileybury Jail in September. I felt I couldn't manage anything more with my students and the ministry.

One of the teachers from the New Liskeard Secondary School was on the Board of the Educational Foundation and they sponsored students to come to Canada and live in the community so they could go to the high school in town. I had filled out the paperwork back in May to have a foreign student come and live in our home. I found out at the end of August we would be getting a young man from Norway named Odin who was 18. He had the spare bedroom upstairs and shared the bathroom with Warren. His English wasn't that good, but we could understand each other and we liked him right away. Warren and Odin got along really well. Odin loved to play table tennis although he had a hard time accepting the fact that I was good at it and could beat him. We had many games where he tried to reverse that situation. Unfortunately, this arrangement with Odin didn't work out as well as I but hoped. But it wasn't all his fault. From the beginning, he told me wanted to be treated the same way as my son was and have the same rules, but he started staying out late and didn't always tell me who he was with or what he was doing or when he would be home so I worried. Under one of the rules of the program, Odin was not supposed to have much money, yet his father kept sending him money time and time again which Odin was spending on all kinds of things. It turned out that his dad either ran a pharmaceutical company in Norway or was one of the top executives in one and he was very well off. Odin's mom and dad were divorced. His dad was remarried, and from what Odin told me, I gathered his mom had some depression issues but he was close to her. Then Odin decided, on his own, to come to church. We knew from what Odin had told us that his father didn't like him going to church because his father did not believe in any religion so when his father called from Norway and found out that Odin was going to church he got really upset and wanted to know what kind of church it was.

The last eighteen months had been the happiest months of my life. I was feeling so good about everything and it was wonderful to see Warren so happy. We were again looking forward to Christmas with Odin and the aunts were planning their usual trip in December to be with us at Christmas. Everything was going so well and then everything changed.

CHAPTER SEVEN

A Terrible Loss

One day at the end of November, Susie called and told me that Louise had had a massive stroke and my world fell apart. She had found Louise unconscious on the floor in her bedroom and called the ambulance. Louise was at the Oakville hospital. I called Dr. Soanes and he told me that the next 72 hours would be critical. I told him I would be at the hospital as soon as I could. When Warren got home from school, I told him that Weisa had had a massive stroke and he was very upset and very anxious to get to the hospital. He ran upstairs to pack while I called Madge and Maarten Hogerland to arrange for Odin to stay with them while we were gone. I had to tell Odin what was happening. Since he had a key to our house, he could come back later to get what he needed. I felt badly having to leave him but I had no choice. He had already met Madge and Maarten and really liked them, so it was a good choice for him to stay there. Madge was waiting for him at her home when we dropped him off.

It seemed to take forever, almost six hours, to get to the hospital and we were both very anxious since we had no idea what to expect. Susie had stayed with Louise in the hospital all that day and was with her when we got to the hospital room. Louise certainly knew us but she couldn't communicate and that broke my heart. She tried to speak to us but she couldn't make the words come out and got very agitated. She was paralyzed on her left side and it was painfully difficult for her to be so helpless and unable to do anything for herself. It was hard to see her like that. Susie had been helping her communicate by having her write down what she wanted to say and Susie made a valiant effort to translate but the words she wrote didn't make sense. We were there for five days but her condition did not change although the nurses told us that, at night, they would find her sitting up humming away with her right hand moving like she was conducting an orchestra. But Louise never spoke again. I went to see Dr. Soanes and he told me that Louise's heart was strong but, at some point, she would shut down when she was ready. It could take a few weeks but it was only a matter of time. Susie encouraged us to go home and said she would be with Louise all day every day to help her communicate with the nurses. She thought we were better off at home and we could call her every evening to see how Louise was. Because Warren was very upset and agitated about Weisa and felt as helpless as I did, Susie and I both thought he would be better off at home and, even though I wanted to stay on, I had to think of Warren and he needed to be with me. It was heart wrenching to leave but I needed to give Warren as much of a normal life in the next few weeks as possible because we both knew we could get a phone call at any moment. Looking back, I don't think I was actually taking it all in at that time because it felt so surreal and I'm still not sure I made the right decision leaving.

Before I left, I had a quiet moment alone with Louise and I told her I had to take Warren home.

I held her hand and caressed her beautiful white hair that I loved so much. I thought about all the things I hadn't said to my aunt about loving her as much as I did and how much she meant to me all those years, even when I was confused and lost as a little girl and a teenager. I didn't know if I would ever see her again so I hugged her and kissed her and told her how much I loved her and just sat with her for a while until Warren and Susie came back from the cafeteria. Our car was packed and Susie went down with us to the parking lot to see us off. I could depend on Susie to look after Louise because, as much as they argued, and argue they did, Susie had never let her sister down. I also knew Susie was strong enough to take care of Louise and help her. We left and I went home to try to keep things as normal as possible as my world slowly fell apart, Odin came home but I couldn't focus on him. He tried to distract me by challenging me to table tennis and, this time, he had more of an advantage. He was a good young man but I didn't have the emotional strength to deal with him and I simply let him come and go as he pleased. Sandy and Don Haslam were in the church and had become good friends. Sandy and I had talked after I got back home and I told her it wouldn't be long before my aunt passed away. She told me that when that happened, her husband Don would drive Warren and me down to Oakville and stay with us as long as we needed him, even if it meant over Christmas. I couldn't believe what she was telling me. Don and Sandy were very kind people and Don was one of the best teachers at the high school. In preparation of what might happen, I had organized the Christmas Eve service and the Council arranged for a minister to lead in the service and do the communion if I couldn't be there. I felt some relief knowing that. At least everything was looked after at the church.

On December 19th I had just performed a funeral when Dr. Soanes phoned me at the church and told me that Louise had gone into a coma and it wouldn't be long. I talked to Susie and she said she would let me know when it was time. Susie called me the morning of December 21st and told us to come. I phoned Sandy and didn't even get the words out. She said Don's suitcase was packed and he will be there in half an hour. Odin went again to Madge and Maarten's home and Bill and Elaine said they would be at our home after we left to get our pets and would keep them for as long as necessary. Warren was very quiet so I knew he was having a hard time with this as well. It was so hard to even imagine Louise was dying and it took forever to get to the hospital. When we got there, we went to Louise's room but no one was there. I went to the nurse's station and asked where my aunt was and she told me how sorry she was but that Mrs. Thompson had passed away two hours earlier. My heart stopped for a moment and I could hardly think. I phoned Susie at the apartment and she said she had been to the funeral home and I was to go there and talk with them. When we got to the funeral home, Don came with Warren and me to the office and I told funeral director that we wanted Reverend Jim Campbell, the minister at St. John's United Church, to do the service. He called Jim and arranged for the funeral to take place on the morning of December 23rd at St. John's. Don was a quiet presence for us both which I so appreciated. Then we went to Susie's. Both Warren and I were still in shock. I was so glad to see Susie and relieved to see that she was at peace in herself about Louise passing away, a place I had yet to find. I introduced Susie to Don and he asked me if I was alright and I told him I was so he said he was going out for a while. I couldn't thank him enough for just being there. I had a lot of phone calls to make so I sat down and called my sister first. We just cried and cried and Warren came over and put his arm around me. Jana and I talked a long time and Jana told me she couldn't come to the funeral. Although I totally understood, I would have loved for her to be with us. I called Bill and told him about Louise and he said he would be at the funeral and was so sorry. It was so reassuring just hearing his voice. Then I called Pierre and told him Louise had passed away and when the funeral would be and hoped he could be there. He got upset and told me that I should be having a memorial service later and I hung up on him. What did it matter to Pierre when it was? But I felt badly and phoned my sister back and told her that I had just hung up on Pierre and would she please call him and explain and she did. After she talked with Pierre, she called me back and said that she told him that Louise was like a mother to me and all I wanted was to let him know when the funeral would be. She also told him that I hoped he would come and he said he would be there. Jana said that Pierre mentioned that I had hung up on him and Jana said she told Pierre I had done that to her too.

I felt so much better that Jana had called Pierre. When I got off the phone with Jana, Don came back and told me he had rented a room at a motel for however long we needed him. I hadn't even thought about where he would stay and I told him how much I appreciated him doing that. I made a few more phone calls to friends and then I couldn't talk anymore. Don and Susie were deep in conversation and Warren had the TV on low. I told them I was going into Louise's bedroom for a while and I went in and quietly closed the door. I felt so sad and broken. I thought about my aunt and how much she had loved me unconditionally. I missed her terribly and talked quietly to her. I truly believed she could hear me. After a while, I went over to the dresser where I saw some papers and on the top of them I saw what looked like a note she had written in her own handwriting. It was written to me and, as I read it, I couldn't begin to describe my feelings.

> *"Dorinda, no matter what happens I can never feel sad for Warren. He is the most wonderful gift that could ever happen to you. He has an unbelievable potential for good in this world. He is such a joy. I have always thought that you belonged to me and Warren belonged to me and that is all that matters. For me you are great happiness. I keep you locked up in my heart and nothing can touch you. I just feel sad for those who have not had this experience.*
>
> *Women were supposed to be mothers and you are. I would like Warren to have all that is good and beautiful in this world but I do not want him to grow up without a knowledge of evil. As Milton said in "Aeropagitica", "if you do not understand evil, how can you appreciate what is good?'" How can you appreciate and discriminate? Give Warren my love and my kisses xxxooo and remember I know you are both the best there is."*

There was no date on the note she left me, but she must have had a premonition and written it shortly before she had the massive stroke. It just took my breath away and I lay on her bed sobbing. When I got up and went out to the living room, Susie told me that Don had taken Warren out for dinner and they would be back later. It was coming up for 7:00 p.m., the time Susie always watched *Wheel of Fortune and Jeopardy*. She made tea for us and we drank our tea and ate cookies as we watched the two shows that she and Louise had watched together for years. It felt good to know that some things stayed the same. The next day Susie, Warren and I went down to talk to Jim about Louise and the service for her. It was nice to see him again, if only the circumstances had been different. I was so glad he was there to do the service for my aunt as he had done the service for Uncle Phil when he died 15 years earlier. The day of the funeral was very hard. Warren, Susie and I sat in the small room off the church waiting for the service to begin until, finally, we were taken to our seats by the Funeral Director. As I sat down, I felt a hand on my shoulder and, when I turned around, there was Pierre. I was so happy to see him and I turned right around and hugged him. Pierre's wife Janet was also there, along with three of their children. Jim did a wonderful service for my aunt but it was very hard for me. Warren put his arm around me but he didn't break down until much later. At Louise's service I had Jim read this poem Louise wrote:

I STAND UPON THE THRESHOLD

I stand upon the threshold of this door,
And ask for gifts that only gods may grant;
Pink apple blossoms with their fragrant store,
Blue skies with clouds, and winds that softly chant
Among the budding trees at break of day,
For tender grasses growing by the way.

I pray for fields of daisies white as snow,
The primrose growing where the shadows run,
The secrets that the gods alone may know,
The clouds of amethyst when day is done,
The light of evening ebbing in the west
When every beast and bird lies down to rest.

And time to worship quietness to think,
The will to fashion some immortal dream;
The silent wilderness where one may drink
Deep draughts of bliss; where truth may rise supreme,
The revelation love alone can give,
The golden dreams by which great spirits live.

For me this poem my aunt wrote, opened a door into her beautiful soul and I am sure the people who attended her funeral and knew her well understood this poem and the person she truly was.

At the reception after the funeral, I was so moved that there were over 20 people there from Grand Valley who had rented a bus to come. Jean Boggs was with them and so many people that I had visited and cared about during my ministry there. I spoke to Pierre at the reception and couldn't thank him enough for coming. I told him that he probably thought I was becoming more and more like my Aunt Louise because I could be stubborn like her and had my own mind set on certain things. He said he had to agree, and we laughed at that. Barbara Ryrie Davidson was there and my dear friend Edythe Harris. I was glad that we had time to visit. When it was all over, we went back to the apartment and I told Don I wanted to go back to New Liskeard the next day. He wanted to be sure that I was ready and I told him I really did want to go home and so did Warren. Susie understood and didn't have any trouble with that. I told her we would be down Boxing Day and stay until the New Year and she said she looked forward to that. Don called Sandy and told her we would be back in the early afternoon on the 24th and that I would be doing the Christmas Eve service. Then he went back to the motel and told us he would pick us up at 10:00 a.m. the next day.

Susie surprised me at how upbeat she was and I thought about that before we left. She had spent her life looking after other people. She looked after me as I was growing up and she looked after Grandma for a number of years when she was not well. She had looked after her husband because of his rheumatoid arthritis for most of the years of their marriage. Susie also had looked after Louise from time to time because of her heart condition and she worried about Louise going to university. Susie was always there to help and I knew how much of her life she had given up to be there for her family. Now she had no one to look after and, from that point of view, she was free. Free to be on her own and look after herself. Now she could do whatever she wanted and she loved that sense of freedom. She was very happy about that and I was happy for her and I told her that before we left. She was very pleased that I understood. When we returned home, Odin came back for Christmas as did our pets and they distracted us which was a good thing. Before I officiated at the Christmas Eve service, Warren told me not to say anything to the congregation about Weisa until I got through the service and that was good advice. The church was packed with well over 200 people and I felt I gave a very meaningful service. I was so happy to be with my congregation. The music was wonderful and the choir outdid themselves. At the end of the service, I thanked my congregation very much for their support and concern for myself and for Warren. I thanked them for their love and their prayers and for their cards. I also thanked Don and Sandy publicly for their wonderful support in our time of need. I told my congregation how much it meant to me to be able to be there to worship together. It wasn't easy for me but I got through it.

After church, we went home and in the morning there were Christmas stockings for Warren and Odin. We had a nice breakfast together and then opened presents. When everything was almost done, I took Warren and Odin into the little room next to my bedroom and there were a couple of large boxes for Warren to open. I had bought him a Commodore 60 computer and he was very excited. Warren and Odin spent the next few hours setting it up as I got the turkey dinner ready. It was hard to celebrate and be really happy without my aunts there and knowing that Louise was no longer with us. Odin knew we were leaving again after lunch the next day to be with Susie until the New Year. The next morning the teacher on the Board of the Exchange Program came to talk with me. He told me that Odin was upset and unhappy about what had happened and didn't want to stay with us anymore. He was having a hard time with all the change. I totally understood and was actually relieved. Warren also didn't seem to mind that Odin wanted to leave. I went to talk with Odin in his bedroom and said how sorry I was that it hadn't worked out but that I understood. He was packed and ready to go and I walked downstairs with him. Warren and I said goodbye to him as he left with his teacher.

After Odin left, we finished packing and drove to Oakville. Susie was very happy to see us, but I could also see that she was a little worried about something and I asked her about it. She told me she had understood that the money Louise got every month would now come to her and asked me if that was true. I told her that I didn't think and that, once Louise died, that money was gone because it had been in Louise's name only. I called Pierre and talked to him about this and told him how worried Susie was. He talked to her and said he would see that her rent was paid for as long as she lived. When she got off the phone, she was as happy and relieved as I was and it was so good of Pierre to do that for Susie. We had a very quiet time together. We all needed to rest and reflect, swim and enjoy our time together. Warren was doing very well in Grade 12. He was very involved in the cadets and he now had the position of Sergeant. He was also very active in the church that year as a member of the senior choir and the youth group. He was a youth Elder as well, which meant he had a district and visited eight families four times a year. He had many friends that he loved to be with and I knew they would keep him occupied and help him heal. As for me, it was so hard to think that Louise was really gone and I knew I still hadn't begun to process what had happened. But even though I felt a sadness deep inside me, I knew a better day would come. I loved being in the church and would not have wanted to be anywhere else. I had a wonderful supportive congregation and wonderful friends in the church and in the community. I tried to look forward but it was too soon to see very far ahead.

CHAPTER EIGHT

Leaving New Liskeard

Everything had been going so well until the day when my world came crashing down with the death of my aunt. From 1972-1981 I had lost my mother, Uncle Phil, Uncle Hugh and then Dad. None of their deaths had the impact on me that Louise's death did. I remember going to the post office to get my mail one day and I just broke down and started crying for no reason. This happened many times over the next few months. I didn't understand what was happening to me. I tried to carry on but I was having a harder time focusing and there was a sadness deep inside me that wouldn't go away. I was also worried about Warren. He told me he was fine, but he hadn't shown any emotion when Louise died and told me that it bothered him that he hadn't cried. It wasn't easy for either of us.

As soon as we got back home in January, I was very busy. Aside from the usual duties of my ministry, I was also Secretary of Temiskaming Presbytery. I was back teaching piano again and I had two Master Classes to prepare for. I also had three new students, Brenda Pinkerton, Darren Miller and Lori Merritt. I was excited to teach Lori, who was in her early 20s and was working full time and wanted to take her Grade 10 piano exam. She was willing to do two to three hours practicing every day. We set June 1989 for her to try her exam. In August I would be going to the General Council meeting at Victoria B.C. for 10 days. There would be about 500 Commissioners from across Canada made up equally of ordained ministers and lay people who represent their churches, Presbyteries and Conferences. It is the highest court of the United Church of Canada. The decisions this Council makes every two years become polity/policy for all the churches in the United Church of Canada. I had never been to a General Council Meeting. The General Council had requested a report on sexual orientation, but it had been in the making for several years. I didn't really think much about it and I was sure it would be business as usual. Then, in early March, this report came out. It was called, *Toward a Christian Understanding of Sexual Orientation, Lifestyles and Ministry"* and it recommended that:

> *"Homosexual orientation be defined as a healthy lifestyle that 'ought to be seen as natural and as a gift of God,' and that self-declared practicing homosexuals be considered eligible to participate in all aspects of the life and ministry of the Church, including the order of ministry. "*

The order of ministry included both Dicaconal Ministers – Christian Education and Pastoral Care, and Ordained Ministers - Word, Sacrament, and Pastoral Care, but everyone was focused on those who could be ordained. Since this was a huge and controversial issue, it was reported in all the major newspapers across Canada and every United Church Conference had to look at this issue at their Annual Meeting at the end of May or early June. Everyone was discussing it and most people got upset just talking about it. I knew this issue was going to be extremely divisive. I am sure that the other Protestant denominations thought the United Church of Canada had lost its mind because it would be years before they would deal with the issue of homosexuality and ordination in their churches. Now that it was on the Agenda of the General Council meeting in August, the pressure was certainly on those of us who were Commissioners. In our system of governance, any local church could send in a petition to their Conference stating clearly what their reasons were for saying yes or no to ordaining people who are homosexual. Thousands of petitions went out from churches across Canada to their Conferences who then had to deal with every one of these petitions. If the Conferences did not agree (non-concurrence), they did not have to send these petitions on to General Council. The conferences only had to send on the petitions they agreed with (concurrence). However, because this was such a huge issue, most Conferences sent on almost all the petitions they voted on, whether they agreed with them or not to the General Council office in Toronto.

We certainly had heated discussions at St. Paul's about this and it soon became the only issue that all our churches were talking about. Everyone was clear on my position. I had no problem with people who were homosexual being ordained. I knew that there were some people in my congregation who didn't have a problem with this but they kept very quiet about it. Dorothy, our church secretary was against it. She was part of a group who were preparing a petition against ordaining people who were homosexual. I explained to Dorothy, very clearly, how important it was that she follow the procedure required for preparing their petition or it would be rejected. I gave her group all the material that explained everything about how to put a petition together properly. Since she knew my position, she was surprised that I was making sure she had all the right information. I told her that we worked in a democracy and we didn't have to agree with each other. She had a right to her opinion even if I didn't agree with it. It was my responsibility, as the minister at St. Paul's, and as the Secretary of Temiskaming Presbytery, to help facilitate the petition process. Dorothy, her brother Ted Simmill and the rest of their group sent in their petition to Conference as did other churches in our Presbytery.

We were all upset having to deal with this issue regardless of what side was taken. I tried to be professional and inform people about the process. It was not my place to ask people what they thought about this issue but the congregation had a right to know my position, that I was in favor of being inclusive. How could we expect someone who was homosexual to sit in our congregation and be active in our church and yet not be allowed to be a candidate for ministry? That didn't make sense to me. I believed that any member of a United Church congregation who felt called to ministry had a right to be heard regardless of their sexual orientation, their race or gender, marital status or not being married and having a child. Doriel and I had discussed the issue and she had an interesting perspective. She was in favour, not only of people who were homosexual being ordained, but of giving them the same rights as heterosexual couples by allowing them to marry. Doriel went beyond what General Council was asking in dealing with this issue.

People were very riled up at St, Paul's. There were even those who said they would leave the church if the Commissioners at General Council voted in favour of ordaining people who were homosexual. Thousands of people in our churches across Canada felt the same way. No congregation could tell a Commissioner going to General Council how they must vote. It is the hope that every Commissioner would take their role very seriously and that the Holy Spirit would work through all of us to help us come to a decision that we were being called on to make, whatever that decision might be. All Commissioners, lay and ordained ministers, would go to this General Council meeting knowing exactly what their congregation wanted to happen and what the consequences could be if the Commissioners voted in favour of ordaining people who are homosexual. There would be thousands of petitions that would have to be dealt with and voted on by those attending General Council.

A group was formed of lay and ordained people within the United Church of Canada who called themselves *The Community of Concern* and it became a very strong voice at General Council for those members across Canada who did not want to see people who are homosexual ordained under any circumstances. Now the lines were drawn in the sand and every Commissioner, like me, going to General Council knew that this was going to be a very difficult and stressful meeting. Whatever decision we came to would affect the United Church of Canada for years to come.

One evening in March, Warren came home after choir practice and I could see he was very upset and had been crying. He said he was singing in the choir and suddenly he became very emotional and had to leave the choir and run outside. He said he had been thinking about Weisa and he walked around for what seemed to him a very a long time crying because he missed her so much. When he went back to the choir, everyone was very concerned and asked him how he was. He told them he was fine but he didn't tell them why he had been upset. After choir practice, Tammy had come over to him and asked him what had happened and he told her. He said that he felt so much better now and I told him that I was very relieved. He loved his great aunt dearly and she had loved him unconditionally.

By the end of March, I was feeling upset all the time. I was having more trouble focusing and I couldn't understand why. It wasn't because of the General Council issue, I knew that much. It was me. We had a new Personnel Officer at Manitou Conference and I went to see him. He told me that he felt I needed a few days away alone and offered me his apartment in North Bay at the end of April while he was on holidays. I went home and talked to Warren about how I was feeling and told I him I had to go away for a few days and get my head together because I was upset all the time. He understood so I took the Personnel Officer up on his offer. I needed to have this alone time to think and reflect and pray. When I got to the apartment in North Bay, I found myself crying for two days straight. I was frustrated and angry at God. Then I started writing poems including one about Louise. That's when the grief and pain I felt started coming out as it had for Warren that night in March. My aunt had been such a dynamic, vital person. Growing up with her was an experience in living and she had certainly left her mark on my life. She was a wonderful support to both me and Warren and to all who knew and loved her. I just wasn't prepared for her death to affect me to the extent that it did. Once I faced my grief and pain, I began to feel more at peace with myself. I realized even though I wasn't feeling as sad as I had been, I was ready to start the process of moving on. I still didn't want to let my aunt go and I struggled with those feelings. I knew that Louise would be in my heart until the day I died. After three days by myself, I knew it was time to go back home. The great sense of loss I had been feeling was still there but at least I had achieved some closure.

It was so good to be home and Warren was so glad to see me. I knew he had worried about me when I was gone. He would never say that but I knew my son. One of the first things I did when I got back was call my sister. We had been talking on the phone more often since Louise had died and Jana knew how I was feeling. She understood because she had had a terrible time dealing with Mom's death. She knew what a great loss this was for me. Jana was so helpful and supportive, and I was so glad she was there. Susie turned 80 on May 3rd and Warren and I went down to celebrate with her and took her to her favorite restaurant, the Mandarin. We had a great time and she told us she was going to live to be 100.

Because I had taken the Supervision course this past summer, I had many discussions with the Council about having a student minister come to St. Paul's for the summer. Our finances were good overall so the Council was willing to do this. They had never had a summer student. A lay supervision team was set up to work with Doug Currie. He would be coming to us from May to the end of August when he would return for his second year of studies at Emmanuel College. I was very pleased with Doug and the ministry he did. I saw him every week from May until the end of July but I was away most of August so I saw him at the end of the month when I went over my final report with him. He was the fourth student I had supervised and again I enjoyed doing this.

On Sunday, May 29th I had the first piano Recital for my students at St. Paul's United Church. We celebrated the performances with a reception afterwards in the Board Room. In the little booklet I handed out at the recital it said, *'I want to thank everyone for coming this afternoon. It has been a pleasure for me this year to work with all these gifted students. To learn to play the piano well is an art as I am sure you already know. Appreciating music and sharing our music with others is what this is all about.'* The weekend after the recital, I attended Manitou Conference for three days along with 350 lay leaders and ordained ministers. Of course, there was only one issue people were concerned about and that was whether we should ordain people who are homosexual. There were over 80 petitions from the congregations across our Conference and a committee had been set up beforehand to put all these petitions into some kind of order to make them easier to deal with. At the Conference, we had lots of debate and heated discussions around this contentious issue and, in the end, we sent all the petitions on to General Council whether we agreed with them or not.

Warren had another good year with the cadets and in June, Nora and I again attended Warren's Army Cadet's impressive year end program where Warren was presented with two awards. I really liked his leaders, Mr. and Mrs. Pelletier both of whom had the rank of Captain. I understood that Mrs. Pelletier had fought long and hard to get one placement in Banff for someone in this cadet group to go to there for the summer and when she got it, she gave it to Warren. He was thrilled. That summer my son would be flying to Banff, Alberta in July and spending six weeks there. What an opportunity this was for him. The program was all about leadership and training the young men who gathered there from across Canada, to be leaders and take responsibility. I was so proud of him. Warren finished Grade 12 that year and did very well. I couldn't believe that he only had one more year to go until he graduated. He still hoped to go to Royal Military College and enter their Engineering Program.

I had no regrets coming to New Liskeard if for no other reason than it had worked out so well for my son. In fact it had worked out well for both of us and I couldn't imagine a better place to live for Warren's last years at high school. At the end of June Warren and I went down to visit with Susie. Then, in July I took Warren to the Pearson Airport in Toronto for his flight to Calgary and cadet camp in Banff. Knowing that Warren would be away for six weeks, I had made plans to go Mexico City in early August for a 10 day workshop just before I would attend the 10 day General Council meeting in Victoria B.C. The program was called G.A.T.E., (Global Awareness Through Experience). I had found the information about the workshop intriguing and it stated:

> *"GATE Offers a Spirituality of Solidarity. Welcomes people from all faith traditions. Stands in solidarity with the global community. Allows the traveler to approach a people as pilgrim, in deep respect for their culture and history. Shows life through the eyes of the poor, women's groups and grass roots communities. Offers insight into the implication of global economics and politics. Integrates each day's experiences with dialogue and reflection. Draws on ... years of experience to offer opportunities that touch the heart and speak to the soul. Unique opportunities that can transform one's life."*

Here was an opportunity for me to see Mexico. The leader of this program was Sister Stephanie, an American Catholic Nun. She had the trust of the Mexican people and was able to take her groups into places in Mexico City that few people ever saw. When I flew into Mexico City, I was met at the airport and taken to the Lutheran Centre compound where we all stayed. There were three Americans in our group, 10 Canadians from Quebec and the Maritimes, and I was the only one from Ontario. Everyone in the group, except myself, was Catholic and only two were ordained, myself, and Father Michel from Detroit, Michigan with whom I had many conversations. We had morning lectures by economists, theologians, teachers and professors talking about Mexican history, Mexican culture, politics, the International Monetary Fund, the Catholic Church, and Liberation Theology - a Latin American movement that embraced the poor and called for social change. The lectures in the morning were interesting and thought provoking and we had opportunities to ask questions.

One morning, after our lecture was over, we were introduced to a 30 year old woman from El Salvador who had fled her country and was now living in Mexico. This woman was one of the tens of thousands of women whose husbands and children were taken from their homes and their wives and mothers never saw them again. The rock band U2 had written a song, *'Mothers of the Disappeared*' that was inspired by Bono's experiences in Nicaragua and El Salvador in July 1986. That song introduced the term *'Mothers of the Disappeared'* which is what these women were now called. She had come to tell us her story. There was a young woman in her early 20s who was translating for us. The older woman told us that she had lived with her husband and two sons in a very small house in San Salvador and, one night when she and her husband and their two boys were asleep, a big truck full of soldiers drove up to their home and broke down their door. They were all terrified, she said, as the soldiers ran in with machine guns and made them all get out of bed. The soldiers put her husband and boys in the back of the truck and tied them up. Then, in a very calm voice, she told us how 13 of these soldiers raped her, over and over again. She said that her vagina was torn so badly that it took more than 80 stitches to repair. You could hear a pin drop when the young women translated for us and she had tears streaming down her face as she described what these men did to this woman from San Salvador. What had happened to this woman was unbelievable. She said she only wanted us to understand what had happened to her and her family and so many other families like hers. She told us she had tried long and hard to find out what happened to her husband and her two boys but was never able to. None of us could imagine such horror and brutality and we didn't know what to do or say. There was a photograph of Archbishop Romero behind her on the wall as she spoke and that was very significant to me. I knew about the wonderful work he had done in El Salvador and how he spoke out against poverty, social injustice, assassinations and the torture practiced by the government while his Church turned a blind eye. Archbishop Romero was assassinated on March 24, 1980 as he was offering Mass in the Chapel of the Hospital of Divine Providence. He had given great hope to the poor and the marginalized and had become a martyr to his people.

The soldiers in countries like El Salvador, Nicaragua, Argentina and Chile roamed the cities and towns late at night to take men and children from their homes to arenas where they were murdered. Sometimes bodies were left on the streets and in ditches. People working for Amnesty International, the Red Cross and other groups and individuals had gone into these arenas to take photos of the tens of thousands of people who had been murdered in these countries. This woman had brought some photo albums with her which we were welcome to look through. In these albums, were picture after picture of tortured and mutilated dead bodies. These albums were only a few of hundreds of photo albums made up of those who had been murdered that had been put together over many years. Women looking for their husbands and children looked through these albums to see if they could find a loved one or loved ones and have some closure. More often than not, they never saw their loved ones again. I will never forget this woman who only wanted us to understand what was happening to her people in her country in El Salvador.

Sister Stephanie also arranged for us to be taken for an afternoon into a barrio in Mexico City. The smog that hung above the city seemed permanent and was so debilitating that one of the women in our group had to wear a bandana over her face every time we went outside because she found it hard to breathe. We drove through the city to the barrio in vans. We didn't know what to expect and started walking down the broken cement steps that opened into the barrio. The poverty was mind boggling, the likes of which none of us had ever seen. People were living in shelters they made of whatever they could find, like wood, aluminum and cardboard that people had found amid the garbage which was everywhere. There were live wires hanging almost to the ground and water and mud everywhere. Children were playing in the squalor and dogs were scrounging through the garbage for food. We were told that 350,000 people made their home in this barrio and that the population of Mexico City at that time was 20,000,000. If the outlying areas of the city were included, the population would be close to 30,000,000. I couldn't begin to imagine that many people living in one city. The population of the whole of Canada at that time was only 26,795,383.

Our translator accompanied us on this outing and she took us to meet one of the Christian workers in the barrio, who took us into what appeared to be a makeshift church but was no more than a room in which there was only a small table and chairs. There we met a local women's group from the Catholic Church and the smiles on their faces said it all. They were so happy to meet us and had made rice pudding to welcome us. Being as poor as they were, it was more than kind of them to offer us this food when we knew that most days they didn't have enough food to feed their own families. We had been told to be careful about what we ate outside the compound so many in our group didn't want to eat the pudding. For me it was important to accept their kind hospitality, so I ate the rice pudding. It was very good. I knew there had been an election in Mexico City July 6. Cardenas was a very popular leader in Mexico running for President at that time, but the Institutional Revolutionary Party under Gortari didn't want to lose the power that party had held since 1917. The election had been rigged with soldiers on the streets terrorizing people during the campaign and people were afraid and, needless to say, Gortari was re-elected. We still saw signs of the election everywhere because many posters had not been taken down. There were soldiers carrying machine guns on the roofs of banks so you could still feel the tension and fear in the air. We had an opportunity to talk with these 10 women through our translator but most people in our group didn't know what to say or ask. Because of my experience with Indian people, it was easier for me. I told the women that, in Canada, we knew about their election and that it had probably been rigged because it had been reported on the front pages of our major newspapers. They were very excited and so encouraged by the fact that millions of people in Canada had heard about their election. It made them feel they were not alone. Maybe there were people in the world who cared about them, even if they didn't know them, and that gave them hope. I asked the women if there was an alcohol problem in Mexico and, if there was, how it affected them. They said all the men in the barrio drank so it was dangerous to go outside at night, especially on the weekends. They said they locked their doors at night to keep the men out and protect themselves and their children. They also told us that their husbands had insisted they not talk to us because they were afraid of reprisals from government soldiers and even other men in the barrio. They also told us that their men didn't like their women going to church but when I asked them about Archbishop Romero, their eyes lit up and they told me he had given them great hope and still did. Everywhere we went in the barrio we saw enclosed statues of Mary, the mother of God, where candles were lit and prayers were said to her. These were wonderful women who had great courage and faith and, given the circumstances, it was really brave of these women to disobey their husbands and meet with us. That barrio, filled with people living in a poverty and squalor we can't even imagine, was, for me, like one huge Indian reserve. A professor from one of the universities told us about the history of Mexico, that the Indigenous Indian people of Mexico were the least respected and the poorest of all the people in Mexico. Most of the people who lived in this barrio weren't Indigenous Indians though many there were of mixed blood.

On Saturday morning, Sister Stephanie told us that we were going to worship at the Catholic Cathedral that evening. I didn't feel comfortable going because I knew that we would be offered communion and only Catholics are allowed to take communion, so I told the group I wouldn't be going and why. The group tried to convince me to go and they told me that there would be hundreds of people there and the Priest that served communion wouldn't know that I wasn't Catholic. I told them that was true but I would know. Father Michel came over to me after that conversation and told me he would stay behind with me but I told him while I really appreciated his concern I was fine. After everyone left for the service the compound felt really empty. I went over to the piano and played for quite a while. Then I sat down and started writing what ended up being some poems about Mexico. I put all my feelings into these poems as I wept for the people of Mexico and the horror of poverty and violence and hatred and racism. This evening alone gave me much needed time to process what I had been experiencing and also time to reflect and write and pray. I made copies of the poems I wrote and gave them to Sister Stephanie when the group returned. After she read them, she told me they were wonderful and said she knew I understood what she was trying to do. As we spoke, I realized the enormity of this ministry she had taken on. I admired her stamina and courage in offering such a program as GATE.

Because it was coming close to the time we would be heading back home, Sister Stephanie arranged for us to go to our respective Embassy. We Canadians met with our Ambassador, Raymond Chretien, who was Prime Minister Jean Chretien's nephew. We had a wonderful visit with him and he told us that Canada isn't always able to do a great deal to help the people in Mexico but he talked to us about what we can do. He told us about something he was able to help with when the Mexican government ordered its soldiers to push back the refugees who were coming into Mexico from Guatemala. The soldiers were using a lot of force to do this and our Ambassador and some of his officials went to the Mexican Guatemalan border where a huge refugee camp had been set up. He and his officials walked along part of the border there and, because of this one simple act, the Mexican government realized that Canada knew what the Mexican government was doing and it made a difference. The violence stopped. After our meeting, he came down to the lobby with us and, on our way out, we had a group photo taken with him. It was wonderful being in our Embassy and having the opportunity to meet Raymond Chretien. That day I was very proud to be a Canadian.

The Americans in our group weren't quite as lucky. They didn't get to see the Ambassador at the United States Embassy, but instead were sent to speak with one of the junior officials. Sister Stephanie had explained to them before they went that when she first started this program, the Americans in her group were able to see the Ambassador but, over the last few years, the

American Government had begun to disapprove of what she was doing in Mexico. As a result, even though she was an American citizen, the Ambassador refused to meet with the people she brought in. It all seemed so unfair to me since the only thing Sister Stephanie was trying to do was inform and educate her own people.

Sister Stephanie arranged a final worship service for our last day and invited Father Michel to lead the service. Later that day, he came and asked me if I would take part in the service and told me that it would be a privilege for him if I would serve communion with him. I considered it a great honour and agreed. That evening, Father Michel caught up with me and I could see he was upset. He told me that he had mentioned to some of the members of our group, that he had asked me to serve communion with him. They were upset with him for asking me and did not want me to participate. He said it shocked him that the Canadian men in the group were the most upset. He was very embarrassed to have to tell me that and very disappointed with the group and the injustice of it all. I told him I understood the situation and would certainly come to the service no matter what. He said he would not be offering communion as part of the worship service and he wanted me to take part in the service by reading a scripture and doing the closing prayer and the Benediction. I told him he didn't have to do that but he said he did because it was right and just and he was very angry with the group. We had our closing worship together without communion. I took part in the service as he requested and found it very meaningful. It had been an amazing and transformational 10 days for me. It was very emotional especially saying goodbye to Father Michel and Sister Stephanie but it was time to go.

Now I realized I had to really change gears for what was to come at the General Council meeting. I headed home to unpack from my trip to Mexico and repack my things for my flight to Victoria. I had spent a lot of time in June and July pouring over the hundreds of pages of documents every Commissioner to General Council had been sent to be ready for the meeting. Just before I left home, Bill Glassford came to see me. He was very upset about what our Church was doing and made it clear to me that, if the Commissioners at General Council voted in favour of ordaining people who are homosexual, he would leave St. Paul's. I was so upset to hear Bill tell me this. We had spent a lot of time together doing ministry at St. Paul's and I had become good friends with Bill and his family.

When I arrived at the University of Victoria in B.C. where the General Council was meeting I was shocked to see the media there and cameras everywhere. It was very intimidating and totally unexpected. It seems the Moderator and other officials of the United Church of Canada had decided they would have a very open meeting and invited the press to come. There were rules the reporters had to follow and only certain places where they could stand with their cameras and the press was very respectful. They seemed to understand how important this meeting was, not just the United Church of Canada but for all Canadians. I decided to sit upstairs where I could get a better view of everything that would be going on, and I got a seat in the front row in the balcony where I found myself sitting next to the Very Reverend Bruce McLeod, a former Moderator of our church from 1972 to 1974. I knew Bruce and admired him. As we were talking and getting acquainted again, someone came and sat down beside me. I had a huge emotional reaction when I saw it was Reverend John Shearman who had been on the Halton Presbytery Student and Education Committee when I went through for the ministry in 1973. He told me how nice it was to see me again but all I could think of is what he had put me through in those interviews. They had felt more like interrogations than interviews. Seeing him again I really resented him sitting next to me and I felt very uncomfortable.

The second day as I walked out of the meeting for lunch, John caught up with me and I finally confronted him. I let it all out and I couldn't believe how emotional I was as I relived that time and told him how he had made me feel so small and insignificant. At first he didn't seem to understand what I was saying to him, which made me even more upset. He told me he had played the Devil's Advocate but that it was only a role he had taken on, not what he believed. I challenged him on that and I told him that I felt what he said to me and how he presented himself to me back then was indeed who he really was. I made sure he realized that the experience had been very painful for me and he had really hurt me. He accepted that and told me how sorry he was, because he hadn't realized at the time how much he had hurt me. I told him I wasn't sure I could accept his apology and that I would need time to think about it. He said he understood. I was proud of myself for being able to address this issue with him and I let the rest go for the time being. I felt so much better after I talked to him and let out my anger and resentment.

From time to time, the debate around the issue of ordaining people who are homosexual got very heated on all sides. Finally, after days of sorting through petitions and hours and hours of debate, we got to the point where we felt we might be able to make a decision. It looked hopeful. We had been meeting since nine in the morning and it was now midnight. When it came closer to making a resolution Reverend Bill Fritz, the acknowledged leader from the Community of Concern, said that, if we were going to ordain people who are homosexual, then they had to be celibate. There was a great deal of discussion around that but the motion was put forward and defeated because of the argument that no unmarried heterosexual person who is an ordained minister in the United Church of Canada is required to be celibate. Finally someone made a motion and someone else seconded the following resolution: "A) That all persons, regardless of their sexual orientation, who profess Jesus Christ and obedience to Him, are welcome to be or become full members of the church B) All members of the church are eligible to be considered for ordered ministry." In this context ordered ministry included both diaconal ministry and ordained ministry.

At some point in the discussion Reverend Bill Fritz said they could live with this resolution. When it came time to vote, you could hear a pin drop. When at least two thirds of the Commissioners present voted in favour and the motion was passed no one cheered or clapped. I was never so proud of my Church as I was that night. The majority of Commissioners had come to this meeting with a bias against ordaining people who are homosexual. Many delegates had probably never met an openly homosexual person before coming to that General Council but we had all sat and listened to the heart wrenching testimonies of devout gay and lesbian church members. We debated little else and searched our souls and prayed to learn God's will. In the end, many of those who were opposed changed their minds. It was a huge privilege to be at that General Council, the only one I ever attended, and help my Church make history and become the most inclusive church of all the Christian churches anywhere in the world. It was almost 1:00 a.m. in the morning and we were all exhausted as we went to our rooms.

That morning, the United Church of Canada was in every newspaper in Canada and on every channel on television and all over the internet. We all knew that, eventually, we would return home to our congregations and it would be especially hard for those of us, like myself, who had voted in favour. At lunch that day, I was sitting with some people I didn't know and one woman who was a lay person from the Maritimes told us that her congregation had told her to vote against the motion no matter what and one person told her not to come back home if she voted in favour. She said she had had every intention of voting against the ordination of people who are homosexual but after listening intently to everyone who spoke on the floor of General Council around the issue she was torn and had no choice in good conscience but to vote in favour of the resolution put forward. She said she knew that it was the right thing to do.

I was looking forward to the end of this General Council meeting. The meeting had been an emotional roller coaster with great highs and great lows and the most difficult, most intense and emotional meeting I had ever attended. When it was over, I got on the plane from Victoria to Vancouver and Warren flew into the Vancouver airport from Calgary to meet me. It was wonderful to see him. He looked fit and handsome and was so excited and happy as he told me all about his trip. They had climbed mountains, rapelled, learned many things and had, as he put it, the best time ever. He showed me pictures of elk that just wandered into the cadet camp from time to time. He wanted to know what had happened at General Council and was pleased to hear about the decision we had made and I told him about my trip to Mexico City. I rented a car and we travelled all over the mainland and I was so happy to be able to take him around Vancouver and Burnaby and introduce him to my friends, many of whom last saw him when he was only two years old. It was a nice break. We flew home the end of August to get ourselves sorted out for September. It would be Warren's last year at high school, and I had to prepare to face my congregation. When we got back home, Bill Glassford was the first person to talk to me about what we had done at General Council. He told me he was leaving the Church, but that his wife Elaine wasn't. After Bill talked to me, I told Warren what Bill had decided and I told him that I hoped this wouldn't affect his friendship with Ronald. He told me they had already talked and decided that, whatever happened, they would always be friends and I was so pleased to hear that. Just when I thought we had put the issue to bed, Reverend Bill Fritz was interviewed by the press and said that he had not said that he agreed with the motion and resolution that was passed at General Council. I was shocked to hear him say that because it wasn't true and I called Bruce McLeod and talked to him about this. He told me not to worry because what Bill Fritz said at the General Council was all on tape and would be aired the next night on television. That was very reassuring.

Warren settled into his last year at high school and was working hard at his studies. He was also playing soccer, going to cadets, playing games on his computer which he loved, singing in the choir and visiting his friends. At the same time, he was also working on getting all the forms and necessary paperwork filled out for the recruiting office. He had decided to apply to the Royal Military College in Kingston for engineering the next year. We did lose a few more members from our church over the issue, but we didn't lose as many members as the country churches around us did. In the end, Bill, like many others, stayed in the United Church, but joined the Community of Concern which was now looking for a place to worship in New Liskeard. Over the next few months, we began to hear that more and more members were leaving the United Church of Canada across Canada and, over the next few years, tens of thousands of members would leave the Church as the United Church of Canada struggled to deal with the fallout from the decision we made at General Council in August 1988. As a measure to combat this development, the Board at St. Paul's thought it would be helpful to offer a workshop in September on the history of the Christian Church and homosexuality. This workshop was mainly set up to be informative but also to provide an opportunity for people to ask questions and have an open forum for discussion about what had happened in General Council. A few leaders from our church took part in helping me put this workshop together and I was surprised to see how many people showed up for it. We had over 40 members come and it went very well. There was lots of interest and discussion and everyone who came told us how helpful it was.

After my eventful summer, teaching piano again was a welcome distraction. It really helped me because it took my mind off all the things happening in the Church and I could simply concentrate on my students whom I really enjoyed teaching. They all wanted to do well and that was encouraging for me. I was working particularly hard with Lori because she still had a lot of work to do to get her Grade 10 piano exam the next June. I also had my four Master Classes to set up and there would be the recital at the end of the year. We had a good life in New Liskeard. There was the Tuesday movie night in town with Sharon and Benica, and even Nora came a few times, depending on the movie. Nora and I had become very good friends and often walked along the park by the lake and talked. Warren and I went for dinner to Doriel and Don's once a month and they invited Susie over when she visited with us. I knew this would be my last year with Warren. I didn't know exactly where he would be in September 1989, but I did know he wouldn't be living at home. One Sunday after church, I saw one of our members sitting alone in a pew crying. She was so upset because her daughter had just left for university and would be gone until Christmas. Even though she still had two daughters and a husband at home, she was beside herself. Seeing her in this state, I made a promise to myself in that moment to work hard this next year to be able to let Warren go, and not be too upset when he left. I knew he would always come back and would always be my son. But I had raised him to be independent and make his own way in life and now he was on the threshold of doing just that. It would be hard for me when he left, but I needed to refocus when that happened and begin a new life for myself. He wasn't mine to hold forever.

Winter started up again in October and, sometime during that month, Warren had an English assignment to do and when he finished it, he asked me to read it. I was shocked to see that he had no punctuation in it and asked him what happened. He told me that, in the midst of our moves, he thought he had missed the grammar classes. I talked to a member of our church who was a retired English school teacher for advice. While she didn't tutor students any longer, she offered to teach Warren the grammar he had missed and refused to take any money. She said it was her way of helping Warren. For about three months, she taught him every week for one hour until he was all caught up. She was wonderful to my son and she thought he was pretty special.

As I was still the Secretary of Temiskaming Presbytery, I knew we had a lot of work to do as a Presbytery. We were prepared for our meeting in September to be divisive and it was. There were people there who were upset and angry and others who really appreciated what the General Council had done. Our Chair was very unhappy with the decision but he did a good job chairing a very difficult meeting and trying to reassure people. There was no doubt that the repercussions of the General Council decision would reverberate for a long time. Then I received a letter from Reverend John Shearman, on October 12th and was taken by surprise. In part, he said: *"I am deeply touched by your witness to our meeting at GC in Victoria. I only wish that I had not waited for twelve years to say how sorry I am for the verbal abuse to which I subjected you to on behalf of the Halton Education and Students Committee. Your letter also helped me realize how painful sexual harassment can be to its victims. Before receiving your letter, I had not seen exactly what sexual harassment is. I hope that you will forgive me for taking so long to learn that lesson."* It was very good of John to send me this letter and I really appreciated it and I did accept his apology.

St. Paul's United Church celebrated its 90th Anniversary that year over two days from October 22-23 and it gave us something to really celebrate in the midst of all the controversy. Members of the congregation found old photos of the church and different activities the church had taken on through the years. We put up displays and invited members who had moved to other communities to come home for this weekend and many did. We hosted a wonderful dinner on the Saturday night and many people got up and told stories of their church and wandered around the hall to look at all the displays we had set up. We had a memorable service with lunch after church and a huge anniversary cake which everyone enjoyed. It was a privilege for me to be St. Paul's minister at this important anniversary service and it was indeed a wonderful celebration.

In November, we had a meeting of Temiskaming Presbytery which upset me very much. I had heard from a couple of members of Presbytery that our Chair, Reverend Richard Lougheed, was talking to the press against the General Council decision. It was one thing to disagree with our Church and another thing to deliberately go against the Church and try to overtly undermine what General Council had done, especially since he was using his position as the Chair of Temiskaming Presbytery to do it. I genuinely like Richard but I felt very strongly that what Richard was doing wasn't right. Not long after we started our meeting, I brought my concerns to the Presbytery. Richard said he was not going to back down on talking to the press and putting forward his own opinion. I told him that his opinion was not reflective of our Presbytery and that was my issue. I had no choice but to ask for a motion to have him removed as Chair of Presbytery. I did not do this without a lot of thought and reflection. I was prepared to resign if he wasn't removed but I didn't tell the Presbytery that because I didn't want to make it about him and me. There were people in Presbytery who were angry at me for even asking for a vote but I thought we really needed to be clear on whether we supported our Chair or not. I knew many people in Presbytery were upset with him but to ask for his removal as Chair as I was doing was taking a real risk. He told Presbytery that he respected me and understood why I was doing this and he was fine with having a vote. Someone seconded the motion and then we had a secret ballot. Stewards were elected to count the ballots and they came back and said the vote was in favor of keeping Richard as our Chair. Then Richard upset many in the Presbytery by asking what percentage of Presbyters voted in favour and he was told by Reverend David Bould that we didn't do that. Richard insisted and in the end, the Court agreed to tell everyone what the vote was. Richard had won the vote by 63%. When he heard that, he said it wasn't enough and resigned as Chair. He angered everyone in Presbytery but he felt he needed 75% to stay on. The lay person who had been our Chair the previous year didn't have the problems with the General Council decision that Richard had, and he was re-elected. I give Richard credit because he came over to me after the meeting and said he had no hard feelings and understood why I had done what I did. I appreciated that very much because, for me, it was not personal. I really liked Richard and was glad that he continued to attend Prebytery meetings.

Back in June, I had talked to Warren about going to California for Christmas to visit with Aunty Jana and he thought that would be a lot of fun and something different to do. I had also talked to Susie about this and told her we would spend Christmas Day with her in Oakville and then fly down to California for 10 days to visit Jana. We would return to Susie's after New Years for a few days before heading back to New Liskeard. Stacy had just had her baby and I was so looking forward to seeing my great niece, Brandi. Stacy was very excited about us coming for Christmas and wrote me a note on November 11th: *"Happy Birthday!!!! Can't wait for you to get here. I can't wait to see Warren. I also can't wait for you to see Brandi. She's getting so big. She weighs 10 lbs. now at 3 months. I don't have much to say because I'll see you next month. See you then. Have a wonderful birthday and take care. Lots of Love Stacy."*

By December, we already had lots of snow piled up high and, with Christmas just around the corner, we did our Christmas shopping locally that year and got a few things for Susie and Jana and her family. We had a wonderful Christmas Eve service again and, after the service, Warren and I went home, finished our packing and headed to the train station. Even though I had arranged a top and bottom berth for Warren and me so we could sleep on the way to Toronto, I didn't get much sleep on the train. We got in about 6:00 a.m. and took a taxi to Susie's. She was already up and so happy to see us. We had a nice breakfast together, listened to the Queen's message, as usual, and then opened presents. After supper we left for the airport. Jana was waiting at the San Francisco airport for us and was as excited to see us as we were to see her. She drove us the two hours back to her home in Sacramento and, because of the three hour time difference between Toronto to California, it was still Christmas Day. When we walked into her home, Stacy and Scott were there and so were Ken and his children, the twins Monty and Nicki, Steve and Derek. In the living room was a huge, beautiful Christmas tree with lights and decorations with many, many presents under it. Warren and I were surrounded by family. It was wonderful to be there. Stacy went into the bedroom where Brandi was sleeping and brought my great niece out to meet us. She was the most beautiful baby and I could see how happy Stacy was. My sister was only 40 when Brandi was born. Jana was indeed a proud grandma and it was a first for her.

Jana was having the family Christmas and dinner the next day and when we got up the next morning, Jana had the television turned on. We saw that the road we had driven on from San Francisco to Sacramento had been closed because the road was slick and people didn't know how to drive in snow. From Warren's perspective and mine it sure didn't look like much but they had never had snow in that part of California and it was a big deal for them. Warren and I had a good laugh about that. We all had breakfast together and then spent what seemed like hours opening present after present, but the best present for me was that all of us were together. After all the presents were opened, we helped Jana set up the table for the 11 of us to have dinner together. When Jana finished decorating the table, it looked beautiful. Jana had Christmas carols playing in the background while she prepared our dinner, made the dressing and getting the turkey and all the vegetables ready. I had lots of time to hold Brandi and give her a bottle and I could see why Jana couldn't get enough of her new grandbaby. Warren had a great time with all his cousins, playing games with Scott, Monty, Steve and Derek and Nicki who doted on him like a little mother while talking a mile a minute. It was the most wonderful day with my sister and our families as we celebrated Christmas together.

The last Christmas Jana and I had spent together was with all our family in Oakville was December 1963, just before Mom, Dad and Jana left Canada for the States in September 1964. The first time I went down to Sacramento for Christmas was in 1970 when Warren 8 months old. We were with Mom and Dad, Jana and Stacy who was two. Now 18 years later, Jana and I were together celebrating Christmas again and we made the most of it. We had a wonderful ten days together but, too soon, it was time to go home and we were on our way back to Toronto and then on to a visit with Susie for three days. Every day, Warren and I went in the pool with Susie and we all had a lot of fun as she sang her heart out. We played three handed bridge and we all missed Louise. We could hardly believe that just over a year had passed since she died. I still missed her terribly and so did Warren. Susie missed her sister too but she kept busy. She continued to go to the seniors' centre and play cards there every week and, of course she swam in the pool every day. She still drove her car and went shopping, made more friends in the apartment building and went down a few times a week to the superintendents' apartment where they talked and smoked up a storm. They were a couple in their 50's who really liked my aunt and kept an eye on her for me which I appreciated.

I came into 1989 not sure of what I wanted to do. I loved being the minister at St. Paul's United Church and I really enjoyed the congregation. I had made many friends and, after those first nine months, the conflict had been resolved there, but now huge changes were coming. This was Warren's last year of high school and he hoped to be going to the Royal Military College. In case that didn't work out, he was also looking at three universities and trying to decide which university would best suit his needs. For almost 19 years I had raised Warren on my own. Soon he would be leaving home and I was already trying to get my mind around this and prepare myself. I was wondering if it was time for me to make a change in ministry. I wasn't sure because there were more reasons for me to stay than to move. Nevertheless, in February, I decided to put my name on the United Church of Canada's national list indicating that I might be looking for a change in Pastoral Relations and every month the National Church sent me the list of pastoral charges looking for a minister. It was a half-hearted effort because I wasn't sure I wanted to leave or even if it was the right time but, after I got the list, I applied to a few places. But nothing really seemed to interest me. By the time April came, I knew that most ministers move into a new pastoral charge in July and that a minister must give the pastoral charge 90 days notice if they are leaving. That didn't seem to give me enough time to make up my mind and I decided, at that point, I would stay at least another year.

Susie came to visit us in April for a week and we had a great time. I took her on trips into the country, which she loved, and every day we went down to the park and walked along the lake. Susie loved visiting us and coming to church and seeing everyone. She was quite the character and at 80 she was still as feisty as ever. She could always drive me crazy with her antics and that twinkle in her eye that told us to watch out. She seemed to be getting shorter every year and she was now slightly stooped over. She had been 5'3' and small but now she was about 4'8". Warren was 5'10" and when he stood beside her he looked like a giant as she looked up at him. She was so proud of Warren. After we got home from church that Easter Sunday, we had lunch and played bridge for most of the afternoon. In the middle of our game, the phone rang. I answered it and it was a woman who told me her name was Eveline McNaughton and, she had seen my name on the national list and was calling from Peterborough Presbytery to talk to me about the Warsaw Pastoral Charge. She said she thought, from the write up I had written, that I might be someone this pastoral charge would be interested in. She told me that it was a four point Pastoral Charge and asked me not to hang up. It wasn't as much work as it sounded, she said, because this Charge only had two services on a Sunday and the congregations attended each other's church. Eveline said she knew that some of the members of the Pastoral Relations Committee would be interested in coming up this next Sunday to hear me preach and would I be open to that. I didn't know what to say and wasn't even sure where Warsaw was. I asked her and she said it was east of Peterborough. That made it at least a five-hour drive for them to come to New Liskeard and I told her our church service started at 10:30 a.m. If nothing else, Eveline was very direct on the phone and told me they would be there. She said that they would be very careful and quiet when they came into the church because five people would be coming. I really didn't know what to say because I didn't know if I was interested, but if they wanted to come who was I to say no. I talked to Susie and Warren about the phone call but I wasn't enthused and I told them I didn't think they would actually come and then we got back to our bridge game. The next day, I went over to see Doriel. She was the only one I had told that I was thinking of leaving and she was a good friend whom I could trust. I told her about the phone call and that these people might come. She said she would help in any way she could if they did. I was busy all that week and I didn't think any more about it.

Susie went back home on the Saturday train and when Sunday came, I drove to the church as usual. When I got there, I could smell food coming from downstairs and realized I had forgotten we had lunch after church. After the service, I went to the back of the church, as I usually do and was shaking hands with people as I invited everyone to go downstairs for lunch. A woman I didn't know came up to me and when we shook hands she wouldn't let go of my hand. "We are here," she whispered in my ear. I really didn't understand at first, so she said it again. In that moment, it dawned on me that this must be Evelyn and that they had come from Warsaw to hear me preach, just as she said they would. I told Eveline they should all go downstairs and have lunch and, after I shook hands with everyone and most people had gone downstairs, I saw Doriel and took her to my office. I told her the people from Warsaw were there but I didn't know how many had come. Doriel said she would talk to all of them during lunch and make sure they got upstairs to my office without anyone seeing them. My mind was racing so I calmed myself down and went downstairs for lunch. As I looked around the room, I saw two visitors at one table and three at another. It was awkward but I consoled myself that no one knew why they were there. I visited with everyone as I always did, and then had lunch. When people finished their lunch, they got ready to go home and as I looked around the room I didn't see the guests from Warsaw. I assumed that Doriel had taken them upstairs and was able to get them all into my small narrow office. I went to my office and opened my door and found five very hopeful people sitting there looking up at me and smiling. I could feel their positive energy as I sat down and we started talking. I asked them how their trip was and they started to laugh, saying that they had gotten up at 3:30 a.m. and were on the road by 4:00 a.m. They were all very chatty and laughing throughout our conversation so I knew they were my kind of people and I liked them right away. They told me they had stopped for breakfast on the way and were making good time after breakfast when they ran out of gas on the highway and went into a panic. Fortunately, someone stopped and helped them but by then they were really running late. They got to the church about two minutes before 10:30 a.m. and three of them sat on the left side of the church while the other two sat on the right side. I told them I had had no idea they had come in and they laughed even harder.

We had a great conversation and I found out there were four active churches: Warsaw United Church was the biggest, then Bethel United Church, Zion United Church and Carmel United Church and they were spread out over a 15 mile circuit. Warsaw and Zion United Churches met every two weeks and then Bethel and Carmel met the other two weeks and that seemed to work out well for them. Donna Hampton, one of the members at Warsaw United Church, handed me a very small piece of paper. She said she had called the bus terminal and wrote out the schedule for buses into Peterborough for when Warren would be coming home from university. I had no idea where he was going to university but I remembered I had told Eveline he was looking at different options like McMaster University in Hamilton and even the Royal Military College in Kingston. It was so kind of Donna to think of that, it really was, and I was impressed. They asked me to come the next day for an interview, but I really wasn't sure and I told them I would call them later that evening. They told me they were really hoping to hear from me as we said goodbye and I thanked them for coming. When I got home, Warren was waiting to hear all about it. I told him what they asked me, what they had said and that they wanted to interview me the next day. He asked me if I was going to go and I said I really didn't know, but that I had to let them know by that evening. I'm not sure how Warren felt about the possibility of my leaving New Liskeard with him going off to university but I did know how flexible my son was. He always wanted me to make the right decisions for what I needed to do and where I felt called.

All afternoon and evening, I thought about whether I should go for the interview or not. It took me a long time to decide but I made my decision at 11:00 p.m. Donna had given me her phone number in Warsaw so I called her. Donna's husband Gerry answered the phone and he told me Donna wasn't home yet and all he knew was that they had gone to a church to hear a minister preach. This committee really took confidentiality seriously but I had to tell Gerry who I was and why I was calling. I couldn't believe they weren't home because they left New Liskeard at 2:30 p.m. He told me that once Donna came home she would call me. Twenty minutes later, Donna called and was so happy to hear from me. She told me they were late coming back because they stopped for a nice dinner and took a couple of trips around the area before finally heading home. I told Donna that I had decided to come for the interview the next day if that was still a possibility. Donna sounded very happy and relieved as she replied that she would call everyone. We would have the interview right after lunch. She asked me to call her when I got into Warsaw and said that she would meet me at the church to show me around. The next morning I left around 6:00 a.m., stopped for breakfast on the way and got to Warsaw just after 11:00 and called Donna. I was beginning to feel that there might be something here. Warsaw is about two hours from Oakville and I knew that Susie would be very happy to have me closer. I also didn't know where Warren would be going to university, but Warsaw was much closer to Kingston and Hamilton than New Liskeard was. The only thing I knew for sure was that I would know by the end of the day if this was a call.

Donna showed me around the church and took me through the manse. We then drove around the circuit to see the other three churches. She told me the interview would take place at the home of a member of the church at Warsaw who lived in Peterborough. I should follow her in my car so I could leave from Peterborough which would make my drive home easier. The interview went really well and it was nice to see everyone again. I was surprised at how much at home I felt with the people interviewing me. They were so enthusiastic and positive and really wanted me to be their minister, of that there was no doubt. At the end of the interview, they asked me to go out for a few minutes while they had a discussion.

I went down to the lobby and, as I walked around, I did a lot of thinking. I believed I was called to be their minister. It would be a shock to move from a one point charge to four churches, but I knew in my heart that this was the right move. Donna came down to get me and, when we came back up to the apartment, they asked me to be their minister. Without a moment of hesitation, I accepted and said that I knew that this was a call. I truly felt this and so did they. It was wonderful to feel so sure. They were very happy and couldn't say enough nice things to me. After we concluded the business end of things, they told me they didn't want to pay for a moving van and wondered if they could help me pack and do the move for me. I knew they didn't have a lot of money and, besides, I could see that this was a hand-on charge that did everything themselves so I told them that was fine with me and I would call Donna to finalize the details of the move. I also told them I had to give St. Paul's 90 days' notice so I wouldn't be able to start until August 1st and they agreed to that.

As I drove back to New Liskeard, reality started to set in. I suddenly felt very sad that I was leaving and didn't know how I would tell my congregation. It would be very hard. All the people at St. Paul's had been wonderful to me. Warren had been so happy in New Liskeard, had come into his own and found friends and interests that made a real difference for him. Yes, the first nine months had been very stressful but we had worked through it together. Then the General Council's decision to allow people who are homosexual to be ministers in the United Church had created new tensions. There had been fallout all across our Church after this decision as thousands of people left the United Church and, yes, even at St. Paul's. That was a painful time but, again, we got through that together. As I thought about all the important things that had happened in the last four years in New Liskeard, I became very emotional on that drive back home.

I got home around 10:00 p.m. and Warren ran to door when he heard me open it. I gave him a big hug and then we sat down and I told him everything. "Mom," he said, "when that phone call came during our Bridge game and I heard you talking, I knew you were going there." "Really?" I asked him, "But you didn't say anything". "Because you didn't think that you were going there." Warren replied. " But I knew." I was amazed at my son's spiritual discernment of my call when I didn't even know yet. When I called my aunt to tell her I was moving to Warsaw, she was thrilled. She loved New Liskeard and the train ride but Warsaw would be so much closer. I also called my sister in California and she was happy for me as well. As far as the congregation was concerned, only Doriel knew that I was leaving. The Pastoral Relations Committee in Warsaw had to call a meeting to discuss their recommendation to the congregations and present my name. This meeting had to be announced two Sundays so I would have to wait two weeks before I would be able to announce to my congregation that I was leaving. I wrote out what I was going to say to my congregation:

> "There is no other way to say this. I am leaving. I have accepted a call to another Pastoral Charge as of August 1st. I need you to understand how this came about. In February I knew it was time to leave. I can't explain how I knew and I didn't know if it would happen in a year or in a few months, but I began the process. Then I had a phone call from the Warsaw Pastoral Charge just outside Peterborough. It all happened very quickly. Five people from the Pastoral Relations Committee came up to hear me give a sermon two weeks ago and I went down the next day for the interview. They asked me to be their minister. Last Sunday they had their congregational meeting and issued me the call. I accepted. I can only say I haven't felt so certain about anything since I came here four years ago and met with your Pastoral Relations Committee and knew this was where I was to come.

It is not easy today to tell you I am leaving. For four years you have been our family. We have shared a great deal. We have had a lot of good times. We have had our ups and downs like in any family. It has been my privilege to have been your minister. I have no regrets. The positive far outweighs the negative and when I leave, I leave only with good feelings about St. Paul's and the ministry we shared together. You have enriched my life and given a great deal to me and to my son. You are wonderful people. You welcomed us into your homes and your hearts. There were those times especially in the first year during the conflict when it was very difficult – you phoned, you came and talked with me, you sent flowers, we prayed together for the ministry at St. Paul's, you cared about your minister and this church. It will not be easy to leave.

Since I was ordained in 1976 I believe I have served where God has called me to serve. And I believe at this time God is calling me to serve the four congregations in the Warsaw Pastoral Charge. I do not pretend to understand. I only know I am being called to leave and go there to serve our Lord. You are a wonderful congregation. I want you to know that any minister coming here will have a great team of dedicated people to work with… …We must begin to make the break. We must begin to look forward, building on the past….. Our family has been blessed by this congregation in so many ways. Together we have served our Lord and tried to do our part. Now it is time to move on. God has something more for us to do. As I have heard God's call and answered, so you must hear God's call and answer as you continue to do God's work here in this congregation…We will miss you all very much, With Love, Dorinda

Once I told them I was leaving on August 1st, I don't think they heard anything else I said. People were visibly shaken and upset as we hugged each other after church. I felt so badly but I knew it was the right decision or I could not have done this. Pearl Winter, one of the members who had been there when the five guests had come to church from Warsaw said, "Now I know who those people were who were visiting. If I had known what they were really there for, I wouldn't have been so nice to them. I would have told them to go home and leave our minister alone." We both laughed but with a touch of sadness.

I knew that many of the older people at St. Paul's, like Pearl Winters, Vi Farrow, Nina McCarty, Lila and Len Fielder, Cliff and Eileen Rhamey, Mil Meisner, Anne Plaunt, Evelyne Taylor, Freda Pearce, Louise and Keith Reid, Mable Keech, had enjoyed my many visits in their home over those last four years, and it mattered to them that I was their minister and I felt badly leaving them. Not long after I got home from the service the phone rang and it was Lila Fielder. Lila and her husband Len were in their 80s and long standing members of the church and highly respected. She told me how very sorry she was that I was leaving. She said that she had never seen the congregation so upset as when I told them that I was leaving and she said that it was about time they felt this way. She had been in the congregation all her life and had seen many changes but, for her, this time had been different. I thought about what Lila said later. Perhaps the conflict we went through during my first nine months of ministry had opened people up to be more loving and caring with each other and with their minister. I truly loved Lila and Len and looked up to them as people who really lived their faith.

On May 14th, Doriel and I gave our last organ piano recital with vocalists Hye-Jin and Mary-Beth Campbell. It was a great evening and, as usual, great fun. On June 4, Nora and I went to hear the original cast of Beatlemania. Nora and I thoroughly enjoyed that concert and I surprised myself because I knew almost all the songs. At the end of May I had my last students piano recital and it went very well. My students outdid themselves at this recital and I was proud of every one of them, especially of Lori. She took her Grade 10 piano exam in June and got 74% which was amazing. She put in many hours of practicing while she had a full time job. I was very, very proud of what she had accomplished and so was she. In the brochure, I wrote this to my students :

"I have enjoyed teaching these last two years. All of you have been very good students and I appreciate the effort you have made. As you know I will be leaving July 30 to move to Warsaw near Peterborough. I am sorry to be leaving because I have enjoyed sharing music with you. If you are ever down my way, I am very easy to find and my door is always open."

I had enjoyed the music Doriel and I had played as well as teaching piano. I loved my students and discovered I was still a good teacher. It meant a lot to me to do this but it was not my real focus. I discovered in New Liskeard how much I loved being a minister and how creative doing ministry could be. I also loved living in New Liskeard where I had made many friends, and once the conflict was over I was very happy to be there. It is wonderful doing ministry when a congregation rises to the occasion, wanting to be a welcoming church and being happy just to come to church. It made my role as their minister so much easier. Yes, we had some rough patches but most of the congregation had such a positive outlook on life and their church. In a way this congregation reminded me of the Monticello United Church congregation which was always positive and lived their faith. Of course, St. Paul's had a much larger congregation but after the conflict, they blossomed and it was a beautiful thing to see. It was very hard to leave St. Paul's because the people there had really become our family and had nurtured both Warren and me.

Warren and I were very busy over the next two months, sorting, throwing things out and packing. Donna told me that her husband Gerry and his buddy Carl would come up the last week in July with a moving van to take our things to Warsaw. Warren had applied to three universities for engineering. He had been accepted by all three but hadn't made a decision. He really wanted to go to the Royal Military College in Kingston and had been down to the college for interviews and done all the paperwork. Now he was waiting for a phone call. I happened to be home when the call came and I went into the kitchen and waited. I wasn't so sure that I wanted my son to have a military career and I had talked to him about this but his heart was set on it. I would support him in spite of my reservations. If this was what he really wanted, I hoped that he would get in. Then he came into the kitchen and told me they said no, not this year, but they would hold a place open for him next year. I asked him what he was going to do and he said that if they didn't want him the first time, he didn't want to go. One thing about my son, he is confident, and had been like that even as a little boy. Things do bother him but he has his own way of dealing with the things that upset him. Somehow he can turn them into something positive. He had made his decision and told me he was going to go to McMaster University. nother major change in our lives had occurred. Warren made his decision as I had made mine. I was there at his graduation in June when he finished high school and what a proud mother I was. It was earlier that month that I had taken Warren to a car dealership in New Liskeard and had him try out a few cars. The deal was this: I would buy him a car and finance it but he would eventually pay me back because I wanted him to be responsible and independent and he wanted that too. He picked out a car he liked for $4,500.00 and he was excited that he could now get around on his own. It gave him a great sense of freedom and independence and I was so happy for him.

Now there were people I had to notify about my move. I wrote to Reverend Don Lockett, who had been one of the conflict consultants at St. Paul's back in the spring of 1986. I wanted to let him know I was leaving and he sent me this letter on June 23rd:

> *"I received……your letter saying that you were changing pastoral relationships. Allow me first to say a word of congratulations. I really admire the spirit of enthusiasm that bursts forth from you. This is all the more remarkable, it seems to me, in light of the fact that you are going to a four point pastoral charge. I can't help but feel that the many and varied gifts that you bring to the ministry will richly benefit the Warsaw Pastoral Charge. And, of course, I pray that our gracious Spirit God will infuse all of your words and work with God's rich blessings."*

Then Jane Sullivan heard I was leaving. She had been a candidate for ministry through St. Paul's United Church and was now ordained and serving in the Brownsburg-Cushing-Grenville Pastoral Charge. She sent me a nice note on June 2nd :

> *"What words can begin to express my appreciation for all you've done for me since you came. Thank you seems to sum it up but it's so normal! Blessings on you and Warren. You're both terrific – a great team ministry!"*

The Charge decided to have a picnic party for Warren and me at the end of June at the lake and Susie decided to make the trip one more time so she could come for the party. I was so happy to have her there and everyone welcomed her warmly. Lots of people from the church came and wished us the best. We all had such a nice time just relaxing by the lake, talking, laughing and having fun together. The official going-away party would be after church on my last Sunday in July, after which I would be driving to Warsaw and my new home. Since Warren was finished at the end of June, he wondered if he could go ahead of me and stay at the manse in Warsaw because he had been offered a full-time job for the summer at the Warsaw Caves that had been arranged by a member in the Warsaw Pastoral Charge. Since my contract with the Warsaw Pastoral Charge didn't start until August 1st, I called Donna, explained the situation and asked her if it would be possible for Warren to come in July and live at the manse. She said she would take it to the Board and get back to me. I could understand their hesitation since the people in the churches weren't sure what Warren was like. After all, he was a 19 year old boy. Only the five people who had come to St. Paul's had seen him, and then only in passing that Sunday in church. Donna told me they were advised by a lawyer to have me sign an agreement that held me responsible for the manse if I would pay $1.00 for its use. It was so good of them to do this and Warren really appreciated it. I signed the contract, paid the dollar and Warren was good to go. Most of our packing was done, so off he went in his new car to Warsaw to work for the summer at the Warsaw Caves.

Of course, as soon as everyone met him, they knew there would not be any problem and he was even invited to Don and Gerry's for supper a few times. The people in the congregations were good to my son that month he was there and I really appreciated their kind hospitality. Before Warren had left we had found a really good home for Frisky with a retired woman who just loved our dog. On July 17, Shelia Draper wrote me a letter. She and her husband were members at St. Paul's and I was very moved by what she said:

"I am happy for you that you have been accepted at a new charge and sad for me (feeling sorry or I guess you could say selfish) that you are moving on......I must honestly say I have never been touched by a minister in this way before. I have always enjoyed your sermons and believe it or not several parts of different ones have stuck with me. I have been touched by your Christmas Eve, Palm Sunday and communion services to name a few. I have enjoyed the times when you have included your experiences with our native people in your sermons. I was especially touched by your service at the funeral for our dear friend Mrs. Wilson. I must also mention how much I enjoyed your piano-organ duets, very touching. One piece that comes to mind and I'm not even sure if this is the title, but I believe it's The Golden City (The Holy City)...I must also tell you I have never done as much at St. Paul's as I have done since you came.. I never sat on any committees before nor did I ever offer to act as an usher. When I was asked by you that first time to do a children's story I was proud, pleased and nervous and being a lay reader was a whole new adventure for me. I feel I got my confidence just by knowing you were close by.... I'm sure you are aware of the fact that Alvin is not a church goer, but he has gone more since you came than ever and when he received your letter about confirmation classes and accepted the offer I felt your attitude had something to do with it. To me this was like a dream come true!! You have done so very much for us all at St. Paul's how does one say thanks. I know there were rough times and it must have been very hard on you, thank goodness you survived. I feel I am a better person from what I have gained by having you as our minister."

I truly appreciated this heartfelt letter from Sheila who, over my four years at St. Paul's, had become a good friend. She spoke for many of the people in the congregation who felt the same way as reflected by many of the cards I received. Many people touched my life when I was at St. Paul's and, as I thought about what Sheila wrote, I remembered back to a service I had conducted at St. Paul's in 1987 when a 90 year old woman came forward and asked me if she could join the church. It was a very moving moment in St. Paul's history to have a 90 year old woman join the church and I have never forgotten her and her faith and courage to come forward in that way. That was a pretty special moment. In the card she sent to me afterwards she wrote,

> *"You have a wonderful way of making a person feel so much at ease. Everything was so much more calm and happy than I expected and beautiful. You are such a caring and loving person….thank you and bless you."* Beth Rice.

The day finally came when Gerry and Carl came to my door. They were ready to pack my things into their moving truck but, when I went out to see what they came in I found a four horse trailer. It was big, mind you, but I knew it was not nearly big enough. I didn't say anything as we walked into my house and I showed them everything that was going. They just looked at each other and knew the four horse trailer didn't have enough room for all my things. They hinted that, because I was single, they didn't think I would have that much and we laughed at that. Before we started loading up, I took them to the church and, when we walked into the sanctuary, they couldn't believe how huge it was and were overwhelmed. The sanctuary at Warsaw would fit into this church twice. Carl's Church, Carmel United Church had a sanctuary that only held 70 people whereas St. Paul's Church could hold over 250. They couldn't understand why I would leave St. Paul's United Church to come to their churches, so I told them, "I felt it was a call." That was all I could say. When we went back to the house and started loading things into the four horse trailer, Tom and his wife Evelyn came over to help and I was truly grateful. Evelyn and Tom were members in my congregation and I gave Tom's son Aaron and Evelyn's daughter Brenda piano lessons. The boxes were easy and most were already packed but Carl and Gerry had not done any moving in a very, very long time and weren't sure what to do with the rest. Tom was a trucker and knew how to pack and make the most of the space he was working with. When he looked at what Carl and Gerry had brought for my move, he knew right away this was not going to work. Carl and Gerry didn't know what to do, but they certainly knew they would have to make another trip. Tom offered to put the things that they couldn't take in his truck and said that, on my last Sunday, he and his wife Evelyn would follow me down to Warsaw with my things. When Tom offered his truck, there was such a look of relief on Carl and Gerry's faces. They couldn't thank him enough. Nor could I. It was so kind of him. We agreed that Tom would take my piano and other heavy furniture and then we all worked together and got the house pretty much emptied out. I had made a map of the inside of the manse and indicated into which rooms I wanted the boxes and furniture to go. Warren was already in Warsaw and he would help them unpack the trailer when they arrived. We all worked hard that day and, after it was over, and Gerry and Carl left, Evelyn, Tom and I just sat around and talked. It was a good day.

My last Sunday at New Liskeard was very hard. Many people were there to say goodbye. Warren had come up for that weekend by train so we could drive back together and it was hard for both of us. We had many wonderful memories and had made many friends in those four years. They had a wonderful lunch and a big cake for us downstairs and all the members of the youth group were there. The congregation gave me an envelope to open and in it was a picture of a barbeque. I didn't know exactly what to make of it until they explained that it was being delivered by Sears in Peterborough to my new home in Warsaw and would arrive the next day, Monday, in the afternoon. I love to barbeque and that was a wonderful and thoughtful gift to give us. It was sad to say goodbye. After the party, most people had left but my friends Doriel, Sharon, Eldon and Benica remained behind with a few others. They walked me to my car and Sharon handed me an envelope from the congregation which I put it in my purse. Tom and Evelyn were there with Tom's truck to follow us to Warsaw with the rest of our furniture and it was so kind of them to do that. Though it was hard to say goodbye to our friends, it was time to go and off we went. In the car, Warren asked what was in the envelope. I said I didn't know and told him to look in my purse and see. As he opened it, money started to fall out. There was over $400.00 and I was speechless. It was so kind of the congregation.

When we finally arrived at Warsaw, Gerry and Carl arrived to help Tom and Warren take the piano inside the house, along with lots of other furniture. It took a while and I showed Tom and Evelyn around the house. It was a very big, comfortable house which the Pastoral Charge had kept up really well. When we first went inside, the stairs were about six feet in front of you and on the right of the entrance was a large room which became my church office where Donna, our church secretary, worked one morning a week. To the left of the entrance was the living room. Walking through the living room, you came right into the dining room where I put my piano off to one side by the window. There was a small addition added to part of the back of the manse with a lovely, bright bedroom with a bathroom. This was where Evelyn and Tom stayed for the two nights they were with us. From the dining room, you walked into a lovely big kitchen which had just been completely renovated. There was a large sliding patio door off the kitchen that you could open and walk out onto the new deck where you could see the river. It was beautiful. There was a carport as well. The partial basement underneath the house was more like a cellar and could never be used for anything except the furnace. Upstairs there was a large bathroom on your left at the top of the stairs. Beyond that were two bedrooms, Warren's bedroom was on the same side as the bathroom. Across from his bedroom, was my bedroom.

We were all up early the next morning and I made us all breakfast and then we started unpacking the boxes. Tom and Evelyn were a great help. After lunch, Sears showed up with my barbeque. I thought barbeques were delivered all put together. We opened up the box and there were tons of nuts and bolts inside. Tom told me he liked a challenge and said he would get the barbeque up and running before they left. When we all went to bed around 11, Tom was still working on the barbeque and told us he didn't need anyone to help him. In the morning, the barbeque was on the deck, all put together. I couldn't thank him enough for doing that. Evelyn and Tom left after lunch and headed back to New Liskeard. I couldn't believe the friends I had. Here were Tom and Evelyn driving a truck down from New Liskeard with our furniture and, on top of that, he put our barbeque together. It was wonderful of them to do that for us and we deeply appreciated it. By the time they left, we were pretty much moved in and I was ready to begin my ministry at Warsaw.

CHAPTER NINE

Warsaw United Church

Once I was settled in Warsaw, one of the first things I had to do was help Warren find a place to live while he would be studying at McMaster University. Living in residence was too expensive so we looked at ads in the paper and went down to Hamilton twice to check things out. The places we looked at were real dumps and Warren and I were shocked, especially by the rents they were asking. He suggested that we look in Oakville. There we found an Italian family who lived near the Third Line and were offering room and board. Warren was happy with that and relieved that he now had a place to stay and would very soon be attending classes in engineering at McMaster University.

The day Warren left home was really hard on me. He was 19 years old and very happy as he was setting out on his own. We were outside on the veranda and, as I was saying goodbye to him, so many emotions were running through me. We had a big hug and when he got in his car and drove away, I had to hold back the tears. I had been thinking of this moment for months, trying to prepare myself because I knew I had to let him go, but can anyone really prepare themselves for the moment when their child leaves home? I was proud of him but my emotions were getting the better of me as I stood outside watching him drive away. I knew I would see him soon but I it would never be the same again. It was very hard and I went into the house and closed the door.

Luckily, I was very busy getting to know the families in the four churches. I was feeling really good as I went about visiting, preparing services and getting into a routine. People invited me over and were very happy to welcome me with a cup of tea or a lunch or dinner. I began to feel very much at home in Warsaw and I loved sitting out on my deck in the mornings and at night looking out at the river. It was very beautiful there. I also met some lovely people at Warsaw. There was Donna and Gerry Hampton, Donna's sister Joyce and her husband Reg Payne. There were lots of Paynes and Clysdales, including Edna and June, two sisters who lived together in Lakefield. I learned very early on that the people in these four congregations were very capable of looking after their church, their finances, their business and all of them had a very strong faith. They just needed a minister to support them, preach the Gospel and be there for them. They all got along really well with each other and it was a joy for me to be their minister and serve among them.

I met Maida Ormsby early on. She was the Clerk of Session at Carmel United Church, the last point on the circuit about 15 miles from the Warsaw Church. At age 70, Maida was quite the feisty character and a woman who would stand out in any crowd. She had beautiful white hair and looked elegant in whatever she wore. She was a force to be reckoned with and we became great friends. We both had a quirky sense of humour and were Sagittarians, one of the fire signs. She had lots of energy and we related to each other very well. We talked a lot on the phone. I often went out and visited her and another member of the congregation, Ruth Gorrod, who lived just up the road from her. Like Maida, she was also a widow in her 70's. Ruth was very independent and could fix most things in her house including her roof and I found that impressive. Also attending Carmel Church was June Drain who was in her 50's and a very active member of the church. I liked her right away. She was a very kind person and couldn't do enough to help her church. Her husband Carl didn't attend church but he was very proud of his Clydesdale horses, which he showed at many of the fairs in the summer and he was the one who brought the four horse trailer to New Liskeard.

Netta and Gerry O'Marra lived across the road from Zion United Church and they had a big farm where they grew all kinds of vegetables and fruit which they sold in the summer. Netta always made sure that their neighbour Bethel United Church had enough strawberries for the strawberry social they held outside their Church at their big fundraiser in June. People came from all over the county to visit for this special social. Gerry didn't come to church, but Netta did and she was very evangelical, more than anyone else raising her hands in church and saying, "Praise You Jesus, Thank You Jesus", which bothered most members in the church. Netta and I liked to go out for lunch once in a while. We had quite the 'theological' conversations because I didn't always agree with her and she liked to be challenged. At one time, she told me she had been part of a right wing evangelical group in the area who tried to ban Margaret Laurence's books and they had a real campaign going against her in Lakefield where she lived. It was hard for me to believe that Netta had been involved in such a hate campaign and she told me she deeply regretted it. Marta and Harry Hamilton were also members at Zion United Church. Harry was Clerk of Session and a wonderful man. He had a woodworking shop where he did beautiful carpentry work. Marta never went to church but I got to know her. She was quite the character and loved to play Bingo and went out every night of the week to play. She would start out in the evening around six or seven and come home about two or three in the morning which meant she slept most of the day. She had lupus and was crippled up with it but managed somehow to hold the bingo cards in her hand when she needed to and put the chits on. Whenever she was in the hospital, which was a few times, and would see me coming, out would come the crib board and I had to play at least four or five games with her before I could leave. I knew she was in a lot of pain most of the time, but she never let on and we would just laugh through the visit. I enjoyed her friendship.

Ron and Mary Frankish and Joan and Laurel Hamilton were two wonderful couples at Bethel Church. Ron was the Clerk of Session at Bethel and I often visited Laurel's dad. I enjoyed my visits with him and once asked him how he had managed to stay married for over 60 years. He told me his secret was that he always told his wife she was right. He was a real gentleman and a very kind man and, needless to say, a devoted husband, father and grandfather.

I got to know Donna and Gerry Hampton particularly well the first month I was in Warsaw and we became friends. Now I thought about the possibility of dating again. I hadn't dated for a few years but out there in Warsaw there was no opportunity and I decided to put an ad in the

Peterborough Examiner. I felt a little embarrassed about taking out an ad when I was in the newspaper office but I told myself many people did this. Donna and Gerry had been married 30 years and when I told them what I had done, they said they found that was a strange way to meet someone and told me to be careful. I had quite a few responses from my ad, which surprised me, Many of the men who responded didn't interest me at all but I picked two that I thought sounded interesting from their letters. I called one of them and we decided to meet at a restaurant in Peterborough and have dinner together. He was a very nice looking man, but I suspected right away that he was a player and looking for a blond bombshell which I wasn't. When I mentioned in our conversation that I was a minister, it didn't go over well. We both knew early on that it wouldn't work but we had a nice dinner and went our separate ways.

The second person on my list sounded nice on the phone and we decided to go out for coffee in Peterborough and talk. He was in his late 40s, over six feet tall, had reddish hair and was of medium build. We actually had a good conversation. He told me he was divorced, that he wanted to find someone and it didn't matter to him that I was a minister. We had a good time and I liked him, so we decided to go out again and I invited him to my home for dinner the next week. I showed him around the manse and we sat and talked in the living room until I went out to the kitchen to get the dinner ready. When everything was prepared, I went in to tell him and found him sitting and reading the newspaper. He had certainly made himself at home and looked very comfortable. We had a nice dinner together but, so far, there was no chemistry. It was a beautiful night, so, after dinner, we went out for a walk. I wasn't ready when he kissed me and he was not a good kisser. I had told Donna and Gerry about this upcoming date and they suggested that, after our dinner we drop over to their house. So, after the ordeal of the kiss, I told him about my friends and he was happy to go for a visit. Donna and Gerry both liked him and I really wasn't surprised. Here was a very nice and kind man who could keep up a conversation but, for me, he was not terribly motivated, had low energy and was not passionate. Even though my friends thought he was great, they also recognized that he probably wouldn't be able to keep up with me. We had a nice evening and then he headed home. He called a couple of times after that evening, but I just couldn't go out with him again. I looked at the other letters from the men who had written me and I threw them all out. In my experience, you just feel that spark or you don't.

At the end of August I decided to have an open house at the manse and I was very excited to do this. The congregations had been very good to me and they had done wonderful work in the manse decorating, cleaning and even renovating, so I wanted to show my appreciation. I had hung my framed art work around the downstairs area but I had not done much upstairs except put up the posters of the horror movies that I had collected over the years whenever I visited my sister in California. I had never put them up before but this house was perfect for them and I put all 24 of these large posters on the walls in my bedroom. I had posters of *Frankenstein, The Werewolf, Dracula, The Mummy, Dr. Jekyll and Mr. Hyde, The Invisible Man* and from the more recent movies: *Freddy, Nightmare on Elm Street, Halloween* and many others. It had not been easy to find these posters, even in California. As a child I couldn't wait for Saturday morning to come so I could see another horror movie from the 1930s and 1940s and I loved them all. The actors like Bela Lugosi, Lon Chaney Jr., Basil Rathbone, Peter Lorre, Boris Karloff, and many supporting actors like Claude Rains and Charles Laughton were wonderful. I am just one of those people who love scary movies and horror movies in particular. I was thrilled to have them up but didn't know what my congregations would think.

One Sunday afternoon from 2:00 p.m. to 4:30 p.m. members of my congregations came to see my home. I had lots of goodies for them and coffee, tea and juice. Everyone walked through my home looking at everything. I did get a few comments on my bedroom, mostly that it was certainly different. Then one of the oldest members of the Carmel congregation whom I really liked came to the door. She was in her 80s and always wore a lovely dress and running shoes which reminded me of Susie who also had trouble with her feet and could only wear running shoes. I showed her around my home and then I took her upstairs and showed her the bedrooms. When she got to my bedroom she stood in the middle of the room looking at all the posters saying, "Oh My! Oh My!" Then she looked at me and smiled and I smiled back. She was a real sweetheart and she had a good sense of humour. It was a great afternoon and was wonderful to share my home with everyone who came that day.

In early September, I decided to take a creative writing course at Sir Sanford Fleming College in Peterborough, something I had been thinking about doing for a while. After all, I had written many poems over the years, articles in newspapers and even had my own column in two newspapers. I had also been writing sermons for 13 years. I had lots of questions and felt there was something more for me to do with my writing, so I signed up. The course was one evening a week over 10 weeks and our teacher was Gail Corbett who had a gift for writing and had written a few books herself. She also worked with many aspiring writers and encouraged her students to think outside of the box and use their gifts. She told us to write something every day and gave us lots of ideas and suggestions and assignments. There were about 15 of us in the class. I liked Gail and she was a very good teacher.

I was really looking forward to Thanksgiving because Warren was picking up Susie and bringing her to Warsaw. Besides I hadn't seen Warren since he had left home. When they arrived, I ran out to see Warren and just hugged and hugged him. It was wonderful to have him back home for the weekend and he was happy to be home. Susie hadn't seen the manse yet and we walked her through it. She loved it even though she wasn't sure about the posters in my bedroom. However, she laughed when she saw them and remembered how much I loved horror movies as a child. She loved the deck and sat there having her coffee and a smoke and thought how beautiful the river was. We had a great time together playing cards and I made a wonderful Thanksgiving dinner on the Sunday afternoon. We had lots of good conversation and I told them about my creative writing course which Susie thought was a wonderful idea and Warren said he was happy I was writing again because he knew how much that meant to me. It was a great visit and Warren seemed to be doing well at university with only a month in. On Monday afternoon, it was time for Warren to take Susie home and get ready for university. I had such a wonderful visit with my son and Susie. It was hard to see them go.

There had been a time, a few years back, when I had thought of adopting a child and had looked into it, but in the end I decided not to pursue it. I remembered this when I received information in the mail shortly after I arrived in Warsaw from the Big Sister Big Brother organization out of Peterborough who needed people to be a Big Sister or Big Brother. I gave this a lot of thought and decided to see what was involved. My Aunt Louise had worked for a few years in the Big Sister offices in Toronto so I knew they were a reputable organization. I called them and one of the caseworkers came to see me and talked to me about their program. I became really interested, especially when she said there was a young girl she would like me to consider who lived less than ten minutes from my home. The caseworker took me out to meet the family and I saw they did not have very much. She introduced me to the mother and father, to their youngest daughter and son, and then to Sarah who was almost 12 at the time. She seemed older and was very cheerful and happy to meet me. I sensed she had great expectations. We hit it off and I became her Big Sister. At first I saw her a few hours a week, but I really wanted to have her stay over once in a while because it would be more fun for her, and Sarah wanted to as well. But, as a Big Sister, I wasn't supposed to have Sarah stay over until we had a year together and Sarah's family knew that. I spoke to her parents about this and her mom and dad were happy to have her stay over at my house once in a while on a Friday night and I started taking her overnight every two weeks on a Friday so we could have all day Saturday together. That worked out really well. She loved coming for a sleepover and, with her parent's permission, I took her to Oakville near the end of October, to meet Susie and they got along really well. Susie loved her energy and enthusiasm and Sarah couldn't wait to go down to the pool. I had already told Warren about Sarah and we all went swimming in the pool and then we had dinner together. Warren liked Sarah but she teased him terribly and I just let them work it out. After dinner, Warren told me he was still trying to figure things out, and it was all so new and different but he loved university life, which I was very pleased to hear, but he said he was having a very hard time with calculus. Overall, Warren seemed happy and, even though I knew it wasn't easy, I was glad he was settling into university. I was a Big Sister to Sarah for three years and took her out to dinner, to lunch, we cooked at the house, we went for walks, she came at Christmas and Easter and we went to the movies, which we both loved. We had great times together. It was one of the best things I did when I was at Warsaw and her parents couldn't thank me enough. I really appreciated their trust.

In the sixth week of our course, Gail asked us to bring in some of our writings to read to the class. I brought three of my poems and, when I read them, it felt really good and I got very positive feedback from the class and especially from our teacher who seemed very impressed. When our writing course was almost over I talked to Gail about my writing and she said she would like to see more of my work. On our last day of class, we agreed on a time to get together when I would take some of my writing to her. She said she was interested in seeing my poems as well as some of the sermons I had written over the years. As busy as I was in the church, I began to feel more and more that my writing was important too. After Gail read what I had brought her, she had many suggestions. She said that perhaps I could write some stories from the manse, or a book of poems or a book of reflections. It was then I decided to take a week off for reflection. I took all of my writings to a Retreat Centre and worked on my writing feverishly, day and night. I had no idea what I was doing, or what I might come up with, but I was excited about the possibilities. It was great to feel so creative and energized. As I went through my sermons and poems, I found writings that stood out and, by the end of five days, I had more than enough material to fill a small book. It wasn't long after I got home that I met with Gail. She was very excited about the work I had done and looked on these writings as reflections that, on their own merit, could be made into a book. I knew she had her own publishing company and she told me she was willing to consider helping me publish a book. I began to think about what this might look like. I had an idea. Edna Clysdale was a wonderful person who had done missionary work in Tibet for many years and was the pianist in the Warsaw church and she lived with her sister June in Lakefield. June did beautiful calligraphy so I went to see them. I told June what I was doing and asked her if she would be interested in working with me on this project. She said she would and wanted to see some of my writing. When I showed her some things that I had brought with me, her creativity kicked in and she gave me some ideas of how the writing would look. I got really excited and so did June. We both knew it was a wonderful collaboration and when I showed Gail some of June's calligraphy, she was very keen on the idea. The three of us got together for a meeting and we were on our way. It was a great start.

Near the end of November, Warren had a car accident. He called and assured me he was alright and told me what had happened. When he was driving to university that morning it was a very snowy, blizzardy day and he had stopped at a stop sign just before turning onto the Queen Elizabeth Highway. He said he looked both ways and then, suddenly, this car came flying down the hill out of the blue just as he started out and hit him on the driver's side of the car. He told me that a bus was coming the other way and the driver pulled the bus off the road and ran over to see if he was alright. Warren couldn't open his door so he rolled down his window to get out of his car. He told the bus driver he was fine but his car was totaled. The police came and Warren was charged, even though the officer said he was sure the young man that hit his car was speeding. Unfortunately, that couldn't be proven. The young man who hit Warren's car was also a student at McMaster and had told the officer that he had an important test that day and was running late. When a tow truck took Warren's car away, he got on the Go Train which wasn't far from the accident site and made it to his classes. I was so relieved that Warren was alright but now he didn't have a car. In that telephone conversation, Warren also told me how unhappy he was with the family he was living with, especially the mother who had all kinds of rules and regulations. He told me he wanted to live with Susie, which would be especially useful now that he didn't have a car and her apartment was only a 10 minute walk to the Go Train. I told him I would come down that Saturday and we would talk to Susie to see if she would like to have him come and live with her. It turned out that Susie was happy to have him come and stay and he could have Louise's bedroom. Warren and I went over to where he was living and I talked to the family. The mother tried very hard to get him to stay but he couldn't wait to leave and ran up the stairs to his bedroom to get all his things. Warren lived with Susie until he graduated in 1995 and it turned out to be a very good arrangement for both of them. He was happy there and she was very happy with Warren's company.

My life was very busy. I was preparing services for Sundays and led in worship and preaching which I loved. I went to the hospital when there was a family member from the congregations there, visited in nursing homes in Peterborough and attended our monthly Presbytery meetings. Then there was the pastoral care and all the visiting I needed to do in my congregations. On top of that, it looked like I might be getting a book published in time to have the book launch in April 1990 and I had lots of work to do before then. When I had the writing ready, June would still need to do the calligraphy.

Back in August, as I was leaving New Liskeard, I had written to Reverend Cliff Plant, the Personnel Officer for Manitou Conference, but hadn't heard back from him until I got his letter dated December 21, 1989 where he said:

> "In June I received your letter telling of your new challenge as you moved to the Warsaw charge. Now this letter does not break any records for a prompt response but it does indicate that you have not been forgotten! You did a significant work in ministry at New Liskeard. You have left your mark in ministry in Temiskaming Presbytery and Manitou. I remember that evening we sat in the basement of the church and heard the overwhelming support for the decision and of your courageous act in dealing with a very insidious situation in the congregation. That one act alone has enriched the life of the congregation and altered the thinking of a significant number of clergy and lay people in the church. You proved that clergy can have creative ways of dealing with intolerable situations."

Cliff's letter made me stop and think about what I had done at New Liskeard as I remembered all my friends there and the wonderful support they had been through a painfully difficult time. It was so kind of Cliff to write me and remind me of the good ministry I had had at St. Paul's and I deeply appreciated his letter.

In early December 1989 Warren wrote his exams but he wasn't feeling very good about his first semester at university. In fact he didn't do well at all, which surprised me. It turned out that his high school didn't teach the calculus or some of the math courses he needed before going into engineering. He came home from university upset about what was happening to him so I arranged for a tutor in Peterborough to teach him over the next few months off and on when he was home, and that turned out to be very helpful. Once he got settled in for the holiday break, we got out the Christmas tree, set it up together and decorated the house like we always had. Susie was coming for a week over Christmas and Warren and I went down and got her on the 23rd, in time for my first Christmas Eve service at the Warsaw Church the next evening. The service was wonderful and Susie and Warren loved it. The congregation went all out to decorate their church and it looked beautiful. Warren sang in the Choir. After the service, we invited people over to our home for hot apple cider, coffee, tea and desserts and about 30 people came. After everyone left Warren opened one Christmas present and then we sat around and listened to

Christmas carols and visited as we played cards. I told Warren and Susie about the book that I might get published and showed them the mock up for it, some of the writings for the book and June's calligraphy. Warren and Susie thought that it was really great. After Warren and Susie went up to bed, I filled up Warren's Christmas stocking and had to laugh to myself as I did it knowing my son wasn't yet old enough to give that up. I also thought about Louise and how much I missed her. She would have loved being with us in Warsaw.

The next morning was Christmas Day and it was a wonderful day with Warren and Susie. When it was time to open our presents there was one little glitch. Susie was very excited to open her present from Warren because it was fairly large and wrapped in lovely Christmas paper. But when she opened it and looked at it, she wasn't quite sure what it was. When Warren told her it was an electric air freshener she wasn't at all pleased. Susie smoked up a storm every day in the apartment but she never inhaled so all the smoke went into the dining room and living room and kitchen. Warren was finding it hard to breathe and he knew that Susie wasn't going to stop smoking. His way of addressing this problem was to give her an air freshener. Well, she was not impressed. Warren told her she had to keep it on all the time and he would make sure to replace the filters. In the end she gave in but, I must say, I enjoyed seeing the two of them interacting in the way they did. After all the presents were opened, I started to work on the turkey and the dressing for dinner. We played bridge most of the afternoon with Christmas carols playing in the background and had a great time. Christmas was a welcome break for me from the busyness of the ministry and I felt very relaxed. My little sister had come over and brought a present for me, Warren and Susie and we had presents for her. We talked to Jana Christmas Day and she was having a wonderful Christmas with her family. By the time I took Susie home before the New Year, the time seemed to have gone by so quickly but Warren stayed on with me and I took him back to Susie's around January 10th so he could get ready for university. We had had another wonderful Christmas together and it felt comforting to know that some things don't change.

So how does one get a book published? Gail had formed a company called Woodland Publishing in Peterborough and she had an ISBN number and worked with a particular printing company whenever she helped someone get a book published. She was willing to do that for me and I really appreciated this. I knew many people, so I was in charge of the distributing and marketing. I knew there would be no money to be made but that wasn't the reason I was committed to writing this book. I believed that I had something to say and that what I was now writing and putting together could help other people. I had asked the Very Reverend Lois Wilson, a friend and colleague in ministry who had been a Moderator of our Church from 1980-82, if she would consider writing the preface for my book and she asked me to send her a copy of my writings for this book. She wrote the preface and I was so pleased that she would do this for me. I called the 63 page book *Reflections - to ease the pain*.

It was a very creative and productive time for me as the book began to take shape. June was wonderful to work with and did beautiful calligraphy for it. When our work on the book was finished, Gail took June and I to the printers that she used. They had huge printing presses which took me back to my Uncle Phil and his work as a newspaperman. He had taken me a few times to the newspaper office where he worked and I had loved the distinctive smell of ink and printing. Here I was again, experiencing that same smell and the excitement of the presses running. But, in this case, it was my book to be published. It was a wonderful feeling as June and I watched this process for the first time.

Before it was published, we discussed how we would try to sell the book. I had written to friends and family, as well as people I knew in the church and outside the church, to ask if they would be interested in buying a copy of my book. It was a lot of work but I wanted to get my book out there. Gail had 300 copies of the book printed off for April and we sold all of them except for the ones we kept for ourselves. The money that we made from this paid for the printing costs and an honorarium for June. The book launch was on a Sunday afternoon in April at Westdale United Church in Peterborough where Reverend Joan Henderson, a friend and colleague, was the minister. As the publisher, Gail looked after the setup for the book launch and was very pleased to see all the people who came. The women at the Warsaw Pastoral Charge, headed up by June Drain and Joan Hamilton, had coffee, tea and desserts there for this special event and my congregations were very happy that I was able to get a book published. There were speeches and introductions and June and I visited with everyone who came. I was especially happy that Warren came for the weekend and he took photos of me and June and Gail. It was a great feeling of accomplishment to have finally finished my book and have it so well received. I was so grateful to Gail for her encouragement and support and to June for her beautiful calligraphy. June's family was very proud of what she had done. It had been a very busy nine months since arriving at Warsaw and having a book published was the biggest surprise of all. Feeling so creative again felt wonderful in terms of my writing, preaching and having a Little Sister, but it all fit together.

Right after the first book launch, Gail suggested we work on another book similar to what I had written for the first one. She knew there were many writings we had not used and so was born the idea for a book I called, *More Reflections – to ease the pain*. Even though I didn't have the writing together yet, I needed to know if June would consider doing the calligraphy for this book too and she said she would. We were so happy to be working together again. It took me a while to focus on this new project but I wasn't worried since Gail wasn't looking to have the second book launch until April 1991. I had a lot of time to work on it.

Warren came home after writing his final exams and said he was sure he had failed some of his courses his first year at university. I was very concerned, but he would be home until the end of August and I knew we would have a lot of time to talk. It was wonderful to have him home and, during this time, he worked at Nephton Mine as an engineering student and was very excited about this internship. He couldn't wait to start. It was great to see him blossoming and being so happy after such a rough year at university. At one point in this internship, his boss had to be away for a couple of days and he put Warren in charge. He was very proud to be entrusted with this responsibility and took it very seriously. When Warren was told by some of the workers that one of the biggest machines had broken down and could not be fixed, he wasn't sure what to do because he knew the cost of a new machine would be around $500,000.00. He called his boss and told him what was happening. The boss told Warren he was in charge and, if this new machine was needed, to go ahead and order it. It gave Warren a huge boost in confidence that his boss would trust him to the extent that he did. On Mother's Day that year, Warren gave me a card that showed his great sense of humour. It said;

"Happy Mother's Day from your son. Mom, you always created such a warm, comfortable home, you're a great housekeeper and cook… you're such an understanding listener… so sensitive and caring.. And you're such fun to be with! Can I move back home? Scared you didn't I? Happy Mother's Day, Love Warren."

When Warren found out he had failed his first year of university as he feared he would, he wrote a letter to the Associate Dean at the Faculty of Engineering explaining why he had had such a difficult time with calculus and math. He also explained that he had had a tutor for calculus from January to April and his marks had come up, but just not enough and that was why he had failed. The Faculty responded that they would allow Warren to come back and redo his first year and he was very relieved about that. At the end of the summer, he got high praise from his Supervisor at Nephton Mine for his work there. All in all, he had a wonderful summer working at the Nephton Mine, being at home, going out with friends and singing in the choir at Warsaw United Church. Now that he would be able to redo his first year, he was ready to take that on as well and would go on to do very well.

My sister had told me, that first Christmas at Warsaw, that she was coming to see me for two weeks in July 1990, and I was so excited to have her come for a visit. I sent Jana a copy of my book when it was published and she told me she was so happy for me and that she loved my book. I met Jana at the airport and it was just wonderful to see her and we talked all the way as we drove to Warsaw. When we got to the house, Warren was home from work and he was very happy to see Aunty Jana and they had a great visit together. She loved the big house I lived in as it reminded her of our home in Oakville. Jana also came to church with me and I introduced her to many of the families at the Warsaw Church. After church that morning, Jana and I sat outside on my deck looking out over the river when she asked me why I had come to Warsaw. She said she liked the people whom she had met and they were all very nice to her but she was wondering why I had come to do ministry here. She said they were very much country people and said it had to be very different for me from New Liskeard which was a much, much larger community with so many things easily accessible. It was hard to explain to my sister why I was here. I told her it was a call and that I was very sure of that. I told her that the people who had come from Warsaw to New Liskeard to hear me preach were wonderful people. I had made a connection that first time I met them and I felt at that time there was something there and so I went down for the interview. I knew Warsaw wasn't a place my sister would feel comfortable living in because she had lived almost 30 years in Sacramento, a huge city with everything available all of the time. I think she thought this was a step back for me coming from New Liskeard to Warsaw. I didn't see it that way and for me it was a call. Jana and I set about making the most of her visit and we went down to Oakville for a few days to visit with Susie who was very happy to see Jana and wanted to hear all the news. We all swam in the pool and had a great time. We also went to Niagara Falls for a day to see Aunty Marion (Keifer), my godmother, and visited Olive and Peter Habjan in Wainfleet and Olive's mother Mrs. Tina Matthews in Welland and Jana's best friend Mary Jane Ferrell in Welland. Of course, we also went to Port Colborne to see all the neighbours on Borden Avenue where my sister had grown up. After we got back home, Jana and Warren and I spent a day at the Sandbanks and went swimming in Lake Ontario. We told Warren about the wonderful times we had had at the cottage there and at the Lakeshore Lodge next door. We had a great visit but, as always, it was way too short.

In early September The Right Reverend Sang Chul Lee, who was born in Siberia and immigrated to Canada, was the first Asian moderator of the United Church of Canada from 1988 to 1990. He came to visit us at Warsaw one day during the week and it was quite an honour to have him there. All the churches in Peterborough Presbytery knew he would be at our church to talk with anyone who came to meet him and he wasn't at the church for very long before Joyce Payne took me aside and said, 'Dorinda, the toilet facilities have overflowed'. She was very embarrassed. Joyce was our representative to Peterborough Presbytery and an active member on the Mission Committee in Presbytery which I chaired so Joyce and I knew each other pretty well. The bathroom we had in the basement was tiny with an earth floor and only had one disgusting toilet in it that didn't flush and had to be cleaned out by hand. For years the women at the Warsaw Church had wanted a new kitchen and proper washroom facilities but the men didn't want to spend the money. Aside from the washroom and the kitchen, we also needed to put a ramp in outside to make the church accessible. There were a lot of steps going up into the church and some people had difficulty getting into the church. Joyce asked me if we could use the washroom in the manse and I of course said yes. I knew how determined the women were to have proper washroom facilities, an accessible ramp and a new kitchen in their church and they had my support in finding a way to make that happen. Since I had done a lot of fundraising over the years, I believed that we could raise the money for the renovations but everyone, including the men, had to be on board. Now with the Moderator there and the washroom facility being in such bad repair, there was even more reasons to push ahead and get this done. Our next Board meeting was coming up at the end of September and I encouraged the women to bring this issue up then. I conducted all the business at this Official Board meeting at Warsaw United Church and there were 20 people present. When I asked for new business, Joyce Payne spoke. She talked to the Board about the church and having the kitchen renovated and a washroom put in as well as an outside ramp to make the church more accessible. The men could understand the issue but were definitely opposed to spending the money. I talked to them about how much this church meant to people in Warsaw. Even though most people in the community didn't come to church, I told them, I was very sure that people all over Warsaw and the greater area would give money to make this project happen. I assured them that we could do this and that our Presbytery would support us in getting a loan up to $35,000.00 from the United Church of Canada. The men reluctantly agreed and a motion was made and passed to proceed with the renovations. The women were thrilled. A Building Committee of eight people was set up which included Joyce and myself. We set about immediately getting two quotes and decided on the one for $109,000.00. Joyce got the forms from Presbytery that we needed in order to ask for funds from the United Church of Canada. The next step would be to start raising money to build in the spring of 1991.

The United Church of Canada approved our loan for $35,000.00 and money literally came pouring in from the community when we put the word out. It was a huge project for this little church but you could feel the energy increasing with every day. The committee worked with the Contractor and we were on site every day to see what he was doing and if he needed anything. This was a struggling congregation trying to keep their church open. In the beginning, the men never believed that we could raise that kind of money, but I knew they could do it. People in the church and community made the commitment and it was amazing to see. When all was said and done, we were able to return the $35,000.00 loan to the United Church of Canada within eight months of fund raising. I felt very proud to be part of this and to be able to help them. The women were thrilled to have a new kitchen and washroom facilities and we had a very solid ramp as well.

Back in January 1990 I had decided to give a full piano concert in October to help raise money for two of my congregations and designated 85% of the money raised for this concert to go to the Building Fund of Warsaw United Church and the other 15% to Zion United Church. We needed a larger church for my concert and St. James United Church in Peterborough had a grand piano so the congregation kindly gave us their church for that evening and the kitchen which would be used for the reception that would follow. There was an article written in one of the local papers about my upcoming concert which said:

> *"The Reverend Dorinda Vollmer, Minister of the Warsaw Pastoral Charge, is a woman of many accomplishments and talents. Her grounding in reality is evident in her ability to relate to people from all walks of life encompassing, as it has, pastoral charges as diverse as the Roseau River Indian Reserve, Grand Valley and New Liskeard. In addition to her calling as a minister, Rev. Vollmer is a pianist, composer, graphic artist, poet and writer… … … Her poetry and visual art arose out of her experience on the reserve. Her poetry is very moving, filled with compassion and understanding for the pain of others. Her paintings are striking, bold representational works of tremendous strength and individuality. 'I wanted to take the pain and suffering that I saw and turn it into something positive and good,' Rev. Vollmer says. Dorinda feels that the measure of a society is determined by how we care for each other… … Rev. Vollmer believes her gifts have been given to her as a means of giving to and sharing with others… … She explains, the music is part of that. Getting ready for a recital is very challenging and exciting."*

I called this concert, *Lightly Classical* because I knew that most people in my congregations loved country western music. So I played easy-to-listen-to classical music by Bach, Chopin,

Beethoven, Mozart and four of my own compositions as well as a few popular tunes. The concert was held at St. James United Church in Peterborough Sunday, October 21, 1990 at 8:00 p.m. and the members of my four congregations had sold tickets for my concert. We raised $1,250.00. The concert went really well and everyone was very appreciative of what I had done. Gerry Hampton told me after the concert how much he enjoyed my music and especially the classical pieces I played since it wasn't the kind of music he usually liked or listened to. For me, that was a great compliment and I appreciated it. Many people at the concert asked me when I was giving another one and I said I would certainly think about it. I remember Donna and Gerry's granddaughter asking me for an autograph and I signed her program. That was a big deal for her and I realized how much this concert meant to her as a young person and that impressed me.

I had had great success and joy with the young people in both Grand Valley and New Liskeard so I decided to open my home to young people ages 12-18 in Warsaw who would like to come for a movie night on Friday evenings twice a month. I started this in September 1990 and I had about 15 young people come including my little sister and they were a great group of kids. I just wanted to be there as a friend to them and I always had lots of snacks and treats for them. We had a great time and, sometimes, before the movie, we would have a discussion on any topic they wanted to talk about. One of the topics that interested them was the Gulf War. Many disagreed with it but a few didn't so we had quite a lively discussion on this and war in general. Most of the young people wanted to watch a horror movie and I let them use my bedroom which, of course, they thought was so cool because I had all those horror posters on the walls. There were always three or four of the young people who didn't want to watch a horror movie so I would watch something else with them in my living room. On occasion, I would quietly go upstairs and bang on the bedroom door and open it to scare them to death. They loved it. They were a great group of young people who came to my home for two years and we had good times together.

I also started writing a weekly column for the *Norwood Register*. The first one appeared on November 7th and I kept this up until July the following year. I called my column, *"It Seems To Me"* after a column of the same title my uncle had in the newspaper he worked for in Oakville. I found it was a lot of work to write a column and prepare a sermon and work on my new book but I was writing and that felt really good. Also on November 7th, I wrote a letter to St. John's United Church in Oakville at Reverend Jim Campbell's request to tell the congregation what had been happening to me since I had been ordained. I brought them up to date and in part said:

> *"The ministry has enriched my life. It has been a privilege to serve God's people where God had called me to go. I enjoy ministry as much today as I did when I first began. I have also done work in the Presbyteries and Conferences I have been in…..and I was a Commissioner to General Council in 1988 in Victoria…..My son Warren is now 20 years old. He is just a joy and such a nice young man. He is attending McMaster University in Hamilton studying Engineering. He has discovered Philosophy and loves it. He sings in St. John's United Church Senior Choir and really enjoys it…...I always come back to St. John's to visit. From a young child you nurtured me and helped me to grow in faith. Reverend*

Terry was a source of inspiration for me as I listened to his sermons as a child Sunday after Sunday. Reverend Jim Campbell was a real source of strength for me. He believed in in me and encouraged me, never doubting God was calling me. You never wavered in your support to me as a candidate for the ministry (1973-76). Thank you again for your love from those early beginnings to the present. You are always in my heart."

I couldn't wait for Warren to come again for three weeks over Christmas. Of course, Susie came for a week and again we had a wonderful Christmas together. Warren was much happier and more confident this year and had done so well this past semester at McMaster. I was so happy to have him home again and seeing him so content really pleased me.

I went down to Oakville in early February 1991 to visit with Susie and Warren. Susie asked me to get something from Warren's room and, when I went in, I saw a woman's bathing suit hanging from the top of the bookcase. I was surprised and wondered if Warren had a girlfriend. When he came home, I asked him about the bathing suit and he said that was just a friend's bathing suit from university and then added, "But I do have a girlfriend. We have just started dating and her name is Susan". There was something about the way he looked at me when he said those words that I knew he was serious about this girl. I was so happy for him and he told me they had met at McMaster through a mutual friend. I told him I would like to meet her sometime and he said I would. From there I went to Sacramento for 10 days to visit my sister. Ken's four children, Monty, Nicki, Steve and Derek lived with them, as well as my niece Stacy and nephew Scott and they were so happy to see me. Jana and Ken and I went out for dinner and the theatre together, saw movies, and went to Old Sacramento to see all the sights and go on the river cruise. I couldn't have had a better time with my family. I drove from the airport to Oakville to see Susie and Warren for a couple of days before I went back home.

I was right back into ministry visiting and attending meetings, as well as getting together with my Little Sister Vicky and I also had work to do for my next book. My writings for the book were done and June had all the calligraphy done except for the preface. Before I left on holidays, I had asked Dr. Anne Squire, who was the Moderator of the United Church of Canada from 1986-1988 if she would consider writing the preface for my second book. I had sent her my writings and she said she would be pleased to write a preface and it was waiting for me when I got home. As soon as June finished doing the calligraphy for that, Gail, June and I went over to the printers and saw some of the pages of the book run off. June and I still had that same feeling of excitement seeing a second book published. Everything had gone very well with this book and the second book launching was scheduled for April 7th, 1991. It was held at Westdale United Church. The women again prepared a tea for everyone and everything went really well.

Back in November I had decided to do another concert for the Warsaw church. Even though most all the money had been raised for their Building Fund, Warsaw United Church still needed financial support. On Sunday, April 14th 1991 at 8:00 p.m., I gave a concert again at St. James United Church in Peterborough. This time I called it *Lightly Classical and Movie Themes*. This concert was as successful as the last one and raised $1,200.00. I told stories and talked about some of the classical composers, which was a little different from previous concerts I had given, but I liked doing this and building a relationship with the audience.

In the meantime, I was anxiously waiting to meet Susan. Warren had dated in the past but I had never met anyone that he had gone out with. From the time Warren had told me about Susan, I just had a feeling she was the one. Finally, Warren called and said he wanted me to come down and meet Susan. I can't begin to describe my joy at that moment and I was so excited to be meeting her. We arranged to meet at the foot of Trafalgar Road in Oakville at Lake Ontario. It was a beautiful spring day and, when I got out of my car, I saw them there. Warren was so happy to introduce me to Susan and I liked her right away. I could see that she was as happy with Warren as he was with her. They just clicked and I could see that. Susan had a lovely smile and was 5'8" with natural curly brown hair. She wore glasses and had a slender build. I noticed she wore a top that said *I Don't do Mornings,* which I commented on and I could see she had a great sense of humor. We had a nice walk along the lake and I was absolutely sure this was the woman my son would spend the rest of his life with. I was so happy that they had found each other. A few weeks later, I went down again. Warren was coming in from the university and Susan and I were waiting for him at a coffee shop near the Go station. We had a great talk and I told her I was so happy for her and my son. I felt grateful that she trusted me enough to share some personal things with me and I appreciated that conversation.

Susie, of course, saw a lot of them together in the apartment and she also liked Susan very much. Susan really liked Susie too and found her to be quite the character. Susie was already over 80 by then, about 4'6" and very stooped over, and like the majority of us she had not aged well. She still had her lovely wavy brown hair but with some white in it and she always had that mischievous look on her face which told you she was up to something. There was one contentious issue however, because Susie loved to go around naked in the apartment, especially after she had a shower. Susan saw her a couple of times like that so Warren had to sit Susie down and tell her that she had to have her clothes on when Susan was there. She understood what Warren was asking her to do so she was really good about it after that.

One day a member in one of our congregations talked to me about her daughter who had been sexually abused by an Elder in this Pastoral Charge 20 years earlier when her daughter was a child. I told the woman I would be more than willing to talk with her daughter about this when she was home for a visit and, that June, she asked if she could bring her daughter over because she wanted to talk to me. When they arrived, I could see that the daughter was very agitated. She told me that, when she was eight years old in the 1960s, the family was living at Nephton where her dad worked at the mine. As in every small community, everyone was very close and knew each other. She said there was a custodian who worked there and it turned out he liked little girls. This young woman had been one of the young children he targeted and sexually abused yet this man was never charged. She told me that what had happened to her as a child haunted her. It was still very much a part of who she was and made it hard for her to trust people. She had always had a lot of problems keeping a relationship but now had finally found someone she had fallen in love with. Still, it was hard for her to trust him. All she wanted was for someone other than her mother to believe her about what had happened to her and to find closure.

Back in the late 60s, early 70s, no one talked about molesting children. We didn't even know there was a term for that - a pedophile. According to her mother, people at the Nephton Mine knew what this man was doing to children but there was this wall of silence and they turned a blind eye because he was the brother of the owner of the mine. People were afraid that if anything was said against him, they would lose their jobs. From the beginning, the girl's mother had believed her daughter when she finally told her what had happened to her, but many parents did not believe their children and that was part of the problem. No one talked about this openly at that time and people wouldn't believe someone would do these horrible things to children. The mother told me he had been an Elder in our Pastoral Charge for years but that he had moved into Peterborough years earlier and had transferred his membership to a church there. Now he was in his late 60's, retired and had grandchildren. I was shocked to learn he was active member in Peterborough Presbytery because I attended Presbytery meetings but I didn't know him.

I felt so badly for this young woman. She was still very angry about the terrible things this man had done to her as a child and no one had said anything and no one except her mother had believed her. I asked her what she wanted to do and she told me she really didn't know. I told her I would be willing to call some of the Elders in our four churches and ask them if they could come to my home the next morning, a Saturday, to meet with her. I asked her if she would be willing to come and talk with them and tell them her story. She was surprised at what I was suggesting but didn't have to think about it for too long. "Yes', she said, "I would come". I told her that her mom was welcome to come with her and that I would set this meeting up and confirm with her later that evening. I spent a long time talking with her and her mom then I closed with a prayer and we all had a hug. She told me that she was so glad she had come to see me and thanked me.

That evening I called five Elders I trusted implicitly. I told them it was important for them to come to my home on Saturday morning but that I couldn't tell them what it was about on the phone. I asked each one if they trusted me and each one said they did. Every Elder I called said they would be there. I then called the mother and told her I had set up the meeting and she said she and her daughter would be there. On Saturday morning, when the Elders came in and sat down, the young woman and her mother were already at my house. All the Elders knew the mother but had not seen her daughter in years. I told them that this young woman had a story to tell them about herself and I asked them to please just listen to what she had to say. This young woman just poured out her heart and her pain and it was hard to hear. It was also hard to bear but she had borne the burden of this all alone since she was a child. Now we were being asked to help her bear the load. It was very emotional and difficult for the Elders to hear what this young woman was telling them. After all, she was talking about a man whom they had known and respected for years. She told the Elders that she had made a decision to come forward and tell her story after talking with me the day before because our conversation had given her courage and hope. She told us she was going to the public prosecutor in Peterborough to lay charges because she believed this man needed to pay for what he had done to her and to other young children at Nephton. It took great courage for this young woman to face these Elders and tell them her story but they believed her and told her they did and that gave her hope. During this difficult conversation, I noticed that one of the Elders was particularly upset and he told me after everyone was gone, that he was a personal friend of this man and had had no idea at all that he had done these terrible things. He was very shocked. This Elder was also a member of Presbytery and always looked forward to seeing his friend at Presbytery and having lunch with him. He told me he often wondered why he never saw his friend alone with his grandchildren. After this meeting at my home, he never spoke to him or had lunch with him at Presbytery again.

This young woman did go to the public prosecutor in Peterborough and he wanted to know who else this had happened to. She told him she knew of at least two other children who had been sexually molested by this man. The prosecutor contacted them and one of them couldn't bear to talk about it. The other woman was greatly relieved to know someone had come forward. She lived out west and the Prosecutor's office flew her back home to give her statement and to testify in court. This pedophile was arrested and charged and the newspapers reported the story, including his name. Many people who knew him were shocked to discover the horrifying things that he had done to children for years. All that young woman wanted was for the truth to come out and to feel some sense of justice so she could begin to heal and move on. It was so sad to think that the people we most trust are often the ones most responsible for the evil in the world.

Being a minister, there were always sad duties I had to perform and funerals were some of them. All the funeral services in my Pastoral Charge were conducted at Hendren Funeral Home in Lakefield and, when I arrived in Warsaw, one of the first things I did was to go over there to introduce myself to the Funeral Director, Larry Hendren and his wife Mary who also worked there. He showed me around and told me about how they did things but there were some procedures they had that I felt uncomfortable with. After the funeral service was over, Larry told me that he had everyone, including the minister, get up, get their coats on and go out. I told him that this was not what I did when I officiated at a funeral. I told him that, at the end of the funeral service, I had people stand and we all processed out with the casket. He didn't want to do that, so we had to find a compromise and that was for me to stay with the casket while everyone else went out. My understanding has always been that, when a minister comes into a funeral home to do a service it is the responsibility of the minister as to what happens in the service but, at Hendren's we found a way that worked for both of us. One of the funerals I presided over at Hendren's was a suicide. I received a phone call from someone in my congregation who said there had been a shooting. When I found out who had died I telephoned this person's wife, whom I knew but she did not go to our church. She asked me to come over. When I got to their home, I could see that the two people there were very distressed and I sat down with the grieving wife privately to talk. She told me that her husband hadn't gone to work that morning because he wasn't feeling well and he was upstairs asleep when her friend came over. They were having coffee and talking when they heard a thump upstairs that sounded like someone had fallen out of bed. She ran upstairs and found her husband on the floor. He had shot himself using a pillow to muffle the sound. She said her husband did have bouts of depression from time to time but she had no indication whatever that he would kill himself. She was shaking as she talked to me and I could tell she was in shock. She told me the police had already been to the house a few hours earlier and interviewed her and her friend. Then her husband's body had been taken to the coroner. She also said she was having cleaners and painters coming in to clean up the bedroom that afternoon because she couldn't bear to go up there again and look at the scene. I couldn't imagine what she was going through. She also asked me if I would do her husband's funeral.

When I arrived at the funeral home in Lakefield to do the service, I could see that the family was still in shock and grieving. The wife seemed so lost. She could hardly talk and just stood at the casket not knowing what to do. I did the best I could in the service and when it was over Larry came to lead all the people out and then came back for the family. The wife would not leave her husband and, if she wasn't leaving, neither were her children and their spouses. She just stood there sobbing and transfixed and I felt so badly for her. Larry didn't know what to do and I took him aside and told him she needed to stay where she was with her children for as long as she needed to and I would stay with them. He was very thankful at that moment that I was there and came back a couple of times to check in. I just stood beside the wife and I told her to take all the time she needed. It took quite a while for her to settle down and, when she finally told me she was ready, I went out with the family. It was the hardest funeral I officiated at because it reminded me of some of the terrible things that had happened at Roseau.

The one other funeral that stood out for me was also tragic but in a different way. There was a lovely woman I knew very well in one of our congregations who couldn't do enough for her church and was a very active member in the United Church Women's group. When her husband had a heart attack and died suddenly, a member of our church called me and told me what happened. When I called this woman, one of her daughters answered the phone and said her mother didn't want me to come over and would let me know when it was a good time. I had to respect what the family wanted but I found that very strange so I asked one of the members of the United Church Women's group who was a good friend of this woman's, if I could ask her some questions that would help me understand what the situation was. What she told me was very helpful.

The next day, the daughter called and asked if she could come to see me. She was very distraught and upset as she sat in my living room. I could see she was trying to tell me something but seemed unable to get the words out as she struggled with what she wanted to say. I knew instinctively that this couldn't be her normal behaviour and I began talking to her quietly. I told her that I knew her mother had been abused and beaten by her father and that, on occasion, her mother's friends at the United Church Women's group had seen bruises on her face but her mother had never said anything to anyone about how she got them. The daughter was so relieved that I knew and that she didn't have to explain. She told me that I couldn't say anything at the funeral about her father being a loving husband and father. I could feel her anger and rage as she spoke about her father and I understood completely. I asked her to trust me that I would do the service her mother needed me to do. It was a very hard service for me to prepare and, as I was working on it, I remembered back to that man in Dominion City who had abused his wife Ann on many occasions and how relieved she felt when he died. After the service was over, the daughter came over to me and could not thank me enough for what I had done for her mother and their family. Even in small communities there is domestic violence but the stress of trying to keep it a secret in a small community is very hard because everyone knows each other and sees each other on a regular basis. I can't imagine what this woman had gone through putting up with this abuse for over 30 years of marriage and trying to keep it hidden. She was not the only one in my Pastoral Charge that I knew this happened to. It is so tragic and I have never understood this kind of behavior and probably never will.

Warren was continuing to do very well in university and had been hired to work at the Canadian Centre for Inland Waters in Hamilton from April to the end of August as their student. He had his own office and enjoyed it there. I was impressed when I went to visit him with how official he looked in his jeans and shirt. He also made good money that helped with his university fees. When Warren told me that he and Susan would be coming home for a weekend in the summer, I was so happy to have them. I cooked up a storm for them and we had great conversations about how they were both doing at university and the friends they had made. I talked about the ministry and my friends at Warsaw and Susan loved to play cards and games as much as our family did. They noticed the canoe by the river and went out a few times in it. They paddled up and down the river and I could see how much they enjoyed each other's company. It was wonderful to have them home for the weekend.

In October, my Presbytery asked if I would consider taking the training for the Interim Ministry course and I said I would consider it. Having the Interim Ministry training meant that I could be flexible in where I went for one or two years at a time, working in a Pastoral Charge helping them sort out their concerns before calling a new minister. By this time, I had begun wondering how long I would stay at Warsaw since I was now in my third year there. Perhaps, I thought, this would be a way to do something different. I decided I would try out the course and see if it was for me. I really enjoyed it and felt I could be good at this kind of work. My teachers at this course thought I would be too. At that time, the United Church of Canada did not recognize Interim Ministers and so most ministers who took this training were, in a way, on their own unless a Presbytery like mine saw the value in having ministers get training for this kind of work. The first step was to take the training, which I did, and the second part would involve me having a Supervisor for three months when I was in a Pastoral Charge who needed an Interim Minister. Now the problem was that there wasn't a Pastoral Charge in our Presbytery that needed this kind of support. Nonetheless, taking the course was a good way to start. I really enjoyed it and learned a lot but I didn't see me going any further with it at that time. Still, it got me thinking about the future and what I would do next, after my time in Warsaw was done.

In November Gail had arranged for a book signing in Grand Valley, following the book launch for the second book we had back in April. I was really looking forward to doing this and seeing all my friends there again. Some of the United Church Women at Trinity United Church had kindly agreed to put on a tea for that afternoon and, since June was unable to go, Gail and I went together. We got there before lunch to make sure we had everything set up for the event since it was scheduled to begin around 2:00 p.m., and there were my friends, Jean Boggs and June Maycock and others from the Monticello and Trinity congregations. It was wonderful to see them again and I had a great time talking with everyone and catching up on all the news. The launch went over very well and there were speeches and introductions. I visited with all the people who came and Gail was very pleased that all the books we took were sold.

The process of writing my two books of reflections was a very rewarding one and, on January 5, 1992, an article was written in the *Oakville Beaver* about the publication of my second book and the article was titled, *Reflections on a Long and Winding Road."*

> *"When Rev. Dorinda Vollmer steps up to the podium every Sunday to address her small Warsaw congregation, she speaks from her heart, and her past. It's a heart that is occupied with compassion and love, and a past that's filled with heartache, suffering and doubt. Without such a warm heart, the past might have won out…….Her soothing poetry, excerpts from her life, her sermons and her faith, was published as More Reflections to ease the pain, a small softcover book… …..is an inspirational package of verses on topics ranging from creation to death and although it is directed at those needing comfort it can be enjoyed by anyone."*

Before we turned around, Christmas was upon us again. The years were flying by. Warren and Susie and I had a wonderful Christmas in Warsaw. Susie was now 83 and still feisty and still loved to laugh and have fun. She was pretty healthy overall and walked down to the Oakville Mall for groceries, which was a good 20 minute walk for her, and always found someone who would drive her back home. Susan had gone home to Ottawa for Christmas to be with her parents, Heather and Tom Wheat, and was really close to them being an only child. Needless to say Warren and Susan were often talking on the phone.

Warren and I had a chance during Christmas to talk seriously about his future. He was doing very well at university but, although he wanted to be in the electrical engineering program they had put him in the civil engineering program which he didn't want. He told me he had a lot of thinking to do that coming semester about what he would do next. He assured me he would complete the year and then decide what he wanted. I trusted Warren and I knew that, whatever decision he made in April would be right for him. With the new year coming, I knew changes would be coming for both of us. Then an Interim Ministry position came open.

Peterborough Presbytery asked me if I would consider going to the Millbrook Cavan Pastoral Charge July 1st 1992 because their minister was leaving in June. Presbytery wanted them to have an Interim Minister for a year before calling a minister. Since I had taken the course which was the first part of my Interim Ministry training I would have to have a Supervisor for the field work. Presbytery would set up an interview at Cavan if I was interested. I told the Presbytery I would go for an interview and they set it up for the end of February. There were about 12 people there from the Millbrook and Cavan churches and the meeting went very well. I thought this was a good representation of people from both churches who just wanted to sort out some issues they had in their Pastoral Charge before they called a minister. I told them I had to have a Supervisor for the first three months I was there in order to complete my Interim Ministry training and they were fine with that. So, with Presbytery representation there, I agreed to work with them. They provided a salary, travel allowance and a manse as well as other benefits and I accepted. I asked Reverend Joan Henderson to be my Supervisor. She was the minister at Westdale United Church in Peterborough and she agreed to supervise me. Everything at that end was now in place. I had a contract with the church to do Interim Ministry for a year and then I would either find another Interim Ministry contract or move on to another Pastoral Charge.

I had already talked with Warren and Susie and my sister about this and now I told them I had signed the contract and was moving to Millbrook in July. Susie said she was very happy because Millbrook was even closer and that made me laugh. She was right, that would make the drive to Oakville easier for sure and just over an hour. Warren thought it was very good I had taken this training and, if I was happy with this change, he was fine with it. Now I had to tell my Pastoral Charge that I was leaving. I told them at our Board meeting in March that I was leaving June 30th and I explained to the Board that since I now had the training to do Interim Ministry, the Presbytery had asked me to accept a one year appointment at the Millbrook Cavan Pastoral Charge and I had accepted. I told them it had happened very quickly and I had not planned for this. They said they were very sorry I was leaving. They told me they had hoped I would stay longer but I told them I knew this was the right place to go.

I also had to tell my Little Sister Sarah that I was leaving and that was hard too. She was 15 years old and we had had three fun-filled years together. She had turned into a very confidant and outgoing young teenager and we had had lots of serious talks about her education and her plans for the future. She wanted to be a lawyer. I told her to dream big and she was doing just that. I felt I had made a huge impact on her life and she was growing into a fine young woman who definitely had a mind of her own. She was still quirky and funny and still had a great sense of humor. I was very proud of her and the influence I had on her life at that time. I went out for lunch with Gail and told her that I was moving. I couldn't begin to tell her how much it had meant to me that she had encouraged and supported me in getting, not one, but two books published. She said she had really enjoyed our collaboration with me and she was very happy for me.

Warren had to make a decision as his university year was coming to an end. He finished his third year in April with two years completed in Engineering but he didn't get into the Electrical Engineering program and told me he had decided not to continue. He would switch to Philosophy, which was another interest of his because he loved to debate. I supported him in this decision. He stayed with Susie that summer and worked at odd jobs like stripping paint off a house and then working at a factory. He had another good summer and was saving his money. Susan had gone home for the summer but they would do their best to find time on weekends to get together when they could.

In the early 1990s Marie Sopinka invited me to visit her in Ottawa. Marie had been my Grade 10 french teacher in high school in Oakville. She was maybe ten years older than me and my aunt taught her children piano lessons. I don't know how we became friends but we did and for many years even after I moved away from Oakville, whenever I returned home I would visit at her home in Oakville and she was a good friend to me. Marie's husband John Sopinka was a lawyer and, on May 24, 1988, he was appointed to the Supreme Court of Canada as a Supreme Court Justice, the first Ukrainian-Canadian appointed to the High Court. John and Marie moved to Ottawa but I continued to keep in touch with her through letters over the years. They had a huge house and it was great to see them again. They had a gorgeous grand piano in their living room and since John was a wonderful violinist, he asked me to play a duet with him on the piano. He was very excited to have someone to play with him and told me he had been practicing this Mozart sonata for piano and violin for quite a while. I told him I loved Mozart and I would try to play this piece with him but we would have to go slowly at first until I learned it. Up until that time, I had done some accompaniment on the piano for individuals and choirs but I always had time to work on the pieces before we practiced. Luckily I was a good sight reader but I was worried I wouldn't be able to do the music justice. However, I did my best and we were playing together beautifully and going along at quite a pace when I suddenly heard a thump and stopped playing. I looked down and saw that the pedals had fallen off the piano. John and I were shocked and we both got down on our hands and knees to see what had happened. The entire mechanism that connected the pedals to the piano was on the floor. John asked if I could fix it but I had no idea how to do that. Then John asked if I could play with him without the pedals and, even though I knew it wouldn't be as easy I said I could, and we carried on. It was wonderful to play with John. He loved music with as much passion as I did.

When Marie called us for lunch, John went out to help and I followed along soon after but since I have no sense of direction, I went the wrong way and ended up in what appeared to be a bedroom. Marie came along and rescued me and we laughed at how I had gotten lost in this huge house. Then she told me the what happened when they first moved in. Marie said she knew that the RCMP was responsible for looking after the safety of the Supreme Court Justices and that there was a connection in their house that went directly to the RCMP. She knew that the RCMP was constantly watching the house and kept surveillance on who went in and out but she worried about how long it would take for them to get there if anything ever happened. One day, John was at work and Marie was having a new carpet laid. One of the workers was working on the rug near the front door and, suddenly, someone knocked at the door. When Marie opened the door, several RCMP officers were standing there and more officers were on her lawn and on the street and they had even closed down their street. The officers came into the house and accosted the man who was laying the rug. Evidently, he had accidently cut through the wire that was connected to the RCMP offices. The officers had arrived in an instant and Marie said that she never again worried about whether the RCMP would come quickly if or when she or her family ever needed help. It was a sad day for Marie and her children when John died on November 30th 1997. The service was held in St. Jude's Anglican Church in Oakville and I attended. I wanted to be there for Marie and Melanie and Randy. It was a very emotional service and a great loss for Canada. Marie and I continue to keep in touch and I have always valued her friendship.

Around the middle of April a woman came to my door. She lived in a community near Newmarket and had family in the Peterborough area that she occasionally came to visit. Her name was Cheryl and she was about 5'4", of medium build with short hair and she was my age. Someone in her family had told her about me and she wondered if I would counsel her. I told her I didn't do counselling but I could listen if she wanted to talk and she said she would like that and I told her I did not charge anything. She came to see me once a week for six weeks and I got to know her and I liked her. She talked with me about her parents and issues she had and about the accounting work she did from home at which she made a very good living. She told me she was fairly well off and had her own home. She also talked about a man much older than herself whom she had been involved with years ago and she talked about her friends and her loneliness. She said she was single, didn't live with anyone and never had. I found her interesting and she reminded me of Lee who had asked me if I would come and talk to her and we had become friends. Well after six weeks I felt that we had gone as far as we could and she thanked me very much. She knew I was moving to Millbrook and she asked me if she was in the area if she could take me out for lunch sometime and I said I was fine with that but I didn't expect to see her again.

I had really enjoyed my time at Warsaw. The people were wonderful, very open and accepting, and we had a lot of fun together. I had a good ministry there and had worked long hours visiting, attending meetings, sharing stories, having dinner with families, preparing services and sermons and attending Board, Session and congregational meetings as well as attending the monthly Presbytery meetings, chairing the Mission Committee of Presbytery, co-chairing and later chairing the Ministry Personnel and Education Committee of Bay of Quinte Conference and attending the yearly Bay of Quinte Conference meetings. I had worked closely with the Clerks of Session at each of the four churches. I had also helped the Warsaw Church with their huge renovation project which had been a great success. In addition I had given two benefit concerts for my churches and had two books published. Without a doubt it had been another very creative period of my life.

The congregations gave me a wonderful party before I left. Some of the young people in the youth group came and it was really nice to see them. Warren came home for this and everyone was very happy to see him again. The congregations presented me with a painting of the four churches I had served, something which I greatly appreciated. This time it wasn't as hard to say goodbye because I wasn't going far and I was still going to be in the same Presbytery.

Trinity United Church, Grand Valley, Ontario 1981

Me and my aunt Louise on one of our many picnics with the family August 1981.

My dear friend Jean Boggs who was the Clerk of Session at Trinity United Church.

Tempus Youth Choir in Oakville celebrating its 10th Anniversary August 19, 1981. From the front row from the left – Fran Lunshot, Cindy Craig, Ellen de Boer and me. At the back row from the left – Mike Dinsmore, Paul Hansun, Marie Donaldson, the Director and Founder of Tempus - Brian Turnbull, Brenda Fredrick and Bill Lemming.

My wonderful neighbours across the road, June and Wayne Maycock with their children, Julie, Adrienne and Warren.

Warren and me in front of Trinity United Church. We were on the front page of The Globe and Mail October 23rd, 1981 titled, "Unwed Mother Wins Respect in Ministry".

Warren with his great aunts. On the left is Louise who he called Weisa and Susie.

On January 11th, 1982 the "That's Life" TV crew came to Grand Valley to do a show on me and my family. Standing is Peter Feniak, the host of the show with one of the crew and Robbie Rowe and Warren on the far right.

Some of the young people who came to my home every Thursday during the school year. There are over 30 children in this photo September 1982.

Back row from the left is Ruth Hunter, her mom, Ursella Woodward, Mrs. Dodd and daughter, Shiela Hunter, a man and Paul Hunter sitting on Warren. Front Row from the left Mrs. Dodd's two daughters and in front Danny Neilsen then Ursala's daughter Cathy, and my nephew Steve Moon visiting us from Sacramento, California in the summer of 1983.

"Duo Keyboards" - the concert Liz Borman (the organist at Trinity United Church in Grand Valley) and I gave at my home church, St. John's United Church April, 1984. It was a benefit concert for Trinity United Church in Grand Valley. I am wearing my brown wig.

April 1984 my sister Jana was visiting me in Grand Valley. To her left is Stan Nelson celebrating his birthday at the church after the Committee of Stewards meeting at Trinity United Church.

I am in Freiburg Germany at the house of my aunt Maria, my father's sister, with her granddaughter Marian, my cousin.

Left to right is Brandon Borman, Warren, Danny Nielsen and Paul Hunter. All the boys are 14 to 15 years old. This was taken in August 1984 after Warren and I went to Europe.

*The tornado hit Grand Valley May 31st, 1985.
Trinity United Church was badly damaged beyond repair.*

The farewell party for me and Warren at Monticello United Church and some of the people there.

Ioan Shortt was reading the poem she wrote for us as Warren and I are sitting on the stage. I have my brown wig on.

St. Paul's United Church, New Liskeard 1985.

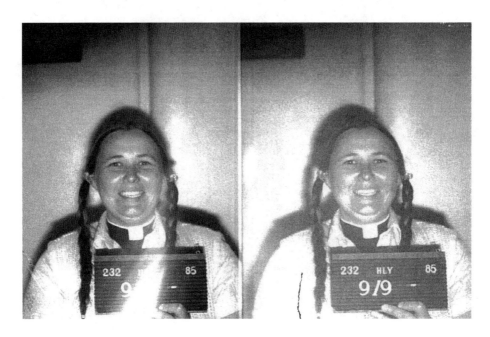

One of the correctional officers took a photo of me September 1985. I volunteered at the Haileybury jail once a week for two years.

Dorothy McClaren our church secretary and me. 1985.

My dear friend Nora Ladoceur and her husband Fern.

Don and Doriel Poupore with their daughter Tammy. Doriel was the organist at St. Paul's. They were wonderful friends. 1986.

Back row from the left Elaine Glassford, Bruce Glassford, Bill Glassford and in the front row my sister Jana and Ron Glassford in New Liskeard. Summer 1986.

In the background far left is Janet Berton. In the front is my nephew Scott Cannon, my sister Jana and behind her Warren and next to her Pierre Berton and my aunt Louise Pierre's aunt. Summer 1986 in Kleinburg, Ontario.

Susie, my sister Jana visiting from Sacramento, California and Louise on the patio at their apartment in Oakville, Ontario.

Pierre Berton and my aunt Louise in Kleinburg, Ontario.

Jana and me with our cousins Jessie and Al Stebbings in the summer of 1986.

At the apartment in Oakville with Warren and my sister Jana and seated on the chesterfield is Susie, Scott Cannon Jana's son and Louise. Summer 1986.

Warren with his great aunt he called Weisa Christmas 1986.

Warren's awards at the Army Cadet ceremonies in New Liskeard, June 1987.

Warren with Susie and Louise after his summer at Camp Borden 1987.

Warren with his cousins, Annie and Jim Nesbit at Carman Manitoba. August 1987.

Reverend Bill Whetter, me, Gertrude Whetter and Warren at their home in Winnipeg, Manitoba. August 1987.

At the Roseau River Indian Reserve, Manitoba in August 1987. Warren is with Chris Hayden.

Me and Betty Martin at Roseau. August 1987.

Warren is with aunty – Joyce Littlejohn McArthur - at the Band Office at Roseau August 1987.

Warren is in Dominion City. Manitoba with Jean Baskerville on the left and Audrey Pearce on the right, August 1987.

Warren is with Nina McArthur in Sperling, Manitoba. August 1987.

Warren is with Stephanie McArthur at Sperling, Manitoba. August 1987.

Brenda Fischer was one of my eight piano students at my home in New Liskeard December 1987.

*December 25th, 1987 at our home in New Liskeard.
Warren is with Odin who was a student from Norway staying with us.*

I went on a GATE program, Global Awareness Through Experience to Mexico City. Some of the group are walking into the barrio there which has 350,000 people living there. August 1988.

At the Canadian Embassy in Mexico City. Behind me is the Ambassador Raymond Chretien, Prime minister Chretien's nephew. We are with our group. August 1988.

I am just about to leave Mexico. On my left is Father Michel who was also in the GATE program. August 1988.

At the 1988 General Council in Victoria, B.C. in August for 10 days. I am with our newly elected Moderator, The Right Reverend Sang Chul Lee.

Best friends in New Liskeard on the left Sharon Reynolds, me, Vi Farrow and Anne Plaunt. In the fall of 1988.

Christmas December 26th 1988 in Sacramento California with my sister Jana on the right and sitting beside her is her step daughter Nicki Moon.

December 26th, 1988 and Warren is holding Jana's first grandchild and my great niece Brandi.

Warren is the leader at the ceremonies in June 1989 at New Liskeard. He just finished his last year of Cadets.

Susie came for Warren's high school graduation in June 1989.

Warren is walking up to receive his high school Diploma at New Liskeard Secondary School June 1989.

The going away party that St. Paul's United Church in New Liskeard had for me at the end of July 1989.

The cake for the party. On the left is Randy Lang and beside me is Tammy Poupore.

Warsaw United Church the first of my four churches at the Warsaw Pastoral Charge August 1989.

Inside Warsaw United Church. Me and Edna Clysdale our organist.

Bob and Joan Hobson from Carmel United Church.

Lu Cooper who lived in Warsaw and was the Treasurer of the Pastoral Charge.

My friends Donna and Gerry Hampton who are in Warsaw United Church.

Me and Maida Ormsby when I visited her in her home in Denman Island in B.C. in the summer of 2007. Maida was the Clerk of Session at Carmel United Church when I was at Warsaw 1989-92.

Ron and Mary Frankish. Ron was the Clerk of Session at Bethel United Church.

The book launch of my first book, "Reflections to ease the pain" April 1990 at Westminister United Church in Peterborough. In the back row left is Joan Hamilton from Bethel United Church, Gail Corbett my publisher and June Drain from Carmel United Church. In the front row is June Clysdale who did the beautiful calligraphy for my first book.

I am at my home in Warsaw at my piano preparing one of two benefit concerts I gave in the three years I was at Warsaw.

Me and my little sister Vicky in the spring of 1990.

Jana came for a visit in July 1990 and we are with Warren on the patio at the apartment in Oakville.

I met Susan Wheat, Warren's girl friend at the foot of Trafalgar Road in Oakville at Lake Ontario April 1991.

I am holding my second book at the time of the book launch in April 1991.

Me and June Clysdale who did the beautiful calligraphy again for my book. We are at the launch of my second book, "More Reflections to ease the pain" at Westdale United Church in Peterborough. April 1991.

On the left Edna Clysdale, June's sister visiting with Joan Hamilton and June Drain who again did a beautiful reception for the book launch.

The building committee of Warsaw United Church. From the back row left to right: Lloyd Payne, Ivan Clysdale, a man I don't remember, Lu Cooper, Joyce Payne, Ann Stabler, Dora Barr, Edna Clysdale, me and Noel Moore. Spring of 1991.

I did a book signing at Trinity United Church in Grand Valley November 1991. On the left is Ross Brown and me and on the far right is Grace Brown

CHAPTER TEN

Millbrook, a Period of Transition and More Changes

Moving to Millbrook was a huge step for me because it didn't offer the financial security I usually had. The contract was only for one year and I knew I would have to look for a Pastoral Charge next July. This was very different from my previous Pastoral Charges where I could stay as long as the congregation and I wanted to be in ministry together. But I wasn't really concerned at that time. The focus of this ministry was to help the congregations understand where they had come from, where they were now and where they wanted to be in the future. I was there to help them really look at themselves honestly and make better choices. Once they understood those things, they could move on and make a plan as to where they wanted to go in ministry. Reverend Joan Henderson had agreed to be my Supervisor and meet with me once a month from July until October when she would give her evaluation to Peterborough Presbytery with her assessment of my abilities as an Interim Minister. The manse where I would be living in Millbrook was a split level house with a lot of stairs. When you came in the front door, there was the church office just down the hall with a separate bathroom and a basement downstairs which I never used. When you went up the first few stairs, you walked into a large living room and dining room and, off that, a fairly large kitchen. Then you went up another few stairs to three bedrooms and a bathroom. There was a nice small front yard and out the back was a partly fenced in, very large backyard. Warren came home to help me move in. We unpacked boxes and organized and it wasn't long before I felt this was my home.

St. Andrews United Church was right across the road and looked like a small stone cathedral with a beautiful sanctuary that had a pipe organ and choir loft. There was also a huge basement which cost a lot of money to heat and look after. Cavan United Church, about 10 minutes away, reminded me of Warsaw United Church because it was an old, small brick church with a small sanctuary and basement. Fortunately, I was able to get to know the congregations very early on because I did what I always do - I visited families. But this time, I visited with more intent because of the focus of this ministry. I was really excited about the possibilities and met with the Official Board of the Charge in July to talk about what they needed to do. They were very open to the discussion and I talked with them about some of the things I hoped we would accomplish over the next three months. This meeting set the tone and everyone seemed very positive.

One of the first things I did when I was settled was call my sister and we had one of our long, serious talks that always helped both of us cope with what was happening in our lives at the time. I told her I was settled at Millbrook and that I felt it was the right place for me because I felt challenged in these congregations. I was doing a different ministry there than I had done before and hoped the Interim Ministry would help them. Jana was happy to hear I was settling in. Jana's life had also been going through changes. She had left Ken in the summer of 1990 after 10 years of marriage and I had been worried about her because she had never lived on her own and didn't like being alone. About a year later, though, she was in a new relationship with a man named George who was from Austria and had only been in the States 10 years. She didn't know if this relationship would work but she was willing to try. This was a very different and new phase in Jana's life because Ken's four children and her two children were grown up and on their own now. Everything was changing for both of us.

She asked me how Warren was and I told her he had come home for the going-away party they had for me in Warsaw and that had really helped me because I felt so badly leaving. The people in Warsaw had been so good to both of us. I talked about Warren's university experience and I told her he couldn't wait to begin his new major in Philosophy in September. Susan had gone home for the summer, I said, and Warren and Susan were both finding it hard being apart and looking forward to being together again at university in September. I asked her how Scott and Stacy were and she told me Scott was working for the forestry at Lake Tahoe and Stacy was doing fine. Her granddaughter Brandy was now four years old which was hard to believe, and Jana said she was as cute as ever and such a joy. Then she asked about Susie and I told her she was very happy I was now closer and looking forward to coming at Thanksgiving.

Over the next few months I really dove into the work of this ministry and had many meetings with members of the congregation. It was unusual to do that in the summer but I really needed to get on board quickly since I only had one year to do this ministry. In July, I presided over four weddings and then there was always the usual administrative work, the services to prepare and, of course, a sermon every week. In that five week period I had visited 76 families, some more than once. I met many wonderful people and some of them became my friends at Millbrook when I was there. There was Gord and Marg Clifford, Wilma Bates, Betty Brown, Leo and Lois Fallis and Cheryl Fallis, Marice Collins, who was the St. Andrew's Secretary and her husband and their daughter Brenda Thackery, Ron and Lorraine Maksymetz, Quentin and Louise Brown, Norma Kennedy, Carol and Trevor Fallis, Nancy Mitchell, Roy Dawson and Bill Morrish.

During my visits, I heard many things about the way things were in this Charge. They felt there was too much backbiting in the church. They told me there were two or three people who always wanted to run things as well as small cliques in the church and families who were interrelated so it was hard for new people to break into the church community. They knew if new people felt uncomfortable in their church, they wouldn't come back. A lot of people had been neglected and hurt by the church and a number of them had indeed drifted away after 1988 so it was now an aging congregation. In addition, there always seemed to be a pull against the minister. They put it this way: "There is not enough listening to the Lord." As I listened to what people told me, it sounded a lot like St. Paul's in New Liskeard when I first arrived. I had also seen and experienced this kind of behavior at Trinity United Church in Grand Valley and I didn't want to think that there were people in almost every church who were negative and controlling. But I knew that my experiences at St. Paul's and at Trinity would certainly help me in this Pastoral Charge and I would be able to be objective and not be influenced by any one point of view. One thing was certain, there was a lot of work to do. I prepared a full report for the Steering Committee for Interim Ministry and for the Official Board of the Millbrook-Cavan Pastoral Charge and presented it to them on August 13, 1992. In my report I included many of the comments I heard from the church community and offered an overview and recommendations to the Official Board. Then I went on holidays for two weeks and spent most of my time with Susie and Warren. I also went up to New Liskeard to visit friends. In the fall, I started back to work and was feeling very positive and confidant about the ministry I was doing and most people in the two churches were beginning to see how important this work was. I attended the last part of the Interim Ministry course from October 5th to the 9th and both Peterborough Presbytery and the leaders at this course had the letter from my Supervisor Reverend Joan Henderson from October 1st, 1992:

"This is a letter of evaluation for the Rev. Dorinda Vollmer. As her Field Work Supervisor I have met with her on several occasions to review how she has been dealing with life on the Millbrook-Cavan Pastoral charge……..Having been in this Presbytery for nine years I have been aware of the Millbrook-Cavan Pastoral Charge and of the different types of ministers that have served there. As with all things, rumours have spread about the people and how they treat their ministers. Dorinda wisely has chosen not to listen to the stories but has entered into the charge with an open mind…..the people have been honest with her in assessing their own behavior and in figuring out why things have happened the way that they have. In the two case studies that Dorinda and I have looked over together it has become quite clear why she is able to be in interim ministry. She has met the persons whom she is dealing with face to face and with her own unique quality has had the ability to start a healing process in a conflict situation. Dorinda has a rare gift in that she can handle conflict very well. She is always conscious of the other person's feelings and considerate of the emotion… I feel with the many qualities that Dorinda possesses she will continue to help the Millbrook-Cavan Charge to grow in its faith. The fact that she has been in ministry for 17 years gives Dorinda a wealth of experience from which to draw on."

I received my certificate from the Interim Ministry Network in Baltimore, Maryland for having completed the Basic Training and I was very proud of that.

Warren had started back at University in September and, even though he had more papers to write that year he was very happy in the choice he had made to switch to philosophy. His relationship with Susan was going very well. Susie loved having Susan around too when she was able to come and visit Warren in Oakville and I got to see them both when I was at Susie's. Warren and Susie came for Thanksgiving. Susie loved our new home. We had a great time together. Then one day in October I had a knock at my door and there was Cheryl. I was surprised to see her. She had been visiting with her family in the Peterborough area and dropped in to see me on her way home. She said she was there to take me out for lunch and we had a great visit. I liked her sense of humour and she loved to go walking. I had found a great place near Millbrook so after lunch we went for a long walk and had a great time. She was looking for something more in her life and wanted to make some changes but found that difficult because she really didn't know what she wanted. I was in the midst of change and next July would bring more change so we talked about that and had that in common. I just liked her and so began our friendship.

I continued to work hard with the congregations to try and find the best way for them to go forward in their churches. I felt good about the progress we were making and, on October 29th 1992 I presented a very detailed, five page report on the Interim Ministry to the Steering Committee. In part of it I said:

> "I think, overall, the Interim Ministry has been going well. It is different by virtue of its intention and therefore more stressful for the minister and the congregation…….. A great deal of visiting is done to try to understand the particular situation and the concerns. This is to help the congregations assess themselves……..From the congregations' point of view, they don't always understand what the Interim Ministry is and why. Sometimes the communication and process around the discussions with Presbytery as to the validity and need for that kind of ministry for their Charge feels laid on and so there is some resistance and that's understandable. Also there is the urgency around, 'let's get on with it, lets get the Pastoral Relations Committee going and get a minister'…….. Having said all of that…. there is a feeling of positive openness and dialogue from our congregations. They are really trying to make the most out of this year."

Cheryl phoned me one day about a month after her visit and wondered if I minded if she came to church. I didn't have a problem with that. She told me that her experience of church was very limited. She said she was searching for something to give meaning in her life and she respected me. So she started coming to church a couple of times a month and we would go out for lunch after. I actually looked forward to those times. People in the church really liked Cheryl and were very welcoming to her. Marg Clifford was very happy to meet Cheryl as was Wilma Bates who became a good friend of hers. Brenda Thackery loved Cheryl's sense of humour and, whenever we had coffee hour after church, she would go right over to talk with her. Donna and Gerry Hampton and I had become very good friends at Warsaw so, about once a month, I went over to see them and stayed for dinner. When I told them about Cheryl who had started coming to church on Sunday, they invited her to come with me because she played euchre and they needed a fourth person. The next Sunday Cheryl came to church I told her about Donna and Gerry and she was happy to go there for dinner and play euchre. Donna was a great cook and we had wonderful times playing euchre which, I have to say, is not as interesting as bridge but we had lots of laughs. I usually partnered with Gerry and Cheryl partnered with Donna. Gerry loved to win and Donna and Cheryl both hated to lose so it got quite intense sometimes but it was really great fun

Millbrook, a Period of Transition and More Changes

Warren came home around the middle of December while Susan was in Ottawa visiting her parents over Christmas and a few days later we picked up Susie. I had prepared a nice dinner and we had a great time. Then we all went to the Christmas Eve service, my first at St. Andrew's. It went very well and that put us all in the Christmas spirit. On Christmas morning we had our usual Christmas Day celebrations and a wonderful Christmas dinner. In the New Year, I took Susie and Warren back home. Warren and Susan were looking forward to going to Orlando, Florida for their February break, a trip paid for with money Warren made from the beer bottles he had collected when he drove the garbage truck for the Town of Oakville that past summer. Warren was always innovative and told me he found it amazing how many people threw out their beer bottles and their Tim Horton's coffee cups without checking for prizes.

Many people in St. Andrew's congregation loved classical music and so I decided to give a benefit concert for St. Andrew's and Cavan United Churches on March 28th at Grace United Church in Peterborough. They had a grand piano. I was very pleased to do this and since Cheryl had never really heard me play except a few pieces on my piano, this was also an opportunity for me to show her something I loved to do. It was a new experience for Cheryl since she wasn't really into classical music but she could appreciate what I did. We had a great turnout and the concert went really well. I was happy to be able to introduce Cheryl to my music and she, in return, shared her love of photography with me. She was a member of a photo club near her home and an active member. I loved photography too but hadn't really done much over the last few years. Cheryl encouraged me and helped me and I began to really enjoy photography in a way I never had before. I was grateful to her for that.

When Warren finished his university year in April, 1993 he was hired again by the Town of Oakville to drive a garbage truck for the summer. He found a bike near the dump which was in good condition and used it to bike back and forth to work. He really enjoyed that work and did it for the last time in the summer of 1994 at the end of which the Town of Oakville and his Supervisor said he was the best summer student they had ever had and made him an open offer for a permanent job working for the Town. For me that was a real tribute to my son's work ethic. In April, 1993 Susan graduated with an Honours B.A. in Modern Languages and Linguistics from McMaster University. Then in May, Susan's maternal grandmother, Hilda Clarke (nee Fisher} died in England. Since she was a young child until she was 16, Susan had spent two months visiting her grandparents in England, both her mother's and father's parents. Needless to say, she was very close to all her grandparents and this was very hard on her.

Around that same time, I started to think about what I wanted to do after my time with Millbrook and Cavan ended on June 30th. Some members of the congregation at Millbrook wanted me to stay, but that past year, the United Church of Canada had made a policy that stated a minister could not continue on in a Pastoral Charge after the Interim Ministry ended. So staying at Millbrook was not an option for me. I put my name out there again and began looking for another Interim Ministry appointment. There didn't seem to be one available so I looked for a Pastoral Charge. I was invited for an interview with a Pastoral Charge about 38 miles east of Millbrook and the interview went very well. One of the men on the Pastoral Relations

Committee was very excited that I had worked with the Orford String Quartet because he loved their music and encouraged me to consider their Pastoral Charge because he saw a lot of potential in me. I liked the people who interviewed me and felt I could do a really good ministry with them but I didn't feel the call and that confused me. I was having a difficult time and I didn't know why. I turned down their offer and felt I needed to take a year off but I really didn't know how I was going to that. I called my sister and talked to her about what was happening and that I had turned down an offer from a Pastoral Charge to be their minister. My sister was surprised and asked me why. I told her it just didn't feel right. I certainly wasn't looking ahead at that moment. I wasn't thinking straight or I would have realized that, making that decision would mean I would not be able to pay into my pension plan anymore or get the extra health benefits once I left full time ministry. Jana told me she was worried about me. Looking back I think with Warren leaving home I hadn't really sorted things out and just went along with what I needed to do. I realize now that I was experiencing burnout. I had had three very busy ministries starting with New Liskeard, Warsaw and then here at Millbrook. I was tired and I needed a break. But I didn't know what to do.

Then Jana told me that George really wanted her to leave California and move to Coos Bay, Oregon with him to get away from all the demands of Ken's children and Stacy. I was very surprised she was even considering this because she had lived in Sacramento for almost 30 years and she had a granddaughter there whom she adored. I told her I was worried about her too and asked her not to make any rash decisions. She said she was worried about this move because George didn't have much money and she only had her job waitressing and had done a little bartending as well. But, she admitted, the thought of moving was exciting except for the fact that she didn't know how often she would see her family if they moved because it was a 10 hour drive to Oregon from Sacramento. Jana had a lot to think about too. As I gave my sister advice about not making rash decisions, I didn't see that I was doing exactly the same thing. We seemed to be at the same place for different reasons and neither of us was really sure what to do. My sister had gone through three marriages and I had gone through three Pastoral Charges and I think we were both emotionally drained. We talked a few times over the next couple of days about our situations.

Cheryl was the one person I could confide in and I told her about the offer I had turned down and I didn't know what I was going to do. She told me that I could move in with her to give me time to sort out things in my life and figure out what I needed to do next. I was very surprised at her offer. She said she had lived alone for 20 years and she was lonely and didn't share easily. She felt I would be easy to live with. Cheryl said that I had really helped her at a critical time in her life and I had not asked for anything in return and now she wanted to help me. Our friendship had grown over the last nine months. She asked me what I might do for work and I said I could probably find part time work in ministry but I wasn't sure what was out there and I could also teach piano again. It was a very generous offer. I needed time to think about this.

I got a call from a couple at the church in Cavan who invited me to come for dinner. It turned out that the husband had a sister whom he had not seen for 25 years even though she lived in the area. He said he couldn't remember what they had argued about and he had tried many times over the years to see her but she had always refused to see him. Now she was in the hospital and seriously ill and was not expected to live much longer. He wanted to see her and asked me if I could help him. I told him I was more than willing to visit her in the hospital if she would see me. I went to see her and she was very friendly. We talked about general things until finally I asked her about her brother and told her he would like to see her. I could feel her close up inside when I brought him up and asked her to only think about it. Then I said a prayer with her. About two days later, her brother called me and told me his sister had asked to see him and it was wonderful to be with her again after all those years. He couldn't thank me enough and I was really happy for him and for his sister that they had some time together because she died a week later. I found that situation so tragic and couldn't imagine not seeing my sister. I knew that nothing could be so bad that it could separate us. I felt badly for that brother and sister who, in the end, didn't even remember what the issue had been that caused their rift and I was so pleased that I was able to help them.

My time as the Interim Minister at the Millbrook Cavan Pastoral Charge ended at the end of June and the congregations had a reception for me to thank me for all the work I had done with them. I was very grateful for their thanks and appreciation and I felt I had done a very good Interim Ministry with them. In early June, the Pastoral Charge had approached me and asked if I could fill in full time as their supply minister from July 1st until September 30th because their new minister was unable to come until October 1st. They said I could continue to live in the manse as part of this new contract. I appreciated being asked and, of course, said I would. It felt good to know that, after I finished my contract as their Interim Minister, I would be doing three months of ministry in the Pastoral Charge as their supply minister and that was a huge help for me financially.

In July I took my holidays and I invited Cheryl to come with me to B.C. for 10 days. I said it would be a good way to see how we got along and she agreed and she had never been to B.C. We went to Burnaby, up to Grouse Mountain and Vancouver Island and she fell in love with B.C. My sister came up to Vancouver by bus to meet us for three days so she and I could visit and she could meet Cheryl and we could talk together. The three of us had a good time and I enjoyed taking my sister and Cheryl around to meet many of my friends in B.C. Jana told me she liked Cheryl and if she was offering her home to me over the next year why not go for it and she also talked to Cheryl about this and it was all positive. Jana also told me that George was still insisting on moving but had decided to put it off for a year so they would moving to Coos Bay, Oregon the summer of 1994. I asked her how she felt about that and she said she was now thinking it might not be so bad an idea though she knew she would miss her family. Besides, she said, she didn't want to create any conflict with George. I told her that was no reason to go with him.

While the three of us were in Vancouver, my friend Helen Robson introduced us to her friend Ann Mortifee, who was a Canadian singer-songwriter born in Zululand, South Africa. She came to Canada as a child and was raised in Vancouver but never forgot her South African roots. I told her I wrote poetry but hadn't done much in the last couple of years and she had asked me to send her some of my poems which I did when I got back home. In August, she wrote to me:

> "Thanks so much for the note. The poems are wonderful. So full of pain and compassion. Thank you for sharing them with me. The struggle that is ours as we journey is so dark, so full, so alone. The beauty and the scar. The wonder that rises from the ashes. We die and are reborn again and again. I support your fullness, your commitment. Bless you for the strength it takes to live who you are. There are so many of us now journeying together."

I found Ann's response to my poems wonderful and surprising. For me it was a sign that I was doing the right thing by letting go and taking a year off to rethink the ministry, to regroup and look again seriously at my writing. I was confidant now that going to stay at Cheryl's was what I should do to have the time and space to have a break and find my way again. Cheryl knew I had lived with different people over the years I was in Vancouver and that I was very flexible. I phoned Cheryl and told her how thankful I was that she wanted to share her home with me. She was very happy that I was doing this and it was as much a change for her as it was for me.

Warren came home at the beginning of September for a weekend to help me finish packing and help with the yard sale I had. I really had to pare down. Then, at the end of the month, Warren came back to help me with the move to Cheryl's home. I rented a truck in Peterborough for the day and Warren went with me very early in the morning to pick it up. It was a huge truck with a gear shift but one of the gears stuck from the second to third gear so Warren had to physically help me get it moved back and forth. He couldn't drive the truck because he wasn't 25 yet and my insurance didn't cover him. It was very annoying for us trying to get into third gear but also quite funny. When we got to Millbrook, Wilma and Cheryl were waiting for us at the manse and Wilma took a photo of me sitting at the wheel of that huge truck. It took us until the early afternoon to load up the truck with friends Marice and Ron, Brenda and Wilma helping Warren, Cheryl and me. Before we left, I sat with my friends, and shared a bottle of wine Wilma brought for all of us. It was hard to say goodbye because they had been such good friends to me but soon we had to go. I drove the truck, with Warren helping me, and we followed Cheryl in her car. When we got to Cheryl's house in Mount Albert, it was quite a job unloading everything and then Warren and I had to make the two hour drive to take the truck back to Peterborough and get my car. It was early evening when we got back to Cheryl's. It had been a huge day and I was exhausted and Warren was too. He stayed over that night, and the next morning, I drove him to the train back to Oakville. I was very thankful to him for coming. He had done this so many times for me - when I left New Liskeard for Warsaw, when I left Warsaw for Millbrook and now, again, helping me move to Cheryl's home. And he never complained.

Then something changed for Warren. Kairos is an organization made up of Canadian churches working together for justice and peace. It sees its mission as a response to the call "to do justice, and to love kindness, and to walk humbly with your God", Micah 6:8. They respond to Christ by engaging in social transformation. Kairos empowers the people of God and is empowered by them to live out their faith in action for justice and peace, joining with those of goodwill in Canada and around the world. In October, St. John's United Church paid for Warren to go to a Kairos youth event for a weekend. When Warren returned from this weekend, he called to tell me that, as soon as he got home, he went to see Reverend Jim Campbell at St. John's United Church and told him he felt the call to ministry. Warren told me that Jim simply looked at him and said, "'What took you so long Warren?" I must say that I wasn't totally surprised by his news. I had encouraged my son not to think about the ministry because I knew how hard and demanding ministry can be but he had seen all of that growing up and, in the end, it was his calling too. I was really happy for him, especially knowing he was going into this with his eyes wide open. He told me he had talked with Susan a lot about his going into ministry and she supported his decision. She had been raised in a United Church in Ottawa so she understood how the church works. Susie was very happy with Warren's decision and was proud of him. He met with Halton Presbytery for an interview and it didn't take him long to be accepted as a candidate for ministry. Warren asked for information on three of the United Church of Canada's theological colleges and decided to apply to the Vancouver School of Theology with the intent to start September 1994. He still had his degree at McMaster University to finish the spring of 1994.

Living with Cheryl in Mount Albert was new and exciting and I was hopeful I would be able to make this new living arrangement a success. Cheryl lived in a small bungalow that had a kitchen, dining room and living room, a small family room where she had her TV, two bedrooms and a full bathroom. The basement smelled damp and had some mould but she didn't use it except for storage. It didn't take long for me to get settled in and, before I could catch my breath, the Sandford Zepher Pastoral Charge found out I was in the area and got in touch with me. They needed a minister to do services for about seven weeks from the end of October until the middle of December while their minister was on medical leave. They had heard I was in their Presbytery and that I might be available. I was happy to be able to help them out. I was introduced to the Pastoral charge Secretary, Nancy Wolfe who was also the organist at the Zepher congregation where she and her husband attended church. I really liked her and I became very good friends with Nancy and her husband Jim who reminded me of my Uncle Phil. Nancy was in her middle 50's and as soon as I told Nancy that I was a pianist, she told me she had always wanted to get her Grade X piano and, talked to me about giving her piano lessons. So, by the end of October, I had my first piano student. She also suggested that I put flyers in the local post office to see if others would be interested in taking piano lessons and I did that and also put out flyers in the Millbrook area. Finding some work had never been an issue for me and, before I knew it, I had 18 students from Sanford, Mount Forest and area, Millbrook, Bethany and Pontypool. I was busy. I went to the homes of all my students from Millbrook, Pontypool and Bethany on one afternoon and evening and I did the same for my other students who were closer to where I lived. I was really feeling energized and happy.

I enjoyed teaching piano again and I had some really good students. One of my students was 12-year-old Colin who was very mature for his age. His piano teacher had moved away but he really wanted to continue to play the piano. He was a dwarf and had very small hands but I showed him that I have small hands too and he thought that was cool. I also encouraged his father to build a box for him to be raised up high enough so he could use the pedals as my Aunt Louise had done for me when I was five years old. Colin was very excited to be able to use the pedals and he did very well. He was very mature for his age and practiced a lot, working hard so he could get his Grade VIII piano exam in a few years.

As the Secretary of the Sandford Zephyr Pastoral Charge, Nancy wrote me a letter December 18, 1993 when I finished my supply ministry at the Charge:

> "I thank you for conducting the services during our minister's absence. It is always reassuring to have someone as capable as you are to fill the need when it arises. Certainly, the past six weeks have gone well as this is a very busy time for a minister and the life in the church. I thank you, personally, for having the Bulletin material ready each week – the procedure was very convenient."

Cheryl and I had worked things out and she was very pleased I was doing part time ministry and teaching. We loved going for walks and took our cameras with us as we both enjoyed taking pictures. Cheryl worked at her bookkeeping jobs at home so she was busy most days during the week. I went out to teach piano and had time now to work on my poetry again and my writing. I continued to see Donna and Gerry in Warsaw and I saw Susie and Warren and Susan often. Warren had been accepted at the Vancouver School of Theology (VST) starting September 1994 and was doing very well at University and loved the Philosophy courses he was taking so I was happy to know he had made the right choice.

That Christmas, I went down to Oakville for our family Christmas with Susie and Warren and Susan was there. She had graduated in 1993 and was now back home living with her parents and continuing her studies at the University of Ottawa. She would continue to live with her parents the first year that Warren would be at VST. There were so many changes happening for me, for my sister and for Warren and Susan that it was hard to keep up with it all. On February 18th, 1994 at 3:00 p.m. Warren proposed to Susan at Toronto Union Station. Susan said she didn't accept right away and made him wait until later that afternoon to say 'Yes'. They called Susan's parents and me to tell us they were engaged and would be married June, 1995. It was just wonderful news. It was great to see them so happy and in love. Susie was happy for them too and so was my sister who had not yet met Susan. I had yet to meet Susan's parents, Heather and Tom Wheat, but, on March 28th I received a nice letter from them:

> "Although not totally unexpected we were nonetheless pleased to learn of Warren's proposal of marriage to our daughter Susan. I am sure that you are aware that over the last two years our energies have been spent caring for our parents in England. Consequently circumstances have presented us from meeting you. As the wedding is planned for next year, we hope we will have an opportunity to meet before then. If you are in Ottawa you

are welcome to join us for a meal. We are looking forward to getting to know Warren better and supporting him and Susan in the future."

I was very pleased to hear from Heather and Tom and, at some point in the next few weeks I went up to Ottawa for the day to meet them. Tom was a scientist who worked for the Government of Canada in Ottawa and Heather had done some teaching but wasn't working anymore. She attended Quaker meetings and was very involved in the peace movement and peaceful protests. She was not only very active in the peace movement but in social justice issues too. Tom and Heather lived a very simple lifestyle and nothing had been changed in their home since the 1950s, including the small black and white TV in their living room. They loved their neighbourhood where they knew all the neighbours on their street and everyone got along really well. I enjoyed my afternoon with Heather and Tom who were very friendly. We were all looking forward to the wedding in June.

The Port Perry Prince Albert Pastoral Charge called me in March to ask if I would consider doing part time ministry there and asked me to come for an interview. At the interview, they told me they would expect me to come one day a week for eight hours doing Pastoral Care, helping their minister, Reverend Bob LePage by visiting families who needed visits on a regular basis and going to the hospital and nursing home. They said they had a list of people who needed this support and that it didn't matter to them where I lived. I agreed to do this but told them I would prefer to come twice a week for four hours each instead of once a week because of my piano teaching and that was agreeable to them. I was happy to work with Bob who was a very good minister and whom I respected. I also met Pat Bird who was the full time Secretary for the Charge and she was a really nice person. I looked forward to working with her as well. On the last Sunday in April, I was introduced at Port Perry United Church by Heather McCrae who had written a short article about me for the community in the local paper. Then I went to Prince Albert United Church to be introduced to that congregation as well. I did do a few services for them over the five years I was there but my responsibility was mainly to visit families in the congregations. It was great to be doing ministry again even if it was only part time and I realized I had missed it. Glen was the organist at Port Perry United Church and was an excellent organist. Over the time I was there, we played some organ piano duets together. It was wonderful to do this again.

Then, in April, 1994, Warren graduated with an Honours B.A. in Philosophy. The ceremony was held on June 3rd at 9:30 a.m. in the Great Hall at Hamilton Place at McMaster University. I picked Susie up and we went to the graduation ceremonies together. I was so proud of my son. It had taken him five years to get his degree but he had persisted and succeeded. Warren was very excited that the Convocation Address was given by Farley Mowat who happened to be Susie's favorite writer. Susie and I sat with Susan, Heather and Tom who were very happy to finally meet Susie. Of course we took lots of pictures and, after the ceremony, went out to a wonderful restaurant to celebrate.

May 16th I received a nice letter from Audrey and Stan Pearce congratulating us on Warren and Susan's engagement. *"I just can't imagine our little Warren getting married. I guess we figure we stay the same and expect the kids to do the same. So glad to hear he is doing so well."* It was nice of Audrey to write. They thought the world of him when we were in Dominion City. I was doing very well in my part time ministry, visiting people in the Port Perry and Prince Albert United Churches and was very busy teaching piano. I had had six students entered in the Kiwanis Festival in Peterborough and they all did very well. Then, in June, I had two students doing their Grade II theory, and three others doing their Grade III, Grade VI and Grade VIII piano exams for the Royal Conservatory of Music in Toronto. I had a recital in June where all my students performed for each other and for their parents. They did really well.

Then Cheryl said she was thinking of moving to Millbrook and I was very surprised because she didn't like change at all. She said she had loved the town and the community when she visited me there. She asked me if I was thinking of going back into full time ministry and I said no, that I was happy with the ministry I was doing and teaching piano for now. She asked me if I would move with her. Millbrook was closer to her family and she would be able to see them more often. She said I had many students there and would be able to pick up even more students in that area. She was right because it would be easier for me. This would be a huge change for her since she had lived in her home for over 20 years. I said I was fine moving back to Millbrook. This reminded me of Barb and her two children and me and Warren who was two at that time. I shared a house with her in B.C. when I was on welfare and she was on welfare too and we needed a bigger house and moved. I was pretty easy that way. Cheryl found a house with about an acre of land and a pond on the property. It was a very large bungalow with a downstairs walkout basement. Cheryl loved the house and the property and she made an offer that they accepted. We were moving into this new house on July 20th almost ten months after I moved into her present home. Cheryl took me over to see the house and when we went to see the finished basement it was huge and she would turn into it into a room with comfortable chairs to sit on in front of the wood fireplace. At the end of the long hall in the basement was another very large room that Cheryl said would be mine where I could put all my things and my piano and TV. It was exactly what I needed and I was very pleased and I could even teach a few students in my studio, office and TV room. It had already been a very busy year for me and now more changes were coming . Cheryl listed her house for sale in May and it sold quickly. Jana was making a major move from California to Oregon but my move was insignificant in comparison.

I helped Cheryl pack and it was a job in itself but she was good to me so I did what I could to make the move easier for her. We moved in July and it took two trucks to move Cheryl because she had so much stuff. The new house was at least twice the size of the other house and she would have more room to breathe there. When you opened the front door, there was a lovely formal living room on the right where Cheryl put all her treasures, beautiful furniture and Arabian horse paintings. Next to the living room, there was a large dining room area that could seat 10 people. If you walked straight ahead from the front door, there was a hall and on the right you could see the large kitchen off which were patio doors going out onto the large deck. Going back to the front door if you went straight ahead and left down the hallway, there was a bathroom on the right and, at the end of the hallway two bedrooms - one on the left and one on the right. The one on the right was the biggest and had a large window which looked out into the back yard. There was also a nice front yard and there was a big garage that was attached to the house that had an electric opener. When you got out of your car in the garage you went up about four stairs to a door that opened into the house and a small landing. Straight ahead you walked into the large kitchen but if you turned left on the landing you went down the stairs to the basement and into a very large room with a bathroom. My room was at the end of the hallway. Off the room in the basement there were also patio doors to the walkout with the deck above where Cheryl put her barbeque and table and patio furniture. There was at least an acre of property which was very hilly in spots, especially where it went down the ravine to the pond with lots of trees. I used the John Deere Riding Lawn Mower to cut the acre of grass and also did most of the gardening which I loved.

Living closer to the Millbrook, Pontypool and Bethany area, I put out more flyers for students and by September I had 45 students in total. I had told my students in the Mount Albert area that I was moving and, starting in September, I would come back once a week on Tuesdays to teach all ten of my students there. I was already spending two half days at Port Perry Prince Albert United Churches visiting families so, starting in September I had a lot of work to do to fit 35 students over the rest of the week. This meant my teaching days would start around 2:30 in the afternoon and I wouldn't get home until 10:00 p.m. or later. I was only able to teach nine months of the year since students had two months off in the summer and two weeks holidays at Christmas and a week at Easter.

Jana and George also moved to Coos Bay in July and rented part of the building that had been the old hospital. Money was very tight and George didn't have a job yet so Jana was looking for work. She soon got a job as a waitress at the best restaurant in Coos Bay, The Hilltop, and the owners, Jodi and Joseph, became Jana's really good friends over time. When they realized she was a bartender too, they hired her for that work which helped to pay the bills. It also had turned out that George was a con man and could talk anyone out of their money. He thought up a scheme in which he took people's money but told them he couldn't guarantee they would get their money back. Life wasn't easy for Jana and now she had no family or friends in Coos Bay to lean on.

Warren didn't come home from B.C. that Christmas and that was hard for me. I really missed Warren and it just wasn't the same. Susan had a serious bout of bronchitis at that time and was sick for over a month so I didn't see her either. I went down to see Susie over Christmas and we had a nice time but I noticed that Susie had changed. She couldn't remember a lot of things. I realized then that Warren had been her memory and even he hadn't realized how much she had gone down until I phoned and told him. I worried about her but I was so busy most weeks that I couldn't visit as often as I needed to. I did talk to the superintendents of the building who really liked my aunt and were very happy to help her out whenever she needed it. In November, I had started ordering food in for her every week. She always asked me to get her two cooked chickens, four dozen oranges, and sometimes, more tea bags. The supers said they would see that the help I got for her from social services could get into the building because often she wouldn't answer the buzzer to let them in. This was a very hard time for me seeing my aunt the way she was but she could still manage in the apartment and I had promised her she could stay there no matter what.

I was now 50 years old and it had been a good year teaching. All my students were doing very well and I was enjoying the ministry at Port Perry and Prince Albert. I was moving into a New Year, 1995, and the changes would keep coming.

CHAPTER ELEVEN

A Wedding and a Death in the Family

I had 10 students in the Newmarket area whom I taught on Saturdays. Nancy, my Grade X student was the first one of the day starting at 7:15 a.m. for an hour. As much as Nancy didn't like getting up that time of day, she was a trooper especially when I would remind her that I had to get up at six in the morning to get there for her lesson. I was still doing two half days of ministry a week in Port Perry and Prince Albert and that left me with five days during the week to teach my other 45 students most of which were half hour lessons at their homes in Peterborough, Millbrook, Bethany and Pontypool. Then there were the yearly recitals in a local church like Prince Albert or Bethany United Church. I loved all of it, as well as being on the road, even though it was tiring to be driving around late at night, especially in very snowy weather. Going into my third year teaching piano, I found it was still my passion and I knew Louise would have been proud of me helping young people appreciate music, something she had done at our home in Oakville for almost 30 years.

I very much appreciated that Cheryl had included me in her new home. I was now able to pay her some rent and I bought a lot of food every month as I had done in Mount Albert. It was a good arrangement and worked for both of us. I had my own place and space and was very comfortable there. I wasn't around a lot because I was busy doing part time ministry and very busy teaching but I did have three mornings free until 1:30 p.m. Sunday was my only day off and I really needed it. I loved being on the go and I was still young enough and healthy enough to keep up the pace.

In February 1995, when I was down visiting Susie, I found her very upset and worried as she sat in front of what she told me was a pile of bills. When I looked at the pile, I realized they weren't bills at all, they were letters from people asking her for money. She was confused and had thought she had to give money to them. I asked her what she wanted to do and she told me she wanted me to look after everything for her. She told me to call her lawyer and take over as Power of Attorney. I went to see Susie's lawyer, whom I knew, and he made all the arrangements for me to do that. When I told Susie it was all arranged, she was so relieved to have me look after everything for her. There really wasn't much to do. Her rent was paid through Pierre's office and the few hundred dollars a month pension she received from the government covered the food I ordered in for her that was delivered weekly, the cleaning woman I hired came once a week, as well as a nurse who checked in with Susie once a month and she still had money left over. I took her to the doctor when she needed to go but she never thought she was sick. Even when Dr. Soanes gave her pills, she would throw them in the garbage. She was stubborn and determined and that's why she was still with us. I wanted my aunt to be as independent as possible. She made me promise that, no matter what happened, I would never put her in a nursing home. She wanted to live in her apartment until the end. I promised her and I kept that promise.

In March, Susan went out to Vancouver for two weeks to see Warren and look over the place where they would be living after they got married. They had a great time together. In April, Susan graduated from Teachers College at the University of Ottawa and became a certified teacher. Also in April, Warren finished his first year at Vancouver School of Theology and came home. I was so glad to see him again. So was Susie and he stayed with her. Susan and Warren had a lot to do for their wedding and they were hands-on looking after everything. After they had announced their engagement in 1994, they asked me to marry them. I felt it was a real honour for them to have asked me to marry them but I had said no because I really wanted to be just the mother of the groom. They were disappointed at my answer but I made them promise me that I could baptize any children they had and they agreed to that. They were being married at Kingsway United Church in Ottawa where Susan had been raised. Susan's parents had given them a choice of a fancy hotel for the wedding dinner in downtown Ottawa or Dow's Pavilion by the lake. They wanted the Pavilion and a buffet-style dinner because all of Warren's friends loved to eat and they wanted everyone to feel comfortable. As an added bonus, this place had no problem with parking. Every decision Warren and Susan made was for the comfort of their friends and family who were coming to celebrate their special day with them. My son is a very caring young man and Susan is too and they really complimented each other and brought out the best in each other.

At the end of April, I received a wedding invitation from my dear friend Helen Robson who was marrying Alastair MacCulloch at Fairview Presbyterian Church in Vancouver B.C. on July 22nd. Theirs was a real love story and I was happy that Helen had found someone. Helen and her mother had gone on a trip to Scotland about two years earlier and while they were on a bus there, they met a Scottish man whose wife had died two years earlier and his name was Alastair. He got on well with Helen and her mother and he showed them around his country. It turned out that Helen and Alastair really liked each other but she made it clear that she would never leave B.C. He told Helen he would consider moving to British Columbia because his daughter was studying at U.B.C. They continued to date and, eventually, Alastair moved to B.C. to be with Helen. Now they were getting married. Helen was a wonderful musician and could play anything on the piano and Alastair was a very good writer and poet and they collaborated, writing musicals together which eventually would be shown at theatres in Vancouver. It was quite the love story and I could not have been happier for my friend. I was disappointed that I wouldn't be able to attend their wedding.

It was almost time for Warren and Susan to be married. I attended the rehearsal which went very well and I met Reverend Doug Carnegie, the minister who would conduct the service, and he seemed very nice. It was wonderful to see Warren's friends, Danny Nielsen and Ronald Glassford who were in the wedding party and even Jay Parnall who flew in from B.C. After the rehearsal, Danny came over to me and introduced his girlfriend Sylvie who was from Quebec where they both lived. We talked a while and then they looked at each other and she said, "Yes."

I didn't understand what Sylvie meant so I looked at Danny. He told me that they were getting married in October in Magog, in the eastern townships of Quebec. He wanted me to marry them but wanted Sylvie to meet me first. Now that she had, she said she would be very happy if I married them. I was so honoured and happy for them and of course, I said I would. After the wedding rehearsal, we celebrated with a dinner at a restaurant Tom and Heather loved to go to in Ottawa. The wedding party was all there, as well as our families, and the food was great. It was wonderful to sit around, talk and visit. Then Warren's buddies had a bachelor party for him. Knowing them as well as I did, I could only imagine what they had in mind. Heather and Tom rented rooms for all the immediate family for the wedding and they didn't ask me to do anything in regards to paying for any part of the wedding. I think they knew I was struggling financially and it was very kind of them. I appreciated everything they did for Warren and Susan.

There were about 90 guests in all, including many of Warren's childhood friends. Warren asked me if I wanted to invite some of my friends to the wedding and I mentioned a few people including Maida Ormsby who was thrilled to be asked and whom Warren knew from Warsaw. But Susie couldn't come to the wedding. She wanted to be there but she wasn't feeling well and didn't want to be away from home. She told Warren she was sorry and he understood. Susan and Warren's wedding took place on June 17th at 3:00 p.m. at Kingsway United Church. Getting ready on the day of the wedding was exciting. It had been a long time since I had felt as good as I did that morning, waking up to know my son had found the woman he wanted to spend the rest of his life with. It was just wonderful and I could not have been happier for Warren and for Susan. I got to the church with time to spare and Maida sat with me. She was almost 80 and had the most beautiful white hair. That was probably why people asked if she was Warren's grandmother. As only Maida could, she said yes she was. When Warren walked into the church for his wedding, he looked right at me and my heart melted. As I looked at him, I could only see him as my little boy and now he was all grown up and about to start his life with the woman he loved. It was wonderful. When Susan came down the aisle, she looked lovely. After they were married and signed the documents, they walked back down the aisle together and everyone clapped and cheered. My son looked so handsome and Susan looked beautiful.

It was a lovely warm day for the wedding celebration. The lake was very still and calm as pictures were taken of the families and the wedding party. I had my camera too and took some of my own pictures. The buffet dinner was wonderful and there were lots of speeches and laughter and great fun. After dinner, there was dancing and even more celebrating. At one point, Danny came over and asked me to dance. While we were dancing, he told me how much it had meant to him that I was there for him when he was a little boy when we lived in Oakville and how hard it had been for him when we moved to Manitoba. He told me how excited he was when we came back in the summers to Oakville and how he couldn't wait to see us. I was deeply moved by what Danny told me. I had no idea he felt this way. I hadn't seen him in years and here he was telling me how much I meant to him. He had been very much a part of Warren's life growing up and when he moved to Quebec, we lost touch. Now our relationship had come full circle.

Later that evening, Warren and Susan left for their hotel and the next morning after everyone was up, we all gathered for brunch with Warren. At brunch, Warren told us that, the night before, his buddies had tried very hard to get up to their room but they didn't know you needed an elevator key for the honeymoon suite where Warren and Susan were staying so no one could get to them. We all laughed at the story, and, knowing Ronald, Jay, Danny and his other buddies, I could imagine how hard they tried. Then Warren and Susan were on their way to the airport to fly to Halifax for their honeymoon. They would be staying in a hotel on the ocean and travelling around the Maritimes. We all said our goodbyes. I got into my car and headed home. It had been the most wonderful weekend ever.

Warren and Susan were back at Susie's for the summer and I went down to see them. They told me all about their trip and how wonderful it had been. They loved the Maritimes. Then I received a nice note from Sylvie on July 31 where she said:

> "Dan has on many occasions shared with me nice memories he has of you and I have wanted to meet you for a long time. My wish finally came true at Warren and Susan's wedding. Meeting you was exquisite. You are just as Dan described: an open mind and open heart. We are both deeply touched and honoured that you will take us through our vows. Please allow us to invite you for the weekend. We will make all arrangements and spend a great time in your company... Thank you Dorinda your gesture means a lot to us both."

At the end of August, Warren and Susan drove to B.C. in the 1967 Aspen Chrysler with a six slant engine which Susan's father had given them. It got them over the mountains and they settled into university life at Vancouver School of Theology for Warren's second year. Susan got a job in the Public Relations department of VST doing Secretarial work. Once my exciting and emotional summer was over, I was also back to work, doing ministry at Port Perry and Prince Albert United Churches and planning for September when my students started back for piano lessons. It certainly kept me busy and I was doing a lot of gardening for Cheryl which I loved, and of course, mowing the lawn which I also enjoyed. The property looked great. Once September came, I started teaching again and still loved doing it.

When the time came for Danny and Sylvie's wedding, I went down to Quebec for the weekend. It was the most beautiful October day in Magog and the colours of the autumn leaves were spectacular. Danny and Sylvie had booked a place for me to stay which was really kind of them. It was great to see them and we had a great visit. Helga and John, Danny's parents, were originally from Denmark and had started up a furniture business in Hamilton that had been very successful. As soon as I got to the wedding venue, I spotted them and it was great to see them again. They were happy to see me and when I talked about 'Danny' they told me that, after Warren and I left Oakville in 1976, no one was allowed to call him Danny anymore. Everyone had to call him Dan. So to this day Warren and I are the only ones who call him Danny. As the ceremony approached, I was very nervous about one passage in the service I was delivering because I wanted to say it in French and my French left a lot to be desired. But I got through it and the wedding went well. Danny and Sylvie looked so happy and I was very happy that I could share in their special day with them. I was sorry that Warren and Susan were not able to come to their wedding but they had had a very busy six months of their own. After the wedding, I got a letter from Susan on October 20th:

> "…We are so glad that you had a good time at Danny's wedding and that everything went well….I have been enjoying my volunteering in the grade 2/3 class. The kids are wonderful and we have fun together. Warren is busy making chocolate chip cookies. He has been wonderful to me while I've been getting used to the move and a new city. Vancouver is so big, it can be quite overwhelming. We have a great view out our window and a cozy apartment. When can you come for a visit? We'd love to have you…...Take care, we are thinking of you."

It was wonderful to get this letter from Susan and I missed them very much. Then there was a terrible tragedy just before Christmas. Reverend Joan Henderson died on December 17, 1995 of a blood clot in her leg that moved to her heart. She was only 37 years old and the minister at Westdale United Church in Peterborough. Joan had been a wonderful support to me when I trained for the Interim Ministry and she had been my supervisor. I was devastated when I heard she was gone. Joan had gone into the Peterborough hospital for a minor procedure and was home recovering. The day she died she had spoken to her husband on the phone at noon and just after that conversation she collapsed. One of the men doing some work at their home saw she was in trouble and called an ambulance but she was gone before they could get her to the hospital. The church was packed for her funeral and all the ministers who came were seated at the front on the right side of the church while the immediate family sat on the left side. Reverend Marion Davies, who had retired back in June had moved to Plaster Rock, New Brunswick with her husband to be the minister in the United Church there for two years. She flew back for the funeral and we sat together. I don't remember much about the service because it was so upsetting but I do remember that Joan's husband Warren was grief stricken. When the family walked down the aisle, Warren was walking wtih Joan's identical twin sister which was shocking because she looked exactly like Joan. It was so difficult to lose such a good friend and such a good minister who had so many more years of service ahead of her. I really missed Joan and still do to this day. She was a wonderful friend and a kind and compassionate minister who was dearly loved.

The next week was Christmas and I spent time with Susie in Oakville because she felt safer at home. She was now 87 and had even stopped going to the pool to swim because she had contracted a serious infection in her foot which turned almost black because she didn't look after it. Dr. Soanes said she had probably gotten it from the pool and he gave her pills to take but she sometimes got mixed up so a nurse came in to help her with her pills three times a week. Warren and Susie did not come back for Christmas and I missed them terribly and I was worried about Susie. It was a very busy year for me right from the beginning. I joined the brave new world in 1996 and bought a computer. It was big and clunky and not easy to use but it was a beginning. I took a couple of courses but still had difficulty. Typing on it made things a bit easier for me but then there was email I had to learn about. I told myself that better times would come for me and the computer.

All of my students continued to do well in their exams, both in January and June, and so did those of my students who competed in the Kiwanis Festival in April. I was very proud of all of them. I also decided to give two benefit piano concerts, one at Mount Albert United Church on March 24 and the other on September 29, at Prince Albert United Church. Music has always been so much a part of me and it has always made me very happy to do this and I was able to help raise money for these two churches. With Warren so far away and Susie getting much older, I felt for the first time a disconnect from my family which was really hard. Playing the piano helped me reconnect and sharing my music at these concerts was important to me. Susie was really happy to hear that I was continuing my music and performing.

Warren and Susan were very busy too. Warren wanted to take the Clinical Pastoral Education training at Vancouver General hospital from May to August, but first he had to get into the training program. But the professor who supervised the students in this CPE program wouldn't take anyone under 28 and Warren was 26. Warren was very concerned about that because he really felt he needed that clinical training before going on his field placement in September. He spoke to one of his professors who then went and talked to the CPE supervising professor about Warren and asked her if she would at least talk with him. She agreed, and Warren went in to see her. He wasn't there five minutes when she told him he could take the CPE Unit. She told him she very impressed with his maturity and that she had never made an exception before. Warren was so happy. When he told me the hospital he was taking this training in, I reminded him that he was born there. At the end of April, Warren and Susan flew to the UK to visit her paternal grandmother, Vera Wheat (nee Poole) and took pictures of their wedding for her to see. Then, on June 15th, Susan's gran passed away. She was the last of Susan's grandparents to go and that was very hard on her. I wished I could be there with her and decided that I'd go out to B.C. for two weeks near the end of July after Warren's CPE was finished. I was so happy to spend time with them and we had a great time together. While I was there, I got the chance to know Susan even better. She was such a lovely person to be around and so positive and she had really good energy. They showed me all around the university and I saw lots of changes since I had been there from 1968-71 when I received my Bachelor of Music Degree. Susan and Warren had told me they were going back to the UK for three weeks in August to meet her mom and dad there, help them clean out her gran's house and visit with many of the family there.

Warren had passed his CPE with flying colours and when his Supervisor heard that I was coming for a visit, she told Warren she would like to meet me. I asked him why but he said he didn't know. We met for lunch and she told me she was so impressed with my son and couldn't understand why he was as mature as he was. I liked her and I told her I was very glad that he had done so well under her supervision. Then she asked me what I had done. I told her that my mother had given me up when I was three years old to her family in Oakville and that I knew what it felt like not to feel loved as a child. I told her I had raised Warren on my own and that all I wanted for my son was to feel loved. Then it was time to go back home.

Susan and Warren moved to Picture Butte, Alberta for his field education from September, 1996 to May, 1997. Picture Butte was known as the Feed Lot Capital of Canada and was close to Lethbridge. Warren was very excited about this posting and Susan got a job as a Teaching Assistant at the High School in Picture Butte. It was another change for them but they had a great time there and Warren did very well. There was an article written up about them in the local Alberta paper, *The Sunny South News*, in September and they sent me a copy:

> "Members of the Picture Butte United Church congregation will be seeing a new face over the next eight months. Warren Vollmer has been taken under the Church's wing as a student intern minister. He will be working under the supervision of Rev. Paul Taylor… .…he will lead worship on occasion, make home and hospital visitations and perform other duties as outlined in a 'learning covenant', Taylor says… ..He also ended up following in his mother's footsteps. A minister herself, she had made her claim to fame as the first single parent ever ordained in Canada… ..He expects to be assigned to a rural church after graduation, so he says he wants to intern in a rural setting as well. He has lived in smaller towns than Picture Butte, but the rural lifestyle will be new to his wife, Susan… .As for how his wife is taking to it, "so far so good," he says. The church arranged to provide the young couple with housing, and they have already been treated to several Alberta beef dinners and housewarming gifts. The Church also helped Susan find her job as a teaching assistant at Picture Butte High School. "The people here have been just wonderful," Vollmer says. "That sense of community is really great."… .He expects it to be a good learning experience where he can "explore ministry and get a good sense of my own gift."

One morning I went down to see Susie and she had a friend visiting. I needed to talk to the community service people about Susie and went to the bedroom to call. While I was doing this, I heard Susie say something about her weighing 10 pounds just as the woman from community service came on the line and we started talking. At that point Susie and her friend walked into the bedroom as her friend said, "You don't weigh 10 pounds Susie. Potatoes weigh 10 pounds." At that point Susie dropped her robe on the floor and stepped stark naked on the scale. I yelled at Susie to put her clothes on but she paid no attention to me. Her friend bent over and looked down at the scale and said, "You weigh a hundred pounds, Susie". The poor woman on the phone didn't know what was going on and I had to tell her that my aunt was standing on the scale bare naked trying to prove she weighed 10 pounds. Susie reluctantly put her robe back on and we all had a good laugh about it.

Jana and I had also talked a lot on the phone. She had bought an Apple computer and George taught her how to work it. She got very creative with it and loved it. George was constantly writing articles for the newspaper he owned and used this format to express his opinion on different things while Jana was typing everything that needed to go into the newspaper. She was also working fulltime at the Hilltop as their bartender and felt that time she worked there gave her much needed time away from George. We were both moving into 1997 with some major changes around the corner.

I had a lovely Christmas with Susie that year and stayed 10 days to be with her and go swimming every day. At Warren's wedding I had had an idea to do something special for his birthday in April, at that time eight months away. I wanted to prepare my family history and Warren's family history on his father's side. It would be a daunting task and now I only had four months left to finish this. I was very busy with the scrapbooks. I had done one on the Kelso Music Centre and one on my family's history and now I was working on Warren's father's family history for which I had help from Barbara Genrich, Bill's cousin. I had copied lots of very old photos of my family and Warren's father's family and made up a family book of photos, including dates and history for Warren. I had undertaken quite the task and was very passionate about this and now, more than ever, I was determined to finish it. When I was done, there would be seven of these large scrapbooks for Warren.

By the end of March, most of the snow was gone and one evening, around 8 p.m., I was driving home on Highway 35 south which ended at Highway 115 going north. I was almost there and was coming down a long hill when I saw a car turning right on the turnoff to 115 south and I thought nothing about that until this car suddenly made a U turn right in front of me. As I tried to stop, I clearly heard a voice in my head say, 'you are going to hit this car and you will be alright'. I couldn't stop in time and I slammed into the side of this woman's car. Luckily, I hit her car between the front door and the passenger door. That probably saved her life but it totaled my car. I was in shock and just wanted to get out of my car but I seemed to be stuck. Finally, I was able to open my door and squeeze out as some people ran over and asked if I was alright. I didn't know if I was but I couldn't stop shaking. Other people stopped and came over and a man came over to me and he could see I was in shock. He said his car was warm parked it on the other side of the road and I went with him. He was so kind and it was very warm in his car. When a couple of tow trucks arrived he asked me if I would like to call someone. I didn't even understand exactly what he was asking but I told him my phone number and he called the house and gave me his phone. Cheryl answered and I said I was in a car accident and told her where I was. Then I saw a police car and thanked this man for his kindness and went over to talk with the officer. The officer had the other driver in his car and she was not injured, nor was her daughter who had been in the car with her. He put me in the back seat with her and then he got in the driver's seat and took all our information. It was obvious what had happened, there was no denying it, and he was quite clear on who did what. The officer charged the woman and then let her go. One of the tow truck drivers came over to try to get some business and I told the police office I was happy to have the help. I got out of the police car and gave the tow truck driver all my information. When Cheryl arrived and came over to see how I was, I was still shaking. An ambulance showed up then but I didn't want to go with them because I thought I was fine so I had to sign a release form. Finally we were able to go to the house but, when I got there, I didn't feel well and asked Cheryl to drive me to the hospital in Peterborough. It was so good of her.

It was a very, very foggy night and a difficult drive for Cheryl but when we got to the hospital they took x-rays and checked me over. My chest was purple from where the steering wheel had jammed into me but they said I was just lucky. They gave me some meds and sent me home. I couldn't thank Cheryl enough for being there for me. The next day, I called my insurance company and was told that I would get a cheque from the woman's insurance company for the full amount I paid for my new Hyundai Accent back in September. In the meantime, I was covered for renting a car for two weeks until everything was settled. A couple of days later, Cheryl took me out to the lot where my car was to get my things. My car was totally wrecked. It didn't take long for me to get a cheque from the insurance company and buy a new car.

After the accident, I was taking physio twice a week at the Port Perry Hospital, but after three months of treatments, I didn't feel I was getting better. A member of the Millbrook United Church congregation told me that 25 years earlier, he needed back surgery because of driving a tractor on the farm most of his life. He decided to try acupuncture first and went to see Dr. Mah, a medical doctor in Toronto who had come to Canada from China where he had studied acupuncture. He took a number of treatments from Dr. Mah. When he went back to his doctor to schedule an appointment for surgery, his doctor had another x-ray done and told him he didn't have a back problem anymore and asked him what had happened and he told him. He was now telling me that Dr. Mah's daughter Angela Mah, had gone to China to study acupuncture and had a practice in Toronto. I set up an appointment with her. I called my insurance company and told them that I wanted to try the acupuncture because the physio hadn't helped me. They said they would pay for nine sessions but it was not a permanent solution. Those sessions three times a week for three weeks with Angela were amazing and, after those sessions, I was back to normal.

Susie was turning 89 on May 3 and I planned a special surprise birthday party for her at the Mandarin in Oakville. I was expecting 20 people to come including Barb and Gerry Genrich, Al and Jessie Stebbings and their two daughters Heather and Diane and other family members and friends. Warren was also coming home for Susie's birthday party and Susan sent me a note before Warren flew back to Oakville.

> "Hi. How's life? I am missing things there already! Wish I could be there – but someone has to work! Warren has a tiny parcel of goodies for you – make sure you get them. Only 40 more days of school left for me. I cannot believe that Warren is done here so fast. Time sure does fly by! Spring is slowly arriving here in Alberta. I miss trees but absolutely love the sky! Hope you are recovered from the accident and that you are healing well. What a shock that was! I hope you have a great visit with Warren. I know he has been looking forward to the trip. Have a SUPER birthday party with Susie. I send her all my best wishes also to you."

I knew how excited Susie would be because she loved a party, especially if she was the belle of the ball. She also loved company and had made some friends in the apartment building where she lived for 19 years. About three years earlier, she had befriended a family from Lebanon who lived on the fourth floor and she would invite this woman and her son for tea when her husband was working. This woman really liked my aunt and Susie loved to learn about different people and cultures. She was very well read and still read every day. Warren came home near the end of April and I was so happy to see him and met him at the airport and took him to Susie's since he was staying with her which made Susie very happy. I brought all the scrapbooks I had made for him with me to Oakville and had even wrapped them up for him. Even though he was tired that first night, he opened them all. When he looked through some of them, he told me he appreciated what I had done. Susie got all dressed up for her birthday with a nice skirt and blouse and scarf and she did love her scarves. She looked lovely. She had no idea who was coming so, when we got there, she couldn't believe all the people who had come to celebrate her birthday. She was really surprised and so happy to see everyone. Her eyes just lit up at the end of the dinner when they brought her a muffin with a candle on it and we all sang happy birthday to her. I was so happy for my aunt. When Warren and Susie and I got back to the apartment I could see Susie was very, very tired but she said she had a wonderful time. The next day was Mother's Day and Warren had been asked to preach at St. John's United Church that day May 4th. Susie and I went with him to church. Susie wanted to sit on the main floor and I sat up in the balcony and had so many emotions on that very special Mother's Day. As I listened to him preach I could not hold back the tears and it was so emotional for me as I thought of him as a little boy, and what a good little boy he was. I thought of all the decisions he had made and here he was, my son, all grown up and preaching in my home church. It was very special. Here is the last paragraph of Warren's sermon that day:

> "For our purpose as Christians is to reach out, to help, to share, to bring love and peace into the world. Whew, that is a tall order if I ever heard of one and it is easy to get carried away, get real full of our own holiness, and become a religious zealot. Again we strive for balance, for the harmony, but for me the call is all. To do other than answer the call is to go against my very nature, and stubborn I may be, and somewhat thick on occasion, I'm not stupid. With all my engineering experience, I have come to realize that much as I find the responsibility of ministry scary like nothing else, it is what I was meant to do. It is what I am called to do. It should be quite an adventure, and I must admit that I am looking forward to it."

We went out for lunch with Susie at the Swiss Chalet afterwards and it was wonderful and very special to be together just the three of us. After we took Susie home and Warren came home with me and stayed with me at Cheryl's for a couple of days. He loved the house and yard and the downstairs with the fireplace. It was great to have him back and then, all too soon I took him back to the airport. It was hard to see him go. I only got down to Oakville to see Susie about three times after her birthday because I was so busy preparing my students for their exams in June. I didn't get down to see Susie as often as I should have. I called the superintendents weekly to see how she was doing and they told me everything was fine. I also called Susie every day to see how she was and she always told me she was fine but it was hard to know because she never complained. Then, on Wednesday, June 11, my whole world changed. It was about 2:30 in the afternoon and, as I was getting ready to leave home to teach, the woman who looked after Susie called me and said my aunt wasn't well and was not responding. She didn't know what to do and I asked her to please stay with her until I got there. I dropped everything and phoned my students and cancelled the next two days and took the parents lists with me so I could phone the rest of them if I had to. I got down to Oakville about 4:30 and went right into the bedroom to see Susie. She was coherent but didn't want to go to the hospital so I didn't call the ambulance. I asked the woman to stay with me and she was glad to. I went in and sat with Susie for a very long time as she just rested. Then I phoned Jana and told her what was happening. We just talked quietly together and she told me she felt so badly for me and wished she could be there. Around nine in the evening I called Warren and told him what was happening. He wasn't sure what to do but I told him to just wait and that even though Susie didn't want to go to the hospital, I told him that I knew she would have to go at some point and I would call to let him know. In my heart, I knew my aunt was dying but I promised her she could stay in her apartment as long as she wanted.

At 10:00 p.m. Susie took a turn for the worse and I had to call the ambulance. Her caretaker left and I was grateful to her for the time she had spent with me helping me with my aunt. When the ambulance came, the paramedics could not have been kinder to my aunt as they gently lifted her up and took her out. I went down with them and followed them in my car to the hospital. They took her to emergency first while they tried to get her a room. They told me it wouldn't be long and I said I would be staying with her. Then the doctor and nurses left us but one of the nurses came back from time to time to check on her. Susie wasn't awake but I knew she could hear me as I talked to her about our family, how much we all loved her and the wonderful times we had together. I also talked to her about Warren and how much he loved her. Finally, they got her a room upstairs and she was settled in around midnight. I called Warren again and, when I heard his voice, I just started to cry and cry. I couldn't get the words out but finally told him that Susie was dying. He said he would come as soon as he could get a flight out but I told him not to since he wouldn't get here in time and I would call him when I knew more. He said he would check the flights in the meantime and wait for my call. I went back to Susie's room and just sat and talked quietly to her about the funny things she did and how much we enjoyed her antics and what a character she was and how much we all loved her. I told her she was going to be with her sisters, Louise and Mom, and Uncle Hugh would be there and grandma and grandpa and Uncle Phil and Dad. It was so hard for me. Susie was the last of my family and I didn't want her to go, but I knew it was her time. Around 2:00 a.m. she passed away. I kissed her and held her hand for a moment and then went out to call Warren to tell him she was gone. We were both upset and he asked me if I was alright and I said I would be fine. He said he could get a flight out around 3:00 a.m. his time and would be into Toronto around 9:00 a.m. my time. Susan would phone me at the apartment with the details. I hung up the phone and went to talk to the nurses about which funeral home to call to take Susie. As I headed out the hospital entrance, a nurse came up to me and said she had been in the emergency room with Susie when I was there and had been so moved by the way I talked with my aunt and the stories I told my aunt of the great times we had spent together. She was so kind to come and tell me what she did.

I got back to Susie's apartment and just couldn't believe that it was over. Susie was gone. I missed her so terribly already and felt I hadn't spent enough time with her. But was there ever enough time. Susan called and told me Warren was at the Calgary airport and gave me all the information I needed. When I called Jana and told her that Susie was gone we both cried. She said she couldn't come and I understood that but she wanted to know when the funeral was and I told her I would call her with the details after I made the arrangements. I really appreciated it. It was very quiet in the apartment with only me there and I felt so lonely and so sad. I didn't think I'd be able to sleep, but, once I put my head on the pillow, I was gone. I woke up at 7:30 a.m. and called Bill and told him Susie had passed away and he was so sorry and asked me if I was alright. I told him I was fine and would let him know when the funeral was because he said he would be there. I really appreciated that and told him that Warren was flying in that morning. I had a lot of phone calls to make and I had to see the Funeral Director but he could wait until after I picked Warren up. I was waiting at the airport for Warren and was never so relieved to see anyone when he came running over to me. We just hugged and hugged and I started crying again.

He drove my car back to the apartment and I told him that I had talked to his dad and he was coming to the funeral. When Warren got to the apartment, he called Susan and asked her to come because his father was going to be at the funeral and he really wanted her to meet him, so she set about getting a flight out. I called Barb Genrich and Al and Jessie and many of our friends. I also made an appointment for Warren and me to go to the funeral home after lunch and make arrangements. I called Pierre and told him about Susie. He said he was away the next few days and was sorry that he would be unable to attend the funeral and told me how sorry he was. I appreciated that. I thanked him for all his help for both my aunts and how much it was appreciated. Susan called and told Warren she would be at the Toronto airport about 7:00 p.m. I was so glad Susan was coming and that they would both be staying for six days.

Warren and I went to talk with the Funeral Director and told him that we wanted an open casket and then cremation. The funeral would take place on Saturday, June 14th at 11:30 a.m. with a reception to follow. I planned that the next time Warren and Susan were down, we would spread Susie's ashes at the cottage at the Sandbanks which she so loved. We wanted the service to be very simple but I didn't know the minister who would be doing it as Reverend Jim Campbell was away so I asked Warren to take part. I let everyone know when the funeral was and then I slept most of the afternoon.

Warren made a bed for him and Susan on the rug in the living room and I slept in what had been Louise's room and we all went to bed. I was exhausted and I just crashed. In the morning I woke up crying and got out of bed and I went and lay down beside Warren. I just started sobbing and couldn't stop. He put his arm around me and just let me cry. When I finally got up, I went to the kitchen to make breakfast and Warren and Susan got up. After breakfast I phoned and cancelled all my piano lessons until the following Thursday when Susan and Warren would be flying back home. I had made arrangements with the funeral home to go down the evening before the funeral to put photos up on their boards for viewing at the funeral and reception afterwards, so I started looking through the apartment for family pictures. Susie had them everywhere in the apartment. Warren and Susan stayed home when I went to the funeral home. I was very upset as I was putting up the pictures but I wanted to do it right. Susie had pictures of all the family, at one time or another, and I wanted to put their names on and dates. It took me about two hours to put everything up but I was so pleased after it was done and it helped me to begin the process of healing. Then I went back to the apartment.

Susie's funeral was hard but Warren did a wonderful job talking about Susie. When he talked about her two favorite shows, *Jeopardy* and *Wheel of Fortune* he even sang the *Jeopardy* theme at which point everyone laughed. I know it was hard for him to do this but he was great. After the service we had the reception and Warren was so proud to introduce Susan to his father. Bill had a big smile on his face when he met Susan and I was so glad he came. Everyone was so nice and then it was over. We were all back at the apartment when the phone rang and it was the woman from Lebanon whom Susie had befriended. I knew she had separated from her husband and had moved to Toronto but she was calling to see how "Mrs. Carson" was. I had to tell her we just came back from her funeral and she was so sorry and told me how much my aunt's friendship had meant to her. She said my aunt was her first Canadian friend. It was wonderful to get this phone call and hear what a friend my aunt had been to her.

Now we had work to do to clear out the apartment. Warren had called his friends in New Liskeard, Dave Johnson and Ronald Glassford, and had asked them if they could come down the day after the funeral and help us clean out the apartment. They knew we didn't have a lot of time and we needed to get the apartment empty in the next few days so they came down from New Liskeard early Sunday morning and we rented a room for them to stay over two nights. I didn't want many of Susie's things but I took a couple of pieces of furniture and told Susan and Warren they could take what they wanted and store them in a storage unit in Oakville until they needed them. By the time Dave and Ronald came, Warren and Susan knew what they wanted and that went first to the storage unit which was just big enough to take all the furniture. Ronald and Dave were a huge help as we worked around the clock. Finally, we were done and the apartment was empty. Susan had done a great job following us around and cleaning up. We couldn't thank Ronald and Dave enough for all their help and support. It was emotionally exhausting for Warren and Susan and me but now it was over and I drove Warren and Susan to my place. They were staying with me for two nights until they flew home. Cheryl cold not have been kinder to all of us which I appreciated. The morning I drove Warren and Susan to the airport to fly back to Alberta was very difficult for me. As we said goodbye, I could see that it was hard for them too. But we all had to get back to our routines and in a way, I was thankful that I had to start back at teaching that afternoon because it helped me focus and keep my mind off things. When Susan and Warren got back to Alberta, she sent me a nice note:

> *"Hi! Thanks for having us both in Oakville and at your home. It was a hard and busy time….. Seeing Susie's apartment brought back many memories which made it all the*

more difficult to clear out. I think we all did a tremendous job by getting it done so quickly. I am so glad that you managed to arrange that birthday party for Susie. She must have loved seeing Warren again. It also must have been wonderful to have had so many family and friends there. And to have done the family history – Wow! What a terrific job you did, Dorinda. I have spent a bit more time looking at the albums and now I understand why you were so overwhelmed. What a big task! I cannot imagine trying to get it all organized and sorted out! I am thrilled to have met Bill and still think about the look that passed between us as we shook hands. I only wish I knew him more – and Warren, I'm sure, does too."

Susan and Warren were winding down their time in Picture Butte, Alberta as they began to pack for another move – this time back to Vancouver. Warren's time at the church had ended and Susan was almost finished teaching. They moved back to Vancouver in early July and Susan told me that it was nice to get back to a larger centre where there were many friendly and familiar faces. Over the summer, she worked at a couple of office jobs for a total of about 15 hours a week while Warren madly wrote papers for the university courses he hadn't finished. It had been hard for Jana when Susie died because she couldn't come for the funeral. Pierre couldn't come to Susie's funeral either but, after I called him to tell him the news, he received a letter from my sister and wrote her back on July 30th and she sent me a copy of Pierre's note:

"Dear Jana, How nice to hear from you after all these years! And I'm only sorry it was occasioned by the loss of Susie. But as I recently wrote Dorinda, I was happy that she went so quietly and peacefully and that Dorinda was with her at the end. It was nice of you to share your memories in Kleinburg with Janet and myself. You certainly had an adventurous life since then and we really appreciated getting all the news. Good luck and all the best."

I was still getting my bearings after Susie's death when I got a phone call on August 6 from the family of my dear friend Jean Boggs. They told me she had died and had requested in her will that they ask me to officiate at her funeral. I was shocked and very upset by the news. Jean and I had been great friends and what a support she had been to me in those difficult times in Grand Valley. I had seen Jean off and on through the many years when we would meet in Orangeville for dinner once in a while and she had even come for my covenanting service in New Liskeard and stayed overnight with Warren and me. The family told me the service was to be at 2:00 p.m. on August 8th at Trinity United Church. I called June and Wayne Maycock who still lived across the road from the manse. I asked them if I could stay with them overnight as I was coming the next day to do Jean's funeral. They said of course I could. Then I looked through all my photographs to find some photos I had taken of Jean. She never liked to have her picture taken but I managed to get a couple of good photos of her and I made copies for her family.

It was wonderful to see June and Wayne and when I got settled in, I went to Jean's home. On the table where she always sat was a hymn book, open at a hymn I didn't know. If it was there,

I knew it must have meant something to Jean so I decided I would sing it at her service. I went to the church and told the organist about the hymn and he said he would be happy to play it for me. When I went back to June and Wayne's, we had a nice evening catching up on all the news. They were really helpful and I appreciated being able to stay with them. Late that night, I wrote out what I wanted to say about Jean. I wanted to pay tribute to my friend and honour her for the wonderful person she had been. The service was difficult for me but, at the reception afterwards, it was really nice to see so many people from the two churches I had served back in 1981 and then it was time for me to go home. It was a good two hour drive and, on the way back, I thought about Susie and Louise and how much they had liked Jean, how well they had gotten along and enjoyed their visits with her whenever they came to visit me in Grand Valley. I remembered the many times Jean and I went out for dinner at the Garafraxa Inn in Belmont. Jean was one of those rare people who just touch the heart and she certainly touched my heart and I dearly loved her and missed her.

I was still grieving after Susie's death and now my dear friend Jean had died too. I was at an emotional low and didn't know what the fall or the next year would bring, but I had to start planning the next year of teaching 55 students and there was a lot to prepare. That kept me busy, as did the part time ministry of eight hours a week at Prince Albert and Port Perry. I still enjoyed my visits with the families there but I was worn down and, deep down, I knew that something had to change.

CHAPTER TWELVE

Another Milestone and Moving on

I have always been very proud of my sister for many reasons but there was one reason in particular. Back in 1996, Jana had told me she was writing about her life which turned out to be a book of 200 pages. She called it, *Remembering Eden* and it was about growing up in Ontario from 1948 to 1964, before she left Canada with Mom and Dad to move to California. She sent me her first draft. She loved writing her story which gave her a very creative outlet and throughout the process I encouraged and supported her. In 1998, she sent me a copy of her finished book which she had had printed for members of her family. I read the story of her life and early childhood and it was wonderful to read about our parents and aunts and uncles and grandparents. I was really proud of what Jana had accomplished and her book took me back in time and gave me a real boost that August, something I really needed.

Many things were on my mind that summer about the coming fall and I certainly had a lot to think about. I was thinking about how hard it was teaching in Mount Albert and Sanford. The long drive was taking a toll on me, especially in the winter, and I decided this would be my last year teaching there. I chose to do one more year because Collin was doing his Grade XIII exam in January 1998 and Nancy would be doing her Grade X piano exam in June. Nancy and Colin were really focused on doing their piano exams and I wanted to finish on a high note with my 11 students. When I told my students and their parents in the fall of 1997, that this would be my last year with them, they were very sorry to hear it. They understood and appreciated the effort I was making to continue teaching one more year. I felt relieved when I finally made this decision.

September was also a very busy time for both Warren and Susan. Warren was in his last year at Vancouver School of Theology and, later that year, Warren had his final interviews with Hamilton Conference. He had no problems and so he would be ordained by the Conference on May 24, 1998 in Mount Forest. Here was another milestone coming in both Susan and Warren's life as well as my own and I had to ask myself where the time had gone. In September, Susan began several new jobs in Vancouver, providing child care for an 18 month little girl named Hannah, as well as tutoring students for Grade IX math. In addition, she was continuing with one of her previous office jobs. Warren began a field placement working 20 hours a week in a church in Vancouver where his main focus was on the youth group and visiting families in the congregation.

That Christmas was particularly hard for me. It was another Christmas without Warren and Susan who stayed in Vancouver, and the first Christmas without Susie. I missed my family terribly that Christmas. All my family that had raised me was gone and I was it. I just felt very sad and lonely. I told myself that I had 1998 to look forward to, because it was going to be a very special year with Warren's ordination which made me feel a little more positive going into the

New Year. I felt very vulnerable and I spent a lot of time talking on the phone with my sister. She understood, and, without her there at that time, I don't know what I would have done. Jana was also having a very difficult time in her relationship with George and things hadn't worked out the way she had hoped.

In January I started thinking about something special I could do for Warren's ordination and I decided to have an 'ordination dinner' and invite many of our special friends and family. Because the ordination service would be held in Mount Forest, not far from Grand Valley, I thought the logical place to have the dinner would be the Garafraxa Inn where Jean and I used to go for dinner. I called the Inn and made sure the place was available for a buffet dinner in their big room. I booked it for Sunday, May 24th at 7:30 p.m. and told them I thought there might be 40 people. Now that I had the place, I could start inviting people and I was quite excited about this. I invited friends from Grand Valley and Monticello, New Liskeard, Warsaw and family from Warren's father's side. It was a lot of fun planning this and setting up a program for the dinner. I asked my friend Cindy DiLorenzo from Oakville if she would be Master of Ceremonies and she agreed. Then I asked many other people to speak at the dinner and told Danny, Ronald, and Tom to feel free to say whatever they wanted to. I sent out invitations in March and told everyone the ordination service was May 24th at 4:00 p.m. and the dinner would be at 7:30 p.m. The best part of all of this was that Warren had no idea who would be coming to this dinner or what I had planned. People were sworn to secrecy and they did that very well.

Not long after I sent out the invitations people started replying. I received a note from Rolla and Ossie Foreman of Grand Valley:

> "Ossie and I were so happy to receive an invitation to Warren's Ordination and also to have the chance to meet Susan…..when Warren stayed at our home we were very glad to have him, even then as a young boy he had his nose in books. Dorinda we always felt good that you have kept in touch with our family…..So on May 24th at 4:00 p.m. we will see you in Mount Forest."

And from our dear friends in Winnipeg Reverend Bill and Gertrude Whetter:

> "We were pleased to receive your letter with such wonderful news and that fine picture of your handsome son. We are all so proud of Warren. I will always remember Warren as the little boy who was extremely fond of fresh buns and fresh peaches!! What a wonderful Ordination Dinner with your host of friends – and what a proud and loving mother. Congratulations plus."

Pierre wrote me from his office in Toronto March 17th:

> "It was very nice to hear from you the other day………... I'm also delighted about Warren's ordination. He's a great boy and I'm sure he'll do well. I'd like to come to the dinner but

I won't be able to make it as we have house guests, first my sister Lucy, whom you know, and later on Janet's brother and his wife, all around that time. Please wish Warren well for me, you must be very proud of him."

Then, at the end of March, I got a phone call that Edythe Harris was dying of cancer. Edythe had been my Guidance Counselor in 1963-64, my last year at high school in Oakville. She had been such a support through all the years and we had often gone out for dinner to visit. I went to see her at her home in Toronto and she told me she didn't want to die and felt it was so unfair. I picked up the bible she had beside her bed, shared passages with her and then said a prayer offering God's comfort. I told her how much she meant to me and how much I loved her. Edythe was buried through her church, Timothy Eaton United Church in Toronto, at the end of April and I took part in the service. She was a true Christian who never counted the cost and was always there if you needed a friend. I found her death very hard and it brought back memories of my aunts and Edythe and the time she helped them move into their apartment when I lived in Manitoba. She was a wonderful friend and I missed her.

Through all the losses, I continued to focus on the ordination dinner and, by April, there were just over 50 people coming to the dinner. From Oakville there were: Walter and Jean Craig, Cindy and Dominic DiLorenzo, Carolyn and John Blakeley; from Sanford: Nancy and Jim Wolfe; from New Liskeard: Sharon Reynolds, Kitty Miller, Ronald Glassford, Elaine Glassford, Fern and Nora Ladacoeur, Donna Ladacoeur, Dave Johnson, Don and Sandy Haslam; from Montreal: Danny and Sylvie Nielsen and from Fergus: Danny's parents John and Helga Nielsen; from Toronto: Paul Hunter and Leslie MacKay; Mary and Danny Lozinski; from Grand Valley: June and Wayne Maycock, Ozzie and Rolla Foreman; from Monticello: Betty and Brian Johnston; from Millbrook: Jim and Wilma Bruton; from Hillsburg: Brent and Jennifer Willson; from Warsaw: Netta O'Marra, Donna and Gerry Hampton, Alice and Les Bryan, Maida Ormsby; from Peterborough: Phil and Doris Lowry; from Bethany: Dale and Peggy Mcquaid. Then there was Heather and Tom Wheat, Susan's parents, Warren and Susan and me.

Now that I knew who was coming I set about designing a program for the event. On the front of the program I put: "Ordination Dinner for the Reverend Warren David Scott Vollmer and Susan Vollmer". Below that, a cross and under that, Sunday, May 24th 7:30 P.M. at the Garafraxa Inn, Belwood, Ontario. Inside the program were listed those of us at the Head table: Cindy and Dominic, me, Warren and Susan, Heather and Tom and Mary and Danny. Below that I listed all the special friends who would be there that night and then our family members who were not able to attend: my sister Jana and Stacy and Scott in the States, Jilli and Paul Jackson in Halifax, Janet and Pierre Berton from Kleinburg and Jessie and Al Stebbing from Barrie. The last list was entitled, "In Memoriam" and included Warren's great-grandparents, his great aunts and uncles, his maternal grandparents and cousins who had all passed on. On the back of the program I had two sections. The first was titled, "Interesting History", and was about Warren's family, especially on his father's side, and ended with:

"On both sides of Warren's family there are eight ministers going back to the Reverend John Kipling in England in the early 1800's, who was the grandfather of Rudyard Kipling. Today there are nine ministers in Warren's family."

The second section was titled, "Some Final Words" where I thanked everyone for their love and support through the many years. This had taken me the first four months of the new year to get organized, working on it in between everything I was doing and it kept me upbeat and positive. I was very happy to do this for my son.

Just before Warren's ordination, I was invited to go back to St. Paul's United Church in New Liskeard to be part of their celebrations for their 100th Anniversary on May 3rd, 1998. It was an honour to be asked and wonderful to go back at St. Paul's and see many of my friends there. Warren and Susan flew home for the last two weeks of May, visited her parents in Ottawa and then came down and stayed with me as Warren prepared for his ordination. While they were with me, they went into Peterborough and bought a new Toyota Corolla. Susan had put away money her grandparents left her when they had passed away and had never used any of this money. Her dad didn't want them to go into debt for a car so, in addition to Susan's inheritance, her Dad paid off the rest of the car. After they got back to the house, I remember Warren standing in the kitchen telling me how strange it felt to have been able to pay cash for their car. "Mom", he said, "we have never been able to do that and we always had car payments". I was glad for them that they didn't have any debt except for his university education. It was wonderful of Tom to do that for them.

As excited as Warren was about his ordination, he was even more excited now that he knew where he would be settled for his first placement. I had thought they would continue to live in B.C. but it didn't appeal to Warren and Susan as much as the Maritimes had and Warren had hoped to get a placement in Nova Scotia so he could see his Dad once in a while since Bill and his wife were now living in Cape Breton. He didn't get Nova Scotia but he did get Berwick, New Brunswick, a four point pastoral Charge and he was very excited about that as was Susan. The Pastoral Charge was made up of four United Churches - Berwick, Pearsonville, Carsonville and Lower Millstream but Warren told me they only had two services on Sundays just like at the Warsaw Pastoral Charge. I had never been to the Maritimes but I knew I would be going there now and looked forward to that.

Warren asked me to lay on hands for his ordination and he also asked Reverend Jim Campbell from St. John's United Church in Oakville who, 22 years earlier, had laid on hands for my ordination. When we all arrived at Mount Forest the day of his ordination, Warren took me into the room where we put on our robes and that's when the reality started setting in that my son was getting ordained. It was a beautiful service. Those of us taking part in the service had to sit together and when Warren was called up to the front, Jim and I went up with him and we laid on hands for his ordination along with officials from Hamilton Conference. It was a deeply profound and moving moment for me. Like my Aunt Louise, I believed in my son's potential to do good and I knew this was the beginning of great things to come for him.

After the closing hymn and our procession walked out, there was a nice reception where family and friends gathered to greet their loved ones who had just been ordained. Then people going for Warren's dinner started leaving the reception to go to the Garafraxa Inn so they would be there at 6:45 p.m. and when I walked into the Inn, I was so pleased at how nice it looked. I had set out place cards for the head table and all the other tables were set up so people could sit wherever they wanted. When Warren and Susan arrived with Heather and Tom, they had no idea who was coming and they were thrilled to see so many of their family and friends there. It was a wonderful dinner. After dinner, the speeches started. Some of Warren's friends were roasting him and told stories about Warren that made everyone laugh. Tom, Warren's father-in-law, made a hilarious speech that showcased his wonderful, dry English sense of humour.

It was a great day and everything had gone so well. Warren and Susan came back with me so they could pick up their car in Peterborough the next day. They were driving to Ottawa to leave their new car with Tom and Heather while they flew back to B.C. It had been an emotional few days for me, filled with pride and love and close friends. The only advice I had given my son was: "Visit the people and then visit again and again; preach the Word with great passion and pray fervently; walk with your people and let them walk with you. Let God's love be your code of honour. Never neglect your wife or your family, for your heart is centered there, and always be true to yourself. Always love justice and walk humbly with God, following where Christ would lead you." It did my heart good to see Warren so happy and it was hard to see them go but it had been a wonderful time for me and for the people who came to celebrate with us. On June 10th I received a nice note from Jeanne and Walter Craig, friends I had known for 25 years:

> *"Thank you very much for the super pictures we received yesterday -a special one to cherish is the one of you, Jim Campbell and Warren. It is unusual that both mother and son were sponsored by the same church and the same minister. You must be very proud of your son and we felt honoured to attend the ordination of both."*

Joyce Stephenson from St. John's U.C. also wrote me June 26th and said:

> *"Thank you so much for sending along the pictures taken at Warren's ordination on May 24th. It was great that Jim Campbell was there to lay hands on him, just as he had for you 22 years earlier! Congratulations to Warren and to you for bringing up such an admirable son! We enjoyed hearing him preach a year or so ago when he was at St. John's one Sunday. These pictures will certainly be a nice addition to our church archives. I am hoping to start work on St. John's history soon, and the more information and pictures we have, the better. All the best to you and Warren."*

As soon as they got back home to B.C., Warren and Susan started packing up and, around the end of June, the movers came and picked up their things. Warren and Susan drove the Aspen to Oakville where they met the moving van at the storage unit and picked up everything there.

From there, the moving van went to Ottawa to pick up the two huge crates that had many things in them from Susan's grandparents. Susan drove the Aspen and Warren drove their new Toyota Corolla to Berwick and met the moving van there. The manse was next to Berwick United Church and there was about an acre of property out the back which, they told me, they would turn into a huge vegetable garden the next summer. They loved their new home and it didn't take them long to figure out where they wanted everything to go. The Maritimes seemed so far away to me and I knew I'd miss them but I kept telling myself it was much closer than B.C. Warren had told me that it was only a 16 hour drive to Berwick so that really wasn't bad and I looked forward to going there to visit them.

I was invited to preach at Port Perry and Prince Albert Churches on June 28th, 1998 which turned out to be very good for me to do. It gave me a chance to reflect on the four years I had been with them and, overall, it had been a very good experience. Over those years, I had gotten to know many families very well, even though it hadn't been easy to do those visits because so many were very ill and others were dying. But that was why Port Perry and Prince Albert United Churches had asked me to make these much needed visits for which I drew on my experiences in other churches and at Roseau. I called my sermon, "Looking Back" and talked about our faith and God's love for us and how, through Jesus, God's love is always present and there for us. I also talked about many of the families I had the privilege to visit. I talked about Lillian Peake who was a special person to me and her daughter Betty Deeth and how she and her brother had been there for their mother in her illness and stayed with her when she died. Lillian was a kind and loving person and I had deeply appreciated her kindness to me. I also talked about Glenn Wannamaker and his wife Marjorie and visiting in their home. Glenn had been one of the outstanding Elders in the church and Marjorie had stood by her husband's side through his illness and never wavered.

I talked about Reverend Charles Clarke and his wife Lila in Prince Albert. Charlie was, without a doubt, a great Christian. I remember sitting beside him one day at their home in Prince Albert when we both knew he was dying. I thanked him for all he had done in his long lifetime and told him how much, as a younger person in ministry, I looked up to him. He was a man of great wisdom and courage and his love for God and for Jesus inspired everyone who was fortunate enough to know him. I also talked about Clarence Fair who was a wise and gentle man and always had that twinkle in his eye and a smile for everyone. He was easy to love. Clarence and his wife Vera lived in Port Perry and had many wonderful years together and I always left smiling, knowing that God was right there with them every step of the way. I remembered Ena Harris who had such courage and love for her husband Gord and all her children and family. Most of us would have given up long ago but Ena believed in God and in God's love and she just carried on through her illness. But when her daughter Wendy died suddenly at the age of 41, both Gord and Ena were devastated and Ena never got over that and passed away about three months later. She was an example to me of courage and faith and an inspiration to me and I will never forget her. Grace Beacock loved me to visit and she was so fortunate to have her daughter Eileen Hodgins and son-in-law Terry just down the road. Grace thought the world of her granddaughter Heather who had married and moved to Australia and Heather had such love for her grandmother. I was privileged to see that when she came back to visit and brought her children with her. Grace loved to quilt and was such a treasure for her church and community. A gentle soul indeed. Les Beacock was a fine man and a good living Christian who loved his wife Grace and all of his family. He was a man of integrity who always thought of others before himself, and was loved by everyone who knew him. Another true Elder of the Church. These are only a few of the many people I visited who had a real impact on my life. I didn't know how much longer I would be in this Pastoral Charge. I felt I could do one more year because the ministry was very rewarding but I knew that I needed to make some changes in the near future. Only I wasn't sure in June 1998 how that would unfold.

I had had another great year teaching and a wonderful recital back in April. My students who had exams in January and June were very successful too. Colin got his Grade VIII piano in January and did well. I was so proud of him. Then, because he knew I wasn't teaching in the fall, he took the next six months working with me on his Grade II theory and did very well at the exam in June. Again I was proud of him. Nancy did her Grade X piano exam in June. She had been in a serious car accident years earlier and had trouble with memory loss from time to time so she couldn't memorize her pieces so I had written a note for her to give to her examiner explaining that and hoped that her examiner would take that into consideration. She was also 60 years old which, in itself, was remarkable. She got 68% on her exam and that was amazing. She was thrilled and I was very happy for her.

The summer seemed to go quickly and in September it was easier teaching since I didn't have to drive to Mount Albert and Sanford anymore. I was just beginning to feel much more positive when I got a phone call from Jessie in Barrie that Al had passed away in January 1999. Jessie had called a few times the week before after Al had been taken to the hospital so I wasn't surprised but I felt so badly for Jessie. She said she wanted me to do the service for Al on January 8 and I said I would. I called Warren and he was very upset. Al was special to Warren and had taken him to Camp Borden to show him around and had told him stories about when he was overseas in the Second World War. Al was so proud of Warren and what he had accomplished and would talk to everyone who would listen to him talk about Warren. He was so, so proud of him now that he was a minister. I wasn't surprised that Warren said he would fly out the next day. I picked him up at the airport and the two of us went up to Barrie for the funeral together. Jessie was so relieved to see us and very pleased that Warren had come. Al and Jessie's daughters Diane and Heather were there with their children whom Al had dearly loved. The Legion was also there at the funeral to honour Al and it was a wonderful celebration of his life. I was happy to see Diane and Heather again. We told stories about Al and Jessie and our families and had a great time reminiscing about all the fun times we had had together as cousins over the many years. I didn't know how Jessie would manage now without Al but Diane and Heather told me they would be with their mom as much as they could. After everything was over in Barrie, I took Warren back to the airport and then returned home. Although I didn't have much time with Warren I was so glad he had come.

Back in November, I had written a letter to Donna Sinclair, a writer for the *Observer*, the United Church of Canada's National magazine to ask if they would like to write a story about Warren and me since we had both been candidates in ministry out of the same church in Oakville with the same minister, Reverend Jim Campbell. In January Donna finally got back to me with the idea that Warren and I would write a love letter to each other as a special 'Mother's Day Message' to put in the May 1999 edition of the *Observer*. I talked this over with Warren and he thought it was a great idea. In March, I wrote a letter to Warren and then he wrote a letter back to me and that was the basis for the article that was written in the *Observer* which Donna Sinclair titled "Letters of Love" and wrote this introduction to our letters:

"When Warren Vollmer asked in 1992, to become a candidate for ministry from St. John's United in Oakville, Ont., its minister, Jim Campbell, asked what had taken him so long. Campbell had been there 20 years earlier when Warren's mother, Dorinda, became a candidate. She was the first ever from that congregation, and the first unwed mother to be ordained in the United Church. These letters between mother and son explore those strong calls that led them into ministry."

This is what I wrote to Warren:

Dear Warren:

My life has always been centered in God. I have not directed my life as much as I have been directed. As a child I would spend hours walking along the Sixteen Mile Creek across from our home in Oakville just talking to God, the way you would talk to your best friend.

My mom and dad sent me to live with your great-grandmother and great- aunts Louise and Susie when I was three. I was gifted in music, and Louise was a fine pianist and teacher. I remember when I was twelve, Susie and my grandma took me to see the opera Don Giovanni in Toronto. I fell in love with Mozart and vowed I would learn every one of his piano sonatas. My grandma loved me to read the Bible stories to her and play and sing those beautiful hymns. She loved Abide With Me and Rock of Ages. My love for music and playing the piano has always been a spiritual experience, grounded in our love for God.

Our family has a great deal of history at St. John's. One minister was outstanding, Rev. Jim Terry. He lived his faith, and as a child I hung on to his every word as he preached the Good News. I wanted to be a minister when I was five. I felt the call when I was 12 and again when I was 21. I had just finished my first year in music at the University of Toronto. I went to Covenant College to discuss becoming a minister. I was asked, "Dear, why don't you be a deaconess?" I was hurt and suddenly felt that being a woman minister must require something different. I chose not to answer the call.

Do you remember when we visited my friend in Hawaii? You were two years old; it was July 1972. One night I walked along on the beach and it was there I came face-to-face with God and knew what I had to do. I was 27 years old and had received the Bachelor of Music degree from the University of British Columbia the year before. We were moving from Vancouver back to our family home in Oakville. In the midst of all of this your grandmother died. It was very hard. After Mom's funeral I went straight to St. Johns' to see Jim Terry. He was no longer there but I was warmly received by Rev. Jim Campbell. So began the process that eventually led to my ordination in 1976.

All through your growing up, the church was our home and our family, from the Roseau River Indian Reserve in southern Manitoba, to – in Ontario - the Grand Valley Monticello pastoral charge, St. Paul's United in New Liskeard, and the Warsaw pastoral charge near Peterborough. The Roseau Reserve and all those congregations treated us as family and helped me raise you. Their values were centered in God and we were blessed everywhere we served.

You know the personal struggles I went through being a woman minister and single parent. I always said what I felt called to say. It wasn't always popular, but that's not why we are in the ministry. Thank you for being there in the very difficult times to hold my hand and give me a hug. You enter ministry knowing the pain as well as the joy.

I have gone back to my roots in music. I teach piano. It is a different kind of ministry; a Mozart sonata, a symphony by Beethoven, this music touches the heart of God. I try to help my students connect with that.

You too have chosen the ministry and have been called by God. I am so proud of you. Thank you for being my son and for serving with me all those years.

Love mom Oakville, Ontario

Then Warren wrote to me.

Dear Mom:

I got your letter the other day and was reminded of all the things we have gone through together and how that influenced my decision to enter ministry.

Do you remember that time in Grand Valley, I was about 12, when one of your parishioners asked me if I was going to go into the ministry? "No way!" was my response. "I know what it's like!"

Reading your letter made me remember my antagonism to the whole prospect of ministry. It certainly made me reflect on why I am here – particularly as the statement "I know what it's like" still holds. I saw a callous side of the church. I struggled with being a Christian in a church that found myriad ways to wound my mother; with living in a "Christian" community where, after a disagreement, someone would write "Go home Reverend Squaw" on the bridge in town. I saw a church Board attempt to tear my mother down. And yet here I am. The little boy that cried out "I know what it's like!" continues to be a part of me. I also witnessed – in a way few are privileged to witness – the power of faith to win out over rejection. I saw in my mother a faith that would not be browbeaten or intellectualized, a faith rooted in a sense of God, Christ and the Holy Spirit. That faith called and continues to call her to bring others into a relationship with the church.

I also saw the side of humanity that is beautiful. There are many people in this church whose faith and caring reminds you why you are a minister. Ministry, like most anything in life, has its paradoxes. We are granted the opportunity to bring the beauty of God to life, but we are also in the unenviable position of seeing how structures and individuals can be abusive. You showed me, Mom, that the beauty outweighs the harsher side by a million fold.

Thank you. You remind me never to be naïve. But you also give me an example that keeps me from being callous or unfeeling. I pray the Spirit strengthens me to live my faith with the courage and integrity you taught me.

Love, Warren Apohaqui, N.B.

I was so moved by my son's letter to me. I had had no idea how he felt about so many things that happened to me in the places I served. It was wonderful to read how he had put everything together and had come to a place where he could do ministry. It was overwhelming for me. I started to think about what I might do next and where God might be calling me again. I wasn't ready yet but writing a letter to my son and him writing back to me and saying what he did, began to help me open myself up to new possibilities. Then on May 27th I received a heart warming letter from a woman named Betty Bowers who had read the article.

"As a Presbyterian, I don't often see the United Church Observer. However, some kind friends gave me the May/99 issue with the article "Letters of Love". What a joy it must be for you and your son to share your faith as well as a calling to the ministry! The Rev. Jim Terry whom you mentioned was my brother and I was touched by your reference to him and of how his ministry had affected your life… … … … .Your first name was also interesting to our family. We have a daughter-in-law with that name… .Again, our congratulations to you and your son – your letters of love were inspiring. We also thank you for the kind remarks about Jim. It really 'made my day' to read that article. "

It was so kind of Betty to write to me and her letter took me back to when I was young child listening to her brother's sermons and the profound influence he had on me.

I was just starting to reexamine my life in May 1999 and where I was going. I was also thinking about what my sister had gone through in 1997 when George had become seriously ill and Jana had stood by him in that time and even helped significantly in his recovery. In January 1998 early one morning a few months after he fully recovered, a knock came at their door. George was picked up by people from the Immigration Department and sent him back to jail in Austria. He had been in the U.S. illegally for 10 years. In the blink of an eye he was gone and Jana called me and told me what happened. She said that for the first two years they were together she had no idea he was in the U.S. illegally. But I could only hear relief in her voice that he was gone. She said that, after he left, she found out he owed thousands of dollars to people he had defrauded. She was very worried that she would have to pay everyone back what he owed them because she knew all these people that George had used. She had become friends with many of them. They came and told her that they knew it was George and not her who had conned them and not to worry. They didn't expect to get any money back. Jana was so relieved, moved out of the old hospital they had lived in and found a small apartment to rent so she could move on with her life.

One night not long after George was taken away Richard Purcell came to Jana at her at work and asked her out. She had known Richard for a few years because he often came into the bar at the Hilltop and he would talk to her about the women he dated. Richard told her that he had seen how George treated her and he didn't like that at all. They started going out but Jana was very hesitant at first. In the spring of 1998, she had moved in with him. Richard had a five-acre home on the river which she just loved and she felt so relaxed and renewed living in the country where she could watch the beautiful birds and the beautiful river running by where, once in a while, a tugboat would float by. She told me she would wake up in the morning and make coffee for them and they would sit at their dining room table, look out the patio doors and watch the deer coming by the deck or walking in the field. My sister was so happy. They had differences, she told me, but over the past year they had worked into a comfortable relationship. They had both come into this relationship with a lot of baggage but I had a good feeling about Richard and thought he really loved my sister and cared about her. If I was right, they would work it out and, in the end, they did.

The bad relationship Jana had found herself in for seven years had ended and she had moved into a new, happier phase of her life. I was very happy for her and I wondered now what changes were coming for me. I had my student's recital on May 16th in Bethany United Church and it could not have gone better. For me, teaching had been the one constant that was so positive and uplifting in my life those last six years from 1993-1999 and I knew that I was really good at it. I also loved visiting the families I visited in the Port Perry and Prince Albert Churches, even when some of the visits were very difficult. I had been doing this ministry for five years (1994-1999) but I knew the Pastoral Charge was having some financial issues and had heard that my contract would not be renewed after the end of June. I was actually fine with that. The time for change was coming.

That summer I went to visit Susan and Warren in New Brunswick for two weeks. I was so happy to go and visit them in their new home to see for myself how they were doing. They had been there for a year by then and, by all accounts, they were very happy. They had a good sized bungalow with three bedrooms and a lovely big living room, dining room and kitchen. Downstairs there was a wood furnace which they told me really heated the house in the winter which had been brutal. They had turned most of their back yard into a vegetable garden and had flower gardens as well. They had done a lot of work and the property looked beautiful. They weren't far from the ocean and they showed me all around the area which was quite beautiful. They were very excited I had come and took me to Prince Edward Island. The ocean there was glorious. It was just wonderful to be with them. The second last day we were there, Warren had a funeral that afternoon and Susan wanted to take me to a special place that had wonderful ice cream. We had to go by ferry for part of the way and it was a lovely drive. Even though the ferry ride was short, it was fun and we enjoyed sitting outside eating our ice cream cones at the store. When Susan drove into their driveway, something didn't look right. My car wasn't quite where I had parked it but I knew that Warren didn't have my key to the car. As we came closer, I saw that my driver's door was bashed in. Warren came running out of the house as we got out of the car and I could see how upset he was. I asked him what happened and he told me that the Aspen, which was a huge car, was parked in the driveway when he came out to go to the funeral. He always turned it around in the yard and was in a hurry so he didn't pay attention and backed up and hit my car. Warren told me he had called the mechanic down the road and I would have to stay for an extra three days so the mechanic could fix it because he had to order in a new door. Warren said he would pay for it because he didn't want it to go on his insurance. I wasn't upset with Warren because Susan was really upset with him. I told him it was fine and I could stay a few more days. The car was fixed and I returned home. I felt so reconnected with Warren and Susan knowing how happy they were.

Back in September I had felt it was time to move on and I talked to Cheryl about this. I explained to her that I wanted to be out on my own again but I didn't want to let her down. She could see that I was restless and wanting a change and she didn't know any more than I did what that change might be for me. I told her I would like to look for an apartment in Peterborough which would be more central to all the students I taught. She was really very kind and understanding and told me she would be fine on her own and appreciated all the help and support I had given to her in her new home. So I started looking for an apartment to see what was out there.

In November I received some lovely flowers for my birthday from Warren and Susan. The card read:

> *"On Your Birthday, Mom. Put your right hand on your left shoulder. Put your left hand on your right shoulder. Now, squeeze! There! That's a hug from me! Happy Birthday. Susan wrote - Wishing you a very happy birthday. Can't believe how soon Christmas will be here. Advent is coming quickly too. Hope your special day is filled with joy. Warren wrote - Happy Birthday to you. Love you lots mom, Warren"*

I found a two bedroom apartment in Peterborough for January 1st. I talked to Warren about this and he said he would come down for three days and be there December 5th to help me move. I thought that was wonderful because I didn't know how I would do this move. He said he would drive down and drive me back to their place for Christmas and I could fly home from there. I was thrilled and excited to spend Christmas with Warren and Susan. He suggested I have the movers store my things and the superintendent of the apartment building said I could have the movers come December 30th. I told Cheryl that I had signed up for an apartment January 1st and that my son was coming to help me and I would spend Christmas with my family. She could see how happy I was about this move. She said that because I had helped her she would help me with the move in any way I needed her. I really appreciated that. It took us the three days to pack and Cheryl was a great help. The moving van was there at 8:00 a.m. and loaded everything up. All my things were taken to their storage unit and we arranged they would move my things into the apartment on December 30th. I called the superintendent at the apartment building to let her know I would be there on the 29th and would sleep on the carpet in the living room. I had already left my car at a parking space at the apartment building which I had arranged with the superintendent. I could not thank Cheryl enough for her help over these last 6 years because it made all the difference to me being able to teach again. I was so happy just to be with Warren, stopping on the road to eat, talking on the way.

When we got to Berwick, Susan was waiting and so happy to see us and I was so happy to see her. Their home looked beautiful. They had a six foot Christmas tree and it looked wonderful. Finally, I was once again with my family for Christmas. Warren did a wonderful Christmas Eve service and, on Christmas morning, Santa left good things in our stockings. We had the most wonderful visit. After paying the first and second month's rent for the apartment and paying for the moving van, I realized I didn't have much money left. Warren paid for the plane ticket and gave me a little extra money until I was working again in January and I paid him back. I had very little money but I was up for the challenge and looked forward to starting all over again. I knew how capable I was and I was so happy to be on my own again. I had the most wonderful Christmas and then it was time to leave. I was very excited to get to Peterborough, get my key to the apartment and settle in.

That evening I made up a letter for my students and their parents December 29th, 1999 newsletter which said:

> *"Warmest greetings and Happy New Year to all my students. I spent three weeks in December with my son Warren and his wife Susan in New Brunswick. I had a wonderful Christmas as I hope you all did as well. Most of you know that I have moved into Peterborough. I have my things in storage until tomorrow when I officially move in to my two bedroom apartment. I look forward to starting up again in January and thank you all for your patience in December. Don't forget that my adult students have a get together and party in February and there is a rehearsal party for my younger students towards the end of May with the recital set the first Sunday in June."*

The moving van came the next morning and the men moved all my things into the apartment. After the movers left, I immediately started sorting and unpacking. The furniture and my piano were already where I wanted them, so I just had to unpack my personal things. It was very exciting. Everything felt so new. I settled in and was looking forward to the challenges ahead. I called my sister just before I went to bed and she was so happy for me and this new adventure. My sister had been such a wonderful support to me through those last six years as I had been for her. I really felt there was a call there for me and I needed my own space to sort that out and challenge myself to see what this new change could be. I was very hopeful.

CHAPTER THIRTEEN

Orono, Coming Full Circle

I woke up on January 1st, 2000 to a new day, a New Year and a new millennium. I felt euphoric and I loved my apartment. I phoned Warren and Susan to wish them a Happy New Year. They wanted to hear how I had settled into my new apartment and I told them everything was just great. Then I phoned my sister. We had a long talk and laughed a lot and had a great visit. She asked me how I was feeling and I told her I felt great on my own again. She told me that she and Richard were getting along really well and she was very happy. I had 55 students, a number of them in Peterborough, some of them in the Millbrook, Cavan and Bethany area. I still went to their homes to teach them. I had also started thinking about going back into a Pastoral Charge because I missed the ministry. In early January, I put my name on the United Church of Canada's national list for ministers looking for a church and they sent me the national list of churches looking for a minister. I updated my resume and applied to a few churches. I was still torn because I felt an obligation to my piano students, many of whom had been with me six years, but I also felt God was calling me again to ministry and I had to test that call.

I heard nothing back from the churches I applied to so, at the end of March, I removed my name from the national availability list and I made a commitment to continue teaching while I tried to find part time ministry instead of full time. It wasn't a difficult decision because I loved teaching and I have always enjoyed young people. I was very much like my Aunt Louise in that way. She had had such a profound impact on my life. She passed on her love of music to me and had often told me that there was no nobler work than teaching, especially young people, because they have such energy and enthusiasm for life. They love to have fun, she told me, and are not encumbered by all the things their parents and other adults feel weighed down by.

All my students had done well at their exams in January and I was especially proud of my adult student Gerri Harvey who did her Grade IV exam which was a huge accomplishment. For an adult to even think of trying an exam is commendable and to do as well as Gerri did was great. Besides the fact that she was such a good student, I always enjoyed going to her home and teaching her because she loved to laugh and have fun and was always positive and upbeat. She was also a great gardener and could make anything grow.

Jana called me in early April and told me she and Richard were coming to visit me and I was thrilled. I wanted to meet Richard and besides, I hadn't seen my sister in a few years so this was going to be a very special visit. I cancelled all my lessons for the 10 days of their visit. When I met Richard and Jana at the airport, Jana and I were so happy to finally see each other again and it was wonderful to meet Richard. I liked him right away, particularly his smile and the way he laughed. I could see he thought things through before he made a decision and he was thoughtful and kind. He was very nice looking with receding white-grey hair and a moustache and he had nice eyes. He was about five years older than my sister, 5'10" and of medium build. We drove back to my apartment which Jana loved and she was happy that I was doing so well. But we didn't stay put for long and were soon off to visit Warren and Susan in New Brunswick. We left very early in the morning and it took us 14 hours to get there, stopping only for gas and meals on the way. Richard insisted on doing all the driving, which was fine with me. He told me he was a longshoreman and had worked very hard for many years, first in California and then in Coos Bay, Oregon where he had moved his family. He told me he drove the machinery that loaded and unloaded the tankers that came in from all over the world. He said that he found the winters especially hard because it rained so much and it was hard to keep warm since he worked outside. He talked about his two children who were raised on the ranch that he owned in Coos Bay and about how much he loved to hunt and fish. He said he hunted with a bow and arrow and could pull 75 pounds. I found that impressive. He had hunted for years with his dad and then later with his son and had always been very careful how he hunted and took only what he needed. The year after his father died, his 21-year-old son was killed in a tragic car accident. It was very hard on Richard losing two very significant people in his life in a year and his marriage broke up after these tragedies. His son had been living with his girlfriend who was pregnant at the time and, not long after this tragedy, she had a baby boy. Although Richard thought the world of his grandson Ryan, he and his mother lived in Colorado so Richard didn't see him often growing up. I felt badly for Richard because life had not been kind to him in many ways but I could see that he was a good man.

We finally arrived at Warren and Susan's and it was a dream come true for all our family to be together. We had such fun talking and laughing and visiting. Richard really got to know more about Jana now that he could meet her family and I had lots of stories to tell him about her. We travelled to PEI and all around New Brunswick and because it is a beautiful province with lots of trees which reminded Richard of Oregon so he felt right at home there. We went to the ocean a few times where Warren, Jana and Richard had lobster while Susan and I settled on hamburgers as neither of us liked lobster. We were also there to celebrate Warren's 30th birthday. I couldn't believe he was 30, but then I was 55 and couldn't believe that either. In the evenings, we played a card game called Hand and Foot for hours on end and it was great fun. Soon enough, though, it was time to head back home. Before we left, I told Warren and Susan I would be coming back for Christmas and they were very happy about that.

Back at the apartment in Peterborough I had a few more days with Richard and Jana. Before they flew home, I had a party for them at my apartment with friends from Warsaw that Jana had met back in the early 1990s when I was the minister there and we all had a great time. Richard had been game for anything on our trip to the Maritimes and it had been great to get to know him. He fit right into our family and I was so happy my sister and Richard had found each other. Even though they were still working things through, I could see they had something special together and I also saw how much Richard loved my sister. I had never been to Coos Bay, Oregon so I was looking forward to visiting them in the near future and having Richard show me his favorite places. The day after I took Richard and Jana to the airport, I was back teaching and then six weeks later there was the piano recital for all my students on Sunday, June 4th at Bethany United Church. The recital could not have gone better. What a great year this was turning out to be.

Near the end of May, I had received a phone call from Myno Van Dyke, Chair of the Pastoral Relations Committee at the Orono Kirby Pastoral Charge. He told me they were looking for a minister to fill in about 14 hours a week, preaching every Sunday and doing some visiting, until they found a permanent minister. I asked him why they wanted only 14 hours a week and he said it was because, that way, the Charge didn't have to pay any benefits. He asked if I was interested and I said I was and we set up a time for an interview in early June. When I got off the phone, I was struck by the fact that the Orono Pastoral Charge had contacted me. My maternal great grandfather, James Cuttell, and his brother John had come from England around 1860 and ended up in Orono. They bought a printing press and ran a printing shop there. My great grandfather married when he was in Orono and they had one daughter, Jessie. In the middle 1860s, they moved to Brooklin where he started the first newspaper for the area. Not long after James Cuttell and his wife Olive got to Brooklin she died and he remarried Maria Curtis who was my great grandmother. Their three sons were all born in Brooklin, my grandfather James Samuel Cuttell being the youngest son. John Cuttell never left Orono and raised his family there. The last Cuttell to live in Orono was Alma Cuttell who died in 1990. Now I was being asked to have an interview in Orono. My Aunt Louise was particularly proud of her family history and this could not be a coincidence.

At the interview I met Myno whom I liked as soon as I met him. I also met Laura Head who had just been hired as the Secretary for the Pastoral Charge and I liked her as well. There were other people there from Orono and two people from the Kirby Church, Bonnie Reid, the Clerk of Session at Kirby, and Brian Colville who was an Elder. Myno told me there were many changes happening in the Charge. Their minister was leaving on June 30th and they had just hired a new organist at Orono United Church whose name was Karen Kastner. They told me they hoped to have a new minister in place by July, 2001 and I said I was glad to help out if they would like me to. I was asked to go out for few minutes while they talked things over and when I came back in and sat down, they asked me to be their supply minister and wanted me to start in July. I was very pleased to say yes. I knew this position was as perfect a situation for me as it was for the Charge. This would not interfere in any way with my teaching and I would not have to attend any evening meetings as they had a Presbytery representative who had been appointed to be at their meetings until a new minister was called. I looked forward to working with the people there and everything seemed to be falling into place this first year of the new millennium. I still couldn't believe I was going to be working as a minister at Orono and, when I talked to Warren and Susan and my sister, they were as surprised as I was and didn't see this as a coincidence either.

The first Sunday in July, I was very excited as I prepared to preach at the Orono and Kirby United Churches. Kirby United Church was a large brick building very close to Highway 115.

Everyone went in the back entrance which led to the basement of the church. It was a good sized basement and had a fairly large room for dinners and a large kitchen. From there you walked up the stairs into the small sanctuary which had a small organ and seated about 90 people. There were 20 people at my first morning service at Kirby United Church and it could not have gone better. Everyone was very friendly and welcoming and very appreciative to have me there but then that is usually the way it is in small rural churches. Brian Colville, who had been at my interview, told me how very pleased he was to have me there as did Bonnie. I loved the feeling in that church.

When the service at Kirby was over I headed for Orono United Church which was an enormous, beautiful old stone building that was very costly to heat in the winter. The sanctuary was beautiful and could seat about 350 people. There were beautiful stained glass windows in the church which reminded me of the ones in St. John's United Church in Oakville. They had had a fire in the old Methodist Church in February 1950 and it had burned to the ground. The present church was built in its place in 1951 and an addition was added in 1962 to accommodate the expanding Sunday School when about 200 people attended church. By the time I arrived, the church no longer had as many people in the congregation. On a really good Sunday, we could have up to 150 people but on average, around 85 came but on Christmas Eve the church was packed. There was an organ, an upright piano and a choir loft where the 15 members of the Senior Choir sat. There were many rooms upstairs, most of which were only used for storage, and offices for the Secretary and the Minister, with a door between them. In the basement there was a huge auditorium with a stage and the kitchen off to the side which was big enough for many events including funeral lunches, Official Board meetings and luncheons. The rest of the basement had rooms that were used for Sunday School classes and storage. Being the larger church, I expected to receive not quite as warm a welcome but that was not the case. There were about 75 people there that Sunday and everyone was very happy to have me there. I met Karen, their organist, who was a bundle of joy and energy and I really liked her. Myno also came up and thanked me after the service and told me how much he appreciated that I was there. I felt a lot of positive energy and enthusiasm in the church and it was a great start. I felt warmly welcomed. It was wonderful to be back doing ministry again.

Warren and Susan came for a visit on their holidays in June. I also saw them again in August at Ronald and Nicole's wedding in Sudbury. Ronald's parents, Bill and Elaine Glassford, were there and it was great to see them again. The wedding was held in the Catholic Church and it was a wonderful day. Ronald and Nicole were so happy and they made a great couple. Overall, I had a wonderful relaxed summer and even spent one week with Sharon Reynolds, a member of the congregation at St. Paul's in New Liskeard when I was there, at her cottage south of North Bay at Loon Lake. I went swimming and canoeing, photographed loons, herons, ducks and anything else that moved while I was in the canoe. It was a lot of fun and a great visit.

On September 4th I sent out a newsletter to my piano families. I told them that everyone had done well. Jonah Clifford deserved special mention as he did his Grade I exam in January and got 73%. He was so encouraged that he decided to try his Grade II exam in June. This was most unusual but he wanted to do it and got 75% on the second exam. He was a very good student and I was amazed at his determination. His family was very proud of him and his dad called him Jonah the Brave. How proud his grandmother, Marg Clifford, would have been of him, I thought. She had passed away when I was at Millbrook United Church as the Interim Minister and she had been a good friend. Around this time, I talked with Warren about doing a benefit concert for Wesley United Church, Warren's Church in Berwick, to help them raise money for renovations. Warren really appreciated that and suggested I do this concert at St. Paul's United Church in Sussex because they had a grand piano. We set the date for December 28th when I would already be in Berwick for Christmas.

I was only four months into the ministry at Orono when Myno Van Dyke, the Chair of the Pastoral Relations Committee, came to talk to me. He said the committee had asked him to find out if I would be interested in applying for the position of full time minister. I was interested. I felt very comfortable in both the churches and I was beginning to feel a call there. As an Elder in the church, Myno was great to work with and I loved working with the organist, Karen Kastner, as well. Both of us being musicians, we had a great connection. She was as high energy as I was, a piano teacher too and we both loved music. Laura Head, who was the Secretary in the church office, had been wonderful to work with over those first four months. She was a fairly calm person which was a good thing since someone needed to be with Karen and me around. I told Myno that I would send my resume to the Pastoral Relations Committee and it wasn't long after that they asked me to come for an interview. I had a great interview with them. I asked them if it would be possible for them to rent the manse and let me buy a house in Orono because I wanted to build up some equity for retirement and they understood that but I could see they were not sure about this and they said they would have to really think about that. On the very difficult, snowy drive home to Peterborough after the interview, I really believed this was the call I had been hoping for. But, when I remembered their reaction to my asking them to consider renting out the manse, I realized that it could possibly be a deal breaker. When I got to my apartment, I phoned the church and told Myno that I would be fine living in the manse. He sounded very relieved when I told him that because the committee was having difficulty figuring out how their finances would work if I didn't live in the manse.

The next day, they called and asked me to be their minister. I said yes and told them I really believed it was a call. The committee thought that as well and, the next Sunday, an announcement was placed in the bulletin for a congregational meeting for both Orono and Kirby congregations at Orono United Church to take place in two weeks' time. The announcement stated that, at this meeting, the Pastoral Relations Committee would be putting forth the name of someone they had interviewed and thought would make a good minister for the Charge. When the time came for the Charge's congregational meeting, for which two representatives from the Presbytery were also present, no one had any idea who the Pastoral Relations Committee would be presenting. A lot of people felt badly for me, thinking the committee would be naming another minister, and many people told me how much they had been enjoying my ministry these last four months and had been hoping I would be their new minister. I kept quiet and had to let them think I would not be the one chosen. When the day came for the announcement, Myno told me not to go home after the service but wait downstairs until the meeting was over. The congregation, meanwhile, was to think I had left.

Myno made the presentation and, while I was waiting, I heard talking and laughing upstairs and a discussion that went on for what seemed a very long time. Myno was quite the character and loved to draw things out. He gave the congregation lots of information and details but did not divulge the name. When it came time to announce the name of the person they were presenting, Myno said, her name was Marion, which is my first name, and then stopped. He told me later that everyone was listening intently to hear who it was and, when he thought he had teased them enough, he said the new minister they were presenting was Marion Dorinda Vollmer. Downstairs, I heard a huge uproar and cheering and clapping at one point but I had no idea why. Many people later told me how disappointed they were when Myno said the name of the minister was Marion and that everyone was very relieved and happy when they discovered it was me. They knew Myno pretty well and were amused by his antics.

When Myno brought me upstairs, the congregation was very enthusiastic and appreciative and I told them I would be happy to continue as their supply minister until Sunday, April 1, 2001 which was when I would begin full time ministry. I had chosen to begin on April 1 because I needed to be fair to my students and take them as far as I could in their piano year and April would give us all enough time to sort things out. Being accepted as the minister for this community was a great moment for me. In that moment, I thought about my family who loved me and had raised me in Oakville and my mother's family who had come so far from England to Orono 140 years earlier. They had once worshipped in the old Methodist Church that had stood on the grounds where this new church stood. I knew how proud my family would have been had they been there, especially my Aunt Louise. For me Orono was more than a calling, it was like coming home – coming full circle. It would be a great new beginning for me.

I called Warren and Susan and told them what Myno had done and everything else that had happened and they could see that these were two really good congregations. I called Jana too and she was so excited for me to be back in full time ministry because she knew how much that meant to me. Without a doubt, the year 2000 had been an amazing year when everything fell into place and I was so happy. To top it all off, I was going to be with Warren and Susan for Christmas which was only around the corner. What more could happen I wondered. But the best news of all was just around the corner. In early December, Warren and Susan called to tell me they were having a baby. That news took my breath away and, to this day, I still get emotional thinking about that moment. How precious and how special that was. My son was going to be a father and I was going to be a grandmother. I was overjoyed. They told me the baby was due the middle of July, 2001. I phoned my sister and she was thrilled for me. Jana still remembered what it felt like when Brandi was born. She became a grandmother when she was 40 and I would be 56. She knew what happiness was waiting for me and was excited that I would soon be experiencing those same feelings she had felt when her granddaughter was born. She confirmed the special bond we had in the Christmas card she sent me that year:

"Of all the friends I'll ever have, not one will ever be important to my life the way you've always been to me. In many ways we're different, yet I always turn to you to put things in perspective with an honest point of view. You take the time to listen with a sympathetic ear and tell me things in gentle ways I really need to hear. A sister is a special gift I'm always grateful for, because there's no one anywhere I trust and count on more."

Truer words were never written, and I could have said the same to my sister. The Christmas Eve service at Orono United Church was wonderful and the church was packed, even in the balcony, with about 250 people. It was a wonderful celebration of faith with the promise of new things to come. I flew to New Brunswick on Christmas Day and Warren and Susan were there to pick me up. Their manse looked beautiful with all the Christmas decorations and the beautiful Christmas tree. We exchanged gifts and they even had a Christmas stocking for me filled with goodies. Later, we had a wonderful turkey dinner with all the trimmings. I was so happy to be there. Of course we talked a lot about the baby and they were so excited and happy. Warren and Susan would soon know the joys of being a father and mother. On Boxing Day, Warren took me to St. Paul's United Church in Sussex to try out the grand piano and I told him it would be just fine for the concert. We had a good turnout for the concert which was a great success and there was a nice reception afterwards. I just loved giving concerts to raise money for local churches and I had done many concerts over the years. The music was much appreciated and it gave me a wonderful sense of satisfaction to give back for the gift I had been given.

I had a great time with Warren and Susan over Christmas but, when it was time to leave, I was anxious to get back home. I knew it was not going to be easy to tell my students and their families that I had accepted a full time position at Orono and Kirby United Churches and that I would not be able to continue teaching. Sunday, April 1st was also the date of my students' final recital. I had already arranged that it would take place at Orono United Church and as soon as I returned home, I talked to Karen Kastner, who I knew was an amazing piano teacher, about whether she would be willing to take on most of my students if they wanted to continue their lessons after I left. She had moved into the Orono area in September so she had only had a few piano students. She was more than willing to help me out and I really appreciated that. It made me feel good that I wasn't letting my students down and that was very important to me. When I finally told my students and their families, they were very sorry to hear that I couldn't continue teaching but 35 of my students did want to continue and looked forward to meeting Karen at the recital. I agreed to continue teaching the 10 students who were doing their exams in June and, then, if they wanted to continue in September, Karen said she would take them as well.

The next three months went very quickly, not only for me but for the people at Orono who were very busy fixing up the manse before I moved in. The manse was an old wood house in good condition with very high ceilings which made the house look much bigger inside than it actually was. The manse used the same driveway as the church and when you walked in the side door, you came into a small room the size of a mud-room where you could hang coats, boots and shoes. There was a space big enough where I could fit my small freezer in. On the left of that there was a door that led into the kitchen which was about six feet wide. There were lots of cupboards on the left and a window that looked out at the front of the church, and on the right, a refrigerator and a stove. At the end of the kitchen, on the left, was the laundry room complete with a washer and dryer and, off that, a small bathroom.

On the right, coming out of the kitchen, there was a long narrow hallway and, in front of the kitchen, there was a good-sized dining room and then, going right out of the dining room and then left was a door that led out to a small room like a porch that was completely closed in but not heated. There was a door there that led you into the large back yard where I could have a flower garden. Coming in from the porch and turning left, there was a good sized living room where I would put my TV and piano. There were two very big windows which brought in a lot of light and plenty of wall space for paintings and photos. Moving out of the living room, you came back to the long hallway and, on the left, was the front door which rarely got used but you could walk outside and down two steps to a small cement walkway about four feet in front of the sidewalk. Right inside the front door was a long staircase and, to the left, a very large room that would be my office and where I would put all my books, papers, movies, computer and a desk and chair. Coming out of this room, on the left, were stairs going up to the three bedrooms. I chose the largest bedroom at the top of the stairs which had, on the left, a full sized bathroom. It was a lovely house and my only concern was that it was really close to the church and shared the same driveway. The people on the Pastoral Relations Committee assured me that people were very respectful and didn't knock on the minister's door very often unless it was an emergency. That turned out to be the case which I appreciated.

All the people who worked in the manse could not have been nicer and couldn't do enough for me. As well as painting the manse, fixing things that needed to be fixed, cleaning windows and counters, they were taking up the very old rugs to be thrown out. Underneath the rugs, they found good wood floors that only had to be cleaned. They didn't put new rugs in the house again but agreed to put a rug in my bedroom when I asked. Once the rug had been put in my bedroom, they were proud to show it to me and it was a beautiful, soft rose carpet. At my interview in November, Myno had asked me if the Charge could help me move my things to Orono so they wouldn't have to pay for a moving van. They even offered to help me pack and I agreed. By March I had already packed many of my things and Myno, his wife Judy, and Sharon and her husband David Staples came to Peterborough to help me finish packing my many books, videos and files. The Charge had rented a truck for the second week of March and we all worked one morning for about four hours to load up the truck and move me to Orono. Once I was at the manse, there were lots of people there to help me move my furniture and boxes into my new home. I served tea and cookies and we had a great time. It was wonderful to have all that help and they were fast and efficient. Myno, Judy, David and Sharon helped me set up my office before they left and that was a great help too. It took me to the end of March to really feel I was moved in and what a great feeling that was. I was no sooner moved in than Warren and Susan arrived on March 31. They had come to Ontario for a short visit and had already been with Susan's parents in Ottawa. Now they were with me to spend a couple of days and celebrate Warren's birthday at my new home on Sunday, April 1 before heading back to New Brunswick on Monday. It was wonderful to have them with me.

Warren's birthday would be a very busy day for me as I had the two services in the morning and then my students' last piano recital that afternoon at 2:30 p.m. The church was packed with all my students and their families who came for the recital and a few people from the church who sat in the balcony. After the recital, I introduced Karen to my students and their parents, many of whom would now have Karen as their teacher. The recital went very well and, afterwards, the families surprised me with gifts and gave me a beautiful book on birds as well as a beautiful bird bath with an angel sitting in it. They also presented me with flowers and four dozen roses. It was a great afternoon but I was sad to see my students go, especially since I had been teaching some of these students for seven years. I had really enjoyed teaching them all, the young students and the adults and I was fortunate to have students who really wanted to learn to play the piano. I was very proud of what I had been able to help them accomplish these last seven years.

I had also planned a dinner party that Sunday evening for my two congregations. They had been so good to me and I wanted to thank them for all they had already done for me. I felt very much at home in Orono before I even moved into the manse. When I told them I was getting 20 cooked chickens for the dinner and a dessert in the form of a huge Batman birthday cake for Warren, the women told me not to worry, they would set up for the dinner and bring salads. I invited a few friends including Donna and Gerry Hampton and Maida Ormsby from the Warsaw Charge. It was great fun and everyone enjoyed the party and my son's birthday cake. It was also a great opportunity for my congregations to meet Warren and Susan. What a wonderful way to begin my ministry with the Orono and Kirby congregations by thanking them for all they had already done to help me feel very much at home. It was great to be doing full time ministry again.

I was tired out by the end of the very busy day and it had been very emotional saying goodbye to my students and their parents. I was still exhausted the next morning when Warren and Susan were getting ready to leave to go home and they hadn't left yet when the phone rang. It was one of the members of my congregation whom I had visited a few times in Orono. She was distraught and told me that her granddaughter's husband had killed his wife, and then killed himself at their home in Pontypool. She said that her daughter had asked her to call me and see if I would come to see her and her husband who lived in Pontypool. I was a little shaken over this and I told Warren and Susan what had happened. They were as shocked as I was and I took a few minutes to see them off before driving to Pontypool. When I got to the house, the mother whose daughter had been murdered was so relieved to see me. She introduced me to her husband who was her daughter's stepfather. I sat down at the kitchen table with them and her two grandsons who were ages 13 and 15. I could feel a real disconnect in these two boys which I could certainly understand. Their father had just killed their mother and then killed himself. The boys were in great distress. When the boys went downstairs to the recreation room, they told me what had happened and they were crying and so upset. I felt badly for them and it was a terrible tragedy.

She told me that her daughter was in the midst of leaving her husband who had been physically abusive for many years and she had told her mother she couldn't take it anymore. She had bought a home in Bowmanville and would have been moving today with her sons. She said that she had often asked her daughter to leave her husband and to come and live with her and her husband who were just up the street, but now realized if she had moved in with them he might have killed them too. She said that when she had not heard from her daughter that morning she and her husband walked down to her house around 8:00 a.m. The garage door was locked but they had a key and opened it. When they went in, they saw her daughter lying on the garage floor and knew she was dead. A distance away her husband also lay on the garage floor with a rifle beside him. He was dead too.

They called the police and when the police got there, they told them to go home and they would take their statements at their house. The mother told the police that her two grandsons had stayed with them overnight and were still asleep at their home when they came to the house. Now she had to go home and tell her grandsons that their mom and dad were gone. She couldn't believe that her beautiful daughter was dead and I can't imagine how anyone could deal with that reality. I felt badly for these boys, for the mother and stepfather who was so helpful and supportive to his wife at this time and to the grandsons and he was heartbroken too. I felt badly for the grandmother who had called me. The mother asked me to do the funeral for her daughter. She said she would make the arrangements through the Morris Funeral Home in Bowmanville but wanted the reception to be at Orono United Church. I did my best to get all the information that I needed and told them the details could be worked out later. I sat and talked with them for a very long time and prayed with them. It was a terrible tragedy and, understandably, their greatest concern now was for the grandsons. After I left them, I went right over to see the grandmother who had called me. She was terribly upset and I sat and talked with her and prayed with her. She dearly loved her granddaughter and could not believe what had happened. She had known some of the circumstances but never thought he would go that far. I told her about the arrangements her daughter would be making for the funeral and she said how much it meant to her that I had come to see her and that I was doing her granddaughter's funeral.

I needed to catch my breath after all that had happened the last few days and I went home. I called the funeral home and talked with them about when the family wanted the funeral. I told them I would work with whatever arrangements the family made with them. They told me the family was coming in that afternoon so everything would be looked after. Later, I went into the church office to see Laura. I explained to her what had happened and gave her the details of the funeral. The only thing that made the situation easier was the fact that I had already been in this Charge for nine months and had done some funerals so I had worked a few times with Morris Funeral home. The funeral director and the staff were great to work with. I also already knew how the United Church Woman worked when it came to preparing a funeral lunch and what information they needed from me.

It was, of course, a very difficult funeral to do because of the circumstances but both families were there, the family of the daughter who had been murdered and the family of the son who had killed his wife. The Funeral Home was packed and I did what I could to help these families who were grieving. To their credit, the mother and stepfather of the woman who had been killed could not have been nicer to the parents of the man who had killed their daughter and the funeral for their son was held two days later. This funeral was also at Morris Funeral Home and again both families attended and I sat with the mother, stepfather and grandmother and I admired their courage just being able to be there. The reception was held at the Legion Hall about a five minute walk from the Funeral Home. It was a harrowing introduction to full time ministry at Orono but I was able to draw on other tragic experiences I had witnessed over my years in ministry and especially what I experienced at Roseau that helped me get through this.

Five weeks into my ministry, I think it was May 7, my life changed. It was a Thursday afternoon and I was getting ready to go out to teach piano. I had felt so tired an hour earlier that I had to go lie down before I went out. I don't remember getting up but I do remember that I felt very strange. I couldn't seem to focus and my head didn't feel right. I had no energy at all. I decided that I needed to stay home and, since I only had two sisters to teach outside Millbrook I called the family and cancelled. I vaguely remember phoning and having some difficulty with my words as I left a message. The family told me later that they got my message and knew it was me but couldn't make out what I was saying. I went back to bed and slept until the next morning. I was feeling better when I woke up but wasn't sure what had happened to me and called my doctor in Peterborough. I got an appointment to see him that afternoon and told him what I thought was happening. He didn't seem too worried but said he wanted to do a Doppler test which he set up for Monday morning. I went back home and worked on the service for Sunday. I felt alright that day but, on Saturday, I wasn't so sure how I was feeling and I called Karen, our organist, to tell her a little bit about what was happening to me. We decided to go out for dinner and were having a great conversation when I felt myself slip. I tried hard not to show it but I had trouble forming words. Karen said afterwards she was worried and knew something was really wrong with me. When we parted, she told me to call her anytime if I needed anything.

When I got home, I decided to check out the Baptism forms I had filled out for Sunday but I couldn't make out anything I wrote on those forms and that scared me. I had called Warren in New Brunswick earlier that day and told him I wasn't feeling well. I wasn't sure what I said to him but his voice changed when I was talking and he spoke slower because he knew something was really wrong. He told me not to do the two services on Sunday and to be very careful. I don't remember a lot of what he said but I could feel his concern through the phone. I was thinking about what my son said to me as I read the Baptism forms I had filled out, which now made no sense to me, and I tore them up. I was really worried so I phoned Karen and said I had to go to the hospital. She was there in five minutes and we drove to Bowmanville Emergency. It was very busy there that evening and, when the doctor on call saw me, he said I wasn't showing any symptoms. He gave me a shot of something and told me to take aspirin. He explained how much I should take and told me to make sure that I get into Peterborough for that Doppler test on Monday. Karen told me later she was really upset that the doctor didn't put me in the hospital.

Sunday morning came and I felt fine. I got ready for church and got through the service in

Kirby. But when I got to Orono, I asked Myno if he would talk with me before the service and he came to my office. I told him how I had been feeling and that I wasn't sure what was wrong with me. He was really kind and said he would look out for me and carry the babies down the aisle for the Baptisms. That was a huge relief. I wanted to hold myself together but I didn't know if I could. I felt like I was in a semi fog but my words were alright and I had redone the Baptism forms and they were fine. I made it through the service but I didn't realize at the time how lucky I was. Afterwards, I called my son and he was glad to hear from me. I could tell that he was still worried and so was I. I slept pretty much the rest of Sunday and that night and I felt better on Monday morning so I got into my car and drove into Peterborough for the Doppler test for 11:00 a.m. I didn't know what to expect so the technician explained to me that it was for the carotid arteries on both sides of my neck. When he finished, he said he needed me to wait there for a minute. He went out and was not gone long before he came back and told me I needed to see Dr. Thompson, the vascular surgeon whose office was just down the hall. I realized then that something very serious had to be wrong with me.

I waited quite a while in the doctor's office and, while I was waiting, I started thinking that I needed to have someone with me when I went in to see the doctor because I didn't know if I would understand what he would tell me. I called George, a friend in Millbrook whose wife and three children I had given piano lessons to so we had become friends over the years. He worked at home and, when I told him what was happening, he said he was on his way. The nurse finally called me in and I told her I wanted to wait because I had someone coming and he was on the way. As soon as George got there, we went in to see Dr. Thompson. He was very nice and said that he was very surprised that I had been able to drive myself into Peterborough because I had 90% blockage of the carotid arteries on both sides of my neck. He didn't think that I should even be standing. He also said I had to go to the hospital immediately and be signed in. I knew then I was seriously ill and had been lucky so far not to have had a massive stroke. He needed to operate on both sides of my neck to put in a stint on each side, but could only do one at a time so he would to the surgery on the left side of my neck first thing in the morning.

I asked George to call Warren for me and tell him what was happening. George said he would call Warren after he drove me to the hospital which was five minutes away. He also told me he would look after my car and make sure it got back to Orono. When we got to the hospital, I had all the paperwork from the doctor and had to wait for a while for them to process the information. George phoned my son and I realized suddenly that Carol Yeo and I had made plans to go out for dinner at five that afternoon. I called her and told her what was happening and she was shocked. She asked me for Warren's phone number because she wanted to talk to him. She wanted to know if I would like her to stay overnight with me in the hospital. That's when I realized this was very serious and told her I would like that. I knew Warren couldn't come and be with me because Susan was pregnant and there had been concerns about her pregnancy so he needed to stay with her. I was very thankful to Carol who was willing to come that evening to be with me. It wasn't long after this that the nurse got me into a room and George went and got me magazines and deodorant and toothpaste and a toothbrush. After he did that, I thanked him for everything he had done and told him I was alright and he left. The woman in the bed next to me was also having surgery the next day and we were both scared. She was very nice and we talked up a storm to pass the time.

Carol came at eight p.m. with an overnight bag and I was very relieved to see her. She told me she had talked to Warren and told him she would be staying with me and would be there when I went in for the operation. She also said she would call him as soon as I was out of surgery to tell him how I was. I was so thankful to Carol because I knew how worried Warren and Susan would be. That night I couldn't sleep because the doctor had explained the risks to me and I knew how serious it was, but, at the same time, he told me he was optimistic. I could hear Carol snoring quietly on her cot in front of my bed and my roommate breathing heavily. Both were in a deep sleep as I lay there wide awake that night. I didn't know whether I would make it through the surgery and I thought about my life. I had a serious conversation with God and told God I just wanted to live long enough to see my first grandchild born. I cried as I thought I might not see my son again or Susan or my sister. In the end, I had to leave it in God's hands and in the hands of my surgeon but I cried for the longest time before I could let go and leave it with God.

Early the next morning, they prepped me for the surgery and Carol was there reassuring me that she would be calling Warren as soon as she knew how I was. Then they put me to sleep. The next thing I remember was being very warm and feeling something heavy on me. I felt like I was in a dark, long tunnel, deep down somewhere, as I tried to wake up. I could feel I was in a deep sleep but kept hearing a voice calling my name from far off. I tried to respond and to say that I was there, over and over again, but I couldn't wake up. I was afraid that maybe I would never wake up again. Slowly, though, I felt myself coming to the surface and, finally, I was able to open my eyes. It felt so strange to be almost awake and trying to wake up but not being quite there. Once I was completely awake, I was so relieved. There were lots of other patients in the recovery room with me and a few nurses. I saw Carol when they took me back to my room. They kept me in the hospital for only one night after the surgery and then Carol came and drove me home the next morning. She had even arranged for people to come and be with me at home for a week and bring food. Everyone, she said, would take a few hours and there would be those who would stay overnight so I would be covered around the clock that first week. The doctor had told me that I had to sleep with my head up but I didn't have a Lazy Boy chair. But when Carol got the word out, one of the families in the church came forward and said they had an old style Lazy Boy chair that they brought to my house so I could sleep in it. People were wonderful.

It was a huge relief to be home. I had a friend in Bethany who was a nurse and whose daughter I had taught piano, and she came to change the bandage on my neck and told me the surgeon had done a great job. I called Warren and Susan and they were so happy to hear my voice and know that I was home. They told me that Carol had told them not to worry because she had people looking after me to make sure I was alright that first week at home and they were so relieved that I was well looked after. They told me they had tried to call Jana a few times and left messages. Finally, I got hold of my sister and it was so good to talk with her. She told me she had been away and when she got home and heard the news she said she was so upset and called Warren right away to learn that I had made it through the surgery. She was very relieved that I was home and recovering. I also called my cousin Diane and her husband Jason who lived in Pickering to tell them what had happened to me. They came out a couple of times and did yard work for me which I appreciated, especially since Diane was the kind of person who could lift a person's spirits because she loved to laugh. I knew I wouldn't be able to stay still forever and do nothing so I asked Laura to come in every morning and bring me up to date on what was happening in the church. She was happy to do that and we had good visits. People came and went and I just felt so reassured to know I had people around me for my first week at home. It was so kind of Carol to make sure I had the help I needed and I could not thank her enough.

My biggest problem after the surgery was that the extra medical coverage I had paid for had not gone through and I needed that coverage. I had started at Orono on April 1st and the Charge had put in all the required paperwork. They were upset that the coverage hadn't come through and couldn't figure out what the problem was. They were getting no information from Presbytery or Conference. I didn't know any of this at the time but Myno called Warren whom he had met at the dinner I had for the congregation back in April. Myno assumed that, being a minister, my son would know the procedures and the right people to talk to. When Warren found out what was happening, he was angry and phoned the staff person in the Bay of Quinte Conference office who was in charge of looking after this. This person knew me personally and had known Warren from the time he was 15 years old but he still gave my son the runaround. Well, Warren didn't take that very well. He took a strip off this staff person and told him to fix the situation immediately. It got done.

I had to go through the second surgery for the right side of my neck in June and Carol was there again for me. We went through the same routine and people stayed with me again for a week. I still continued to do some work as I recuperated but I was careful and made sure I got lots of rest. Warren wanted to send me a Lazy Boy and I said that would be wonderful but I would pay for it. He knew what I wanted because I loved the one they had at their home. It was so comfortable and very easy to sleep in. One couple who came and stayed with me one Sunday morning was Isabel and Don Hamm, members of Kirby United Church. They were the salt of the earth and wonderful people. They were then in their 80s and, when they arrived, Don stayed in the car and read the newspaper while Isabel sat with me in the living room and we talked for a while. Then I dozed off and when I woke up, I heard music down the road at the park where they were having a community service that Sunday morning. Then I heard snoring. I looked over and there was Isabel stretched out on my chesterfield sound asleep. When she eventually woke up and saw me, I had to smile. Here I was, I told her, the one who is supposed to be sick, and she fell asleep on me and was snoring. We both had a good laugh.

I made a quicker recovery after the second operation and started preaching again at the end of June. My granddaughter, Rachel Anne Vollmer, was born on July 16th and I was so excited and so grateful to have made it through the two surgeries and now I had this beautiful granddaughter. I so badly wanted to see her and couldn't wait so, when I felt well enough at the end of July, I took my holidays and drove to New Brunswick. I can't begin to describe my feelings when I saw this beautiful baby. She was perfect in every way. As I held Warren and Susan's daughter - my granddaughter – in my arms, I thanked God for her and that I was alive and able to experience that moment. I stayed with Warren and Susan for a couple of weeks and, during that time, I went with Susan to the baby shower the Pastoral Charge gave for her. It was a great celebration and they gave Susan lovely gifts for Rachel. It was the first time in that Charge's history that their minister's wife had a baby. Warren's half-sister Jilli invited me to come to Cape Breton and visit for a few days and, since I hadn't seen them in a long time, I was looking forward to that. I took a few days and went down to visit with Jilli, her husband Paul and their two children, Elizabeth and Andrew. I knew Jilli's parents were living in Sydney, Cape Breton but I didn't expect to see them. When I arrived, Jilli told me her mother had invited the family for dinner and I was welcome to come. I asked her how she felt about that and she said that, if it is alright with her mother, she was also fine with it. So I went. Her mother was very friendly and it was wonderful to see Bill. He was bent over and crippled with rheumatoid arthritis by that time, the same illness his father, my Uncle Hugh, Warren's grandfather, had suffered from as well. We had a nice dinner together and we all played cards after dinner. Bill and I never needed words and I still loved him dearly. I was at peace with how it had all worked out, raising my son on my own, and it did my heart good to see him.

The next morning when I woke up at Jilli and Paul's, Warren called me and said he had received a call from Myno to tell me that Marie Tamblyn had died. I was totally shocked. Marie was our Clerk of Session and only in her 50s. She hadn't been well in July with what they thought was some kind of virus but it didn't seem serious to her or her family. I had gone to see her in the hospital before I left and she was looking forward to seeing me when I returned from New Brunswick. Warren said that the Charge had been very anxious to get hold of me but Carol was away and she was the only one who had his phone number. Being a police officer, Myno was able to find Warren's number and called him. Myno wanted me to know that Marie had died before I got back home because he knew it would have been a huge shock for me. I felt terrible that I couldn't be there and, as soon as I got off the phone, I phoned Marie's husband Bill in Orono. One of the family members I knew answered the phone and told me Bill was at Morris Funeral Home and gave me the number so I called and I talked with him there. It was good to connect with him and I really felt for him and all of Marie's family, her children and grandchildren. After I spoke to Bill, I called Marie's dear friend Donna Scott and we talked for a while. All I could do then was send them both a card. It was hard to believe that Marie was gone. She was one of the beautiful people in heart and mind and soul. She helped everyone and was there, even before they knew they needed help. She was loved and respected in her community and church. It was a huge loss for her family and all her friends, her church and her community.

Hearing about her death made me look back over the previous three months of my own life. I had had two major surgeries at a time when I was going to have my first grandchild. I knew I could also have died but I wanted to live. I was so grateful that I made it through and lived to see my granddaughter. Marie was too young to die and I had more long conversations with

God about that. I went back to Berwick and spent more precious time with my family and my beautiful granddaughter before returning home. Rachel brought me so much indescribable joy. She made me think back to when my son, her father, was born and how that felt, those very similar feelings of pure love that I now felt for Rachel. Life goes on and there is such joy in a new life, a granddaughter. But sadness was there as well, knowing that Marie, who still had so much living to do and had been so deeply loved, had died. It wasn't fair. It could have been me. But it wasn't! I was grateful to God that I was still here but it was hard to understand why someone who still had so much to give was gone.

At the end of June when I had felt well enough, I had planted a garden on the east side of the house and put in a small garden on the west side very close to where I parked my car. It was good for me to be physically active after my surgeries and I loved gardening but it was a big job getting the property cleaned up and ready to plant flowers. Coming home from my holidays near the end of August, the gardens looked beautiful and the congregation at Orono was very pleased that I had planted them. They couldn't remember the last time a minister had done that. It was good to get back home and settle in. I felt it was a privilege for me to serve in this Pastoral Charge and there was so much positive energy in both the churches. Everything was running smoothly because both Sessions had wonderful Elders who really cared about the people in their congregations.

There were wonderful people in Kirby United Church and I really enjoyed my visits with them. I enjoyed working with the Clerk of Session there. Bonnie had lots of ideas and suggestions and we worked well together and often talked on the phone. Don and Isabel Hamm were such a wonderful older couple who truly lived their faith and loved their church as did Leland and Betty Ball. Brian and Ruthe Colville were a couple who were the salt of the earth. Brian was an Elder in the church and they had four children, Mellissa, Kyle, Adam and Kaiti. I also got to know Ruthe's mother Mary Henderson. I loved visiting Jim and Joan Ard, Loreen Ball, Iris Lambier, Dick and Janet Rutherford and their four girls Erin, Stephanie, Andrea, Lia and Janet's mom Jean Duvall. There was also Annie Fischer who was a joy to visit as was Hilda Tamblyn and Mac and Norma Ransberry. Then there were was John and Martha Conrad and their four children Aidan, Morgan, Harriet and Grace and also Clair Chapman who couldn't do enough to help his church. In many ways Kirby United Church reminded me of Monticello United Church. Both were small but mighty. They had wonderful fellowship and the members of the church always pulled together to put on bazaars, talent shows and other events to raise money for their church. They had many active groups like the Session, the Committee of Stewards, the Board of Trustees and there was an organist and a Senior Choir. In September, 2002, when Kirby United Church had their 122nd Anniversary service, something that was very important to them, the church was packed.

Orono United Church had about 130 families and I enjoyed my visits at Orono and getting to know the families. Fay and Glory Adams were really good country western singers and I told them that they reminded me of Roy Rogers and Dale Evans when they sang. Joyce Willis, Minnie Taylor, Wayne and Carol Bailey were very kind to me. I often visited Orville and

Isabelle Challice and she became a devoted friend. I loved Grace and Ed Coatham and Grace couldn't do enough for her church. I visited Faye and Carman Cornish regularly and they were a wonderful couple as was Francis and Joyce Cowan and Betty and Jim Major. Muriel Patton and Muriel Patterson both lived alone and loved to have me visit and we became good friends. There were Ed and Olive Millson who were devoted to their church. I had met them right after I started at Orono as the supply minister. Their daughter Cathy, who was only in her 40s and lived with them, had been a passenger in a car that had a terrible accident about a month before I arrived and had almost died. The accident was not the fault of the person driving the car but Cathy was seriously hurt. The Millsons told me that she was still in the Oshawa Hospital and now doing physio but it was a very slow and painful process. They asked me if I would visit her in the hospital and I went in every week over the next few months until she was able to come back home. I really liked Ed and Olive and visited them often, but Ed had a routine, and this happened every single time I visited them. When our visit was over, I would say a prayer with them and then start to leave. That's when Ed would bring up something that was on his mind about the church. He could have brought up in the first hour of our visit but hadn't. He was sure I would disagree with him on whatever he had on his mind, and I usually did, so this church concern would take us at least a half hour to discuss. He didn't back down and I didn't back down. Olive would just sit there quietly and smile as she listened to our discussion, which sometimes got a little heated. But he respected me and I respected him and, every time I left their home, I had to smile because he got me every single time.

I enjoyed my time with Francis and Janice Quantrill, Shirley Moffat, Alison and Randy Cowan and their children Erik and Taylor, and my next door neighbours Jack and Elaine Mercer. Dorothy and Robbie Robinson were good-hearted people and, of course, I loved working with Laura Head and knew her husband Brian Malcolm and their children Emily and Hilary. I also worked with Don and Donna Scott and they had two older sons, Kevin and Andrew. There was Helen Schmid who was the town historian and had my mother's family, the Cuttells, recorded in her history of Orono. There was Roy Scott, his wife Marion and two daughters, Ruth Gray and Anna Marie Allin and her husband John and children Tanya and David. Their whole family was committed to their church and we became very close friends. There was David and Sharon Staples and his mother Vera Staples who never missed a church service if she could help it, and my neighbours across the street Lloyd and Flo Sharpe. Flo was a very good seamstress and I often took my slacks to her to turn up. There was Don and Jeanne Staples. Don was a very good artist and his wife had been a very fine musician.

I visited Edna and Earl Taylor, Cliff and Eleanor Terrill, Thelma Vagg, Shirley Williams, and Alvin and Ruth Yeo. Ruth was very helpful to me when I was first visiting the hospital in Bowmanville because she was the receptionist there and knew everyone. Carol and Grant Yeo were a wonderful couple. They were both very active in our church as were Dorothy and Derek Barnett, Margie and Clarence Gunter, Brad and Vickie Heard and their children Elizabeth and Rebecca. There were wonderful visits with Ruth Grady, Gary and Marilyn Hancock, Connie and Bill Hooey, and Dave and Audrey Kilpatrick. There were many more families I visited.

I met Gary Armstrong at his grandmother's funeral in the summer of 2000. Gary worked for the family's Armstrong IGA in Orono and was about 40 years old, over 6' tall, had long curly black hair just below his shoulders and had the build of a gentle giant. We became good friends. I loved his sense of humour and, as we got to know each other better, I found I could talk to him about anything. I have a silly side to me and I could really get Gary laughing. He didn't drive, so once a week we would go shopping and have lunch or dinner together. I felt very fortunate to have such a good and loyal friend who was my confidant and never let me down.

As a minister I loved to visit and hear people's stories which I found so interesting. I was lifted up by the hope they had and the faith we shared and the love they had for their church. It gave me hope as I listened to people tell me about the struggles they had, the grief they have suffered through in their lives, and still felt to some degree, but still managed to go on with hope and love. It was these visits that kept me going. I visited these families over and over again and always came away feeling what a privilege it was to be welcomed into the homes of the members of my congregations at Kirby and Orono. These visits set the tone for my ministry and some of their stories became part of my sermons. Early in the week, I would read over the three Scriptures set out for that Sunday in our Lectionary and, by the end of the week, after having done many visits, I began to write notes on my thoughts and ideas about the scriptures while also reflecting on the visits I had made and what Jesus might say to me about my week. That's how I wrote my sermon. I loved leading in worship and preaching and visiting. Those were my strengths and my calling.

Orono United Church had celebrated its 150th Anniversary on October 19th, 1997 when the Reverend Dr. Mervyn Russell was their minister and the former Moderator, the Very Reverend Dr. Sang Chul Lee, preached on their anniversary. Those who attended church were very active, in one way or another, like the committee of six who painted the inside of the manse in March, 2001. They had many groups, like the Committee of Stewards, a very active Session, a Board of Trustees, a Senior Choir and a Junior Choir. They had three United Church Women's groups with 29 members and a Ladies Time Out which was made up of five younger women. The Orono Fair was a huge event in September with the Orono Parade leading off the activities, and many organizations including the church, had a float in the parade. There were tractor pulls, a carnival and competitions for the best desserts, quilts, photography and the biggest pumpkin. There was also a Vacation Bible School which 48 children attended every summer. In 1995, Orono United Church had an active Sunday School with 25 children but numbers decreased every year after that. By the time I got to Orono there were only 10 children on a good Sunday.

On October 21, 2001 we celebrated the 50th Anniversary of our church building, with a committee of eight people organizing a special service made up of the combined choirs of the Orono and Kirby Churches and friends, for a total of 23 members. Our Moderator, The Right Reverend Dr. Marion Pardy, was the guest speaker for this service and, at that service, Myno van Dyke, who was now our Clerk of Session, presented Hilda Caswell with a certificate for being as the oldest member in our church. He also presented James Lowery with a certificate for saving our stained glass window when the old former Methodist Church burned to the ground in February, 1949. Dave Forrester, my neighbor, and Ed Millson drove the fire truck to the church the morning of the service and it was the same fire truck that had been used to try to save the old church in February, 1950. When the people at Orono Church set their mind to do something they did it to perfection and this Anniversary celebration was one of many examples of that quality. They had fun doing what they did together and they loved and appreciated their history.

Just before Christmas, I had an open house and invited everyone from my congregations to come if they could. I had lots of food and treats and over 100 people came through my home and everyone had a great time. It had been a long time since I had been so happy and at home. We had a wonderful Christmas Eve Service at both our churches and then, on Christmas day, I flew to St. John's, New Brunswick to spend Christmas with Warren and Susan and baby Rachel. It was during this visit that I baptized Rachel in the Lower Millstream United Church. She looked so beautiful in the amazing baptismal gown that Vicki Heard, a member in the Orono United Church, had made for her. It was a stunning gown and we could not thank Vicki enough for making it for Rachel. There was a lovely reception after the service to welcome Rachel and I felt so honoured to do this Baptism for my granddaughter. I was just so proud.

When I got back home in early January, I heard that Aleck Moffat had died very tragically. He was one of the older members of Orono Church and lived on the east side of Highway 115. He had a habit of walking across the highway, which was illegal of course, but he had done it for years and everyone worried about him doing this. Just after Christmas, Aleck crossed the highway to visit with his friends in town. By the time he headed back home to his family for dinner, it was very dark outside. When he didn't come home at his usual time, his family became worried. His son went out to look for him and saw police cars and an ambulance on Highway 115. It turned out that a woman driving north on the 115 didn't see Aleck until it was too late and he was killed instantly. This shocked the community. His funeral was held on December 31st and that is how we ended the year. For me, this past year had been miraculous. I had made it through two major surgeries and had been blessed with a beautiful granddaughter who made me so happy. I loved living in the manse and the people in both my congregations were wonderful to do ministry with. Considering my mother's family had originally settled in Orono in the early 1860's and there were Cuttell's buried in the Orono Cemetery, I felt very much a part of the Orono Community and was looking forward to another wonderful year in 2002.

CHAPTER FOURTEEN

A Wedding and More Funerals

I WAS READY TO START my second year at Orono, but I did wonder how many funerals I would have. The death of Marie Tamblyn had been an especially terrible loss for her family and our congregation because she had been so active in our church. I have always encouraged families to have their loved ones buried through the church but, since I started in full time ministry at Orono, I had already officiated at far more funerals in the church than I had ever had in all my previous Pastoral Charges. From my experience, this was very unusual but families asked for the church and we were there for them. It was harder to do services in the church because there was so much more involved than through a funeral home. When services were done at the funeral home, they were limited, which was what most families expected, and the service was shorter than at the church, usually about half an hour. When the funerals were done at the church, families hoped that the choir would be able to sing at the service, the custodians had to clean the church before and after the service, and the United Church Women were often asked to look after the reception. I had more to do too since I had to prepare a full service, which was usually an hour and included hymns and an anthem, with our Music Director playing the organ. I had to do up an order of service and our Secretary had to run off the bulletins in the office.

I was very good at doing funeral interviews with families and conducting the funerals for their loved ones and was happy that I could help families in their time of loss, but I found it emotionally draining. I had been visiting families in Orono and Kirby since July, 2000 but my visiting had been very limited with part time ministry at 14 hours a week. Since I had started full time in April, 2001, I had been doing a lot more visiting so I knew many families well and had made some real connections. It wasn't always easy to do a funeral service for someone I had made a connection with because it was more personal for me. In the rare case of a funeral for someone who had become a dear friend, it was even harder to keep my own emotions and feelings in check while conducting the funeral service. As ministers, we are supposed to keep some distance from the people we serve but sometimes it is very hard to do that, and the longer we are in a Pastoral Charge the harder it can be. Aside from visiting families in my congregations, I also enjoyed the preparation for worship on Sunday and writing my sermons. I loved to lead in worship and preach and I enjoyed the fellowship we had at both Kirby and Orono United Churches. The key element in any church's life is family and the families in the community are the life blood of any congregation. I was thinking about that and my own family, particularly my sister and one of the visits we had together. As I reflected on the past, I wrote an article for the Orono Times in February under the column "It Seems To Me". Here is part of that article:

"My sister came to visit. She did not walk across the road or even drive to Orono. Since we were children, we have always been separated. In 1964 my parents and my sister moved to the United States, California…..The distance became greater. As the years progressed, the bond we had only grew stronger… …We have visited over the many years. I want to share one of the family visits we had. My sister and I have wonderful memories of Uncle Phil and Aunt Louise (Thompson) visiting with Pierre and Janet (Berton) and their children at our home in Oakville and at their home in Kleinburg from the early 1950s….. Janet and Pierre were so glad I called and so pleased to see us (Jana and me) when we visited at their home. I saw the old player piano I used to play on. I could see our grandmother Marion Cuttell standing by their window looking out over the valley. I saw the old pictures, silhouettes that my Aunt Louise gave to Pierre when my Uncle Phil, also Pierre's uncle, died in 1973. We saw again the very large old music box we used to play with at the house in Oakville…..Pierre's grandfather T. Phillips Thompson had owned that house in Oakville that Uncle Phil grew up in and later I was raised there. Our Uncle Phil's sister, Laura Beatrice Berton, would come from Vancouver to visit us in Oakville. She was Pierre's mother and was a great friend of our grandmother Marion Cuttell. Pierre and Janet, Jana and I talked about the family and the memories. I gave Pierre his grandfather's book, one of the original ones, "The Politics of Labour" published in 1887. It had been passed on to me by our family… … We shared stories of our children and grandchildren. It seems to me that family is very important no matter how they come to be our family. They have stories and memories that only we know and they bring to life for that moment those we so dearly miss. I thank my sister for the month we had where we were like children again, playing, laughing, remembering, valuing everything we had and everything that was passed on."

I had decided, back in November 2001, to give a benefit concert for the Orono and Kirby United Churches on April 6. I gave this concert in memory of my friend, Dr. Fraser McKenzie. He was a member of Orono United Church and had been the only medical doctor in town for over 40 years. He loved classical music and encouraged me to play for him every week when I went to see him. It was a wonderful feeling to give this concert in Orono United Church, the place where my great grandfather James Cuttell who lived in Brooklin, took his family to visit his brother John Cuttell in the 1870s, 80s and 90s. They worshipped together in the old Methodist Church which was renamed Orono United Church in 1925. This concert was a great success.

Warren and Susan came for a short visit around the middle of April with Rachel and I had a birthday party for my son. It was great to see them and I marveled at how Rachel had grown. I couldn't get enough of her because I had missed her so much and she was so adorable. I really wished they were closer because Rachel was growing so fast and I hoped that maybe, in the next few years they might move back to Ontario. In the meantime, all I could do was visit them when I could and enjoy their visits when they came to see me.

In August, I visited my sister in Coos Bay, Oregon and we had another wonderful visit. Richard took me everywhere to show me his favorite places and the scenery was spectacular. While I was gone, Marion Scott passed away. Her husband Roy was heartbroken as were her daughters Ruth Gray and Anna Marie Allin. I had visited them often and enjoyed my visits with them. As soon as I got back home, I visited Roy. I felt very badly for both Ruth and Anna Marie who loved their mother very much, but it was Roy who suffered greatly because now a part of him was missing with the loss of his beloved wife. I began visiting him on a regular basis and he really appreciated that. Roy was such a fine man and always had great stories to tell.

Back in May I had talked to both Sessions about us having a photo directory. I had made some calls to companies who did this for churches and told the Sessions that it wouldn't cost us anything to do this Directory but it would help all of us to see who our members were. We chose the company we would like to work with so in September, I was busy making all the appointments that had to be set up for the company to take photos of everyone in our two churches. There were many people to call but I saw this as a wonderful opportunity for me to have conversations with families I didn't know who didn't attend church but were on the church rolls. I was very excited about this and the possibilities. We had lots of people in the church helping to organize the days and evenings that appointments had been set up and I was there for every family who came to have their photos taken while Donna Scott and some of the United Church Women had coffee and cookies for the families while they waited for their turn. It was everything I had hoped it would be and the Elders were pleased that so many families turned out for this.

I had already conducted a number of funerals that year and then, on November 4th, Bev Cowan died suddenly. His passing was a shock, especially for his wife Diane and their children and grandchildren. The Cowans were a close family that had deep roots in Orono. Because his death was totally unexpected, I knew how emotional this funeral would be. I knew their son Randy and his wife Alison and their children Erik and Taylor who were a joy to have in our congregation and lived in Bowmanville. Randy was an Orono boy at heart and they were very active in Orono United Church. The service went well. The church was full as the community came out to support Bev's family.

Then, on November 16th, there was another tragic funeral in Orono United Church. Robbie and Dorothy Robinson were, without a doubt, two of the kindest and most generous people in our church and, even as seniors, they continued to be very, very active. They could never do enough to help. When their son Matthew was dying of cancer, Robbie and Dorothy asked me to visit him at his home near Haliburton. His 11 year old daughter Natasha was there. I could see that this young girl was just devoted to her dad. She insisted that they tell her everything that was happening to him and that he talk to her about his illness. This was a father and daughter who were so close and so connected and it was heartwarming to see the love that was there. I spent time with Matthew, who wanted to talk to me about his death, his partner Cindy and his beautiful little girl. Matthew's death was tragic. Dorothy and Robbie had such love for their son and granddaughter and I couldn't imagine how it must have felt to lose a child. It made me think of my own son. Because I had such a strong bond with Robbie and Dorothy and I felt so badly for them, this was the hardest and saddest funeral I had yet to do at Orono and it was all I could do to hold back the tears as I conducted the service.

Then on November 30th Vera Staples died. She was, without a doubt, one of my favorite people. I just loved seeing Vera in church at Orono on Sunday mornings. She always sat close to the front on the right side aisle seat when I was in the pulpit, and she would just sing those hymns with every fibre in her body because she sang from the heart. She loved to have me visit her and she was just one of those people you couldn't help loving. She reminded me of my grandmother because she always had a smile and was very generous and kind. In July 2001, when I announced in church that I now had a granddaughter, Vera went out and bought a stuffie for me to take to Rachel when I went down to see her in New Brunswick shortly after she was born. It was a doggie stuffie, and, to this day, Rachel still has it and it is the only stuffie she takes everywhere with her - on trips and for sleepovers at grandma's and nana's. Again, the church was packed for Vera's funeral and we sang some of the hymns she loved. I really missed Vera because she was such a vibrant and positive person who just loved life and loved people. All in all, I had conducted 23 funerals that year. Thirteen of those funerals were held in our church, and I conducted the other 10 funerals at a funeral home. None of these deaths were easy for anyone and, in one way or another, everyone in the church including myself were emotionally drained. The choir and our organist had come out for all of the funerals in our church. Our organist Karen was wonderful to work with and had a refreshing sense of humour which helped me and the choir during those trying days. She always had so much positive energy which we all felt. The United Church Women prepared the food for every funeral reception they were asked to do and that took its toll on them too because they were older women but they always rose to the occasion.

Not long after Vera's funeral, I was relaxing at home when there was a knock at my door and I opened it to find a man standing there. He told me his name was Lorne and that Frances and Joyce Cowan had suggested he come over to see me. He was there, he said, to ask me to go out on a date with him to the General Motors Annual Christmas dance and said he had already purchased two tickets. I didn't know him at all but he had a nice smile. Besides, I thought the world of Frances and Joyce so he came highly recommended. He was about 67 years old and very friendly, 5'10" with a slender build and a receding hair line. I remember feeling very flattered and surprised that he was asking me out so I said yes. Lorne picked me up the night of the dance and we drove to Oshawa. When we got there the place was packed but Lorne knew lots of people because he had worked for years at General Motors before retiring. It was a fun evening and I enjoyed the music and being with Lorne. I enjoyed dancing with him and he told me I was good dancer. He was surprised at how well we got along and I told him I felt the same way. When he took me home, he asked me out again and I said yes. I liked his energy and enthusiasm and I was having fun with him. It all happened so fast but I liked him and he took my mind off all the sadness I had felt throughout that year with the funerals.

I didn't make the connection the first time I went out with Lorne but I had met his wife Vicky in the hospital back in August just before she died. I didn't officiate at her funeral because I was visiting my sister in Oregon at the time. She had been ill most of her life and that had been hard for her and her family, especially Lorne. After her death, he continued to live in the seniors' complex in Orono where he and his wife had lived. We went out a few more times that month and then he invited me for a family dinner and introduced me to his three children. They all seemed nice enough but I was very aware that their mom had just passed away in August and this would be their first Christmas without her so I could understand if they felt a little uncomfortable.

I had another very successful open house at the manse around the middle of December and again about 100 people came from the churches and surrounding area. It was very festive and everyone was in such a good mood. The Christmas Eve services went well in both the churches and again I went to New Brunswick on Christmas Day to be with Warren and Susan and Rachel who was now one year old. She was getting bigger and I missed seeing her. Warren had already been in New Brunswick for four and a half years and he seemed happy and content with his congregations. I couldn't help wondering how much longer he would stay there and, if they moved, where they would go next. I enjoyed another wonderful Christmas with my family and I told Warren and Susan about Lorne and what a great time we had together at the General Motors Christmas Party and how nice it was to be out dancing and having fun. I also told them I liked him and that he had invited me to a dinner with his family and introduced me to his two sons and his daughter and their spouses and grandchildren. Warren and Susan just wanted me to be happy and they could see that I was.

Coming into 2003, I hoped this new year would be less about funerals but then I had one straight away on January 6th and, on January 12th I had the funeral for Bill Hooey. I remembered meeting him not long after I became the supply minister at Orono United Church in July 2000 when he was in one of the hospitals in Toronto. I knew Bill and his wife Connie didn't come to church but he was well known in the community and Connie was very active in the community and close to many people in the Orono Church. I talked to Connie about visiting him in the hospital and she was surprised I would do this but said it was fine with her. I had my collar on as I walked into his hospital room and I could see the look of surprise on Bill's face. He didn't know who I was so I introduced myself and told him I was the supply minister at Orono United Church. I had been warned that he could be a bit crusty. Well we had a great connection from that first visit when he told me how he loved horses and horse racing. Bill was a good man, one of the boys, and I understood him. He was quite ill at that time and had had his legs amputated. His wife Connie was loved and respected in the community so she was able to get him a lot of help, including a van that was refitted so he could drive it using only his hands which I thought was amazing. Connie knew he needed to be independent and she knew he could drive anything so the van was going to be a huge help. Bill made a good recovery and got out of the hospital and a few weeks later was driving that van around town to visit his buddies. When I learned that Bill was dying, I called Connie to see if it would be alright to visit Bill at home and she said I could come anytime. I felt that was a privilege and, whenever I went in to see Bill, Connie would leave us alone to talk. The church was overflowing at his funeral with people who came to say goodbye to Bill. There was a lot to like about him and I gave the best service I could for him, out of the respect and admiration we all had for his courage to fight the good fight.

Lorne had been really glad to see me once I was back home after Christmas and we continued to date and have a lot of fun together and I looked forward to seeing him and being with him. He took me to visit his sister and her husband in Scarborough where we had a nice dinner and played euchre. For the first time in a long time, I was dating and it felt really good. I could depend on Lorne and he was easy to talk to. We didn't have a lot of chemistry, but we were working into a comfortable relationship and we liked each other. He had retired from General Motors three years earlier and told me he wanted to travel. I told him I wasn't ready to retire for at least another six years and he understood that. We wanted to have time away together so we went down to Niagara Falls for a couple of days to relax and spend quality time together. It was good for me to get away from the church and we did have a really good time. We swam in the swimming pool at the motel and, before we left, he asked if we could go to the hot tub one more time so we did. In the hot tub, he asked me to marry him. That blew me away and I didn't know what to say. I had only known him for six weeks and I wasn't crazy in love with him. I just felt he was someone very nice whom I liked and we got along really well. We liked some of the same things. I saw a future with him. He had lost his wife and my family were in New Brunswick and in Oregon. I had to admit that there were days when I really felt as lonely as he did. I had almost died in 2001 and, in the back of my mind, I saw this as a new beginning. Saying that now feels strange to me, but that's what I thought back then. Every year I was dealing with so many deaths in my two congregations and some were very tragic. As a minister, I knew that funerals were part of ministry but I wanted to live and have fun and enjoy life and here was someone who didn't have any great expectations of me. He wasn't demanding and we had a lot of fun together. I also wasn't getting any younger and neither was Lorne. I really thought we could make this relationship work and have a good life together. I said yes.

We set the date for October 25th, and told our families. Warren was never one to question me about what I was doing and this time was no different. He said that, if this felt right and I was happy, that was all that mattered. I had talked to my sister about Lorne after I met him and she thought it was great that I had met someone. When I told her he had asked me to marry him, she was very happy for me and told me that she and Richard would come for my wedding. That made me so happy. I had told both Warren and Jana that we would be married in my home church, St. John's United Church in Oakville, and that Lorne had no problem with that. Lorne and I both agreed that we wouldn't live together before we got married and we didn't want to live in the manse as a married couple either so I would have to talk with the Official Board because that would mean a change in my contract with the Pastoral Charge. When I told the Official Board that I was getting married, everyone was very happy for me and for Lorne. They could understand why I was asking not to live in the manse and, since I was willing to take whatever rent they would be paid when they rented the manse, they were agreeable to it.

It was a fun time and we were both excited. We had a lot of planning to do and had to decide who we would be inviting to the wedding. Besides, I wasn't thinking about the church all the time, which was a good thing. Most people in the congregations knew who Lorne was because he had lived in Orono for years. He had also started coming to Orono United Church for Sunday services in January. I told him he didn't have to on my account but he told me he wanted to and I was really pleased he did. In the midst of all this, Warren phoned me out of the blue one day in February and told me he was leaving his Pastoral Charge. They were coming back to Ontario and he was looking for a new Charge. He had enjoyed being a minister there for almost five years but it was time to move, he said. I have to say I was really happy they were coming back to Ontario. He told me he would line up some interviews and then use my home as a base. I told him that was fine with me and I was excited because he would be meeting Lorne. By March, Warren had set up six interviews in one week so Lorne and I decided we would take a week's holidays in New Brunswick flying there the day after Warren returned home. Warren and Susan thought that was a great idea. The evening I picked Warren up at the airport I had Lorne over for supper. We had a nice visit and Warren and Lorne seemed to get along well. Warren told me he liked Lorne and I was very happy to hear that.

Warren's first interview was at Lakefield and Young's Point Pastoral Charge. I knew Lakefield United Church from having been the minister at Warsaw and I was aware of some of the concerns the church had had over the years. I was surprised this was one of the churches he was applying to but it was the closest one to where I lived and that was a good thing. When he came home from that interview, he told me all about it and I was very impressed. He sounded excited but it was only the first of six interviews so he would see how the rest went. During our conversation about Lakefield, I felt a chill go up my back. That is the only way I can describe it. I believed in that moment that Lakefield was where he would be going but I said nothing to him.

He came and went that week, doing five interviews in the Ottawa and Waterloo area and drove over a thousand miles. Then it was over and time for him to go back home. Every one of the six Pastoral Charges he had interviews with asked him to be their minister. That was amazing and a real testament to who he is. He knew for sure that four of the Pastoral Charges were not a call for him and telephoned them right away to pass on them. He also sent each one of them a letter thanking them and evaluating their interview process. Again, my son was really impressive. That left two Pastoral Charges – Lakefield and one other near Waterloo. He felt that the call for him was to the Pastoral Charge near Waterloo but he wasn't completely sure so he needed time to think because he also had an excellent interview at Lakefield. It had been wonderful to have him with me and to hear about the interviews but now it was time for him to go home and think about where he felt he was called. He had a week to decide.

Lorne and I were very excited to be going to New Brunswick for a week. I was so happy to be with my family again. Susan liked Lorne and we all got along very well, playing cards together in the evenings and visiting. Warren was struggling with what to do about the two Charges he was considering and he had phone calls back and forth with the people in the Waterloo area. At one point, Warren asked me to read over the two resumes on those Pastoral Charges. I made notes and was shocked at what I found. I pointed out at least eight concerns to Warren about the charge in the Waterloo area. I looked at Lakefield's resume and was surprised again because I couldn't find one issue that needed to be addressed. Warren knew me well enough to know I was not stacking the deck. I was just trying to be very honest.

Then Warren received an email from the Pastoral Charge in the Waterloo area. It was not a nice letter and it upset Warren very much. Warren decided to call the Chair of the Pastoral Relations Committee in Lakefield and told the Chair upfront that he was feeling a call to another Pastoral Charge. The Chair told Warren that they had been looking for a minister for about two years and that the whole committee felt he was called to be with them. They would do whatever it took to make Warren and Susan feel as comfortable as possible. Warren thanked him and told him he would get back to them. He came upstairs and told us what the person at Lakefield had said. "If Lakefield feels I am called to them, I have to consider that," he said. We talked for a while and then Warren went back downstairs to his office and phoned the Pastoral Charge in the Waterloo area. He told them that he had to turn down the call. They said they were very sorry and had been so upset at the person who sent him that email. Warren then called the Chair of the Pastoral Relations Committee in Lakefield back and told them he accepted the call. The Chair hadn't expected Warren to call back so soon and he told Warren the committee had not yet discussed the terms and conditions, things like salary, benefits, travel and housing allowance. Warren asked if they would be fair and the Chair said they would and so Warren agreed. When Warren came upstairs and told us that he had accepted the call. Susan was so excited and relieved that they were going back to Ontario. She called her mom and dad to tell them and they were very happy too. Warren had taken this so seriously and it had worked out for him and his family. I told him how I had felt after he came home from that interview in Lakefield, that I believed it was the call. I was overjoyed for them and, of course, for me too since they would only be 45 minutes away. Now Warren had to tell his congregations that he was leaving as of June 30th.

Lorne and I had a wonderful visit with Warren and Susan and they took us to all their special places in New Brunswick and PEI even though there was lots of snow. Lorne and I returned home and, not long after, Warren called to tell me his congregations were very sorry to lose him because they had been so happy to have had Warren and Susan and Rachel with them. There would be many wonderful memories for all of them of their time in New Brunswick. Lorne and I were very busy getting the invitations for the wedding ready to send out and then we had to look for a house in Bowmanville which is where we decided to move. At the same time we were looking at houses, Warren and Susan were looking on the internet to see what was for sale in Lakefield. He had phoned to ask me that, if they found something, could I check it out for them and I said I would. Two weeks later, Warren called and said they had found a house. It was a century old brick home that they were looking at and he asked me would I go and see it. I met the real estate agent at his office in Lakefield at 7:00 p.m. The agent took me over to view the house and it was a huge old home. It looked lovely from the outside with a driveway long enough for three cars and a carport as well. I met the owner who was a very nice man in his 80s who had recently lost his wife. His daughter and granddaughter lived with him but the house was far too big for them. I walked through it and loved it but saw it needed a great deal of work, inside and out. It had a very large back yard and I could already see the vegetable garden and the wonderful flower gardens Warren and Susan would have there. The outside of the house had a nice veranda with huge old posts all around it that held up the roof over the veranda area.

It was a huge house with lots of space. When you walked into the house, on your left you saw a winding staircase that was in excellent condition. On the right was what could be a large, formal living room. When you walked down the hall from the front door, there was a good-sized dining room on the left with the rest of the formal living room on your right. Going further, there was a good-sized kitchen on the right, and on the left, a table and chairs for five people. Off this area facing the kitchen there was a door going out into a mud room and, on turning left again, there were very old stone stairs going down to the cellar/basement which had a washer and dryer, an old oil and wood furnace and a cold room. Going back up the stone stairs and straight ahead, you opened the patio doors onto a very large deck with a barbeque and hot tub and a very large yard with three small storage buildings. Going back inside the house into the kitchen and turning left, there was a door that opened into a very large family room and off it a new extension that had been added to it a few years ago. Above this room was an attic that was very big. Going back to the front door if you went upstairs to the second floor and turned left you immediately saw a door on your left going up to a huge attic. On this second floor were four small bedrooms and a very large bathroom with a shower and Jacuzzi.

The gentleman who owned the house could not have been nicer and I thanked him for letting me go through his home. He told me he just wanted someone to buy his home who would love it as much as he and his wife had. I told him about Warren and Susan and Rachel and how much they appreciated history and old homes. I told him about the old house in Oakville where I grew up and that it had meant so much to me and to my son and that, as a little girl, Susan had gone every summer to visit her grandparents in England. When we got back to the real estate agent's office, I called Warren. I told him and Susan all about the house and the property and described it in great detail. I also told them about the gentleman who lived there. I told Warren this house was perfect for them and that rarely did a home this old come on the market. Warren asked to speak to the real estate agent and made an offer $10,000.00 lower that what was asked. The next day, the owner accepted the offer. Warren had a week's holidays left and they drove to my place. Susan said she couldn't believe they were buying a house sight unseen and I took them to Lakefield to show it to them. They loved the house and the property. It was everything they were looking for. The added bonus was that the house was across the road from the public school. It didn't even faze them that the house and property needed a lot of work. They enjoyed meeting the gentleman who was selling the house and he was very happy they were buying his home. Warren also met with the members of the Pastoral Relations Committee while he was in Ontario and all the details were sorted out in regards to his salary and benefits. We had a nice visit and then they went up to Susan's mom and dad's in Ottawa for a visit before returning home. Warren and Susan would be moving into their new home sometime in July and it was almost May. Everything had happened so fast.

Lorne and I also found a nice home, a bungalow across the street from the hospital on Liberty Street in Bowmanville and the owners had already moved out. It had everything we wanted.

When you came in the front entrance, you were right in the living room which was a good size. Then you could walk from there right into the small dining room area on your left or you could go into the kitchen on your right. Going past the dining room, there was a small bathroom on the right and two bedrooms. I turned the bedroom on the right into my office and the large room on the left would be our bedroom. If you came into the house from the back entrance, you saw where we planned to have the hot tub. For now it was just an open space. We would also have to put all new windows in that area. A few steps up from there, a door opened into the house and you could either go up into the kitchen or turn right and go downstairs where there was a bathroom on the left and, at the bottom of the stairs, a huge family room. Almost at the end of it was a small cold room on the left and, at the end, a door that opened up into another room which we turned into a spare bedroom. At the side of the house there was a carport and, since we were worried about the traffic on Liberty Street that could be very heavy in the later afternoon until early evening, I was able to get permission from the town to put in a roundabout so we wouldn't have to back out onto Liberty Street. I moved into the house at the end of May while Lorne stayed on at the seniors' residence in Orono until we were married. The Charge rented out the manse in June and paid me the rent they received from the family there. Everything was working out well. We sent out the invitations for our wedding and some of the members of the congregation had a shower for us that summer. I was so happy that my cousins Diane and her sister Heather were there. They were very happy for Lorne and me and we all had a great time.

The house needed work and Lorne told me he had two friends who were very good carpenters who helped us with whatever renovations we wanted to do while I was on my own in the house. Lorne and I had a lot of fun renovating the house, deciding what we wanted, and Lorne's two friends were a great help and good to work with. I really liked them and we all got along well. I also worked hard on the garden in the back as there was a lot of property there. I had asked people in the church about taking some of the flowers I had put in at the manse and they told me I was free to take whatever flowers I wanted and replant them at our house which is what we did. It was a lot of work but when we finished the gardens looked beautiful. When the renovations were all done and the gardens were coming along well, I had a barbeque at my home for members in my congregation at the end of August. They loved seeing all the gardens and Lorne and I gave them a tour through the house.

I really liked our new home and Lorne was very pleased. I had had to get rid of a lot of things at the manse because this house was much smaller but I settled in nicely. Lorne didn't have much in his very small unit at the seniors' residence so I was able to put most of my furniture in the huge family room. We decided to buy a dining room table and chairs and some nice furniture for the living room on the main floor. It took us until August to do all the things we needed to in the house. Because Warren and Susan would soon be arriving in Lakefield, Lorne and I had told them we would go up and help them unpack. I was so happy to have Warren and Susan and baby Rachel back in Ontario and it didn't take long for them to settle in and have Heather and Tom come to see their new home. Warren and Susan and Rachel also came down and saw our new house and loved it and stayed over a couple of times that summer.

In the midst of all this, on July 4th I was called to do a funeral which was held at Newcastle United Church. The local minister was on holidays and I was on call for him. The funeral was for a 21 year old young man named Craig Codd who had tragically taken his own life. His mother Patty had come home from work to find that he had shot himself in his room. What a terrible thing for her to see. How lost she looked when I met with her for the funeral interview. She didn't know what to say or do. Her former husband had come from Toronto and he was also at the interview. Craig's older brother Aaron and his sister Lily who were there were in shock. Craig had friends in Orono, Newcastle and Bowmanville, most of whom he had gone to High School with, and when I went to the wake the day before the funeral, there were almost 100 young people there who were very upset and crying. Some of his friends came and talked with me. They told me that they had been to many parties with Craig. He liked his beer and they asked if, at the end of the service, they could each have a bottle of beer ready to open and give him a toast and they said they would be very respectful. I didn't hesitate to say yes. The service was at Newcastle United Church and it was packed. It was very moving to watch as each one of his seven buddies toasted him.

Not long after this funeral, we had a very happy event at Orono United Church when I married Charlie and Esther Campbell. This wedding had been a long time coming. Charlie had been married before and had a son. When he and his first wife divorced, he had eventually married again but, in between those two marriages, he had also met Esther with whom he had a son and daughter. Esther lived in Toronto at that time and was a nurse in one of the Toronto Hospitals. She had grown up in Barbados and told me she could remember sitting on her grandma's knee as she told Esther what it was like to be a slave in Barbados. Esther had moved to England to get her nurse's training and then came to Canada on her own. At some point she met Charlie, and even though he promised to marry her, he had married someone else. Esther raised her children on her own and never asked Charlie for anything. Years later, her son, who now had children of his own, wanted to meet his father and asked his mother if that was alright. She said yes and he went to Orono to meet Charlie. Esther never stopped loving Charlie and it was their son who got his parents back together. It was a real love story and I had the privilege of marrying them. Esther became an active member of our church and an Elder on Session. She loved to laugh and have fun and I enjoyed her great sense of humour. We became very good friends and are to this day.

I wanted to be married in my home church and I hoped that Reverend Jim Campbell would be able to marry us. He said he would be very happy to marry us and talked to the present minister at the church who had no problem with Jim doing the ceremony. Lorne and I went down and met Jim and had a good interview and visit with him. Laura, our church secretary, offered to decorate the big hall where the reception would be held and said her family would help. We also had other friends from Orono United Church like Don and Donna Scott who said they also would help. One of the members of Orono United Church had a catering business and agreed to do the catering for our wedding. She gave us a really good deal which was very much appreciated. I really wanted to have a white wedding dress so I went with a friend to try on wedding dresses and found the one I wanted. It was wonderful to think that people from Orono United Church would not only be at my wedding but helping with my wedding and Lorne was happy to know we had this kind of support. Everything was set to go. I was having so much fun and felt like a young woman again just starting out. Lorne was into it as much as I was. By September, 95 people had responded that they were coming to the wedding and Jana and Richard would be arriving a week before the wedding and I was so looking forward to that. Lorne and I had talked about our honeymoon and came up with lots of ideas but finally settled on Coos Bay where we could stay with Jana and Richard. October, when we were getting married, was also the time of year Richard went hunting. Lorne hadn't gone out hunting for a long time and I thought it would be really nice for him and Richard to do that together and Richard agreed.

Everything was going really well except for one issue. Lorne's children were not happy that their father was getting married again. I had been to a few family dinners with them and I was beginning to wonder what Lorne told them about us. The issue at the time for his children was that for them, it was too soon after their mother died for their dad to get remarried. I really understood that and I even wondered if maybe we should have gone slower. But Lorne really wanted this and at that time I did too. I really cared about Lorne and had feelings for him but it wasn't the passion or chemistry I had had in other relationships. Emotionally, I was worn out with all the funerals I had, almost one a month in the church, and Lorne took my mind off all of that. It felt good being with him and he was supportive. We worked well together and I enjoyed being with Lorne and doing things with him. I felt badly for his children but I had no reason to question Lorne about his family and I had to trust that he would work this out with them. Lorne didn't ask any of them to be in the wedding party but that was his choice. His children, in turn, said they would not be there for the rehearsal but would come to the wedding. When he told me that, I was relieved for him because it meant a lot to Lorne to have them at the wedding. I liked Lorne's children and grandchildren but it was hard to really get to know them in the family dinner setting where I always saw everyone together.

In the meantime, I was still busy doing the ministry, attending meetings in the Charge and Presbytery meetings, and doing lots of visits in Kirby and Orono, a fair bit of administration work and preparing services and sermons. I also had funerals to conduct. The funeral for Carman Cornish was held on September 30 and that was a hard one for me to do because I had become very close to Faye and Carman. They were both not well and I had been visiting them almost weekly since I had come to Orono. Faye was a lovely person and Carman had had the grocery store on the main street in town for many years so everyone knew him. They appreciated him as a businessman too since he was very generous and fair. Their son had lived in Germany at one time with his wife and children but, after their marriage broke up, he returned to Michigan to work for the company that had sent him overseas. Then he had a terrible motorcycle accident and was laid up for months with no family to help him. As ill as they were, Faye and Carman drove to the hospital in Michigan to see their son and help him in any way they could. They went back and forth to Michigan many times over the months their son was recuperating and many of us in the community worried about their health and what might happen to them. Their daughter lived in B.C. and was a nurse, but Carman and Faye had no family to help them in Orono and people like Donna Scott and others stepped up to help them when they were home. I saw this community step up over and over again to help one of their own especially seniors like Faye and Carman, who had given so much to their community and their church. They were not forgotten. The church was packed for Carman's funeral and this was very hard on Faye and her children who were there. But after the funeral, when her son and daughter returned home, Faye didn't have family near her and she was lonely. I continued to visit her weekly as did her friends in the community.

Jean Bemrose's funeral was the last one I did before our wedding on October 25th. Jean and I had become very good friends and she reminded me of my dear friend Jean Boggs from Grand Valley. She had been a school teacher for many years and I could see what a wonderful teacher she had been because she loved teaching. I visited her every week and looked forward to my visits with her because she was still interested in many things, even though she was now 90. She loved the Indian people and had a wonderful picture of an Indian woman in her living room which reminded me of my friend Rosie Nelsen from Roseau. She said that she and her husband had been on a trip to Manitoba in the early 1970's when they saw this painting and bought it. She said her husband, who had died a number of years earlier, loved the Indian people as much as he did. One day, when I went to see her, I saw that the painting she had that reminded me of Rosie Nelsen was no longer on her living room wall but I didn't want to ask her where it had gone. Just before I left, though, she asked me to wait for a moment and went into another room. She came back with this painting and gave it to me. I was very surprised. As a minister you have to be very careful when someone from your congregation wants to give you a gift because a minister is in a position of trust, especially with older people. It could be seen as the minister taking advantage of a particular situation. I didn't want to accept her generous gift but Jean told me she had called all her family members and asked if they wanted this painting. No one wanted it and she told them that she wanted to give it to someone who loved Indian people as much as she and her husband did and her family said they were happy for her to give this painting to me. I was so deeply moved by this gesture because Jean knew I loved that painting and she also knew what it represented for me. I agreed to take it and was very grateful to her. That Sunday, I put the painting up in the Orono Church and told my congregation the story of this painting and why Jean had given it to me. This painting still hangs on a wall in my home to this day and I see it every day as a reminder to me of my Indian friends at Roseau and my dear friend Jean Bemrose. I really missed Jean after she died because she was the one person in the Pastoral Charge who really understood about Indian people and loved them for who they were. I missed that connection.

As our wedding approached October 25, I was so excited that Jana and Richard coming. Lorne and I picked them up at the airport and I was so happy to introduce Lorne to them. Jana and Richard stayed with me at the house but Lorne was over a lot and Jana and Richard really liked him. We had meals together and played cards. He was giving up his apartment at the end of October and Richard even helped him move a few of his things to the house. Much of what he had his family was taking or he was giving away. I took Jana and Richard up to Lakefield to see Warren and Susan and meet Rachel who was now two years old. We had a great time together and then Jana wanted to see Pierre and Janet again so we drove to Kleinburg and saw the family there and had a wonderful visit. We had some really good times and Lorne was a good sport about it all.

Finally, the day came. We booked a number of rooms at a hotel in Oakville and went up for the rehearsal the night before our wedding so we could also help decorate the hall for the dinner the next day. Heather and Tom were coming to help and, of course, Warren and Susan and Rachel too. Fifteen people from Orono were already in the church hall when we got there and Rachel had a wonderful time running around. Some people were setting up the tables and chairs and about 10 people were already decorating. Laura Head was there with her husband Brian Malcolm and their two girls, Emily and Hilary, along with Don and Donna Scott and other friends from Orono. Three friends, Eldon and Benica Barton and Sharon Reynolds, had come to help too from St. Paul's United Church in New Liskeard. The decorating was great fun and it was wonderful to see everyone. They all told me to just stand around and let them know what I wanted. I had no idea what to do and depended on Laura who was great at decorating and organizing. In the middle of all the decorating, those of us in the wedding party had to stop and go to the rehearsal. The minister was waiting for us and Jim got us organized. Warren walked me down the aisle, Rachel was the flower girl and Jana was my matron of honour. Lorne had his best man beside him and his wife stood beside Jana. Richard was also in the wedding party and stood beside the best man. Richard had bought a new suit for the wedding for which Jana was very grateful. He didn't like wearing suits but he looked very handsome in it. From the beginning, Richard had always been very open and accepting of me and he knew how important family was and understood the bond that Jana and I had. He was the best brother- in-law. By the time the rehearsal was over, we all knew what we were doing. I felt wonderful being in my home church and having all my friends and family around me whom I cared so much about.

There was a lot to do the next day to get ready for the wedding. I arrived at the church with my sister, Lorne's best man's wife and Rachel who looked very cute. When we got out of the car, Warren was there and I took his arm. Then it was time. Just before Warren walked me down the aisle, he asked me if I was sure about this wedding and I said I was. As we walked down the aisle, I saw friends from Grand Valley and New Liskeard and Warsaw. I saw Lorne waiting for me at the front and he had this big smile on his face. Then I took his hand. I felt secure with Lorne and I felt he loved me because he had told me he did and that he wanted to be with me. I had much the same feelings at that time and thought we complimented each other. As a young girl, I had thought about getting married at St. John's. I had the same dreams that all girls have. I had read all the fairy tales about meeting their Prince Charming but life had not taken me in that direction. I was certainly not naïve about where this wedding would take me but I wanted simple and uncomplicated. I wanted easy, not hard. I wanted a companion to share my life with.

Perhaps my son understood better than I did when he asked me if I was sure about the wedding before we walked down the aisle. Looking back, I don't regret marrying Lorne, but I realize it was not the best decision I ever made. I just know that, in that moment, I was happy walking down that aisle towards Lorne and holding his hand. It felt right, and looking back and knowing what I know now, I have that moment when it felt right and I was happy.

When the ceremony was over, Lorne and I went up into the sanctuary to sign all the papers and then Jim announced us and people clapped and cheered as we walked out. People came outside and greeted us and we visited for a while and then had a photographer take family pictures in the church. That took a while because Lorne was having difficulty getting his children to come forward and have pictures taken. His younger son was very upset because he was still grieving for his mother and I felt badly for him. All Lorne's children and grandchildren were at the dinner but they left early. It was not a happy time for them and they were angry with their father. I didn't take that personally and, at the time I didn't know all the issues and concerns they had. The reception went very well. The decorations were beautiful and Laura and everyone who helped her outdid themselves. I had asked my friend Cindy Di Lorenzo to be the Master of Ceremonies and she did a great job. The dinner was excellent and after dinner there were speeches by my sister, Lorne's sister, Warren and Lorne's best man. Lorne was warmly welcomed into our family as I was welcomed into Lorne's family by his sister. Then Lorne and I went up to the microphone and Lorne graciously thanked everyone who had come and said how much we appreciated all the help and support. We cut the cake with Rachel helping, and afterwards, Lorne and I danced to an Anne Murray song we both loved, *Can I have this Dance*. When it was over Lorne and I went back to our hotel. We had a very good night together and it felt right. In the morning we had a breakfast for our family and all the people who had helped with the decorations. We then left for home.

Lorne had finished clearing out his apartment with Richard's help the morning before we left for Oakville so now Lorne was with me at our home. We opened our presents with Richard and Jana looking on and we also had about 35 bottles of wine left from the wedding which we put in the cold room. We finished packing for our trip to Oregon as we were flying out the next day with Jana and Richard. Everything happened quickly and soon we were in Coos Bay for eight days. Lorne liked Oregon and was very excited to be going hunting the next day. While the men were gone, Jana and I had a good visit. We planned a dinner for when they returned that evening and did some shopping. The next day when Richard and Lorne went out hunting, Jana talked to me about Lorne. Apparently, Lorne had upset Richard. He hadn't wanted to say anything to me but he told Jana that Lorne was very controlling and had tried to tell Richard what to do. This surprised Richard because, up to that time, Richard thought Lorne was a really good guy and was genuinely happy for me. But, now, Richard told Jana that he really didn't want to take Lorne out again but was only doing it for me. I was surprised to hear this and didn't know what to say. I had not seen that side of Lorne and didn't know what to think. Jana and I agreed that perhaps Lorne had just been excited to be out hunting with Richard and it had been a long time since he had had that opportunity. Nothing more was said about that and Richard took him out again on the third day which was their last day of hunting. Overall we had a great time with my family and Richard took us for drives to see how beautiful Oregon was. Soon we headed home and got settled into our new life together.

I was very busy and I had a lot to do in the churches. Lorne was retired but had friends in the backwoods he liked to visit and help. He also had his two sons and his daughter whom he could visit so I assumed that he would keep himself busy. We soon bought the hot tub and had it installed. It was wonderful to go into it at night and relax. Before long, we were in the process of getting our house dressed up for Christmas, our first Christmas together. Lorne was a great help in putting up the tree and decorations and the house looked lovely. I was also so happy that Warren and Susan were in Lakefield and also getting ready for Christmas. This would be Rachel's second Christmas. I was still seeing my very good friend Gary every week for lunch in Orono and sometimes shopping after in Bowmanville. We had done this for a couple of years. He was a good friend and had come to my wedding where he sat with our family. I was so happy he was there and he had even worn a suit. Gary was the one person I could say anything to and, as much as he made me laugh, I can also be very silly and get him laughing too. We just had a nice, easy kind of friendship and we both loved to shop. I had told Lorne from the beginning about my friend Gary who was 17 year younger than me so there was no issue. Or so I thought.

I always talked to my sister a couple of times a month and we both looked forward to our conversations about our families, our marriages and generally how we were doing. It was Christmas and I had just got off the phone with my sister where we had talked for well over an hour. I looked over at Lorne and he seemed upset. He asked me why I was talking for so long on the phone with my sister and I told him that we always had lots to talk about and left it at that. Lorne and I had spent time with his family at Christmas but Lorne didn't talk much about them. I never felt completely comfortable with them but I didn't think too much about it. We had our first Christmas, 2003, with Warren and Susan and Rachel at Lakefield and it was wonderful. After Christmas, I called Warren a few times to see how they were. Again Lorne approached me and asked me why I was talking to my son since I had just seen him. That made me begin to wonder if Lorne had enough to do with his time. Now that we lived together, I had also found out about his drinking. He would pour an eight-ounce glass of wine and just drink it down. However, I never saw him drunk and I wasn't about to be critical or tell him how much he could drink. I didn't want him telling me who I could talk to or visit with and for how long either. I let it go.

I had been very busy that year in my two churches and I had done 20 funerals as well. Coming into 2004 and a new year, that didn't seem to be changing. I had Margie Gunter's funeral on January 3rd. She was 90 years old and a lovely person who had been very kind to me. I had buried her husband in July, 2002 and she had had a hard time without her husband but still carried on, always with a smile. Donna Scott had been such a support to Margie and checked on her regularly to see how she was or if she needed anything. That was a great help for her and I went in fairly often to see her as well. She was always so gracious and brought out her teacups and cookies as soon as I came in.

Through January, everything seemed fine with Lorne and me, but then I wasn't looking for anything to be wrong. One day, though, I was out having lunch with Gary as usual. I always told Lorne what I was doing when I went out and he showed up at our table in the restaurant. I asked him if there was anything wrong and he said no and then tried to stare me down. I felt uncomfortable and embarrassed and wasn't sure where Lorne was coming from. All I could say was I would see him later at the house and that he knew I had visits to make that afternoon. After he left, I didn't know what to say to Gary but, again, I let it pass. I phoned Jana and told her about what I thought was strange behaviour on the part of Lorne. She said that Lorne had said some things to Richard about me that made him feel uncomfortable when we were in Coos Bay. She wouldn't tell me much but it was along the lines that, now that we were married, he was the man of the house and things would change. Richard also told Jana that obviously Lorne didn't know me very well. I was surprised but I believed my sister and told her that I was just beginning to feel that controlling side of him which, up until then, I hadn't seen or maybe wasn't willing to see. Lorne showed up again in February at the *Dutch Oven* where Gary and I were having lunch. This time he was a little more threatening and overt in his tone and it took some doing to get him to calm down and leave. Luckily, in the end, he did leave but I was very upset by this and wasn't sure as to what I wanted to do about it.

Then one day when I came home, Lorne's friends from the backwoods were in our house. I had met them before and had a very bad reaction to these two men. I had also heard from a reliable source about their family and that they could be part of the Russian mob. I hadn't worried about it because they were Lorne's friends but now they were in our home. I tried to be friendly but I had a very bad vibe and, when they went outside to do something, I talked to Lorne and told him I did not want them in our home again. I was very forceful and direct when he argued with me but I didn't let up and they didn't come back. It was then that I really started to see a different side of Lorne. He was controlling and I didn't understand why or what useful purpose that would serve. If he really knew me, he had to know you can't fence me in and that's what I felt he was trying to do. I also had heard stories about his wife and how lonely she was, how Lorne controlled the situation but then she had been very ill for many years. That made me begin to think about how he might have treated her but I really didn't know. All I knew was that he was trying to put a wedge between me and my family and my friend Gary and that was never going to happen. At that moment, I didn't have the time or emotional energy to deal with the situation but the time would come when we would have to have a very serious conversation and that time came sooner than I expected.

While I was thinking about all of this, Warren called in February and told me that Susan was two months pregnant and the baby was due in September. I was very excited to think that I would be a grandmother again and was very happy that Rachel would be having a baby brother or sister. They were so happy and I was so happy for them and my sister thought it was wonderful that I would have another grandchild. But my joy was tempered by my developing doubts about my relationship with Lorne. Their wonderful news was the one bright light in that darkness that was beginning to loom over my marriage.

The year before, Kirby United Church had had a lot of concerns over how much longer they could keep going. Over the past seven years, they had seen their congregation continue to lose members through death or people moving out of the area. Now, only 14 people were coming out to church on Sundays. It was a wonderful congregation and I enjoyed being there but it wasn't up to me to tell them whether to close down or not. Whatever they decided, it had to be their own decision. There were many meetings around this concern the previous year and many talks with Oshawa Presbytery since the Kirby United Church congregation couldn't do anything without the approval of the Presbytery. At a congregational meeting on December 9, 2003, the congregation had made a motion to have joint services with Orono United Church in the month of January. Then, at their Annual Congregational Meeting on February 2, 2004, the congregation made a motion to dissolve their church. It was very sad and very hard for the people who made this decision but, looking back, they made the right choice. It was time. Most of the 10 families left in their church did go over to Orono United Church and I was proud of the decision they made. Because Kirby United Church was a historical building, they hoped that they could raise enough money to move the church across the road to the museum and the pioneer village that was there but, as hard as they tried, it didn't happen. The Presbytery sold Kirby Church for $1.00 which would be held in trust by the Trustees at Kirby until such time as it might be moved. I was very emotional when they closed Kirby Church and I knew how much this church meant to the people. Kirby United Church went back to 1880 when it was first a Methodist Church so they had 124 years of history. I now had a one point Pastoral Charge, Orono United Church. This was a big change for our Charge.

In early March, we had a Session meeting at Orono United Church and all the Elders were there including Carol Yeo who had just come back from a trip to China to visit friends. We had a good meeting and everything was fine, or so it seemed. Two days later, on Thursday, I got a phone call that an ambulance had taken Carol to the Kingston Hospital and it looked like she needed a heart transplant. I couldn't believe what I was hearing. How was this possible? She looked so good when I had seen her two days earlier. I called her husband Grant to find out what was happening. He told me they were transferring Carol to a hospital in Toronto that was better equipped to deal with a transplant. He was very upset. I went down the next day to see Carol and, when I walked into her hospital room, she looked up at me and I stopped in my tracks. The fear I saw in her eyes was so palpable it literally took my breath away. She was terrified. I walked over to her, sat on the bed with her and took her hand. I told her she had been so good to me in my illness and had helped me make it through my two surgeries. I told her that she would make it through too, but as I talked to her, I soon realized she was in shock. She couldn't believe what was happening to her and she didn't understand why. I couldn't answer any of her questions because I didn't understand either. I felt terrible and had this sinking feeling in my heart that I can't describe. It was horrible. I stayed quite a while with Carol and then I said a prayer with her and told her I would be back.

Very quickly after that, Carole was put into an induced coma and an iron lung as doctors searched to find a transplant in time. It all seemed surreal. I went down many times in the next

A Wedding and More Funerals

three weeks to see Grant and I met his sister and family. Their son was there too as well as Carol's two daughters from a former marriage who had flown in from B.C. Everyone was in a state of shock and didn't understand why this was happening. In the meantime, my congregation was also very upset and worried and it was a very hard few weeks for everyone who loved Carol. I was distraught but Lorne was no support to me at all during this time when I was so worried about Carol. While I was away more, he seemed to be drinking more and at one point he asked me why I had to be away so much. I told him he knew I was in Toronto at the hospital with Carol and her family. Emotionally, I couldn't deal with Lorne and I was running on empty. On Sunday, March 28, near the end of the service at Orono Church the phone rang in the Board Room. I told the congregation that I had to take this call and ran to pick up the phone. It was Grant's sister. She was very upset and told me Grant had asked her to call me and tell me I should come right away because it wouldn't be long now. She asked me if I would pick her up at her home in Oshawa on my way and I said I would be there within half an hour. I came back and told my congregation the situation, said the Benediction, drove to pick up Grant's sister and we headed to the hospital. When we got there, I asked the nurse where Carol and her family were. She said that she was very sorry to have to tell me that Carol had just died and the family had just gone back to the hotel. Those words ripped through my soul. Grant's sister was in shock as we drove to the hotel. Grant wanted to talk about the service and he said he wanted it at the church. I told him that I would do whatever he wanted and we scheduled the service for the following Friday, April 2nd. When I got home, I felt terrible. I didn't know what to do and called Warren to tell him what was happening. When I was so ill, Carol had stepped up and Warren and Susan were so grateful to her for being there for me when they couldn't be. Warren asked me what he could do and I said the service would be on April 2 at 11:00 a.m. with visiting from 10:00 a.m. – 11:00 a.m. I needed him just to be with me at the front of the church and sit with me in the pulpit and he said he would be there. Not only was our church in mourning but our whole community was. Her death had a huge impact on everyone. Of course, it affected her family the most but everyone in every school Carol had taught in or been the principal of, felt her loss.

I was at the church at 8:30 a.m. the day of the funeral. Morris Funeral Home was looking after everything for the family in the church which was such a big help to all of us in the church. Grant and his family were at the church about 9:30 a.m. and, shortly after they arrived, people started to come into the church to pay their respects. Many teachers who had worked with Carol took what time off they could to come to the wake and then go back to work. They had wanted the day off but, in fact, everyone who had ever worked with Carol wanted a day off to attend this wake. If the school board had allowed that, they would have had to close down all the schools in the whole district. She was that well loved and respected as a teacher, a Principal and a friend. For over an hour and a half, hundreds of people came to pay their respects. Our church knew there would be a huge crowd and had set up a microphone system in the basement as well as in a room upstairs for people to sit and be able to hear the service. Myno told me that, if this service had been on a Saturday, they would have had to close down the town. Over 750 people came that morning and they were lined up outside the church and around the block. It was the largest funeral I had ever presided over. We had over 350 people in the church, at least 200 downstairs and another 80 in the room upstairs with more people standing at the back of the church and everywhere else they could find a place to stand.

As it was almost 11:00 a.m. when the service was to start, I went to the entrance of the church and looked outside where there were people still lined up around the block. I told the funeral director that we needed to start on time if we could because Grant and his family had been there meeting people since 9:30 a.m. and they were exhausted. We couldn't bring more people into the church as it was already packed so they would have to go downstairs. He asked me to direct them. I had my robes on and was ready to start the service so I talked quietly to people coming into the church and showed them where to go downstairs. It took 10 minutes to do this because there were so many people still outside but, between the funeral staff and myself, we got all the people into the church.

Lorne sat with Susan and Rachel at the back of the church for the service and Warren was waiting for me in my office. When the funeral director came and told me that the family was seated, Warren and I went into the sanctuary where he sat with me. He was a huge support to me because I didn't know if I could get through this service alone with all the feelings I had for Carol and her kindness to me. I could only do my best and I was fine until her nephew got up to sing, "You Raise Me Up". There wasn't a dry eye in the church when he sang that song and I had to really struggle to get control back. I still get emotional when I hear that song today. The service went well and the organist and choir were very emotional as they sang the anthem, but they did really well. After the service, there was the reception downstairs, which was very crowded but I visited with as many people as I could. Rachel came over to see grandma and my world changed as I held her. Just seeing her completely calmed me down. People came and went and had their visits with the family until, finally, the family was able to sit in the auditorium and have something to drink and eat. The women in the kitchen outdid themselves that day even though they were run off their feet.

Warren and Susan and Rachel came and said goodbye to me before they left for home. Lorne decided to go and see his family, but I stayed at the church until the family left. It was a very long and emotional day and when I finally got home Lorne wasn't there. I sat and thought a lot about everything that had happened since we got married. I had had so much to deal with in the church, especially all the funerals, and I was emotionally distraught after the funeral I had just done for Carol. Perhaps if I hadn't had such a trying day, I might have overlooked some of the things that Lorne was doing but that day, I was past the point of no return. Life is too precious to be wasted and I knew my marriage was over. It wasn't about blame or confrontation, it was just over. When Lorne came home, I told him our marriage was over. He blamed a couple of people but that didn't matter to me. It was over. I told him we needed to sell the house. I knew that if I decided I wanted to stay there, it would really set him off. Besides, I didn't want to live in that house on my own. I also knew I wouldn't go back to the manse though I had the right to do so. A young couple was living there with their four children and that wouldn't be fair. I didn't worry about where I would live. I would find my way. In the meantime, I knew that Lorne and I would have to live in the house together over the next two months and I moved to the bedroom downstairs until the house was sold. I told Lorne that I was going to tell my congregation that our marriage was over at the service on Sunday, two days after the funeral for Carol, and he asked me what I was going to say about him and I said I didn't know. He turned up with his daughter at the church that Sunday and, at the end of the service, I simply told the congregation that sometimes things don't work out and our marriage was over. Lorne left with his daughter right after the service and, when I went to the back of the church to shake hands with people, everyone was very kind and I appreciated that. I had already called Warren and Susan and told them that the marriage was over and they were sorry, as was my sister, but I don't think my family was surprised. Certainly Richard wasn't. He had told Jana that the marriage wouldn't last six months, based on what Lorne had said to him, and he was right. It was almost six months.

I went to Lakefield for a couple of days after that to just get away and spent time with Warren and Susan and Rachel. They were wonderful to me and so supportive. Driving back home, I dropped in to see Charlie Reid who was in our congregation and worked for a real estate firm. I told him what was happening and asked him to sell our house. He was happy to see me and said he was very sorry about my marriage and would help in any way he could. He told me that, if I needed a place to store my things, he had a big barn out back that I could use. He was very kind. He came to see us the next day and I asked him how much the house was worth and he told me. I said it wasn't enough since we had put $35,000.00 into it and were going to lose money if we didn't recover some of that. I asked him to list it $30,000.00 above what we bought it for. He was surprised and tried to discourage me but I stood my ground. In the end he did sell it for $28,000.00 over what we paid for it and even Charlie was surprised at that. I wasn't.

I made a list of all the things we had in the house: what Lorne brought, what was mine and what was ours – things we had bought together and the wedding gifts. We sat down one Saturday morning and worked out everything. All the while, he kept saying what a shame it was that it hadn't worked out. As for me, I just didn't care anymore. It was over. I started packing right away because the house closing would be the end of June and I had to look for a place to live. I checked out a motel on the highway halfway between Bowmanville and Orono for the interim and they said they would rent me the room for $150.00 a month. When Warren found that out, he was upset and told me I would be coming to stay with them. I hadn't wanted to bother them but now that Warren had asked I said I would stay with them until I found a place and I would store my things at Charlie's. I needed to get away so I went to see my friend Sharon in New Liskeard for a few days and we did a lot of talking about what was happening to me. Sharon was always a good listener and a great friend. I had a really good time away and when I got home, Lorne wasn't there and I couldn't get in because he had changed the locks while I was gone. I went to the back door and broke a window so I could unlock the door and called a couple of friends who came right over and stayed to help me pack up more of my things and to be with me when Lorne returned. Lorne came home and told me he noticed the window had been broken and I said nothing. Then he gave me new keys to the house and I thanked him.

We both went to lawyers to get our divorce. His lawyer was paid for through his union at

General Motors but I had to pay for my own lawyer. More friends came in to help me pack but neither Lorne or I wanted the new furniture we had bought, so we had an auctioneer look after that for us. One day, Donna, a member of our church was in helping me pack and I told her I wanted to go down the street to look at the big apartment building at Baseline and Liberty to see if they had anything available. I asked her if she was alright staying alone with Lorne who was watching everything I did. She said she was fine with that and I went to see the superintendent of the apartment building who was very nice and showed me three different apartments. I wanted to get out of the house as soon as possible. The real estate deal had gone through so I had nothing to stay for. I really liked one of the apartments where a young couple had moved out without paying the rent before their lease was up. The superintendent said they needed to fix it up before I could move in but I told her it was fine for me the way it was. I was willing to take the apartment starting May 1 and give the young couple a break. I signed all the papers and gave her the first and last month's rent. Everything fell into place as it was meant to and I had a new home. I was relieved and actually quite excited. I was moving in less than a week. I was so ready and went back to the house to tell my friend Donna that I had signed up for an apartment. She was happy for me and suggested that maybe I should have friends sleep over with me until I left because she was worried about what Lorne might do. I thought that was a good idea and arranged for my dear friends Laura and Karen to take turns staying with me for the four nights before I moved. I told Lorne I was leaving and that I would be having friends stay over. Laura and Karen slept on my chesterfield in the family room and the sleepovers were fun. They made me laugh a lot.

Warren, and four men from the church who were helping and watching out for me, came down to help the morning of the move which was easy since I was only moving down the street. Lorne was there too watching everything we did. Lots of people helped to move me into the apartment. It felt wonderful driving away from the house for the last time and, when I got to the apartment everyone was there helping to put the kitchen, my bedroom and living room together so it really didn't take long. I so appreciated all they did for me. I still had lots of boxes to open but there was time for all that later. I couldn't thank everyone enough for helping me and Warren had been a wonderful support through all of it. I was determined this would be my last move. I was so tired of moving. Life was good and I had physically and emotionally moved on or so I thought. It was sometime in June, 2004 that I got a phone call from the superintendent who lived in the smaller apartment building around the corner. He told me that his wife was upset because she could see that I was being stalked by my husband. I didn't know what to make of that and talked to Warren about it. He was concerned and told me to call the police. I did that and called more than once but they didn't do anything. I talked to Jana about it too and Richard wanted to know if Lorne had access to a gun or a rifle. I knew he did but I didn't believe he would do anything to me. He had had many chances at the house and, besides I knew he worried too much about what people thought of him.

I continued to have lunch and go shopping with Gary once a week which was really fun for both of us. I enjoyed his friendship very much, especially after I left Lorne and felt so free. I

A Wedding and More Funerals

was glad he was there to be my friend. Then one day, Gary told me that Lorne was hovering around his house and following members of his family in his car which made his mom very nervous. Lorne was still following me around too and I felt so badly for Gary and his family. I didn't know what to say about that. One Sunday morning, Gary called me and said that Lorne had pulled up beside him while he was walking to the store and made a death threat against him. Gary was scared and called the police. He was letting me know that someone from the police would probably be there to talk to me after church. A police officer came to the church just as people were shaking hands with me and leaving so he told me to take my time and he would wait. After everyone left, we went into my office and he wrote up a report. I don't know exactly what happened after that except the police found Lorne and picked him up. I never saw him again and neither did Gary or his family. Although I had been excited and happy when I moved out and closed the door on my marriage the month of August was my holiday month and it was really hard for me. I came crashing down. I closed in on myself and didn't go out much. I tried really hard to pick myself up but I couldn't and went into what I can only describe as a deep depression and really hit rock bottom. It was very hard for me to look at that last year with Lorne and see all the mistakes I had made. I didn't blame anyone, not even Lorne, only myself. There had been warning signs that I ignored and I wondered why, and felt like a fool. What had I done?

But it wasn't like me to stay down and I decided I had to move on. I just had to. I focused on the good things I did, the wonderful family I had and my faith which was still intact. I knew I had to reach deeper and pull myself out of this black hole but it was hard, very hard. If my marriage was really over, and it was, then I had to find positive things to focus on and I made a list. The first thing on my list was my beautiful granddaughter who brought me such joy. Also Warren and Susan and they were expecting another baby and I was going to be a grandmother again. There was my sister Jana and Richard who I loved very much. I also had wonderful friends. I had the most wonderful congregation who were loving and caring and were there for me in all the ups and downs. I told myself I could come back from this but it would take time and I would have to be patient. Before August was over, I was finding my way back and stopped beating myself up. I knew I was still called to serve at Orono United Church and there was more for me to do. People needed me and I had to be there for them.

I was thankful that I didn't have any major funerals after the one I had for Carol because I was still reeling over Carol's death and the breakup of my marriage. By the time Jean Staples, Don's wife, died and I had her funeral on August 28th, I was back and was ready to do the ministry God was calling me to.

CHAPTER FIFTEEN

A New Baby and Conflict in the Church

Warren, Susan and Rachel had been away on holidays for the month of August while I was in a tailspin over the breakup of my marriage, But once I started to come back to myself, I couldn't wait to see them and this new baby that was coming. Warren called me on September 9th and asked me to come up to stay over because the baby would soon be here, and he didn't have to ask me twice. Rachel had just turned three in July and knew she was going to have a baby sister or brother. She couldn't wait to be a big sister. Susan went into labour that evening and Warren took her to the Peterborough hospital while Rachel and I waited for news. When we heard nothing that evening, we went to bed in great anticipation. In the morning around 8:00 a.m., Warren called and said their baby girl had been born a few hours earlier and her name was Sarah Catherine Vollmer. Sarah was born September 10th, 2004. We walked into Susan's hospital room to find Warren and the baby with Susan, and my heart just exploded to see this most beautiful baby, Sarah, my second granddaughter. Warren lifted Rachel up to see her sister and then Warren asked me if I would like to hold my new granddaughter. He brought her over to me and in that moment the world seemed so beautiful. Here was another miracle, another granddaughter, and I was so happy and proud. Susan and Warren were both so relieved that the baby had finally come but they looked very tired since they had been up most of the night. It was a great day and I had those same feelings for Sarah that I had when Rachel was born - just pure love and joy.

September is always a very busy month in the church and I had a lot of work to do, but I stayed a few days to help with Rachel at the house. I called Jana and told her about Sarah and she thought it was wonderful that I had another granddaughter. We also talked about my holidays in October when I would be going to visit her for two weeks. I was really looking forward to that. Heather and Tom came down from Ottawa to see their new grandchild and they were so happy to meet Sarah. When life settled back down, I went to Lakefield whenever I could to see Sarah and she was just a joy to be around. Rachel wanted to hold her all the time and I could see that she was going to be a really good sister.

Now I had to deal with a serious issue at the church when it became clear that Orono United Church had a financial problem. I had to bring this matter to the Official Board at their meeting on October 6th. I knew some of the church's financial history and how their finances had been managed in the 1990s. Before I came to Orono, they had a Treasurer who had done a great deal of work for them but there had been a misunderstanding about a payment and, depending on who talked to me about this after I became their full time minister, most of the Board did not side with the Treasurer. The Treasurer had told the Official Board that the church could get a great deal of GST money back for the past 10 years on purchased items and the Board told the Treasurer to go ahead and do this. It took a lot of work to prepare for the refund and the Board appreciated the thousands of dollars they received back from the government. They offered to give the Treasurer a substantial honorarium for doing this work but the Treasurer had kept track of the hours it had taken to do this work and had already written a cheque for the amount owed, more than twice what the honorarium would have been. The Treasurer insisted that the Board had agreed to this but there was nothing in any Official Board minutes to prove it. The Committee of Stewards, who oversaw the work the Treasurer did, was really caught in the middle of this disagreement. Unfortunately, the Board had not followed the procedures and guidelines set out by the United Church of Canada. As a result, the only person who had authority to sign the Orono United Church checks was the Treasurer who resigned over this but kept the money. There was a lot of anger over this and there were people on the Board who wanted to call the police and bring charges but, in the end, that didn't happen. The congregation didn't really know exactly what had happened so there was mistrust and anxiety everywhere. Many in the congregation could not understand how the Committee of Stewards could have let this happen.

Things changed in 2000-2001 when a couple took on the job of Treasurer for Orono United Church and the Charge books. The two Treasurers signed all the checks along with two people from the Committee of Stewards. From 2002-2004, we had another Treasurer who took on the Orono and the Charge books. To add to the instability of the finances, the Committee of Stewards had three different Chairs from 2000-2004. There was no consistency or continuity in the Committee of Stewards or the position of Treasurer and, without that firm foundation, things can go terribly wrong which they did.

I had reason to be concerned about all these changes and I didn't want things to get out of hand again, so I attended the Committee of Stewards meetings for continuity and stability, something I had never done before in any church where I had served. Unfortunately, most of the time, my presence was seen as interference by a few people on the committee. I asked a lot of questions at their meetings because I wanted to be informed as to what our financial situation was but no one could answer many of the questions I was asking. For example, I was upset over the fact that money from the Sunday morning offerings was not being deposited in a timely manner. Three weeks or more would go by without a deposit and that was a huge concern. I knew this was happening because, once in a while, I visited the Treasurer late at night because it was the only time the Treasurer could see me. The fact that this Treasurer had a full time job and a part time business, in addition to looking after the church's books meant the church was paying a price for that. But the Committee of Stewards wouldn't do anything about this problem when I talked with them about it. To make matters worse, the committee didn't get accurate, up to date financial statements for their monthly meetings and that was a very serious concern. I knew we were in trouble.

Before the Official Board meeting in October I talked to one of the former Chairs of the Committee of Stewards and said I was going to ask the Official Board for the resignation of the Treasurer but I was asked not to do that. I did a lot of soul searching in regards to this and decided I was prepared for the Board to ask me to resign and, if the Board did, I would but I was not prepared to allow the situation to continue without some resolution. The Committee of Stewards didn't know where we stood financially and Sunday offerings absolutely had to be deposited in the church account every week and cash could not be sitting on the desk in the Treasurer's basement for days on end which I saw. It was that serious!

The Treasurer was not at the meeting when I brought up this issue and the Board asked me to state my case. I told the Board that I had been at the Treasurer's house more than a few times asking that the Sunday offerings be deposited but there were weeks when no offerings were deposited. I told them there was no balanced statement at the Committee of Stewards meetings or at our Board meetings. No one could tell the Board where we stood financially. I also told them we had an absolute right to know what state our finances were in and this situation had gone on for far too long. I reminded the Board that we had been paying the Treasurer $7,500.00 a year for doing two sets of books but now that Kirby United Church had closed there was only one set of books to do and the Treasurer was still being paid the same amount. It was not usually the policy of a United Church to pay a Treasurer that amount of money. The position of Treasurer was considered a volunteer position but, in a larger congregation like ours, the Treasurer was usually paid an honorarium. Orono United Church was paying their Treasurer a great deal of money yearly to look after our books. What I did not tell the Board was what I would do if the Board refused to do anything. I would have had to have the Presbytery step in and that would have created a huge issue for all of us in the church.

The Board listened to me and then there was a very open discussion around these serious concerns. Finally, the Board brought a motion that the Treasurer be advised that the Board was reviewing the position of Treasurer and applications for the position would be received and a contract would be in place by January 1, 2005 to be signed by whoever was appointed to be the Treasurer. The motion passed. Right after the motion was passed, a member of the Board volunteered to do the books for the church and didn't want any financial remuneration. The Board thanked her for her offer and asked her to put in her application to the Ministry and Personnel Committee.

As it turned out enough members of the Board trusted and respected me and did the right thing and the matter was resolved, at least for the time being. But I knew then, if I hadn't known already, that the Stewards at this meeting were furious with me. As they saw it, I had overstepped my authority. I also knew that, down the road, I would pay for it and it would happen in the next year. The Board asked me to inform the Treasurer about the decision of the Board and suggested that the Chair of the Ministry and Personnel Committee go with me. They asked if we could to do this right after the Board meeting even though it was late in the evening. I said it wouldn't be too late, because the only time I ever got to see the Treasurer was after 9:00 p.m. When I knocked on the door, the Treasurer was surprised to see me there with the Chair of the Ministry and Personnel Committee. I asked if we could talk, and we went down to the basement. The Chair of the Ministry and Personnel Committee could see right away that the church's bank statements and cash from the church offerings were just lying around. We told the

Treasurer about the Board's motion and that this Treasurer was free to apply for the position. This wasn't easy to do but my responsibility as a minister in a Pastoral Charge is to protect the congregation and the Presbytery expects me to do just that. The Treasurer was very upset with me. I was glad the matter had been resolved for now and I was proud of how the members of the Official Board had handled the situation.

Dealing with the Treasurer and the Committee of Stewards had created a lot of stress for me. Of course, I prefer working through problems with people and being supportive, but when a few people in our church were determined to get their own way over and against their congregation and their minister, that put me in a very difficult situation. I either had to back down or be very direct, which is not my style. The sad part is that this takes away from the overall ministry and creates conflict. I don't know why some people on the Committee of Stewards thought the minister had no business in the financial aspects of the church. If what was being done was right and in the best interests of the congregation, I would have gladly stepped aside. I would have been happy to just do the ministry and not have to be concerned with the finances. I found it very, very stressful and it took a lot out of me.

Back in September, I had been visiting more at the hospitals in Bowmanville and Oshawa, often going in twice a week. Anna Marie Allin was one of the people I visited often. The cancer she had came back and things were not looking good. Anna Marie was on the Committee of Stewards and I loved working with her. She was so positive about everything and was always smiling and could lift anyone's spirit. We had great visits. I would ask how she was doing but she would brush that aside and always wanted me to talk about how I was doing and how things were going in the church because she knew about the issues I was dealing with concerning the Committee of Stewards even though she had been unable to attend their meetings over the last few months. Anna Marie knew how important it was to keep things stable in the financial area and she knew that I continued to attend most of the Stewards meetings. She knew I had a responsibility to the congregation to make sure things were alright and understood what a difficult position this put me in as the minister. In spite of being very ill, Anna Marie worried about her church and after the last Official Board meeting she wanted to know what had happened. I told her and assured her that everything was being taken care of and that she just had to look after herself and get better. Anna Marie was the kind of person who always thought of others before herself. She was also very brave trying to tell everyone she was fine when we all knew she wasn't.

When the hospital sent her home in October, she knew she was dying. She also knew I was going to be away on holidays for two weeks and wouldn't be back until October 27th. I was feeling terrible about going on holidays when she was so ill and went to tell her that I would stay and not go if she wanted me to. I could see my sister another time. She thanked me for offering to stay and told me that she would be fine whatever happened. She knew the stress I was under and told me I really needed to get away and that she wanted me to go and have a good time with my family. I knew she had a minister in place to do her funeral service if I didn't get back in time. Still, I felt very badly leaving her. She had become a dear friend and one of the few people who really understood what ministers go through and have to deal with on a daily basis. She was a wise woman and a deeply spiritual person. I appreciated her friendship and her counsel. I went on holidays as I had planned and had a wonderful visit with my sister and Richard, but I was worried about Anna Marie. I talked to Jana about her and I called her husband John a few times to see how she was. The day before I flew home, I called her husband one more time and he told me Anna Marie was in the hospital in Bowmanville. I told him that when I arrived in Toronto, I would drive straight to the hospital and John told me the family would be there. When I got to the hospital, I could see that Anna Marie was not doing well, but she had this wonderful smile on her face and welcomed me back. Her husband John and their children Tanya and David, were there, as well as her sister Ruth and her father Roy. I felt very badly for Anna Marie and her family. She wanted to know how my visit had gone with my sister and I told her some of the things we had done. Then she got very tired so I said a prayer and, when she fell asleep, I spent time with her family and then I went home.

It was her sister Ruth who called me the next day to tell me her sister had passed away. We both believed she had waited for me to come back. I had her funeral on November 1st and it was one of the hardest funerals I had to do. The church was full since the Allins and the Scotts were families whose roots went deep in Orono and they were known by everyone. Anna Marie's death was so hard on her family. Her father was devastated as was her sister Ruth. I couldn't imagine losing my sister. Her children Tanya and David had a very hard time and I felt so badly for all the family. John was lost without his wife and never really recovered. The congregation was devastated and had lost in Anna Marie another person who, like Marie Tamblyn and Carol Yeo, had put their heart and soul into their church. They had many more years of service to give to their church. You can't replace people that have that kind of love and respect and history in their church. On the heels of that I had Hazel Pigott's funeral November 17th. Hazel and Alf were a great couple and always so happy together, so positive and a joy to visit and I had conducted her husband's funeral July 2nd, 2001. After Alf passed away, Hazel moved from her home in Orono into a house in Bowmanville that had been turned into a residence for seniors. The staff was wonderful there and she loved it. She was the type of person who just appreciated whatever you did for her.

As I thought about Hazel, I remembered that, not long after Sarah was born, I was able to take Rachel to my apartment to stay overnight for the first time. On the way home, I decided to drop in for a visit with Hazel because I was worried about her. She was so happy to see me and meet Rachel and we had a nice visit. I was glad, at that time, to see that she seemed better than the last time I had visited. When Rachel and I left her and went to the car, I saw a glow in the sky over where I lived and it looked like it could be a fire. Driving south down Liberty Street from Highway 2, the glow seemed to grow much worse. As we approached my apartment building, I could see it was dark and no lights were on. I could now see that there was a huge fire south of the 401. I didn't know at the time that propane tanks had exploded and there was great fear that the largest tank could also explode and firefighters were trying desperately to stop that from happening. I tried to remain calm with Rachel in the car and talked quietly with her. I told her I was going to find a phone booth and call the superintendent to see what was happening.

When I called, the superintendent said there were still some people in the apartment building but, because I had Rachel with me, she wouldn't advise me to come home. I didn't know what to do and was really tired so I headed for Laura's home in Orono. When I got there, I told her what was happening and she said she had seen it on the news. As we spoke, I glanced over to where her daughter Hilary was introducing Rachel to the cat and the guinea pig so I knew that Rachel was doing fine. Laura said we were more than welcome to stay overnight with them and I called Warren and Susan and told them what was happening. They didn't seem the least bit worried because Rachel was with grandma so I didn't worry either. I slept on the chesterfield and Rachel slept on the floor beside me and we were both just fine. We returned to the apartment the next day when the fire had been put out and the huge propane tank had not exploded. The next time I visited Hazel, I told her about everything that had happened and we had a good laugh about all the excitement around the fire which had been all over the news.

As usual, I was very busy in the church doing a great deal of visiting every week, attending monthly Presbytery meetings, Session and Stewards meetings, preparing the bulletin every Sunday and working on my sermons. There were phone calls to be made, emails to be written and other correspondence to look after. In addition, I had wedding interviews to do as well since I had about eight weddings to prepare for every year and I met with each couple at least three times. That alone took a lot of organizing. I also had many Baptisms every year which required me to visit with the families.

In November I was on a continuing education course for a week and I had no idea that a couple of people from our church had been talking with Presbytery while I was gone. They told Presbytery that our financial situation was strained now that Kirby United Church had closed and suggested that maybe Orono United Church should go from having a full time minister to half time ministry which would be 20 hours a week. They asked two members from the Presbytery to come to the November Board meeting to discuss this with them. I was not informed about any of this so I was very surprised to see Presbytery people at our Board meeting. Someone from the Board asked one of the Presbytery people to chair the meeting. It was very hard for me to sit through this meeting. I slowly realized that a few people from the Committee of Stewards had gone behind my back while I was away and set this up. This pointed out to me that they were still determined to make it difficult for me. The Board asked me if I would agree to part time ministry. I knew the congregation would never have agreed to have half time ministry so it was really a non-issue. I told the Board that I worked 60 hours a week on average, which did not include funerals. I pointed out to the Board that I didn't count my hours when I was working full time so, if they cut back to 20 hours and I was contracted for that, all I would do was 20 hours. I reminded them that, in that case, my hours would drop not from 40 hours to 20, but from 60 to 20. That seemed to end the conversation. I knew for a certainty that if Marie Tamblyn or Carol Yeo or Anna Marie Allin were still alive, this situation would never have come up but they weren't there to be that calm voice, that steady hand.

In spite of all that was going on, I continued to look forward to my weekly outings with my buddy Gary. He was good at lifting my spirits and making me laugh because he had a great sense of humour. I could just be myself with him as he could be himself with me. We became great friends and I trusted him absolutely and could talk freely with him. When we went out, I would take him wherever he needed to go to shop because he didn't drive and whatever we did, we always had a good time together. I always appreciated his friendship. I must say that I don't know what I would have done without him being there to take the edge off what I was going through in those dark times at the church. He was a great support to me.

I often talked to Warren on the phone about what was happening in the church and he was a good listener and a wonderful support to me, especially in these last two months at Orono Church. I always knew my son was there to talk to about anything, and he knew I was there for him as well. Over the years whenever I was at Lakefield staying over which I did at least once or twice a month, we had some good conversations about the church. We really tried to understand why there were always a few people in the church that make it not just hard on their ministers but also make it hard on their congregation. Susan was a wonderful support to me as well and sometimes we talked about the church but mostly other things, especially Rachel and Sarah. I felt very fortunate to have the wonderful son I have and the most amazing daughter-in-law, Susan, and of course my two beautiful grandchildren. They kept me grounded. There was also my sister and her husband Richard. I felt very blessed.

I was so thankful for Laura, our Church Secretary who I could talk with about the church. We trusted and respected each other. I could tell her how I was feeling and she could talk to me about anything that bothered her and we both knew it never went further. Our organist Karen Kastner was a wonderful support to both Laura and me because she had a great sense of humour and could get us laughing. Laura and Karen didn't have an easy time of it either, because these same people made it very hard on them from time to time. I had to keep telling myself that there are always those people you can't please no matter what you do. But I wasn't there to please them. I was there to do what I believed God was calling me to do. I had a feeling that this latest issue wasn't resolved yet and unfortunately I was right.

Rachel and Sarah could make me forget everything else when I was with them and that was a good thing for me. I went up to see them as often as I could and really enjoyed playing with them and feeding Sarah. Babies grow so fast that first year and it is hard to keep up with them if you don't spend time with them. I was looking forward to a wonderful Christmas with the family in Lakefield and a really special Christmas with a new baby. I was also looking forward to the Yuletide Feast again, a huge fundraiser for our church, which was scheduled for the first Saturday in December. This event had been started by Marie Tamblyn as a simple Christmas dinner but, after she passed away in 2001, we continued this dinner in her memory and offered a full Christmas dinner with entertainment, Christmas music and an auction. We had put the word out for this dinner at the end of October. All 100 tickets were sold within a week so we had a waiting list. It was the dinner of the year and Laura and friends did the most beautiful decorations for this event. When you walked into the hall it was magical.

There was some good news in early December. The Ministry and Personnel Committee reported to the Official Board that they had interviewed the person who had volunteered at the Official Board meeting back in October and recommended to the Board that this person be our Treasurer as of January 1, 2005. The Board approved and the former Treasurer had agreed to work with the new Treasurer to help with the Annual Report and financial statements which was appreciated. We had moved on.

Pierre Berton died on November 30 at the age of 84. I was not expecting this when his family called and told me the Celebration of his Life service would be held on Tuesday December 7th from 4:00 to 7:00 p.m. at the CBC Atrium at 250 Front St. W., in Toronto. I called Warren and told him about the service for Pierre. I also called my sister and told her about Pierre and the service the family were having. I was surprised when Jana said that she and Richard would be coming and would stay for a week but I was so pleased that she was able to come and when the time came we all attended the service. Of course, Pierre's wife Janet and all of Pierre's children were at the Celebration as well as his sister Lucy Woodward from B.C. Many people spoke at the Celebration: The Honourable Betty Kennedy, Elsa Franklin Pierre's Creative Business Partner, Lister Sinclair, June Callwood, Margaret Atwood, Alan Fotheringham, Vicki Gabereau, Rick Mercer and Her Excellency The Right Honourable Adrienne Clarkson the Governor General of Canada, to name a few. What a tribute this celebration was for Pierre. There were hundreds of people there to pay their respects. It was a wonderful celebration and I am sure Janet was very pleased with everyone who spoke so eloquently about her husband and his great contribution to Canada as a journalist, a TV personality and writer. He had written 50 books over the many years. Pierre had been wonderful to our family and I so appreciated him helping my aunts. He would be dearly missed by all his family.

Sometime that December, I officiated at the marriage of my cousin Jessie and her fiance Bill. When Jessie's husband Al died in 1999 she found it very hard to be alone and needed a companion so I was happy to do this for her. So, a death and a wedding in the family all in one month. As Christmas 2004 approached Warren and Susan decorated their home and I went to their first open house on a Sunday afternoon in early December. They made most of their own desserts, from cheesecakes to rum balls to an assortment of cookies to an amazing dip, and they had many kinds of cheeses. About 100 people came from Warren's churches and I always loved that time at their home which put us all in the Christmas spirit. At Orono United Church, the Clarington Band gave a Christmas concert every year and split the offering with us which we appreciated. There were many people who helped decorate our church and put up the Christmas tree so our church looked beautiful. The concert was wonderful. Then we had our Christmas Eve service. It was always such a moving service and, as usual, the church was full as we sang many of the wonderful Carols. Right after the service I headed to Warren's for our second family Christmas together at Lakefield and Sarah's first Christmas. Rachel was three years old and Sarah was four months and we had the most wonderful Christmas together.

Unfortunately, I had to come home earlier than I had planned because the Newcastle Funeral Home called me on December 25 at Warren's. It was very unusual for them to do that but Jeffrey Gray had died that day at the age of 39 and I was asked to do Jeff's funeral on December 28th. I didn't know Jeff but his parents, Anne and Jim Gray, attended our church and were good people.

The funeral interview at Anne and Jim's home was very hard for them. They were very open with me as they talked to me about their son. I felt so badly for Ann and Jim who dearly loved their son and had tried so hard to help him. It was particularly hard on Jeff's 11 year-old son Lucas who was very close to his dad. What a tragedy to lose a loved one and it was especially hard at Christmas.

The year of funerals wasn't quite over, though, when Jean Crossley died December 27th. I had met Jean at Captain George's Fish and Chip restaurant in Newcastle. I went there once in a while for lunch and she was often there. She was a lovely person who had moved to Newcastle in 2000 and bought her dream house. She had two children as well as grandchildren. Her daughter Nancy who lived in Toronto didn't know what to do about a service and turned to Lorna, the owner of Captain George's Fish and Chip restaurant. Since Lorna knew me and knew I was a minister, she mentioned this to Nancy who called to ask if I would take her mother's service. The family wanted a memorial service at the Carfrae Chapel in the Mount Pleasant Cemetery in Toronto on January 4th. Jean was 64 years old when she passed away and had had a very interesting life. She had been raised in Winnipeg, Manitoba and had gone to cosmetology school when she was 16. When she was 17, the CBC came to the school looking for two hairdressers to train as television makeup artists. Jean was picked as one of them and ended up working for the CBC in Winnipeg and later in Toronto. She did the makeup for many well-known personalities like Harry Belafonte, Kenny Rogers, Lloyd Robertson, Brian Lineham, Sonya Smits and even my cousin Pierre Berton to name only a few. As a minister, you never know who you are going to meet or what you may be asked to do but it was a privilege for me to be able to help this family.

In January, 2005, I wrote my message for the Annual Report for 2004:

> *"This past year was a painfully difficult year for me personally (my marriage had ended). But one event which stands out that brought our family great joy was the birth of my granddaughter Sarah on September 10th. There is nothing like a new baby that helps us forget sad things. We all lost a dear friend when Carol Yeo passed away the end of March. We also had our struggle in the church with the finances. Something had to be done. It became increasingly clear that if we didn't make some changes we could lose our church. The members of the Official Board rose to the challenge and made decisions that opened the door to new ideas. Letters and flyers were sent out and articles were written in our local paper about the financial concerns of our church. The members and adherents of our church listened as did people in our community near and far. We heard nothing but positive feedback, and financial help came pouring in that put us over the top for 2004. We can't begin to thank all those who helped and supported us……We move into 2005 feeling positive and hopeful and looking forward to seeing our church an active participant of the Orono community for many years to come."*

Aside from all the deaths that happened so often in our community, my family life was busy and wonderful. I was now having Rachel over to my place about every two months and I so looked forward to those times with her. I would take her to dinner and a movie, we would go to a playground, go walking at the river or the lake and have fun together. She certainly kept me busy. I also went up to Lakefield a couple of days twice a month to stay over and I had a wonderful time with my grandkids and with Warren and Susan. In addition, three times a year Warren and Susan came to my apartment for three days and I looked after the grandkids while they went off and did their errands and shopping. In the evenings, after the children were in bed, Warren and Susan and I would play Wizard, which we loved to play, and had coffee and muffins from Tim Hortons. We were also always together for Easter and Thanksgiving and Christmas and sometimes Heather and Tom, Susan's parents, would join us as well as family friends from Ottawa, Montreal or Sudbury who would drop in. Those were always special times too.

But, by far, the biggest event in 2005 for our family was the Baptism of Sarah at Lakefield United Church on April 10th. I performed the Baptism for Sarah, as I had done for Rachel in New Brunswick. Sarah was a smaller baby than Rachel so we had to wait until she could fit into the baptismal gown that Rachel had worn at her baptism. She looked beautiful in it and, when I look at pictures today of Rachel and Sarah in that baptismal gown, I have a hard time figuring out who is who. They looked so much alike in those photos. It was as special for me to do Sarah's Baptism as it had been when I did Rachel's.

On July 20, 2005 Canada officially became the fourth country in the world and the first country outside Europe to legalize same-sex marriage nationwide with the enactment of the Civil Marriage Act, which provided a gender-neutral marriage definition. Don McKenzie, Dr. McKenzie's son, called me in August to ask if he and his partner Michael Lord could be married at Orono United Church. Both men worked and lived in Toronto and had been living together for over 25 years. After Don's father died, they bought his house in Orono and used it as a weekend retreat. Don wasn't sure whether the Session would approve his wedding in the church because it would be the first gay marriage for Orono United Church and I told him I didn't know either but, if the Session approved, I would be very happy to marry them. Don told me that, if they didn't approve it this time, he would continue to ask because his church meant a lot to him and they wanted to be married there. I was asked by Don to take his request to be married in Orono United Church to the Session meeting in September. I called Bill Tamblyn, who was now our Clerk of Session, and told him about Don's request and asked him for his advice. Bill suggested that we needed to give the members of Session time to think about this before our meeting and asked me to send information to our Elders about this matter. I did that and everyone who came to the meeting knew ahead of time that this request would be on the Agenda. I had no idea what any of the Elders would do. At our meeting, we discussed Don and Michael's wedding and it was unanimously agreed that they could have their wedding in our church. I honestly had no idea what the outcome of this discussion would be but I was never as proud of my church as I was that day. After this discussion, I mentioned to Bill that we needed to let the Official Board know at their September 20th meeting about this wedding. I also told the Elders that when the word got out that we had approved this wedding, people in the congregation would be asking questions. The Elders said that they were prepared to have that conversation with people should they ask them about this wedding. I called Don as soon as I got home and told him the decision that Session had made and he couldn't believe that they had approved his wedding. He was so excited and happy and proud of his church. I also called Warren and told him, and like me, he was surprised and wasn't sure his Session would approve if they were asked.

In September we celebrated Sarah's first birthday. It seemed to me she had just been born and now she was walking. At her party, she just looked at the lit candle on the cake, wondering what it meant and why everyone was blowing it out for her. She did love opening presents and, when they were all open, she looked around to find more. I think she enjoyed opening the presents more than playing with the toys she got. It was wonderful to see her so happy.

We had our Board meeting on September 20th and Bill made his report from Session. After he finished, I reminded him that he hadn't said anything about the wedding, so he told the Board and sat down. I asked the Board if they had any questions about this wedding and I asked more than once until, finally, someone asked me if I had a problem doing this wedding. I said no, not at all, but I wanted to remind them that we were setting a precedent and needed to be clear that we are all on the same page. The Board members said they were fine with it. I married Don and Michael who were so delighted. It was a first for Orono United Church and a first for me. While I had been away in August, Karen put in her resignation as church organist. She gave her letter to someone on the Official Board and said she would be leaving as of July 31st, 2006. I was very upset when I heard she was leaving and asked her if she would meet with me. It was clear to me that she was feeling pushed out of the church by a couple of people who continually complained about how much we pay our organist and I suspected they had finally worn her down. I asked her to reconsider but she didn't want to. I told her it would be better if she resigned on her own terms and not when she was feeling the pressure from a few mean spirited people so she agreed to take back her resignation which was going to be discussed at the September 20th Board meeting.

At that Board meeting, I told the Board that Karen had withdrawn her resignation and I was shocked at the people who spoke out and said that was too bad but she had already resigned. There was a very heated discussion around that. Karen was an exceptional musician and I was furious that a few people would gripe about the money we paid her which was actually thousands of dollars less than what the Organ Association recommended based on her experience and training. Besides, I reminded them we were going to save $7,500.00 in 2006 as our new Treasurer was volunteering her time. The Board accepted Karen's withdrawal of her resignation. Karen put in a new resignation to the Board the following year on November 22nd 2006 for June 30th, 2007, and this time her resignation was on her own terms. When the time came for her to go, I was very sorry to see her leave because I knew how good she was and how hard it would be to get another really good organist. Sometimes I just don't understand people and I especially have little patience for mean-spirited people in the church. The sad part is it only takes one or two to spoil it for everyone.

Then something else happened in my family that was very difficult for me to deal with. Back in

January, my cousin Diane found out she had brain cancer. She did everything the doctors told her to do and she came through with flying colours. By the summer, she was cancer free. She and her husband Jason went out west for a few weeks to spend time with her son Josh and her grandson Hayden and they had a wonderful trip. In October, Diane had tests to make sure everything was alright and went in to see her doctor. The cancer had come back and there was nothing more they could do except keep her comfortable and free of pain. She was shocked and called me. I went over to see her and I couldn't believe what was happening. Everything had been going so well and now she was dying and only had a few months left. Jason and Diane had been so good to me in 2001 when I had my two surgeries. She had called me many times to talk to me and get me laughing and they had come over a few times and had done yard work for me. I found it so hard to understand why this was happening to her. Jason couldn't conceive of his life without his wife and I could only imagine what Jessie, her mother, and her sister Heather were feeling. I visited with Diane in Pickering and her mom, Jessie a few times over the next three months and Diane and I talked many times on the phone. I called Jana and told her what was happening and she was as shocked as I was. Diane's son Josh came for Christmas and he could see how much his mom had failed which was hard on him as it was for Jason, Jessie and Heather. I found it particularly hard to accept what was happening to Diane since I had known her all my life.

Jason called me in December to tell me that Diane wanted to see Warren and I told Warren but he was really busy in his two churches at that time. We had our usual family celebrations over Christmas and it was wonderful to be at Warren and Susan's for Sarah's second Christmas but I was still worried about Diane and all her family. In early January, Warren called me and told me he was coming down so we could go together to see Diane. When we walked into her bedroom, Diane was sleeping and Jason, Heather, Josh and Jessie were there. Soon as she heard us come in, she woke up with a big smile for Warren. She was so happy to see him. She wasn't able to talk very much and soon fell back to sleep but we had a good visit with the family. I could see the toll this was taking on Jessie and Jason and Heather but all we could do was offer our support and love. No sooner did I get I home when the phone rang and it was Heather. She said we weren't gone five minutes when Diane passed away. Heather and I both knew that she had been waiting for Warren to come, the only person in the family she had not seen. Looking back, I don't know how Jessie survived all the tragedies in her family. Her brother Ross had the worst form of diabetes and went blind and died when he was 33 years old. Ross's son Bruce, Jessie's nephew, died in a tragic car accident with his girlfriend in 1983 when he was only 21 and then Jessie's husband Al died in 1999. Now Diane was gone. Jessie's heart was broken and I know she never got over the death of her daughter.

Conducting Diane's funeral was very hard but I was so glad Warren was there. I missed Diane very much and her funeral brought back memories of my own family, good memories, but they had all passed on. Now Diane, who was only 48 years old and had been so full of life, was gone too. Jason had dearly loved Diane and he was heartbroken. After the funeral, he sold their house, and found a good job in Bermuda. It would be a fresh start for him and he stayed there three years before returning to Toronto.

In January, 2006, I wrote my Minister's Message for our Annual Report 2005:

> *"Another year has come and gone. January is feeling like spring has arrived. There are always changes we have to deal with in our life and adjust to whether it be the climate, a personal crisis, getting older, or moving to a new community. I'm sure you can think of changes that have happened in your life this past year and in our church. Our church remains open and welcoming and inclusive and is much appreciated by those who come…. Financially we are beginning to establish a solid financial base. More people are attending church services. New families have come to our church this year and stayed and some have joined. We've had a great music program this past year thanks to the openness of our music director Karen Kastner whose positive response to any suggestion is, the more music, the better. We were so fortunate to have had the inspirational "Himig Singers" from the Phillipines….The Sunday School continues to create an atmosphere of having fun while learning about God and Jesus and their Christmas program was great as we sat around tables and had tea and coffee. What a neat idea. The United Church Women do outstanding work for our church. I thank them so much for their dedication and love for our Lord. It has been a good year even with the usual ups and downs every church experiences. Again we have come out on top and in better shape financially and spiritually than we have been in the past."*

Our new Treasurer had a very difficult time in 2005 trying to sort out our finances and, at the end of that year, she had put in her resignation but said she would do up the financial statements for the Annual Report. I started to worry again because we had to get the Annual Report ready which was always a huge job and notices were put in the bulletin for a Treasurer. Also, the two people who were co-chairs of the Committee of Stewards in 2005 resigned from that position, and we had no one who would take the Chair for 2006. Again, too many changes. I went to see Gord Werry to ask him if he would consider coming on the Committee of Stewards and being the Chair and was so pleased when he said he would. He was just the person we needed and he was respected by the congregation. He served as Chair for one year and brought us much needed stability. I could not thank him enough for doing that. There was more good news. Scott Seigneur, a chartered accountant and a member of our congregation, kindly offered to take the position of Treasurer and he was nominated and elected. He literally spent hundreds of hours on our books and had his hands full. I felt so badly for him but Scott was determined and got the books organized even though it took him over a year to do that. He stayed on as Treasurer until 2009 which gave us the stability and information we needed for the Official Board and the Committee of Stewards to make informed financial decisions. It was Scott who set the record straight because none of us realized until he became Treasurer just how badly the books had been kept over the last few years. We could not thank Scott enough for what he did for our church and we were truly indebted to him, especially since he asked for no money in return for his services. Scott insisted that we have an independent chartered accountant examine our books every year and Mark Hendrick in Newcastle, a respected Chartered Accountant in the area, agreed to take on one more set of church books. He charged Orono United Church nothing for doing this and he continued to do it for the next few years. We had definitely turned a corner and were moving ahead.

Just as I thought things were going to calm down, I had three large funerals in a row: February 10, for Diane Greenwood and February 13 for her mother-in-law, Gladys Greenwood. I felt really badly for Ralph Greenwood because, in a very short time, he had lost his wife and his mother. Then I had Ross Mercer's funeral on February 25th. The Mercers were an old Orono family, with a lot of family history in the town. Ross was well liked by the community and his father Harry had had the only garage in town which had originally been a carriage house. One of Ross's brothers, Jack, was my next door neighbour and I had become good friends with his wife Elaine and we often went for lunch together. The Mercers were good people and loved their community and were all liked and respected. So many deaths of known and well liked people in Orono was taking its toll on our church and our community. I was exhausted by all the stress of ministry so I took a much needed break in March and met my dear friend Sharon, who had been in my congregation in New Liskeard, in Toronto and we spent four days together going to the theatre and movies and walking for miles in the snow. It was great to have that time out and I felt back to my old self when I got home. Being away for a few days had helped me relax and made me realize how much I loved being at Orono in spite of the problems and difficulties I had faced over the six years I had been there. I truly loved the people and it was a wonderful congregation and we had had some great times together. Since my mother's family had settled in Orono in the early 1860s I felt even closer to this community than I normally would have. Everything was good.

Then, one Friday not long after my trip to Toronto, I came home from visiting in Orono to find a message on my machine from the Chair of Oshawa Presbytery telling me she was going on holidays for a week and was very upset to tell me that the Presbytery was doing a 363 at Orono United Church. When she said that, I couldn't think, I couldn't breathe. It was like a death toll. I knew what it meant. When a Presbytery comes into a Pastoral Charge to do a 363 it is usually for the removal of that minister from the Pastoral Charge. I was beside myself and tried to calm down because I couldn't understand how this could have happened or who had done this. I listened to her message a second time and finally understood that three people had approached the Chair of the Pastoral Oversight Committee and sent letters basically saying I was doing inappropriate things in the Pastoral Charge. The Chair of the Pastoral Oversight Committee had then gone to the Executive of Presbytery to say this matter was serious enough to call a 363 which they were now going to do.

I knew there had been no Pastoral Oversight visit to our Pastoral Charge in a few years and I also knew that three people's complaints couldn't cause this to happen. I wondered if the Elders were a part of this, but I didn't think that could be possible because we had a wonderful Session and it was the Session that got the congregation through all the problems we had had. I got into my car and went back to Orono to see David and Sharon Staples. David was an Elder and, when he came to the door, he could see something was very wrong. I went inside and sat down but didn't know what to say. I was so upset I couldn't get the words out. Finally, I caught my breath and told them about the phone call from the Chair of Presbytery. They were stunned and shocked and asked who had done that. All I could say was that it was the Executive of Presbytery through the Chair of the Pastoral Oversight Committee that had decided that the situation at Orono United Church was serious enough to warrant a 363 to remove the minister. David asked me what I wanted him to do and I told him that we had to have a meeting of all the Elders and all the members of the Ministry and Personnel Committee. David got on the phone and called everyone and set the meeting for the next day, Saturday morning at 10:00 a.m. in the Board Room. He didn't tell them what the meeting was about but only that I was there with him and it was an extremely serious matter that had to be dealt with immediately.

I went home and called Warren. I felt so badly calling him because he was in Ottawa visiting with Susan's mom and dad but I just had to call him. I was so upset when I talked with him and I told him about the 363 and he couldn't believe it. He said he would come right away if I needed him and I said that we had a meeting first thing in the morning and I would talk to him after that. My son could not have been more supportive. I couldn't sleep that night so I went through the message on my phone and wrote down on paper every word of that message for the meeting. I also wrote down my thoughts about all of this because I knew I would not be thinking clearly at the meeting. Every Elder and every member of the Ministry and Personnel Committee was there the next morning. I could see that they had no idea what this meeting was about and they could see that I was very upset. I read them what I had written, including the Chair of Presbytery's message on my phone and my thoughts about it all. I found it hard to read and get through it all because I was so emotional. Everyone there was stunned and upset and angry. Not one of them knew anything about what had been done nor had they been consulted about it. I had to explain to them what a 363 was and, when I told them it was to remove the minister from Orono United Church, they became livid. On the word of three people, the Presbytery was going to do a 363.

When they tried to figure out who those three people were, names were mentioned and, as it turned out, they nailed it. I was sure too that I knew who they were. Everyone wanted to know what they could do and I said that the Pastoral Oversight Committee had to come to Orono and listen to the leaders, the staff and meet with the Board. We had a very long discussion as everyone tried to understand how this could have happened and they knew they had to act. Don Lycett was the Chair of the Ministry and Personnel Committee and he said it was his committee's responsibility to look after this and call the people who needed to be called. I had all the names and phone numbers of the Presbytery people he would need to call. Brian Colville, who was my support person on the Ministry and Personnel Committee, said he would work with Don. They took over and looked after all of it. Don was furious so I knew he would take care of it and he did.

It was announced in church the following Sunday that the Pastoral Oversight Committee of Oshawa Presbytery was coming to visit our Pastoral Charge on April 17th at 1:00 p.m. to talk with the minister, all the staff and then would meet with the Ministry and Personnel Committee at 6:30 p.m. and with the Official Board at 7:30 p.m. Anyone from the congregation was welcome to attend the Board meeting. The Chair of the Pastoral Oversight Committee called me and I said all our staff members wanted to meet with the committee individually and there were other key members in our congregation who also wanted to meet with them individually. I knew I was required to meet with them first, at 1:00 p.m. and that the Ministry and Personnel Committee would have a meeting with them at 6:30 p.m. before the Board meeting at 7:30 p.m.. I followed this up with an email to the Chair of the Pastoral Oversight Committee to establish a time for Karen, Laura and three other people to meet with them individually from 2:00 – 5:00 p.m. The word spread in our congregation that this matter was very serious and not a normal Pastoral Oversight visit. I was in shock but I was held up by my anger and by the Elders and the people on the Ministry and Personnel Committee. We were going to have our day in court.

In the middle of all this, Loren Dent died. I liked Loren and I had done the funeral for her mother Mildred Dent in September, 2003. Loren had been very close to her mom and now, this past year, she had cancer and knew she was dying. I went in often to see her at the Oshawa Hospital and on my last visit with her she stopped talking in the middle of our conversation and stared at the wall by the door. Then she turned to me and asked if I saw something at the wall. I said no I hadn't and asked her what she saw. She said it was her mother waiting for her and asked me if I believed her. I said, yes, I did. She seemed different after that, very much at peace, and died the next day. We can't presume to know what anyone else goes through or sees because we have enough trouble figuring out life for ourselves. I have seen enough in my life to respect that what another person sees or understands is what they see or understand. Loren felt so at peace after she saw that vision of her mother and she was ready to go. I officiated at her funeral on March 31st.

Finally April 14th arrived and almost everyone on the Pastoral Oversight Committee was there, about eight people, as well as the Chair of Presbytery. Donna from the UCW had made coffee and tea and snacks for them because she knew it would be a long day and, as it turned out, it lasted from 1:00 p.m. to 10:00 p.m. I was called in first and went in to meet with these people whom I knew and trusted in Presbytery. The Chair of the Pastoral Oversight Committee tried to ask me questions but I stopped him in his tracks and told him that I was there to tell them, as the minister at Orono United Church, what had been happening at our church and what I had been going through. I talked about everything - the good, the bad and the ugly. When I finished, the Chair of the Pastoral Oversight Committee said that what I had shared with them was very different from what he had heard. I said, "I'm sure it is". The Pastoral Oversight Committee had no idea what the issues were that I was dealing with at Orono United Church as the minister, along with the Session, and the Board. The Chair had only heard from three people who had their own agenda. I found out later there was a fourth person involved but who was never named and who had left the church but was a key player in bringing about the 363 because she knew how to work the system. The members of the Pastoral Oversight Committee didn't seem to be on board with their Chair and I had to wonder if he had even met with his committee about this 363 or how he had presented this situation to them. But I had my say and then procedure dictated that the minister must leave the Charge. This would give people the freedom to say what they wanted to say about their minister without the minister being present. I went home and didn't return to Orono until the next day.

Karen went in after me and I knew she had a lot to say, as did Laura. Both of them were also angry and upset and they were sure they knew who was behind this. The individuals from the congregation who met with the committee afterwards had a lot to say too. The next day I heard about the Board meeting with the committee and that there were a few people at the meeting who had a lot to say against me. The Presbytery listened to them and then said that Presbytery expects ministers to know what is going on in their church, in every area of church work and ministry, which includes finances. If something goes wrong in a church, the Presbytery asks the minister what is happening and why. There were a lot of people from the Official Board at that meeting and their voices were heard. The Presbytery did a very fair assessment of the ministry at Orono United Church. They sent a report to the church which was very fair and the Session and Official Board were very satisfied with this report. There was no 363 called. Through all the concerns I had to deal with in the church that year, I was glad Warren and Susan were there for support. Visiting with them was a wonderful diversion for me. Rachel and Sarah could always make me laugh and get me doing silly things with them. It took my mind off the church and the ministry and helped me regroup and head home refreshed and more relaxed. I wrote to my sister on May 9th, 2006 and said in part:

> *"I have had a very hard year in this charge and almost resigned twice over someone who was very controlling and manipulative. I did a lot of soul searching I can tell you and prayed a lot but I am here for the long haul. It feels right. We have had a lot of meetings and all the Elders and the members of the Ministry and Personnel Committee supported me and the ministry we do together. Through all the stress it was very hard on me."*

It is hard being a minister and having to do what I do on a regular basis. Ministry is hard enough, with funerals and visiting people who are sick and dying. Emotionally, that part of ministry is draining. From the beginning of my full-time ministry at Orono in April 2001, the Committee of Stewards were not following procedures that are there for a reason. Then we lost three people from our congregation, Marie Tamblyn, Carol Yeo and, more recently, Anna Marie Allin who were all fair minded and would have been instrumental in helping us find a way through this issue, but there wasn't anyone to take their place who people would trust and respect the way these three people had been trusted and respected. It was a huge loss for our church and I was certainly feeling that. I was very stressed and upset over all that had happened. But I didn't leave because most of the people in the congregation were wonderful. Most of our members had no idea what was going on in the running of the church. I also knew how hard it was on them when someone from the congregation passed away and we had so many funerals. The Orono United Church and community pulled together to be there for one of their own at every funeral. In spite of everything that had happened, I still felt I was called to serve at Orono United Church and do the ministry there.

Back in November 2005, the Official Board of Orono United Church had agreed to have another Photo Directory done and, this time, we would do it in the last week of May and the first week of June, 2006. It was going to be a lot of work but there were a lot of people who volunteered to help when families came in to have their photos taken. Again, I enjoyed phoning the families and setting up appointments. The Photo Directory was a great success and, over the next few years, many more of the older members of the church, whose pictures were in this Directory, would pass away so this Directory became an important historical record for Orono United Church. By the time all the stress of the 363 meeting was over and done with and the Directory was finished, I was thankful that I had six weeks of holidays every year plus three weeks continuing education, should I choose to use those weeks. My normal church year started on July 1 and ended June 30 and I badly needed a break so I took the last of my holidays in June and I went down to Coos Bay to visit Jana and Richard. A few days after I arrived, Jana and I drove the 10 hours to Sacramento, California where her daughter Stacy was living to attend her grandson Cameron's graduation from Grade VI. We then attended her granddaughter Brandi Eszlinger's graduation from High School. Brandi's graduation from the El Camino Fundamental High School was held at Abbott Field in the football stadium with about 1,000 family and friends there, and 410 graduates. I have to say it was an amazing graduation ceremony. It was extremely well done and I was very proud of Brandi, as was her grandma and her mom Stacy. I had a great time with my sister. In October, I took a two week trip to B.C. I stayed at Gail and Harold McDonald in Burnaby for the two weeks I was there and got to see all my friends: Vene and Phillip and her family in Gibsons, her son Jay and Kate and their two boys in Vancouver; my university friends: Signe Palmquist on Bowen Island, Helen and Alastair Mccullough in North Vancouver, Vicki Hansen and Julia Dower. There were other friends like Vicki – originally from Grand Valley- her husband Andy and her mom Irene. Then there were my Greek friends Katina and George and also Elena, all of whom lived in Surrey. It was so good to connect with everyone, especially in that setting with the ocean and the mountains which are so majestic and breathtaking. I found it so relaxing to be there and came home feeling refreshed.

When I got back, the funerals started up again. First was Isobel Hamm. She was the one who fell asleep on my chesterfied when she and her husband Don had taken a turn looking after me when I was so sick and recovering from my surgery in 2001. They were a wonderful couple. Don was lost without his wife. Not long after she died, the family helped Don sell his house and move up north to be with his family. Meanwhile, Warren was doing very well at Lakefield and Young's Point Churches. The Peterborough-Lakefield Police Services wanted him to get the training to be a Police Chaplain so he had taken continuing education courses to be able to work with them. His swearing-in ceremony with the Police Services was in December, 2006 and I was thrilled to be invited. Warren looked very handsome in his police uniform with his collar on. The ceremony was very formal and official with many police officers there for the swearing-in ceremony but it was also very moving. I was very proud of Warren and so was

Susan. Aside from watching Warren at the ceremony, I had to help Susan with Sarah who was a great bundle of energy. It took both of us to amuse her but she was good and didn't get too rambunctious until after the ceremony was over.

Christmas celebrations again meant the Yuletide Feast dinner and, of course, the Clarington Band Christmas concert, as well as the open house at Warren and Susan's and our very special and inspirational Orono United Church Christmas Eve service. This was Sarah's second Christmas as she had turned two in September. She had the hang of it by now and was as excited as Rachel to open all those presents on Christmas Day.

As the new year, 2007, rolled around, I looked back at the past year where so much had happened. Things had come to a head in a very real sense and now I felt the worst was over. The Church's finances were good and our books were starting to get in shape and the leadership provided by Gord Werry, the Chair of the Committee of Stewards, was excellent. We were moving forward but I was also aware that there were still a few people who were not going to give up and let things be. At least now they were a very dull roar and I could live with that. I am not naïve about church life because in every church I have served there has been that very small group of people who just want things their own way at any cost and will even run the minister out of town if that is what it takes. I loved the people in the congregation at Orono United Church and many had become my friends and I valued those friendships. Respect for the position of the minister was still rock solid in the congregation and they appreciated the ministry I did with them. I looked forward to even better times together. I had wonderful support from my family, from Warren, Susan and my grandchildren, who knew how to make grandma smile, and from my sister Jana and Richard and my best friend Gary. Laura, Karen and Don and Donna Scott and I had become really good friends over my years at Orono. There was so much to be thankful for and I was hopeful that the next year was going to be a really good year.

CHAPTER SIXTEEN

Retirement

I was feeling more centered in my life as I came into this new year. I had two beautiful granddaughters; Rachel was five years old and Sarah was two, and they brought me such joy. I was proud of both Warren and Susan for being such great parents and they were very happy with their growing family. Susan wasn't working because she had enough to do at home with the children and she also helped Warren with the ministry he did. Many times when I visited, I could smell the marmalade, blueberry or strawberry jam being made. My favorite was marmalade. Susan and Warren's Million Dollar relish was also a huge hit with the family and their salsa was very good too. Their cold room was always full of jars of jam, relish and salsa. Many jars were given out as gifts and as fundraisers for the church. Warren's specialty was making the most amazing desserts and, at every birthday we could ask him to make whatever delicious cake we liked. They also had the wonderful vegetable garden and beautiful flower gardens they planted every year. The maple tree they tapped in their yard allowed them make their own maple syrup which was really good.

We had had some rough patches over this last year at Orono, but we had weathered them together. I know how hard the ministry can be and, even after 30 years, it doesn't get easier. It is not possible for people to agree with everything everyone does or wants to have done and not everyone agrees with the minister or what the minister wants to do. We were coming into a new year, and I really hoped that things had settled down. I wanted to move on from all the stress I had experienced the year before.

January was a busy month and things were going along as well as could be expected. Again, Laura and I were very busy working on the Annual Report that had to be put together for our Annual Congregational Meeting in February. I sat down in January, 2007 and wrote my message for the 2006 Annual Report:

> *"2006 was an interesting year. Sometimes very stressful, sometimes very joyful, sometimes very difficult and for many reasons. Fortunately we had a wonderful team of leaders on Session and on the Ministry and Personnel Committee who held up our congregation and the ministry this past year. Without their leadership and love for their church.... I don't know where we would be today. I take this opportunity to thank every Elder and every member of the Ministry and Personnel Committee for their willingness to make important and tough decisions so that the ministry of Orono United Church could continue. I also want to thank three other people for the wonderful work and leadership they offered this past year. They went beyond what was expected, to do an amazing body of work for our*

church. First, our Treasurer Scott Siegner…. He had no idea nor did we, what a job it would be this year to put our books in order. He stepped up ….sacrificing time with his family to sort out our financial books. We can't thank him enough for what he did to help us get through 2006, bringing us into 2007 feeling very secure about our finances. Janet Standeven accepted the position of Envelope Secretary which was time consuming. She spent hours updating, correcting and putting things in order. She couldn't do enough to help us and we deeply appreciate everything she did. Gord Werry took on the Chair of the Committee of Stewards at my request. Gord made the commitment, did the work and followed through, offering wonderful leadership to our church. The hours he put into this work were legion… ….I hope and pray this is the year we can consolidate and build on what has gone before.

Not long after I wrote this report something significant happened to me. It happened at 4:00 a.m. on February, 7th, while I was asleep. I felt like someone was with me. I was in a dream-like state but it also felt very real. Warren's father came to me in my sleep and I knew in the certainty of my heart it was Bill and that he had come to say goodbye because he had passed away. I woke up and found myself crying as the love I had felt for him from the very beginning just poured out of me. I can't begin to describe how that felt but I knew he had come to me. I felt sadness as well as a great feeling of peace. Then Bill was gone and I fell back to sleep until I was awakened at 8:00 a.m. by the phone ringing. It was Warren calling to tell me that Mary, his half-sister had called to tell him that their dad had passed away. I told Warren I would come up to Lakefield as soon as possible and I phoned Bill's wife in Sydney, Cape Breton to tell her how very sorry I was about Bill. She told me he had died at home at 4:00 a.m. When I got off the phone, I knew what I had to do. I sat down and, for the next two hours, wrote out Bill's obituary to be put in the *Orono Weekly Times*, the *Lakefield Herald*, the *Oakville Beaver and the Toronto Star*. I included a write-up of Bill's family history, something he was very proud of, and I put my son's name in the obituary as one of his children. Then I phoned Barb Genrich, Bill's cousin in Oakville, to tell her Bill had died and read her what I was putting in the newspapers. She was so pleased that I was doing this and we talked about Bill for quite a while. Then I went to see Warren.

Warren was very upset, of course, but glad to see me. He told me he was flying to Sydney for the funeral and had a flight for 2:00 p.m. He had already talked to Mary about this and she was flying out that morning. He told me later that, when the plane landed, he went right to the Sydney Memorial Chapel where Bill's wife was with Mary and his wife asked him to do the service. Warren said he would. After Mary and her mother left the chapel, Warren asked the funeral director if he could see Bill. The funeral director asked Warren how he was related to the family and Warren told him that Bill was his father. It was very hard for Warren to do his father's funeral because it was very complicated but, knowing my son as I do, I know he would have put his heart and soul into the service for his father and his father would have been very pleased.

Bill's wife also decided to have a memorial service for her husband at St. Jude's Anglican Church in Oakville on Saturday, April 28. She was coming back to Oakville for the service where Bill had grown up and where they had lived together for most of their marriage. Many of Bill's family would be able to attend this service to have some closure and I would as well. Bill's daughter Jilli flew in from Australia for the service with her husband Paul and their children, Andrew and Elizabeth. Mary called me and asked if she and her sister could come over to see me. Jilli had written a song for her father and she wanted me to play the piano for them at the service. They both knew that Warren was their half-brother and they had often seen each other through the years. I told Mary I would be happy to do this for them so they came over and we had a great visit. The song was very good and I was honoured to participate.

I met Warren and Susan and the girls at St. Jude's Anglican Church and, when it was time for Jilli and Mary to sing, I went up with them and accompanied them on the piano as they sang the song Jilli had composed for her father. It was very hard for me at the funeral as all the memories I had in my heart of Bill came flooding back. I thought about all the love we had shared and about our son who was so much a part of that. I often say there are no words but, sometimes, there really are no words and nothing needs to be said. It was a good service and after it was over there was a lovely reception. It was heartwarming to see so many of Bill's family and friends there. I had a really nice visit with Bill's cousin Barb and her husband Gerry, with Mary and her husband Danny, and with Jilli and her husband Paul and their children. Danny and Sylvie were there from Montreal to support Warren and my friend Barb Davidson was there too. She was a great support for me because we had been friends for many years. After everything was over, it was hard going back home, but I felt everything had been done for Bill that needed to be done and we all had closure.

This was the year, too, when my creative juices were flowing again and I looked for ways to use my gifts. Back in January I had decided that I would give two benefits concerts, one on June 9 for Orono United Church and the other one June 10 for Lakefield United Church. I called them *"Dorinda in Concert"* and I was very pleased to be able to raise money for both churches. The proceeds from the concert at Orono would go to the church and the money raised at Lakefield United Church would go to the Lakefield Primary Healthcare Campaign and programs at Lakefield United Church. At both churches there was a reception afterward. I played the classical music of Bach, Mozart, Rameau, Chopin, Beethoven and Schubert and some popular songs too and one of my own compositions. The concerts went very well at both the Orono and Lakefield Churches. Over the years, I had given about 18 benefit concerts. I just loved giving these concerts as it was a way for me to share my music with others. Bill had loved my music and loved to hear me play and I thought of him as I performed these concerts. After the concert at Lakefield, there was an article written in the Lakefield Herald with a picture of me with my son at the piano. The paper came out June 15th, 2007, and it noted that the concert had brought in $1,575.00.

At the end of June, Karen Kastner left Orono United Church after seven years as our organist and I was very sorry to see her go. It had been wonderful working with Karen and I appreciated her exceptional musicality. We had become very good friends and continued to visit. There was a lovely going away party for Karen given by the senior choir and members of the congregation.

A committee had been set up to look for another organist and they had someone in place for July, but I missed Karen after she left and so did Laura. We had made a great team. I continued to see my grandchildren at least twice a month and, in July, I took Rachel, who was now six, and Sarah, who was almost three to the Circus in Toronto. They both loved all the animals in the circus and the trapeze act and the atmosphere. I had loved watching the circus on Saturday mornings on television when I was a child, but I had never had the opportunity to see a live circus before. It was as much fun for me as it was for my grandchildren.

In October, I went for two weeks to B.C., rented a car and went to Courtney on Vancouver Island. I stayed one night at a bed and breakfast and then headed north across to Malcolm Island where I had booked two nights at a chalet where the owners had oxen and other animals. I took two lessons in blacksmithing and received a certificate from "The Black Booger Forge", for completing the Introduction to Blacksmithing. It was a lot of fun and the instructor took a picture of me in my blacksmithing outfit which I found hilarious. I headed back to the mainland to visit with all my friends in Vancouver, Surrey, Bowen Island, Gibsons and Burnaby before returning home. Again, I had a wonderful time with all my friends and took lots of photos of beautiful B.C. As the end of the year approached, I didn't feel the stress that I had experienced the year before and still loved visiting the families in our church and leading in worship and preaching. 2007 was a very good year. We had a wonderful congregation and some of them even made an impact on the world at large. Lieutenant-Colonel John Conrad was one of those. He was a member of our congregation who was serving as a peace-keeper in Afghanistan and our congregation had written to him over the previous year. John, his wife Martha and their four young children lived just east of Kirby Church where they had been members and later joined Orono United Church when Kirby closed in 2004. John had over 28 years of experience in the Canadian Forces and was a veteran of both the United Nations and NATO doing peacekeeping. He had served in Cambodia, Bosnia and, more recently in Afghanistan. Bev Oda, who John mentions in his letter below, was our Member of Parliament at that time and Michaelle Jean was the Governor-General of Canada. I received this letter from John on December 6th where he wrote:

"Dorinda, Thank you so much for your kind congratulatory letter of 5 Oct. 07. I apologize at taking so long to reply. 90% of the letters I write seem to get done in December – shameful etiquette. Thank you again for your prayers for me and my soldiers last year. They were both needed and appreciated. Martha, the boys and I had a great time in Ottawa. The Governor General is a lovely and elegant lady. Bev had this picture taken and I thought you would enjoy a copy. See you in church! John"

We again celebrated Christmas, the most wonderful season of the year and In January 2008 I sat at my desk and I wrote my Annual Message looking back at 2007 and this is what I said:

"We had our struggles and concerns last year as we thought about our faith and what our church means to us. People in our church gathered…..to discuss, share ideas, dream and

begin to believe in a much more concrete way that we can move forward......it was at the roast beef dinner in October that the Committee of Stewards organized with the help of everyone in the congregation that you could feel something was happening. There was a marvellous feeling of energy, openness and newness ..... I thank God every day for Orono United Church and this wonderful congregation I still feel called to serve. May we move into this New Year with joy, hope, love and faith. And may the friendship and love we feel one for another mirror that love and friendship Jesus has for us."

We continued to have wonderful leadership in our church going into 2008. Bill Tamblyn had been Clerk of Session since 2003 and stepped down at the 2008 Annual Congregational Meeting but stayed on Session and Ruth Gray became the new Clerk of Session. She gave wonderful leadership and I enjoyed working with her. Don Lycett had come on as Chair of the Ministry and Personnel Committee in 2004 and agreed to serve another year. Tammy Coad was our new organist and seemed to be fitting in very well. Scott Seigneur continued as our Treasurer with Viola Vanderveen as his assistant. She would take over as Treasurer the following year and would continue to serve in this position for many years. Ron Landry came in as Chair of the Committee of Stewards in 2008 and was still the Chair in 2010.

Then there was a terrible tragedy in Orono. In early February my next door neighbor, when I lived at the manse, Elaine Mercer, was walking from her car to her house and had a very bad fall on the ice on the sidewalk. She had to be helped to get into her home. She was in terrible pain and had trouble breathing. Her husband Jack phoned for an ambulance and she was taken to Oshawa Hospital. I was called by the family and went to the hospital to see Elaine. I didn't know what was happening when I met Jack and other members of the family in the waiting room but Jack was really upset as we walked together to Elaine's room. I didn't recognize her when I saw her because she was so bruised and swollen and the nurse told me almost every bone in her body had been broken. I was so shocked to see her in this state and she passed away the next day. It was tragic, just a simple fall like that. Jack was devastated by his wife's death and no one in Orono could believe what had happened because it was so unexpected and tragic. Elaine had not had an easy life in many ways but was such a nice person, easy to talk to and a good friend to so many. You would see her a couple of times a day in town having coffee with friends. Our community was in shock and the church was packed on February 9 for Elaine's funeral. What a tribute to her. She was a kind and good woman and a very good friend to me and I missed her.

As a minister, it is overwhelming to be dealing with families who lose loves ones but, when the circumstances are tragic, it is really that much harder for everyone involved and Orono had so many tragedies. Because of all the funerals in our church, I felt the need to write about people in the community. I love when people tell me their stories so it seemed the next logical step to write articles about people I knew had a story to tell. This took a lot of time but I was learning and I was writing. From April to November 20, I wrote a bi-monthly article for the *Orono Weekly Times* called, "We Pay Tribute". I interviewed 13 people in our community to tell their story and I also took their photographs for each article. These articles were very well received by the community. Aside from music and writing, I have had a love affair with photography since I was 10 years old. It took me many years to focus on my photography and take seriously the fact that this is an art form. From the summer of 2005 up to this year, I had been showing my photography at the Orono Art weekend. Every summer the main street was closed for a weekend for artists and artisans who set up booths to sell their art. It was a lot of fun doing this and meeting other artists. Henry Lorrain invited me to set up my photography in his barn for a weekend. His business was called, "We're in the Hayfield Now," and sold his daylilies. Henry's daylilies were beautiful and sold all over the world. I would go out and take photos of his daylilies to make up cards and I did well there. I appreciated Henry asking me to take part in this and I did it for a few years and I met so many interesting people.

Kate and Ian Moore had recently come to our church and I showed Kate some of my photography. She was very impressed and encouraged me to do even more. She had me go on a photo shoot for her at Bloom Field Farm which is a garden centre near Newcastle and I took pictures for the article she wrote. She was a freelance writer and editor. That article went into the July 2008 issue of *Active Adult Magazine*. This was a magazine which had been in circulation for 23 years and they put out 100,000 magazines every two months. Kate also told me about the new Clarington Magazine called *Surfacing* that was looking for artists and writers to showcase their photographs and articles. I sent them an email and four photos and they wrote back saying my photography was of the quality their magazine was looking for and asked me for a biography and a picture. My photos were in the premiere issue of this new magazine that showcased Durham's artistic and creative people. The magazine's launch was on September 18 at the Station Gallery in Whitby and it was a great day. I was proud to be part of it. Henry's Camera Store in Oshawa asked their customers to send in photos and I sent in four. They picked my baby lion, blew it up to 16x20, framed it and put it on display in their store along with other photographer's photos they had chosen. When they finished with all the photos they displayed, we got the framed picture. I was very excited about all these artistic endeavours and felt like I was starting out again on a road and a journey that had no beginning and no end.

Coming into this next year I had been doing a lot of thinking about when I might retire since I would be 65 in November 2009. But I didn't know what I wanted to do because, in the United Church of Canada's new rules, you didn't have to go to Presbytery to get approval to stay on in the Pastoral Charge after you turned 65. At the end of April, I invited Warren and Susan and the girls to lunch at the Mandarin Restaurant in Oshawa. We loved going there and at lunch I told them about all the writing I was doing and the photography and my music and that I was feeling so creative. I thought, maybe, it was time to retire. Warren said, "Mom you can do it. Retire November 23rd, 2009 on your 65th birthday. Go out with a bang." There it was. The words said it all, and it fell into place for me. The more I thought about it, the more I was excited about retiring from full time ministry. I would have time to write, do photography, music and art and, of course, I had my two beautiful grandchildren to play with. Rachel said she couldn't wait for me to retire. She was an up and coming artist who, at seven, had won an important award for her art at the Lakefield Literary Festival. She told me she wanted to be an artist and photographer like her grandma when she grew up. I told her that would be great but she would need a day job.

The same evening that I had lunch with my family at the Mandarin happened to be a Session meeting at my church and I wrote a letter saying that I was retiring on November 23rd, 2009. At the meeting that night, after our business was almost finished, I read my letter to shock and disbelief around the table. The Elders were so appreciative of my ministry and I told them, out of fairness to the congregation, I wanted to give plenty of notice so they had 17 months to sort out what they wanted to do. I knew the Session would give strong leadership in this matter as would the other members of the Official Board. Most importantly for me, I knew that when I retired I would be leaving the church in a very stable financial situation with positive leadership from the Elders and the Committee of Stewards. I still had a lot of work to do over the next 17 months at Orono United Church but now I could move forward and I didn't regret my decision.

In June, 2008 my sister came to visit me and it was so wonderful to have her. Around that time, the *One of a Kind Art Show* in Newcastle was being held on July 12. There were 50 artists participating and I had been invited to be one of them. Ann Harley invited some of the artists taking part in this show to meet with her in June before the event and Jana and I went. Ann wanted to discuss with us some kind of co-operative. We had lots of discussion and we came up with the name, "A Gift of Art", which would be Clarington's first artist and artisan's co-operative and Ann would be our benefactor. There were about 20 of us at this meeting and Jana thought that what we were thinking of doing was great. We had many more meetings and everything went really well over the summer. All of us could see the potential and were very excited. Ann rented a place for us in Newcastle and there was a big opening September 26-28 with music and speeches where we displayed our art in the store Ann rented for us. I was involved with the co-operative for almost two years. All the artists were great to work with and I did well there. I felt so blessed to have all the talents I had, the photography I was doing and the writing and music. For the first time in my life it all seemed to flow together as one. I was also doing a lot of scrapbooking for all the many articles I had written over the years and articles that had been written about me. I had also put important letters and papers and documents into these scrapbooks. Kate had been instrumental in helping me get back to my writing and encouraging me to do more with my photography.

Back in February, Karen Smart, the Secretary of Presbytery, had asked me if I would consider being Chair of Oshawa Presbytery. She said she would love to work with me and I said I would. I was nominated at the next Presbytery meeting and elected as incoming Chair. At the June meeting of Oshawa Presbytery, there was a covenanting service and I became the Chair of Presbytery for one year, until June 2009. Being Chair of a Presbytery was a lot of work. Since the Chair of Presbytery makes a presentation to the Bay of Quinte Conference at their Annual meeting, which would be the first weekend in June 2009, I decided to visit every minister in the 31 Pastoral Charges in Oshawa Presbytery and take pictures of all the churches and ministers in our Presbytery. I loved visiting with the ministers, had a great time doing this and I learned a lot.

On July 8, Susan's parents moved to Princess Gardens, a retirement home in Peterborough. The year before, Tom hadn't been well. He had Parkinson's disease and they were having a hard time managing his illness. Warren and Susan had been going up a few times over the last year and a half to help them and, finally they made the decision to move to Peterborough to be closer to the family. Susan and Warren were busy in August trying to clean out Tom and Heather's home in Ottawa to be ready for renting or, possibly, selling it in the future. I felt badly for them and for Heather and Tom having to go through all this but when they finally moved, it was a lot easier on everyone and a great relief.

I enjoyed Chairing both the Presbytery and the Executive meetings. It was a challenge that year because we had a very serious 363 we were dealing with and another possible 333 and or 363 at a church in Oshawa. Presbytery usually calls a 363 in a Pastoral Charge for the removal of the minister and a 333 is called because the congregation is in serious trouble. I decided that Karen, the Secretary of Presbytery, and I needed to visit this congregation in September but they were very upset with us coming to see them. Through our Conference, I had arranged for a conflict consultant to be there on the off chance this could be the way to go to head off the Executive of Presbytery calling a 363 to remove the minister. I certainly knew how that felt. It was a very tense meeting and stressful for everyone there. As the Chair of Presbytery, I chaired this congregational meeting and the Secretary of Presbytery was there to record the minutes. The meeting started out with everyone upset because they were angry that we had come. It was hard for me as Chair to just listen and let people talk but the end result was that they realized we were there to help them and the congregation agreed to talk with the Conflict Consultant we had brought in. He set up appointments that night, talked with many people in the congregation, including their minister and wrote up a report for us. The matter was resolved to everyone's benefit and there would be no 363. The minister and his wife were very relieved and so was the congregation. Again, it had been two or three people who weren't getting their own way and making it very hard on the minister and the congregation.

Near the end of September, Don Lycett came in to see me and he was very upset. I hoped it wasn't something in the church again, but, looking back, I wished it had been. He came to tell me he had just found out he had cancer and, from what he said, it didn't sound good. It was the last thing I expected to hear Don tell me. I appreciated everything Don did for Orono United Church, especially back in 2006 at the emergency meeting with the Elders and members of the Ministry and Personnel Committee there. Don was Chair of that committee then and took charge. I really liked and respected Don and felt so badly for him at this untimely news. He was devoted to his church and a strong and stable voice in the church, like Marie Tambyln, Anna Marie Allin and Carole Yeo had been. I went to his home every week to see him and his wife Betty would give us time alone to talk. Don went into the hospital and it wasn't long before he passed away November 20th. He was only 66 years old and had only recently retired. I officiated at his funeral in the church on November 22. The community was in shock and, again, our church was packed. As much as Don had helped our church, he did even more for the Orono community, helping at the Orono Forestry and the Orono Crown Lands as well as the Oak Ridges Moraine Trail. He volunteered to help wherever he was needed. He was also very proud of " We're in the Hayfield now", the business his brother Doug Lycett had started with his partner Henry Lorrain. It was because of Don's leadership and counsel to me that I was still the minister at Orono United Church. I looked up to Don and trusted him implicitly. I sought his advice many times in difficult situations and he was always there, never letting me down. In my 32 years of ministry, Don was one of the finest men it had been my privilege to serve with in the United Church. Don's death was a huge loss for our congregation, the community and, especially, his family. It was so sad that Don didn't have the time to enjoy his retirement with his wife and his family.

I had received a really nice letter from Reverend Brian Gee on October 21st who wrote to me about our last Presbytery meeting where, at the very end of our meeting, I honoured all the retirees in our Presbytery and I had a big cake there for them in appreciation of all their years of service. He wrote:

> *"I wish to thank you for the very fine gesture you initiated in honouring us retirees! It was the highlight of the evening……And thank you for that great picture of me. It was most thoughtful of you. It is good to know that you are now leading our Presbytery—a good successor to Ted's strong leadership!"*

I was very proud of the ministry I was able to do when I served as the Chair of Oshawa Presbytery and it happened during my last year at Orono United Church. Karen Smart was really good to work with and a huge help and support to me as the Chair of Presbytery.

I had had Muriel Patton's funeral on November 15th. She was 89 years old when she died and had become a very dear friend. I had visited her every week when I could over the last three years and we had lovely visits. I can still see her sitting in her chair at her farmhouse when I visited. She was so kind to me and I appreciated her hospitality and friendship. What a beautiful soul she had and she was a woman of great faith. I still miss her today. The more I visited people and got to know them, the more deeply I cared about them as their minister and loved them as my friend. It is such an honour to be welcomed into people's homes. I was really feeling an emotional heaviness that year with the 19 funerals I had in 2008. Don's was the last of them and certainly his passing had the biggest impact on our congregation. After Don passed away, the Ministry and Personnel Committee asked Brian Colville if he would take the Chair which Brian graciously accepted. It felt good to know that, again, we had strong leadership on the committee. I appreciated that but it was hard thinking that Don was no longer with us. I missed him and his wise counsel.

In November, I began to organize my Christmas letter which I sent out every year to about 180 friends in Canada. I really enjoyed doing that and it included a Christmas picture of me with Rachel and Sarah. I valued and treasured all the things that I loved about the Christmas season, particularly that year because I knew it would be my last time enjoying this season with my congregation as their minister. I wanted the Christmas Eve service that year to be particularly special and it was. My photograph of a beautiful stained glass window depicting

Mary and Joseph and baby Jesus was used for the Christmas Eve bulletin and, again, the church was packed and it was wonderful to see everyone come out. As I left to spend Christmas with my family, I thought about this being the last time I would need to drive to Warren and Susan's on Christmas Eve night in order to spend Christmas with them. I knew there were going to be many changes for me in 2009 but I was positive about it all as I sat down to write my 2008 Minister's Report for the Annual Report in January 2009:

> *"This is my last report to you as I retire November 30th, 2009. My last worship service will be November 22nd. It has been a wonderful journey of faith that we have been on together. I have no regrets whatsoever and my life is so much richer for having had this opportunity to share in ministry with you. This past year, 2008, we did more amazing things. One that comes to mind is the "Celebrate Stewardship Campaign". Willis Barraball really wanted us to do this and it was a great success under his capable leadership. Families in our congregation pledged a total of $10,000.00 of new money in their offerings to their church for 2009....Then there is the Resale Shop, the brainchild of our Office Administrator Laura Head. Dorothy and Robbie Robinson spent hours in the Resale Shop getting it organized....The Resale Shop and Yard Sale brought in over $10,000.00 in 2008 and it has filled a great need in our community....We have had lots of fun together and great fellowship......I want to thank all of you for helping and for doing those simple and kind acts that build up our church in this community. You all have a very special place in my heart and you always will. Orono United Church is a very special place for me. My family, on my mother's side, came from England to Orono in the early 1860's. I did not think in coming to Orono that this community would have as profound an effect on my life and my ministry as it has. I thank you for taking me into your hearts and into your homes. I will never forget you, any of you."*

I still had 11 months to serve and I would finish my term as Chair of Oshawa Presbytery in June. There were still lots of people to visit and meetings to attend and office work to do and I thought it might be an easier year but it was just as busy a year as any other. The Joint Needs Assessment Committee (JNAC) was working very hard for our congregation to put together all their thoughts and ideas for their vision for the kind of ministry they needed in the future and what qualities, faith and leadership, the congregation was looking for in a new minister. The JNAC committee worked long hours so that, when their report was brought to our congregation and approved, members from the congregation were elected to the Joint Search Committee to find a new minister for Orono United Church, another daunting task. This committee would have to do a lot of work to find ministers they felt were suitable to interview in the hope that they would find a minister to have in place when I retired.

Along with the usual ministry work of meetings, visiting and committee work I was doing, I was still very busy with funerals in this, my last year at Orono. We weren't long into 2009 when Flo called me and asked me to come to the hospital to visit her husband Lloyd. They had been my neighbours as their home was directly across the road from the manse when I lived there. Flo did sewing for me and Lloyd had made me some wood boxes for my photography and he did excellent work. I went in to see Lloyd in the hospital and he was very ill with lung cancer. He was glad to see me and I had a good visit with him and his family. I could see how hard his illness was on his family because they knew he was dying. He died on January 15 and I officiated at his funeral in the church on January 19 and again the church was full. Lloyd had done carpentry work for most people in town over the many years and Flo was a seamstress who did beautiful work and probably everyone in town used her services at one time or another. My heart went out to Flo.

Two days later, on January 17, I had another funeral, this time for Francis Cowan who also had lung cancer. This was another huge funeral in the church. The Cowans were longtime residents of Orono. After Francis retired, he had done electrical work for people in town and he was well liked and respected. I had always enjoyed my visits with him and his wife Joyce and they were down home country people. We had become good friends and I had been invited to their home for many family socials over the years. Joyce took his death very hard because they had been very close as a couple and devoted to each other. She remained very active in her church but it was a very difficult adjustment for Joyce without her husband.

From the middle of January to the beginning of February I had six funerals in 16 days. I can honestly say that, when they were all done, I felt like a truck had run me over. I couldn't catch my breath and I was emotionally drained. It was very hard to do that many funerals in such a short time because I had to interview the families and prepare the service. I was exhausted and we were going into February when we had our Annual Congregational Meeting for which I had to be positive and in top form. I only hoped I wouldn't have another funeral for a while. I continued to visit families in our church and I enjoyed my weekly visits with Roy Scott who was a wonderful man and a veteran from WW II. He had moved into Marnwood Seniors Home in Bowmanville. I had been on holidays when his wife passed away in 2002 but I had officiated at the funeral for his daughter Anna Marie Allin in 2004. Roy never recovered from the death of his wife and, when his daughter died, it broke his heart. Roy was dearly loved by his daughter Ruth and his son-in-law John Allin as well as his grandchildren Tanya and David. I had become very close to this family and Ruth and I had become great friends. When Roy passed away, I felt very badly for his family because it was another significant loss for all of them. It was another huge funeral in the church and I conducted the service on February 28th.

When Ruth called me two weeks later to tell me that John Allin, her brother-in-law had died, I simply couldn't believe it. John had just been at his father-in-law's funeral. The funeral was on March 17 and we had the service in the church. Again, it was a huge funeral. It was a tragic situation because now Tanya and David had lost their grandmother, their mother, and their grandfather and now their father. Ruth had lost her mother, her sister, her father and her brother-in-law. Her niece and nephew looked to her in that time for answers. As hard as it was for Ruth, because she was still grieving the death of her father, she was there for them. Ruth was also our Clerk of Session and she had a lot of responsibility in the church, especially since

I was leaving in November. Thankfully in April there was some good news. I was very surprised and pleased with the article written about me by Reverend Phil Hobbs, Conference Minister Personnel, Bay of Quinte Conference in regards to my upcoming retirement. It was put in the Bay of Quinte section of the United Church Observer's magazine and it was nice to be appreciated:

"Rev. Dorinda Vollmer has been a pioneer. She was the first unmarried mother to be ordained in our United Church of Canada. Now that doesn't seem very remarkable. In 1976 it was indeed unusual….Dorinda was determined to raise Warren. She was also strongly committed to responding to God's call to Ministry in the UCC. It was Hamilton Conference that allowed her to put these two vocations together. A career of 33 years valuable ministry to congregations followed. In looking back on her years of ministry it seems that Dorinda… has lived out her passionate devotion to the gospel of Christ. She has lived out of her passionate love of all God's people. She has lived out of her passionate care for the earth. During the past year Dorinda has served the church as Chair of Oshawa Presbytery. As Chair she has sought to help the members of the Court to do Presbytery differently. This has involved a change in the format of meetings. People sit at table groups in the church hall. Significant time is spent in conversation aimed at building community.

Dorinda's creativity also showed itself in her preaching style. She began by preaching from a manuscript. Over the course of the years the papers were set aside. She now delivers her message without notes, standing at the front of the sanctuary on the same level as the congregation….

Remember Warren mentioned above? That would be Rev. Warren Vollmer, our Conference President Elect… … … Artistic creativity is also important to this retiring minister. This is exercised through photography and through creative writing… ...Her pictures are much sought after….. With several other Durham Region artists she has established a co-operative art shop. Dorinda especially loves nature photography. It is her memoirs that are the current medium for Dorinda's creative writing. She has already written fifty pages! Featured are stories about people who have impacted her life….. Like many of us in paid accountable ministry, active or retired, Dorinda Vollmer feels close to God when surrounded by flowers, butterflies, birds and trees. But then we are in good company as The Bible begins and ends in a garden."

I attended the Retirees Banquet on Friday, May 22 as part of the Bay of Quinte Conference meeting of May 22-24 at Pembroke Memorial Centre. It was a great celebration of all of us who were retiring and we all had an opportunity after dinner to say a few words. Warren was with me and it was wonderful to have him there because it made my retirement seem more real. I would be retired in just over five months which wasn't that far away.

Not long after conference was over, on June 4, I went to the Newcastle Public School for a retirement tea in honour of Ruth Gray who taught there for many, many years. It was a wonderful party and I was so happy for Ruth. Something wonderful to celebrate after going through the funeral for her father and her brother-in-law earlier that year. This was a happy time and people were there to celebrate her many years of faithful service as a teacher. She had the reputation of being one of the finest teachers in the whole School Board. The parents of the children she taught had the greatest respect for her, as did her students.

On Thursday evening, June 11, I had a phone call from Lorraine Martin. I was very surprised to hear from her and she was calling to tell me Joyce Littlejohn (McArthur) had died. I couldn't breathe when I heard those words as memories flooded in on me from my time at Roseau. I asked her what had happened and Lorraine said it was her heart. She was only 60 years old. Lorraine told me the funeral would be on Saturday June 13th at 10:00 a.m. We talked for a while longer but nothing seemed to register because I could hardly take in the news of Joyce's death. When I got off the phone, I called Warren and he was shocked to hear aunty had died. He asked me if I would be going to the funeral but I hadn't even thought of that and I told him I'd have to think about it. I was so upset about Joyce that I didn't know what to do. Finally, I picked up the phone, called the airlines and booked a flight out the next day. Next I called Jill Pearce who lived in Winnipeg to tell her about Joyce whom she knew well. She said she would pick me up at the airport and take me to Roseau. She said we could stay over at her mom and dad's in Dominion City since her mom would want to go to the funeral as well. I then called Philip Cheng, Warren's best friend whom he had met at Crane Public School in Winnipeg in 1980-81. I had seen Philip and his wife Miranda a few times over the years. I told him what was happening and asked Philip if he would drive me to the airport if I came to his place on Saturday afternoon and he said he would. When I called Warren back to tell him of my plans and he told me he knew I would be going.

As I flew out to Manitoba I thought about Joyce and Roseau and Betty and all my friends there. I felt so sad. Joyce had been a wonderful friend. I knew the issues she had and the difficulties she faced every day but she was my friend and I dearly loved her and her children, as she loved Warren. It was hard. I had done so many funerals at Orono for people I cared about but this was different because Joyce and I had shared so much over those few years even though it seemed like a lifetime ago. Jill was at the airport to meet me and I was so relieved to see her. We went right down to Roseau. I had told her that Lorraine knew we were coming and there she was waiting for us. I was so happy to see her. Joyce's two children Stephanie and Nina were there but I didn't recognize her youngest daughter Cory because the last time I saw her she was a baby. Now she was all grown up. We sat around and shared stories of Joyce and the good times we had together and her children talked about all the things they remembered. Nina didn't really remember me or Warren but Stephanie did. It seemed surreal on one level but the reality was that Joyce was gone. I felt a part of me was missing and I was overwhelmed with a great sense of loss and sadness. So much time had passed since we were together at Roseau. Now I was retiring and Joyce was gone, even though she had so much more living to do.

A few hours later, Jill and I left and went to her mom and dad's. It was wonderful to see Audrey and Stan again and they were so supportive. We had a great visit and they wanted to know all about Warren and Susan and Rachel and Sarah. We told stories of the old days, over 30 years ago, and laughed and kept saying, "Do you remember when…." and on we went. Because I had to preach on Sunday and had to go back Saturday I had only had that evening with Stan and Audrey, but it was good to be with them. When I went to bed, it all came crashing in for me and I found myself crying and couldn't stop for the longest time and then I fell asleep. The next morning Audrey drove her car to the funeral and Jill drove her car too because I had to go back to Winnipeg after the service and the lunch.

It wasn't easy walking into the Catholic Church in Letellier because it brought back the stories Joyce had told me of how the Catholic sisters in the Residential School had beaten her whenever she spoke her language or did anything that pertained to her culture. The church was burying her but somehow it didn't feel right. Joyce too understood what didn't feel right because she had lived that most of her life. When Joyce's aunty saw me she came right over. She was so happy to see me, and we just hugged each other. She asked me to say a few words and I said I would but I knew how hard that would be. Then I saw Betty Rance and her husband and I went right over to see them. They had taken in Joyce's baby back in in 1977 and raised her. She was so kind in her words to me and I really appreciated that. The Priest introduced himself and he seemed nice but he didn't know Joyce at all. At some point in the service, he asked me to say a few words and it was painfully hard for me to speak. I told her children how much she loved them but couldn't raise them because she didn't know how to do that but she had loved them passionately. I talked about how intelligent a woman Joyce was but she never had a chance to learn. Still, she was instrumental in getting the Children's Centre started with me and Betty Martin. I talked about how much Joyce loved life but life had not been good to her. As I spoke, my heart was breaking because I felt I had let her down years ago when I asked her to leave my home, but I had been so tired and I just couldn't cope. This was one of the biggest regrets of my life. Joyce and I had remained friends through the years and I was so happy I had come to pay my final respects to my friend. There was a nice reception after the service and I visited with everyone from Roseau. Joyce's aunty thanked me for saying what I did and wished she had asked me to do the service but she didn't know I was coming. I told her I didn't know I was coming either and we both laughed. I was so glad I was there and I know Joyce would have wanted me to be there. She was a deeply spiritual person, as most native people are if they are allowed to be who they are, and Joyce was proud of her heritage and never allowed anyone to put her down. That took enormous energy and strength and courage when all around her was hatred and prejudice, the kind of poison that weighs on the soul.

I was so glad Jill and Audrey were there and Lorraine Martin and Joyce's aunty and her children and it was great to reconnect, but we had to leave and it was all over too soon. Jill dropped me off in Winnipeg at Philip and Miranda's and I had a lovely visit with them. Their children, Jasmine and Justin, asked me all kinds of questions about the reserve so, for two hours, I told them stories of Roseau. Miranda and Philip couldn't believe how quiet they were as they listened to me while Jonas, their youngest slept. When it came time for me to go to the airport, Jasmine and Justin wanted to come too so Philip took them and Miranda stayed with Jonas. When I got home, I called Warren and we talked for a long time about aunty and about the funeral and everything that had happened. I know he would have liked to have gone but it all happened so fast and I was thankful that I had been able to go. I also phoned my sister and talked to her for quite a while about Joyce. Jana had never met her but she had heard so many things about Joyce when I was at Roseau. It was like closing a door abruptly, like a chapter ending, as the rest of life goes on.

It was hard to settle back at Orono after returning from Roseau but I was glad to have to focus on the ministry again. Charlie Campbell was very ill, so one of the first things I did the day after I returned from Roseau was call Esther, Charlie's wife, to see how he was. I went over to see him and found him weak and tired. I could see how he was failing but we had a good visit. He was a character, he really was, and I liked him. Esther was the best person he could have looking after him because she had been a nurse. We had become very good friends and I thought the world of her. Everyone in Orono knew Charlie Campbell. He had a good heart and loved Orono United Church, so the church was full on September 19 when I had Charlie's funeral. His family was there to celebrate his life and we gave him a good send off.

Over the 11 months of my last year of ministry at Orono, I had 17 funerals. Many people I really cared about had passed away but they left their mark on the community and on me and I have not forgotten them. I went into the sanctuary one evening and sat alone in one of the pews to think about my time at Orono and all the people who had meant so much to me and were no longer there. For almost nine and a half years, I had had many funerals for people I really felt close to and some of those funerals had been tragic. I also remembered all the wonderful services we had, Baptisms, confirmation, communion services, the Christmas Eve services and Easter services. I thought about Karen and all the wonderful music she brought to the church. I thought about Laura and what a wonderful support she had been to me as I had been to her and the friendship we had and the talks we had when things got tough. Laura was wonderful to work with and it meant the world to me to know she was there. I thought about some of the leaders in our church who had passed on far too soon. Through all my years at Orono United Church we had good solid leadership on Session. The Elders were dedicated men and women whom I respected and trusted and listened to. We had young families in our church who contributed and sat on the Official Board and helped us weather the storms that came and went., but I had a special place in my heart for those older men and women who were in their 70s and 80s in 2000 when I first came, who valued their church. Their faith had held us all up and they remained faithful, not only for the joyous celebrations, but through all the trials and tribulations we had. I felt very good about the ministry I had done at Orono. I thought about my maternal family, the people I never knew but who were my ancestors, like Alma Cuttell and the many Cuttells who are buried in the Orono cemetery. I had no regrets about coming to Orono and I knew this was the place God had called me. Now it was time to leave, to retire, and to look to a promising future of new horizons. I had my conversation with God that night and told God I was grateful and thankful for the congregations at Kirby United

Church and Orono United Church who had remained faithful through it all.

My retirement party took place Friday, November 20th. Ruth Gray and friends from the church helped her plan this. I had no idea what to expect but I had been asked if there were special people I would like to invite other than my family. I invited Reverend Sue Genge and her husband Glenn and Sue said she would bring greetings from Presbytery. There were others too, including Jim and Nancy Wolfe from Sanford. I walked into the basement of the church around 6:30 p.m. and the place was packed. I was shocked but it was wonderful to see all the people who were there. Ruth came right over to me and pinned a retirement brooch on me. They had a chair set up at the front for me to sit on and a podium with a microphone for people to speak. They even had Hillary, a member of our congregation, taking photos and Jim DeCosta doing the videotaping. Warren and Susan were bringing Danny and Sylvie from Montreal with them whom I had invited. The children were all staying at the house in Lakefield but they would be in church on Sunday morning.

Ruth knew I loved to visit so I went around the hall for half an hour talking with people and then Warren and Susan and Danny and Sylvie arrived and then the speeches began and many people spoke: Laurie Heard, Donna Scott, Brian Colville and Reverend Sue Genge. Ron Landry and his son spoke and made a presentation of the 10 best things about Dorinda and there was lots of laughter. Danny was asked to speak because I knew him as a little boy and he was very funny, Randy Cowan spoke and Taylor Cowan, whom I had taught for a few years, played the piano for me. Susan came up to speak and she also read a letter from my sister which I appreciated. Gary also spoke and he was impressive and hilarious so we laughed through his whole speech. When he finished, he gave me a gold watch from the dollar store and everyone laughed even harder.

Then presentations were made: Ruth had bought 80 roses for me that were spread out in vases on all the tables. Kate Moore presented me with a stained glass window with the dove of peace design from the congregation. Laurie Heard made me a beautiful ceramic white dove in front of a cross. The congregation gave me a beautiful water colour painting by Don Staples. Laura gave me a pink cell phone which I used for many years and then presented me with a wonderful laptop and case from the congregation for my travels. I was overwhelmed with the generosity and love I felt that night from the more than 80 people who had gathered. Ruth said a few words and then invited Warren to speak. I was asked to say the last words but I could hardly speak because I was so emotional. What an evening it had been and I could not imagine anyone having a better retirement party. I couldn't thank the congregation enough for what they did and especially Ruth Gray who organized it.

On Sunday morning, my last service at Orono, many people came to church. It started with "Music that Celebrates'" from 10:30 -11:00 a.m. while a power point presentation was shown of my life. William Jones, 17 years old, played some pieces on the piano and then Joyce Gray was on the organ. During the service, Mandy Dolley was the soloist accompanied by Karen Kastner our former organist who had come back for this service. Karen and I played an organ piano duet together. That was really special. Patrick Dewell outdid himself with the two pieces he played on the organ and, for the Postlude Willam Jones played, *You Raise Me Up* on the piano. I would challenge anyone to play that piece better. It was deeply moving.

It was wonderful to see everyone. Danny and Sylvie's two daughters Audrey and Marie, and Sarah sat with me at the lectern because they wanted to. Rachel and William, Danny and Sylvie's son, stayed in the pew. It was a very emotional service and I was glad to have the children with me. Mary, Warren's half-sister and her husband Danny came to the service and he took pictures and later gave them to me in a framed collage which I so appreciated. Myno and Judy Van Dyke had been unable to be at the Friday night celebrations but they were there Sunday. At the end of service and after the Benediction, Warren asked me to sit down. Then Myno Van Dyke, formerly the clerk of Session at Orono Church, said some very kind words and presented me with his 27th year pin as a police officer and that was such an honour. Warren then spoke and it was so heartfelt. I felt so grateful and so blessed to have had the privilege to serve our Lord at Orono United Church those past nine and a half years.

It was hard to say goodbye. There was a wonderful lunch downstairs after the service where I could visit with everyone and that felt good. Hillary had taken lots of photos on Friday night and gave me a disc with everything on it. Jim also gave me a copy of the videotaping he had done Friday evening. Finally it was over and I was back home. It felt right but strange. I didn't know what the future would bring but, the week before the retirement party, I had been thinking about that and waiting for a sign. I felt a call to go to Cuba and I have no idea where that came from. I wasn't even sure where Cuba was to be honest, but I had a strong sense that I needed to go to Cuba and that God had something for me to do there. I went to a travel agent in Bowmanville to see how I could get there and booked a flight to a resort in Varadero for December 3-10th. I had no idea what that meant or why I felt I had to go but I was flying to Cuba and about to start a new chapter in my life, a new adventure in ministry. That chapter is for another time.

Playing at the concert I gave to raise money for the Millbrook and Cavan United Churches I served at from July 1992 to the end of September 1993 as a trained Interim minister. I gave this concert at Grace United Church in Peterborough because they had a grand piano.

Wilma Bruton a members of Millbrook United Church and me outside the manse at Millbrook spring of 1993.

My party at Millbrook United Church the end of September 1993 as I was leaving the Millbrook Cavan Pastoral Charge. I am cutting the cake.

Driving the truck from Peterborough to Millbrook with Warren helping me with the third gear on the truck that stuck. Moving from Millbrook to Mount Albert the end of September 1993.

On holidays I am visiting with my dear friends George and Katina Kostalis in Vancouver B.C. October 1993.

Some of my friends from the University of British Columbia in October 1993. From the left Julia Dower, Barb Palmquist who is now called Singne, me and Vicki Hansen who is now called Victoria. We had a great visit.

Me and Gail McDonald another long time dear friend from university. We are at the new mall in Burnaby B.C. October 1993.

Jim and Nancy Wolfe in their beautiful gardens at their home in Sanford Ontario. May 1994.

Warren's graduation from McMaster University in Hamilton, Ontario walking up to receive his certificate for his Bachelor of Arts Degree. June 3, 1994.

Warren after his graduation with Susie and me. June 3, 1994.

Warren after his graduation with Tom and Heather Wheat and his fiancée Susan. June 3, 1994.

Warren and Susan at their wedding in Ottawa June 1995.

Our Cousins Al and Jessing Stebbings. Standing on the left their daughters Heather and Diane. Spring of 1997 at Heather's home in Courtice.

Warren's cousins on the left Barbara and Jerry Genrich with their daughter Kim at Susie's birthday party May 3, 1997.

Susie's at her last birthday party at the Mandarin. She was 89. May 3rd, 1997.

Reverend Jim Campbell the former minister at St. John's United Church laid on hands for my ordination in 1976. Now he was laying hands on Warren for his ordination at Mount Forest, Ontario June 1998.

Warren and Susan after Warren's ordination June 1998.

At Warren's dinner party after his ordination at the Garafraxa Inn in Belmont, Ontario. Left to right is me, Warren, Susan and her father Tom Wheat. Above them is a photo of Warren on the wall when he was eight years old.

I am with Susan and Warren after the concert I gave in Sussex, New Brunswick December 2000. Sussex United Church had a grand piano. This was a benefit concert for the Millstream Pastoral Charge that Warren was serving after his ordination in 1998.

Orono United Church at Orono, Ontario 2000. I served the Orono Kirby Pastoral Charge.

Kirby United Church at Kirby, Ontario 2000. I served the Orono Kirby Pastoral Charge.

Carol Yeo painting the kitchen early March 2001 before I moved into the manse the end of March, 2001.

Laverne and June Heard with Dorothy Robinson also working on getting the manse ready for me to move in the end of March, 2001.

On the right Eleanor Shetler, Nellie Mereweather and Dini Schoenmaker helping me unpack and sort out my things the end of March 2001.

Me and Myno Van Dyke, the Clerk of Session at Orono United Church in the living room of the manse with me all moved in, April 1st 2001.

Church service April 1, 2001 when I began full time ministry at Orono and Kirby United Churches. It was a combined service and after there was lunch and a cake that Muriel Patterson from Orono United Church and Don Hamm from Kirby United Church cut.

*At Warsaw with Donna and Gerry Hampton
and my sister Jana and her husband Richard the end of April 2001*

*I baptized my granddaughter Rachel at the Lower Millstream United Church near
Berwick, New Brunswick December 2001.*

I am on the left holding Rachel and Susan is beside me with Pierre and Janet Berton at their home in Kleinburg, Ontario in the spring of 2002.

This is the United Church women unit 3. In the back row left is Muriel Patterson, Doris Kingman and Elearnor Terrill. In the second row left is Marilyn Major, Isabelle Challice and Margie Gunter. In the front row left is Jean Bemrose, Olive Millson and Hilda Wright. 2002.

This is the United Church women unit 4. In the back row left is Anna Mae Barnard, Lynn Rod, Joyce Cowan, Merridy Burt. In the second row left is Betty Chatterton, Doreen Wood and Donna Scott. In the front row let is Audrey Young, Shirley Williams and Thelma Vagg. 2002.

My sister Jana with her granddaughter Hailey and in the back row her granddaughter Brandi, her daughter Stacy and her grandson Cameron. This is in Sacramento, California August 2004.

This is me with my granddaughter Rachel three years old and my granddaughter Sarah born earlier that morning on September 10th, 2004 at Peterborough hospital in Ontario.

Grace Coatham on the left with Joyce Cowan working in the Orono United Church kitchen. 2004.

I baptized Sarah in the spring of 2005 at Lakefield United Church. Warren was their minister since July 2003. From the left is me holding Sarah, Heather and Tom Wheat and Warren holding Rachel.

This is our staff at Orono United Church. In the back row left is Laura Head our secretary and Don Scott our custodian. Front row left is Donna Scott also our custodian with me and Karen Kastner who was our organist. 2006.

This is the manse committee. From the back row left is Cliff Terrill and Laverne Heard and in the front row left Carole Bailey, Marie West and Janet Rutherford 2006.

This is our session. Back row from the left is David Staples, Yvonne Maitland, Laura Head and Ruth Gray. In the front row left is me, Esther Campbell and Bill Tamblyn, Clerk of Session. 2006.

This is the Ministry and Personnel Committee. From the left is Shirley Moffat, Linda Hansen, Don Staples, Don Lycett and Brian Colville. 2006.

This is me and Brandi my great niece, June 2006 before her graduation from High School 2006.

My sister Jana and her granddaughter Brandi after her graduation from High School.

There is Susan and Warren is holding Sarah who is 2 years old and Rachel was there who is 5 years old. This photo was taken after Warren's swearing in ceremony as Police Chaplain of the Peterborough Police Service December 2006.

I gave two benefit concerts in June 2007. One at Orono United Church and the next day one at Lakefielf United Church where this photo was taken.

Warren and me after the concert sitting together at the piano in Lakefield United Church June 2006.

I am on Malcolm Island in British Columbia having completed my introduction to blacksmithing. This is the outfit I had to wear. Summer 2007.

Our church group at the Mandarin in Oshawa where we went every November. This photo was taken in 2007. First row left is Loreen Ball and across from her is Joan Ard. Next to Loreen is Claire Chapman and they are from Kirby United Church. Next to me are Brian Malcolm and Laura Head and Robbie Robinson and they are from Orono United Church.

Me with my two grandchildren Rachel who is 7 and Sarah who is 4, December 2008.

Olive and Ed Millson at their home in Orono 2008.

People from our two congregations at my retirement party Friday November 29th, 2009.

More people from my two congregations at my retirement party Friday November 29th, 2009.

Willis and Marilyn Barraball one of many people who spoke at my retirement party. Friday November 29th, 2009.

Don Staples presented to me one of his paintings on behalf of the congregation. Friday, November 29th, 2009.

Me and my buddy Gary Armstrong at my retirement party.

Sunday morning November 22nd 2009 was the lunch downstairs after the last church service I conducted. I am with Sylvie and Danny Neilsen with their children William, Audrey and Marie.

Warren and Susan, me, Sarah is 5 years old and Rachel is eight years old.

Epilogue

After I retired I went to Cuba for a week in December 2009 because I felt a call. I didn't know anyone there but the first day I was walking in Varadero I met Reverend Joel Ortega Dopico who happened to be the minister at Varadero Presbyterian Reformed Church. So began my ministry in Cuba. Two days later, that Sunday, I was invited to speak at the Presbyterian Reformed Church in Jaugey Grande. Later that afternoon, I was asked to speak at the Presbyterian Reformed Church in San Jose de Los Ramos. That evening I was invited to serve the wine in the communion service at El Forte Presbyterian Reformed Church in Cardenas.

I went back to Cuba many times over the next five years, anywhere from two to six weeks. Cuban people love classical music and I gave concerts at the Presbyterian Reformed Church in Cardenas, at the Pentecostal Church in Jaguey Grande as well as at the Seminary in Matanzas. I also did many photo exhibitions with Chuchi, a well known photographer in Cuba from the seminary in Matanzas. I went wherever Dopico, whom everyone calls by his last name, said I was needed - taking photographs for him, preaching in churches as well as visiting families and staying with families in local communities. Dopico was wonderful to do ministry with and later became the President of the Cuban Council of Churches. This journey and my experiences in Cuba deserve their own book and would include many photographs of the wonderful people and their beautiful country.

In April, 2013 I was attending a conference meeting where Reverend Jean Wilson announced that Alderville United Church was looking for someone to preach 10 Sundays while they were searching for a minister. I had no idea where that was and I spoke to Jean. She told me that the church was at Alderville First Nation, north of Cobourg, which is a 45 minute drive from my home in Bowmanville. I felt a chill go up my back. I knew I was going there. I called the person looking after this at Aldervile and they invited me to preach those 10 Sundays. That first Sunday I preached, they asked if I would consider being their minister. I felt it was a call and I applied. After meetings with Hills and Shores Presbytery, the congregation and myself, I accepted the appointment for 14 hours a week starting September 2013 and I am still serving there.

I love being at Alderville. My son Warren pointed out to me that I had come full circle, beginning my ministry at the Roseau River Indian Reserve and now preaching at Alderville First Nation. He was right, I had come full circle. I have made wonderful friends at Alderville and the congregation I serve is very faithful and committed to their church, their community and their culture. I have included a few photos of our church and of some of the members of our congregation.

I feel so blessed in my lifetime to have known all the wonderful people I have been privileged to meet and serve with in ministry for over 40 years. It has been for me an amazing journey and one that continues to this day. I am open to whatever challenges lie ahead. In spite of all the ups and downs in my life I can honestly say that I have had a wonderful life with no regrets. That is the best any of us can hope for.

The beginning of my ministry in Cuba a few weeks at a time from December 2009 to the spring of 2014. I am in the Varadero Presbyterian Reformed church with their minister Dopico and Omelio who was the minister at Jaguey Grande Presbyterian Reformed Church.
This photo was taken December 10th, 2009.

Alderville United Church, Alderville First Nation north of Cobourg in Ontario. The church was built in 1870. This picture was taken in 2013.

Sheila and Ray Stanlick members at Alderville United Church at their home in 2013.

This is a photo of the Homemakers Group at Alderville United Church. Back row left is Evelyn Jewell, Randy Parker, Elgie Cormier, Audrey Smoke, Mary Crowe and in the front row left is Tina Whetung, Evelyn Wannamaker and Lois Heafield in the fall of 2013.

Evelyn and Richard Jewell members of our congregation at Alderville First Nation 2013.

*Fran and Alton Bigwin at their apartment in Cobourg 2013
who were also members at Alderville United Church.*

Wendy Gail Worrock at the lunch at the community centre at Alderville First Nation after our 176th Anniversary service September 2016.

Our former Moderator The Right Reverend Jordan Cantwell who attended our Anniversary service and spoke at Alderville United Church is helping Elmer Marsden, a member of our church cut our Anniversary cake September 2016. This photo was taken at the community centre at Alderville First Nation September 2016.

Mary and Glen Crowe members at Alderville United Church.
This photo was taken at our church September 2018.

Elgie and Bud Cormier also members at Alderville United Church.
This photo is taken at our church September 2018.

This photo was taken September 2018 at Alderville United Church. From the left is my sister Jana visiting from Coos Bay Orgon, my granddaughter Rachel who is 16, Audrey Smoke a member of our congregation, and my granddaughter Sarah.

Printed in Canada